Accounting
for
Management
Control

Accounting
for
Management
Control

SECOND EDITION

Clive Emmanuel
University of Glasgow

David Otley
University of Lancaster

and
Kenneth Merchant
Harvard University

INTERNATIONAL THOMSON BUSINESS PRESS
I ⓣ P An International Thomson Publishing Company

London • Bonn • Boston • Johannesburg • Madrid • Melbourne • Mexico City • New York • Paris
Singapore • Tokyo • Toronto • Albany, NY • Belmont, CA • Cincinnati, OH • Detroit, MI

Accounting for Management Control

 A division of International Thomson Publishing Inc.
The ITP logo is a trademark under licence

British Library Cataloguing-in-Publication Data
A catalogue record for this book is available from the British Library

First published by Chapman & Hall 1985
Reprinted by Chapman & Hall 1986 (Twice), 1987 (twice)
Second edition published by Chapman & Hall 1990
Reprinted by Chapman & Hall 1990, 1991, 1993, 1994, 1995
Reprinted by International Thomson Business Press 1996, 1997 and 1998

Typeset in Aster by Best-set Typesetter Ltd, Hong Kong
Reprinted in the UK by T J International Ltd, Padstow, Cornwall

ISBN 1-86152-272-X

International Thomson Business Press
Berkshire House
168–173 High Holborn
London WC1V 7AA
UK

http://www.thomson.com/itbp.html

TO OUR WIVES,
Gill, Shelagh and Gail

Contents

Preface

The success of a business enterprise depends upon how well it adapts to the environment in which it is set. But success is a multidimensional concept and the aspects of success that are considered most important will differ from time to time and from one participant in the organization to another. To attain satisfactory levels of performance in each of these dimensions requires the control and coordination of a variety of activities carried out by different people. In a large organization this is a substantial task involving the activities of many different specialists to support and inform the line managers most directly involved. A wide definition of the subject matter of this book is that it is concerned with the mechanisms that organizations use to ensure that they remain well-adapted to their environments.

Management control may be defined as the processes by which managers attempt to ensure that their organization adapts successfully to its changing environment. These processess will range from formally specified control devices, such as the allocation of authority and responsibility, to *ad hoc* enquiries into the state of the environment as, for example, when a manager attempts to discover the price actually paid by a customer for a competing product. Not only do a range of possible controls exist, but the mix and manner of their use will vary from organization to organization and from time to time. However, one set of formal controls appear to be used, albeit in differing ways and to differing extents, in all business organizations (and in many non-business organizations as well). These are the formal controls inherent in the use of an internal or management accounting system.

The primary focus of this text is to study how accounting systems should be designed so as to enable effective management control of organizational activities to be achieved. Inevitably the wider context in which the formal accounting controls are set must also be studied, as must the way accounting information is actually used by those to whom it is provided. But the central theme is the provision of accounting information for management planning and control. Given this emphasis on management, the concept of behaviour congruence provides the overarching guideline to the design of accounting information systems. Results, action and personnel controls provide the means of operationalizing the behaviour congruence concept. The distinction which is made between programmed and non-programmed decision-making situations offers a basis for analysing specific situations to ensure that appropriate results, action and personnel controls to achieve behaviour congruence are applied.

Our aim is therefore to complement traditional management accounting textbooks which are primarily concerned with the development of technical competence in performing accounting calculations and which may, in addition, develop relevant economic concepts to ensure that the calculations performed are appropriate to the decisions for which they are being used. However, it is increasingly recognized that economic concepts represent only one part of the foundation upon which management accounting rests. The internal functioning of the organization, the ways in which people react to information and the design of control systems to affect human behaviour are also fundamental to the operation of a complete accounting system. The design of an effective management accounting system requires knowledge obtained from the behavioural sciences and from the principles of organization and management as well as from economics.

The major part of this text concentrates on the applicability of traditional management accounting techniques to business enterprises and the ways in which they can be developed to serve these purposes more effectively. In Part One, the context in which management accounting information is used is described and analysed from a control perspective. Part Two considers the foundations of traditional management accounting techniques and the circumstances in which they are most applicable, namely the relatively simple, centralized organization operating in a stable environment. These restrictive conditions are relaxed in Part Three where more flexible uses of accounting information, as aids to control rather than as total control devices, are developed. The threads are drawn together in Part Four and the prospects for the development of management accounting assessed. Finally, Part Five consists of some case studies in which the principles outlined earlier can be applied.

CLIVE EMMANUEL,
DAVID OTLEY AND
KENNETH MERCHANT

Preface to the second edition

Over the past five years, it has become evident that this text has filled a gap, in that it has been used on accounting degree courses at most universities and many polytechnics in the UK, and in a surprising number of institutions overseas. It has been used both as a supplement to traditional accounting texts by those teaching a broadly based intermediate management accounting course and as a final-year undergraduate text in its own right. It has also played a role in postgraduate courses, both specialist accounting courses and MBA programmes. Indeed, it has attained the ultimate criterion of acceptance into mainstream thought (or the sign that the authors are now over the hill, as one of our unkinder colleagues put it) by appearing as recommended reading for professional accounting examinations.

During the life of the first edition, we have benefited from the many comments we have received from users, and hope that we have incorporated many of the suggested improvements in this second edition. We have also invited Ken Merchant to join us as a co-author in order to take advantage of his expertise in the subject area. In this revised second edition, we have kept nearly everything that appeared in the original edition, changed a little, and added a considerable amount of new material. In this way, we hope to have preserved those features which have made the book so popular while increasing its usefulness to even more teachers.

The main changes, apart from general revision and updating, are as follows. Chapter 2 has been extended to include a more detailed discussion of the contingency theory of management accounting, and Chapter 4 now includes discussion of more radical perspectives on the practice of management. But we have tried not merely to review material which may yield useful insights; rather we have tried to assess the utility of alternative approaches to the role of accounting information in the management control process. To that end, a new Chapter 5 has been included which outlines the control tools available to a manager and discusses how an appropriate choice might be made.

In Part Two, Chapter 6 has been extended to elaborate the concepts used in more detail than before, and it now assumes less familiarity on the part of the reader with both cost accounting concepts and linear programming techniques. However, for a full understanding of its contents, it should be studied in conjunction with a cost accounting text that develops linear programming concepts (e.g. Ryan and Hobson, 1985). Chapter 7 has also been lengthened somewhat to include some more recent empirical material, and also to clarify the transition which takes place here from the programmable to the less programmable situation.

Similarly, Part Three contains additional material, plus a new chapter on rewarding managerial performance. The initial chapter now incorporates a worked example, illustrating the aggregation effect on budget plans, and Chapter 9 likewise provides an appreciation of the divisional cost of capital calculation. The present popularity and growing significance of managerial incentive schemes make the inclusion of the new Chapter 10 timely and essential; in many large companies these schemes are an integral part of the management control process. Chapters 11 and 12 concern the complexity of operations in the multidivisional company, where recent theoretical and inductive studies relating to divisional autonomy and a 'new' form of performance measure to provide consistency between the short and long term have been added respectively.

The 'Framework for Analysis' in Part Four is extended to address expressly three fundamental aspects in the design of any management control system, namely what to measure, at what standard of performance and with what associated incentives. Finally, a new chapter in Part Five introduces seven 'tried and tested'* case studies. All are concerned with the management control system in specific organizational settings, although each concentrates on one or more different issues effecting the AIS. Hopefully, these cases will test the relevance, or otherwise, of the concepts introduced earlier in the book.

The intention has been to provide an up-to-date, more broadly based edition which may be used as a 'stand-alone' text. Only the reader can tell us if we have succeeded, and to what degree. Hence, as with the first edition, we welcome comments and criticisms on this the second edition.

---

* The Scovill Inc.: Nutone Housing Group, Altex Aviation, HCC and ES Inc. cases are reproduced by kind permission of Harvard Business School and Permaclean Products plc, BBR plc and Beech Paper Company by kind permission of Philip Allan Publishers plc.

Acknowledgements

This second edition of *Accounting for Management Control* follows and expands the themes contained in the 1985 edition. The collaboration of Ken Merchant has allowed the introduction of results, action and personnel controls (Chapter 5) to complement and operationalize the behaviour-congruence concept. A new chapter on managerial compensation and incentive payments (Chapter 10) has been included, together with seven cases which enable the broad issues of management control systems to be analysed (Chapter 14). All the original chapters have been updated and revised, as have the exercises and questions.

We are indebted to the adoptors of the first edition for their helpful comments and suggestions and trust that this edition goes some way towards satisfying their wishes. In particular, David Cooper, Neil Garrod and Trevor Hopper must be thanked, together with John Perrin, our consulting editor, and also the many students who have made helpful comments.

As readers of the first edition will be aware, the preparation period to complete the manuscript was not without delay. Coordinating the efforts of three co-authors on two continents has stretched the patience of our long-suffering publishers once again. However, the result is an integrated treatment of management control embedded in organizational, behavioural and economic theory. Placing management accounting and accounting information systems in this wider context is, we believe, a rewarding exercise, especially when students begin to identify and analyse connections between various issues.

Students at the Universities of Lancaster, Aberystwyth and Glasgow have tested the text and new questions in this edition, and the majority of cases have undergone the strenuous attention of Harvard business graduates. We also thank those who have transformed scribbled thoughts into neat typescript, especially Ruth Johnstone, Jacqui Goldthorp and Moreen Cunliffe.

Finally, and by no means last, the continuing efforts and forbearance of our wives must be acknowledged. Extended release from taxi-driving duties, do-it-yourself repairs and schools liaison has ensured that a certain level of output has been maintained. Again, it seems fitting that we should end by echoing the prayer, attributed to Sir Francis Drake, that 'it is not the beginning, but the continuing thereof until it be thoroughly finished, which yieldeth the true glory'.

Part One

The Context of Management Accounting

The aim of this book is to evaluate the role played by accounting information in the effective management of an organization. Although the primary focus will be on the business enterprise, initially a more general approach, encompassing a wider range of organizational forms, such as public sector and not-for-profit organizations, will be taken. In Part One, the context in which management accounting information is used will be described and evaluated, so as to provide a framework within which the overall operation of an accounting system can be assessed.

Accounting information is provided within organizations as a means of assisting them to adapt their activities so they can continue to achieve their objectives in the face of environmental and internal changes. Management accounting is part of the process of organizational control. It is far from being the only control mechanism used by organizations, but it is a ubiquitous and important one. In the first chapter the role of accounting information as part of an organizational control process is analysed by examining in detail the nature of control and some general features of the organizational environment in which it is exercised.

Accounting control systems cannot be developed in isolation, but must be designed in conjunction with expectations of how people in organizations will use and react to them. Historically, accounting systems have been designed on the basis of a highly mechanistic model of organizational functioning. The second chapter reviews more modern theories of organization and relates these to the choice of an appropriate accounting system. Organizations consist of people, and can act only insofar as the people within them choose to act. The ways in which organizations encourage and motivate participants to act in ways that advance overall aims and objectives is the concern of the third chapter. This reviews theories of individual motivation and analyses the impact of specific accounting controls on how people behave.

Organizations require management. The function of management, as distinct from the role of managers, is that of control in its broadest sense, namely ensuring the adaptation of the organization to the circumstances in which it is set. If accounting information is to be of use to managers fulfilling their control function, it is necessary to relate it to the manner in which managers are observed to work. In Chapter 4 the role of management accounting information is assessed in the context of managerial work and the wider information needs and control activities of managers.

Accounting controls are only one of a wider variety of controls available to managers, and the selection of appropriate controls for particular circumstances is a key managerial decision. The fifth and final chapter of Part One reviews the types of control that are available, and develops guidelines for managers to assist them in making a good choice.

The focus of this Part is on the provision of information that is useful in promoting organizational effectiveness. However, this can be assessed only when the wider context in which the organization exists is appreciated. We therefore spend some time describing the organizational context in which accounting information is used and analysing some of the roles it plays in organizational functioning. This material provides an essential foundation for subsequent chapters on the design and use of accounting systems for management control.

Accounting for organizational control

SUMMARY

This chapter sets out the main features of the organizational context within which accounting controls operate. Organizations use many different types of control to coordinate their different activities, but accounting provides a convenient language for discussing the impact of a wide range of disparate activities. However, accounting information is inevitably used in conjunction with less routine, more informal and more qualitative information in decision making and control. A model of control is advanced which allows four necessary conditions for control to be derived; the adequacy of accounting controls is assessed against these four criteria.

A predictive model is central to every controlled process. Where such a model is weak, decisions become non-programmed and control becomes more dependent upon managerial judgement. Clear objectives are also necessary for effective control, but in most organizations goals are ambiguous and subject to political compromise. In these circumstances, control is effected by ensuring that agreed plans of action are implemented rather than by the use of guiding objectives.

The patterns of organizational control observed in practice vary according to the nature of the organization being studied. Business organizations are predominantly utilitarian in nature, and thus reliant on negotiated bargains as their main control device, although this varies across organizations and with managerial level. Control at lower levels is often more coercive in nature; at higher levels it may become more normative.

Finally, issues in the measurement of performance are discussed, together with the meaning of notions such as economy, effectiveness and efficiency. Accounting information serves a central role in organizational control where it provides a means of quantifying overall performance. By contrast, in organizations where performance cannot be captured in accounting terms (e.g., public sector services), its role in control is much more restricted. However, even in business organizations having overall profit goals, accounting information is only an imperfect measure of performance and needs to be used with a degree of sensitivity and care.

INTRODUCTION

Organizations display remarkably consistent and stable patterns of behaviour in their interaction with a constantly changing environment. In cybernetic terms, they appear to be ultra-stable systems; that is, they are capable of adapting their behaviour so as to protect their integrity despite facing a wide range of external conditions. Such stability of behaviour is strong evidence that they possess effective control mechanisms, and one such control mechanism is the organization's internal accounting system. It is argued in this chapter that, for business organizations at least, management accounting systems are of major importance because they represent one of the few integrative mechanisms capable of summarizing the effect of an organization's actions in quantitative terms.

Although the focus of this book is on accounting for management control in the business enterprise, much of the early material is applicable to a wider range of organizations. The business enterprise may be defined as an organization whose *raison d'être* is the provision of goods or services for which it is paid directly by the consumer of its products. Thus some nationalized industries (e.g., coal, electricity and railways in the UK) fall within the ambit of this definition, as well as privately owned enterprises. However, organizations that dispose of their product other than for payment (e.g., local authority, health services and charities), even if privately owned, are not specifically dealt with. Although they have accounting systems, these will often be different in their design and function from those described here. In the first four chapters we will tend to use the term 'organization' when discussing concepts having a wide applicability, and the more restrictive term 'business enterprise' when the ideas involved have a more limited applicability. In later chapters we confine our discussion to large business enterprises.

In this chapter the major function of internal accounting information is viewed as that of aiding the processes of organizational control. The nature of control is examined in detail, and four necessary conditions for control are derived and applied to organizations. One of these conditions, the existence of organizational objectives, raises some important conceptual issues that are dealt with at length. Finally, the measurement of organizational performance is discussed with particular reference to the role of accounting information in promoting organizational effectiveness.

ORGANIZATIONS AND ACCOUNTING

Modern business enterprises display some important characteristics that profoundly effect their behaviour. Perhaps the most obvious feature apparent to the casual observer is the complexity of their activities. In manufacturing industries materials are bought and transported from many parts of the world; sophisticated components may be acquired from other business enterprises; people with various skills are gathered together to transform the materials into products; these products are advertised, distributed and sold. The operation of the transformation process often requires highly advanced technical knowledge and many different products may be involved. In service industries an array of expertise has to be coordinated to provide customers with the services they require at a particular point in time.

To deal with this complexity, the enterprise relies heavily on the mechanism of specialization or differentiation. Different sections of the organization, and different people within those sections, deal with only a small part of the total operation. Yet despite this fragmentation a high degree of regularity of overall behaviour is usually observed. People turn up to work at specified times; materials are available when required; the individual parts are combined into working wholes; customers receive their goods as required. Admittedly such smooth running does not occur all the time, yet it is nevertheless still true that it is disruptions to the process that are unusual and form the news that is reported in the media; the underlying regularity is assumed to be normal.

The maintenance of such regularity is all the more surprising when it is realized that many of the activities required for the successful operation of a business enterprise are subject to a considerable degree of uncertainty. The supply of raw materials is affected by political conditions around the globe, and their price by the demands of other users. The technology of the product may be novel and orders may be accepted before it is known that the product will work (e.g., in industries making products such as computers, aircraft engines and pharmaceuticals). The demand for the final product may also be unknown or volatile, depending upon the preferences of fashion-conscious consumers. Yet, even in the face of such uncertainties, the business enterprise continues to operate with a high degree of regularity.

It is apparent that to achieve such stability in the face of complexity, differentiation and uncertainty requires some powerful integrative control mechanisms. What are these and how do they achieve the desired results? There is no simple answer to this question, because a huge variety of mechanisms exist that help promote stability, some emanating from the shared-value system, or culture, of the society in which the organization is set and others being more consciously designed to achieve this purpose. But many of the mechanisms are, in part, based upon the transmission of information. Integration, coordination and control could not be achieved without information. In a very real sense, information is the cement that binds the organization together and enables it to act in a coherent manner. But even here, we need to be careful with the metaphors we use. 'Cement' implies a solid and unchanging organizational edifice that is fixed for long periods of time. In reality, organizations are much more fluid, and emphasis needs to be given to the processes of interaction that take place within organizational structures, as well as the structures themselves. Such processes inevitably involve the exchange of information.

The flows of information within a large business enterprise are themselves complex. Information may be systematically gleaned from pre-determined sources and reported via formal information processing channels; alternatively it may be obtained in a haphazard fashion by organizational members who pass it on by word of mouth to others to whom they consider it will be of interest. Both the formal and the informal transmission of information are important for the smooth running of the organization. In addition, relevant information may or may not be quantifiable. Sales and production performance can be expressed in numerical form, either in terms of units of products or of money. The reaction of a competitor to a sales promotion campaign or the effect of government plans for new legislation have aspects that are better discussed qualitatively.

Information may thus be:

routinely generated	or	ad hoc
formally transmitted	or	informally transmitted
quantitative	or	qualitative

All these types of information serve important functions in the overall control of the success of the enterprise. Nevertheless an important and basic integrative function is served by accounting information that is routinely generated, transmitted through formally defined channels, and quantitative in nature.

In fact, the accounting system is often the only source of quantitative information that combines the results of the activities of all the different parts of an enterprise. There are two basic reasons for this. In the first place, the maintenance of profitable performance is a prime concern of those who have invested their money in the enterprise. Even if, as we shall argue later, profitability is not necessarily the sole objective of the enterprise, it is an important constraint, for without adequate profitability the flow of funds would dry up and eventually lead to cessation of activity. Secondly, accounting information is of central importance because it represents the only way of assessing the results of the diverse activities in terms of a single dimension. Money is an important measure because it is capable of summarizing the impact of a wide variety of activities. Accounting information serves both as an integrative mechanism used to co-ordinate diverse activities and as a measure of overall performance and viability. For both of these reasons it has a central role to play in the control of organizational activity.

The primary function of all accounting information is that of control. External financial reports provide a means whereby shareholders can monitor the ways in which their funds have been applied and, in principle at least, exercise control by appointing and removing directors. Internal accounting information assists those who have the responsibility of ensuring the continued success of the enterprise to monitor and coordinate its activities and to ensure that it adopts an appropriate stance towards its environment. Management accounting is thus fundamentally involved with the processes of organizational control. To study it, we must therefore first consider in more detail both what is meant by control and also how general concepts of control can be applied to human organizations.

1.3 THE CONCEPT OF CONTROL

The term 'control' is probably one of the most ill-defined in the English language, having a wide range of connotations. Rathe (1960) listed '57 varieties' of its nuances ranging from 'prohibit' to 'manipulate'. Within this variety are two major themes. Firstly, there is the idea of control as domination; the person 'in control' is the one who has the power to enforce his will on others. Secondly, there is the idea of control as regulation: here the controller detects a difference between 'what is' and 'what ought to be' (Vickers, 1967) and this difference acts as a stimulus for action. Business usage includes both of these strands of meaning as is indicated by Webster's Dictionary definition:

Application of policies and procedures for directing, regulating and coordinating production, administration and other business activities in a way to achieve the objectives of the enterprise.

In a more general sense, control is concerned with the processes by which a system adapts itself to its environment. That is, in a self-regulating system, such as a business enterprise, both the specification of objectives and the means of their achievement are internally generated and form part of the control process. This point of view is reflected in a definition of management control put forward by Lowe (1970) where he defines a management control system as:

a system of organizational information seeking and gathering, accountability and feedback designed to ensure that the enterprise adapts to changes in its substantive environment and that the work behaviour of its employees is measured by reference to a set of operational sub-goals (which conform with overall objectives) so that the discrepancy between the two can be reconciled and corrected for.

Management control is therefore concerned both with strategic issues (the general stance of the organization towards its environment) and with operational issues (the effective implementation of plans designed to achieve overall goals). Planning and control are two sides of the same coin and must be considered together.

In order to understand the nature and meaning of control in organizations, it is first necessary to understand what is meant by control more generally. To do this, a general model of a control process will be developed based on the cybernetic literature (cybernetics being defined by Pask, 1961, as the study of 'how systems regulate themselves, reproduce themselves, evolve and learn'). This general model, which is intended to be applicable to any kind of controlled system whether physical, biological or organizational, will then be applied specifically to organizations.

A general control model

In general terms a controlled system can be considered as a 'blackbox' converting a stream of inputs into a stream of outputs, with the internal details of the process being ignored for the present. The process being controlled may be any system, ranging from a simple mechanical device (e.g., a steam engine controlled by a Watt's governor or a heating system controlled by a thermostat) through a biological system (e.g., a single cell or a plant or animal) to a human organization (e.g., a football team or a multinational corporation). Although the control requirements of such a process will be considered in general terms, the reader may find it helpful to keep a specific example in mind, such as a simple manufacturing process.

There are four necessary conditions that must be satisfied before any process can be said to be controlled (Otley and Berry, 1980). First, objectives for the process being controlled must exist, for with-

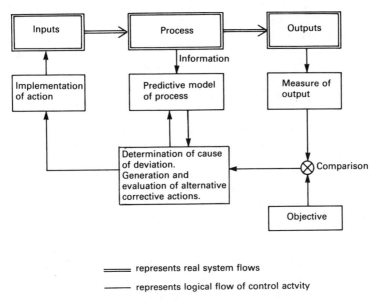

Fig. 1.1 Necessary conditions for control.

out an aim or purpose control has no meaning. Secondly, the output of the process must be measurable in terms of the dimensions defined by the objectives. That is, the degree to which the process is attaining its objectives must be assessed. Thirdly, a predictive model of the process being controlled is required so that causes for the non-attainment of objectives can be determined and proposed corrective actions evaluated. Finally there must be a capability of taking action so that deviations of attainment from objectives can be reduced. If any of these conditions (shown schematically in Fig. 1.1) fail to be met, the process can no longer be said to be 'in control'.

Let us now apply this model to simple system consisting of a motor car and its driver. The driver will have an objective, let us say the transportation of himself and passengers from A to B. Indeed, within this overall objective he will also have subsidiary objectives or constraints. For example, he will wish to proceed without accident, without committing a traffic offence (or, at least, not being caught so doing) and within certain time constraints. Thus even such a simple system can have a complex structure of objectives. Without any such objectives, progress will be aimless and the concept of control inappropriate.

As he progresses, the driver is continually monitoring the world around and comparing his current state with his objectives. Is he on the correct route? Is his speed within the appropriate speed limit? Is he avoiding colliding with other traffic and street furniture? These observations are made either by direct observations or via the use of measuring instruments (e.g., speedometer and odometer). If he were blindfolded so that he obtained much reduced information about his current state, it is unlikely he would remain in control for long. Measurement of actual performance in terms of objective attainment is thus essential for control.

When a discrepancy between the actual and desired states of the system is noted, the cause of the error has to be determined and an appropriate corrective action generated. This requires use of a pre-dictive model of the system being controlled both to determine causes and to evaluate the likely effects of potential corrective actions. Suppose our driver notices that the red lights at the rear of the preceding vehicle are lit; his predictive model, based on his previous experience, indicates that it is likely that it is braking. He further predicts that unless he takes some evasive action his objective of not colliding with other traffic will not be met. Rapidly he generates some possible control actions and predicts and evaluates their likely outcomes. Steer around the obstruction; no, there is oncoming traffic. Slow down; yes, this is feasible. The process of converting an error signal into a corrective action involves extensive use of models that predict the effect of input conditions on the output of the process being controlled. In the absence of an ability to predict, control degenerates into random action.

Finally the decision to take action must be implemented. Our driver decides to brake as a means of slowing down and depresses the brake pedal (one of the car's 'controls' in popular parlance, but in our terms only part of the control system; one might equally talk of the speedometer as a 'control'). Inability to implement this control action would again leave the situation out of control, but successful implementation will eliminate the error between actual and objec-tive and restore control. However in this case the driver applies his brakes but observes that he is still continuing on a course that he predicts will involve impact with the braking vehicle. Why? His pre-dictive model, armed with additional information about the state of external environment, such as the fact that it is raining and autumn leaves are covering the road, explains the paradox that braking is not having the anticipated effect by suggesting that he may be skidding. Further associated observations confirm this to the driver. What can he now do?

At this stage an inexperienced driver may not have an appropriate response in his repertoire; he goes out of control for want of being able to think of a feasible control action. A more skilled driver may think of a possible response (e.g., convert linear momentum into angular momentum by spinning the car), but he is unable to implement this action adequately. He goes out of control for want of the ability to implement the action and hits the vehicle in front sideways! An expert driver may successfully carry out the manoeuvre and remain 'in control'.

It may be seen that failure of any of the four defined components of a control system can cause the system to go 'out of control'. Observation and comparison with objectives generates 'mis-match' signals that alert the controller to the need for action and direct his attention to currently important areas. Other information is processed by his predictive model to inform him about the causes of such deviations and the likely outcomes of potential control actions. Finally, a decision is taken, a control action implemented and its effect on the system monitored.

The model of control that has been developed here is recursive in nature and can be applied at any level of analysis. We may thus talk about an individual's control of mechanical devices or his own actions, a group of people controlling each other's behaviour (social control), an organization controlling its internal activities in response to the environment in which it operates (organizational control) or a society controlling the activities of organizations or individuals within it (social or governmental control). Indeed there is considerable confusion in the literature caused by a lack of precision in the identification of an appropriate level of analysis, in addition to confusion over the meaning of control. In this book, we shall be primarily concerned with analysis at an organizational level, rather than at either an individual or societal level. Thus we will concentrate on organizational control, by which we mean the processes by which organizations govern their activities so that they continue to achieve the objectives they set for themselves. Organizations are thus treated as self-regulating systems both affected by, and affecting, their environment. By adopting this approach we do not mean to deny the utility of work at other levels of analysis. Indeed we will ourselves examine the impact of organizational controls on the individual, and also briefly consider some of the ways in which governments attempt to regulate the activities of business enterprises. Nevertheless our prime focus of attention will be the control of organizational activities by the organization itself.

Boulding (1956) identified a hierarchy of systems consisting of nine levels, each having different control characteristics. These were:

1. static structures or frameworks, e.g., a bridge;
2. simple mechanical systems, e.g., a clock;

3. cybernetic, or closed-loop systems, with given goals, e.g., a thermostat;
4. open, self-maintaining systems, e.g., a cell;
5. plant, or society of cells;
6. animal, characterized by the brain;
7. human, characterized by language and self-consciousness;
8. social organizations;
9. transcendental systems.

The control model developed here is essentially cybernetic in nature, and is most evidently applicable at levels 3 and 4. Its application to human organizations at level 8 is not self-evident, although we would argue that it gives considerable insight into their operation. However it must be stressed that human systems have important characteristics, such as self-awareness, not incorporated into the cybernetic model. In particular, the control of such systems involves the control of self-regulating sub-systems (individuals) that respond to system changes by adapting their own behaviour. Organizational control is a complex and ill-understood activity precisely because it involves an attempt to control a complex network of self-controlling human beings.

It may be thought that our cybernetic model is inappropriate for the analysis of any self-regulating systems, but this is not so. Although in our example of the car and driver we treated the movement of the car as the process and the driver as an external controller, the split between controller and the system being controlled is not essential. Further, it should not be assumed that the process of control is necessarily embodied in a person (the controller). A system may be maintained in control by mechanisms that do not involve a dominant controlling group. For example, a Watt's governor on a steam engine operates in such a way that speed control is built into the mechanical system: an increase in speed automatically results in a reduction in steam supply. Social systems are much more complex, but many examples of self-regulating groups of people exist, ranging from Israeli kibbutzim to business partnerships.

Indeed, all human systems are self-regulating in the absence of any consciously designed controls, although not necessarily at the level of welfare which could be obtained by the addition of more explicit controls. For example, traffic in towns regulates itself in the absence of entry and parking controls, for as traffic jams increase in severity some motorists will use other means of transport or even avoid making a journey at all. Traffic congestion thus stabilizes at a point which those involved find minimally acceptable. The main purpose of designing explicit control arrangements for human activities is to increase overall welfare to a level above that which would occur in the absence of such controls. Thus parking controls, although reducing the welfare of some (e.g., those who would otherwise arrive early and park on the street all day) are intended to increase the welfare of many (e.g., those who drive through the streets all day) and provide a net benefit to society as a whole. A control system must therefore be evaluated against what is expected to occur if it were not implemented.

The general cybernetic control model therefore provides a framework that can be used to analyse the design and operation of management control systems and the role of accounting information within them. Evidently such a simple model, derived from level 3 of Boulding's hierarchy, cannot be expected to capture the full complexity of organizational control processes, categorized at level 8 of this hierarchy. But, used with care, it can provide valuable insights into the nature of management control, and provide guidance as to how such systems can be designed and improved.

Feedback and feed-forward control

The basic model described in the preceding paragraphs is essentially error-based. A deviation between the actual result and the objective set for a process (an error) causes a control action to be implemented that will, it is hoped, reduce this error. This is described as negative feedback control, and it is evident that one objection to its use is that errors are allowed to occur. This is particularly important in systems where time lags occur between the occurrence of an error and the implementation of corrective action. Such time lags are an important factor in the control of human organizations, where an error may not be detected for a period of time and its correction may also be a lengthy process. In such cases there is a need for anticipatory or feed-forward control.

In feed-forward control instead of actual outputs being compared with system objectives, predictions are made of what outputs are expected to be at some future time. If these expectations differ from what is desired at that time, control actions are implemented that will minimize these differences. To the extent that the actions are effective, control is achieved before any deviation from the objective actually occurs. The difference between feedback and feed-forward control is that the measurement of actual process output is replaced by a prediction of expected output at some future time. Such prediction obviously requires the use of a predictive model that is sufficiently accurate to ensure that the control action will improve the situation rather than causing it to deteriorate further.

It is arguable that the time lags that occur in human organizations make feed-forward control equally, if not more, important than feed-back control. Indeed it can be seen that the activity of planning is an example of feed-forward control. The production of plans is essentially an iterative process in which expected outcomes of current actions are compared with aspirations; to the extent that the outcomes fall short of the aspirations, alternative actions are considered until a set of actions is produced (the plan) that is expected to result in a satis-factory set of outcomes. However, for such a process to be effective requires a reasonably accurate predictive model. Unfortunately our predictive models of organizational behaviour are generally weak, and in some circumstances planning may be counter-productive, because it suggests remedial actions designed to avoid situations that would not, in fact, have occurred. For example, the person who throws salt over his left shoulder every morning in order to keep the lions away, may claim that he has good evidence for the efficacy of his action; after all, he has never been bothered by lions in his life! But neither has he taken any action to experiment and to try to discover whether his predictive model is true, or merely a myth which he happens to believe. It has been suggested that much organizational planning and most national planning has been ineffective because the predictive models used have suggested quite inappropriate actions (Wildavsky, 1975).

We shall thus be concerned with both feed-forward and feedback control or, in more conventional terms, with both planning and control. Unfortunately, both of these conventional terms have mis-leading connotations, with planning being seen as the process of setting objectives and the means of their attainment, and control as the process of ensuring that plans are achieved. We shall continue to use the term 'control' to encompass both the activity of planning and of ensuring conformity to plan including, if necessary, the generation of new plans.

It can be seen that the effective operation of an anticipatory con-trol system requires considerable predictive ability. The expected performance of the system through time must first be forecast. To the extent that this deviates from what is desired, control actions must be generated and evaluated. In complex situations the necessity of predicting such outcomes with some degree of accuracy often restricts consideration to incremental actions only (i.e., actions that differ from current actions by a relatively small amount) as more radical alternatives are highly unpredictable in their effects (Lindblom, 1959). In business enterprises the major barrier to more effective control is a lack of predictive ability. Where predictive ability is absent, it is often replaced by assertion and belief, so that action is based on assumptions that may prove to be unwarranted. Improvement of control in such circumstances is possible only by testing the validity of the underlying assumptions and coming to a better understanding of the reality of the situation being faced. Improved information is of value only to the extent that it is appropriately converted into reliable predictions. It may thus be seen that improved predictive models are crucial to the development of improved control systems.

Programmed and non-programmed decisions

There is an important distinction to be made, which is fundamental to the structure of subsequent chapters in this book, between programmed and non-programmed decisions in the control process. A *programmed decision* is defined as one where the decision situation is sufficiently well understood for a reliable prediction of the decision outcome to be made. A *non-programmed decision* is one that has to rely upon the judgement of managers because there is no formal mechanism available for predicting likely outcomes. That is, in programmed decisions the means – end relationships involved are sufficiently well understood for instructions to be confidently given as to how tasks should be carried out in order to achieve a given objective. In non-programmed decisions, the causal relationships are less well understood so that it is possible only to instruct a manager as to what he is expected to achieve; the means of achievement have to be left largely in his hands.

In terms of the control framework, the difference between programmed and non-programmed decisions lies in the location and nature of the predictive model of the process being controlled. In programmed decisions, the predictive model is explicit and available to managers; their subordinates may thus be instructed what to do, and how and when to do it. They can be held responsible for doing what they are told and acting within prescribed procedures, rather than for achieving given ends. By contrast, in the non-programmed situation, predictive models are only implicit in the minds of individuals and may be better developed at junior rather than senior levels in the organization. Here the subordinate cannot be told *what* to do, only the result that is desired. He is held responsible for his results; how they are attained is left to his discretion, because his understanding of the situation and how it can be controlled is better than that of senior management.

Programmed situations can be treated as non-programmed, but the reverse is not true. In the former case, for reasons of complexity and because of difficulties in assembling information a potentially programmable decision may be left non-programmed. For example, it might be possible to devise job schedules for a machine shop using computer-based algorithms that yield optimal decisions and to instruct the job-shop manager to implement them. However considerable savings in data collection effort and increased flexibility may be obtained by leaving it to the job-shop manager's own judgement, with perhaps only a small loss in optimality. However, in the latter case, if means – end relationships are not understood, it is not sensible to instruct the manager what to do, only what should be achieved.

The distinction between these two types of decision situations affects the type of accounting information that is appropriate for control. In the programmed situation, it is possible to specify the inputs necessary to produce a given output. The accountant is thus able to construct a detailed budget itemizing appropriate levels of spending: such costs are described as engineered being based on industrial engineering measurements, and standard costing methods may be used. In the non-programmed situation it is possible to specify the inputs required to produce desired results only in the most vague manner. Here a manager may be allocated a lump sum that he may spend as he judges best. He is held accountable only for achieving the results within his budget constraint. As an example, the construction of a product can often be costed to a high degree of accuracy; the steps involved in making it are programmed and well specified. By contrast, the amount of money required to be spent on advertising so as to increase sales by a given amount is difficult to forecast, and the optimal combination of advertising media is largely an intuitive matter.

Earl and Hopwood (1981) have suggested that management accounting systems have been designed on the basis that decisions are programmed, although they are used, in practice, in non-programmed situations. They identify two types of uncertainty: uncertainty in cause – effect relationships (analogous to the adequacy of the underlying predictive model), and uncertainty in objectives. By combining these as two independent dimensions, they construct a diagram with four boxes (Fig. 1.2).

In the top left-hand box objectives are known and cause – effect relationships are well-understood. Thus, decisions are programmable and the accounting system can act as an 'answer machine'. That is, information is provided which enables a clear and optimal decision to be arrived at. An example is the use of net present value methods in capital investment appraisal: cash flows and discount rates are known so that the NPV model can produce a clear decision rule. If the NPV is positive, then the project is worthwhile and should be undertaken.

		Uncertainty in objectives	
		Clear objectives	Ambiguous objectives
	Good predictive models	Decision by computation Answer machine	Decision by compromise Dialogue machine
Uncertainty in cause – effect relationships			
	Poor predictive models	Decision by judgement Learning machine	Decision by inspiration Idea machine

Fig. 1.2 Uncertainty, decision making and ideal information systems (based on Earl and Hopwood, 1981).

When objectives become ambiguous, no clear-cut decision rule can be provided. Rather, decisions emerge by a process of negotiation and compromise. In these circumstances, decision making should be oriented towards opening up and maintaining channels of communication. Information systems can be used to assist this process by helping managers to develop and argue different points of view which are conflicting, but consistent with the underlying facts (Boland, 1979). Here the accounting system serves as a 'dialogue machine' designed to encourage exploration and debate, rather than providing answers.

Alternatively, objectives may be clear but predictive models may be poor so that we do not know which courses of action are most likely to yield the optimum results. Here it is important to learn from past actions which have not always led to the desired consequences. The accounting system serves as a 'learning machine', enabling managers more thoroughly to assess alternatives. The accounting system is often the only formal record of the effectiveness of past decisions and therefore can serve as an important database for learning about the true state of the world and the way in which it responds to actions. Decision support systems are another example of learning machines, which seek to advise managers on the basis of what is shown, but which are also programmed to learn from the results of previous actions.

Finally, both conditions may apply together; objectives are ambiguous and predictive models are poor. Here, it is argued, accounting systems can serve as an 'idea machine', enabling creative solutions to be found to messy, ill-defined problems. This is possibly an ambitious and unrealistic role to expect a formal information system to play, although Hedberg and Jonsson (1978) have speculated upon the design of semi-confusing information systems deliberately designed to shake organizations out of rigid behaviour patterns in times of changing environmental conditions.

Even if one does not fully accept the above ideas, it is certainly true that accounting information systems often appear to have been designed *as if* they were operating in the top left-hand box, under conditions of absolute certainty. In practice, both types of uncertainty exist to a greater or lesser extent, and it is therefore necessary to use the accounting information system in a more flexible manner than its original design might imply. In the real world, objectives are usually conflicting and ambiguous, and predictive models imperfect. Managerial decisions are therefore often non-programmed.

Although the distinction between programmed and non-programmed decision situations has been described in dichotomous terms, it is in fact a continuum ranging between the extreme points described. Thus a decision situation is programmed to the extent that the manager taking the decision has a detailed predictive model that allows him to specify the means that should be used to achieve the desired result. It is non-programmed to the extent that he is unable (or is unwilling) to specify means, but only desired ends. This concept is closely associated with the exercise of managerial judgement and discretion that has been seen as the heart of managerial work (Jacques, 1961) and which is discussed in more detail in Chapter 4. The accounting implications of exercising control in non-programmed situations are the subject matter of Part Three.

ORGANIZATIONAL CONTROL

Having developed a general model of the overall process control, we will now begin to apply it to analyse the processes of planning and control that are observed in organizations. As has previously been stated, our model is not sufficiently complex for it fully to represent all facets of the exercise of control in human organizations. Nevertheless, we believe that it captures sufficient of the essence of the control process for it to be a valuable tool in aiding us to understand many of the issues involved in the design and operation of management planning and control systems. In this section we will examine the nature of organizational objectives and their impact on the measurement and control of organizational performance. It will be argued that practical planning and control systems focus on plans of action rather than on objectives, and that such plans are more the result of political compromise than of an optimization process. This conclusion reinforces our view of the importance of accounting standards, such as budgets, in the evaluation and control of organizational performance.

(a) Organizational objectives

The exercise of control implies the existence of an objective. If you do not know where you want to go, then the process of getting there cannot be controlled. Yet it is by no means obvious in what sense organizations can be said to have objectives. For example, Cyert and March (1963) begin their classic article with the blunt assertion:

Individuals have objectives; collectivities of individuals do not

although it should be noted that the remainder of their argument is actually devoted to an analysis of how the concept of an organizational objective can be made meaningful.

Even the concept of an individual objective may be problematic. It has been argued, notably by Weick (1979), that objectives are primarily post-rationalizations used to generate explanations for past experiences. Certainly individuals seem far more capable of describing how they took past decisions in terms of an objective-seeking model than they are when attempting to explain how they are making a current decision. Even if it is accepted that the concept of objectives is useful in explaining and predicting individual behaviour, there is a serious problem involved in converting objectives held by a set of individuals into an organizational objective.

Consider a group of nine people, such as a Board of Directors, who are attempting to choose a course of action they, as a group, wish to undertake. They agree that there are three alternative and mutually exclusive courses of action open to them (which we shall label A, B and C), but the Board members have different preferences concerning which should be adopted. In fact, 4 members prefer alternative A, with B as their second choice; 3 members prefer alternative C with A as second choice and 2 members prefer alternative B with C as second choice. The problem for the Board is to determine an agreed course of action; the nature of their problem can be seen as soon as it is attempted to construct a preference function for the group from the preference functions of the individuals.

The individual preference functions are:

$$A > B > C \qquad \text{4 members}$$
$$C > A > B \qquad \text{3 members}$$
$$B > C > A \qquad \text{2 members}$$

By comparing each alternative we find that:

$$A > B \qquad \text{by 7 members to 2}$$
$$B > C \qquad \text{by 6 members to 3}$$
$$C > A \qquad \text{by 5 members to 4}$$

The preference function of the group is therefore:

$$A > B > C > A$$

which is circular (or intransitive).

Thus, even although each of the group members has a well defined and transitive preference function, in this particular case the group has a composite preference function that is intransitive and appears irrational. Moving from individual preferences to a group preference is not a simple mathematical process even when it is assumed, as here, that each group member carries equal weight (Arrow, 1951).

This is not to imply that the situation cannot be resolved. It may be that the group can agree upon a general means by which their conflicts are to be resolved and will agree to abide by its results in each particular case where it is applied. For example, they might agree to abide by the result of a straight vote. If each person votes for his most favoured alternative (and avoids so-called 'strategic voting') the result will be clear-cut, with A being selected. Unfortunately, different methods of resolving the conflict can produce equally clear-cut, but different results. Suppose a single, transferable vote system were to be adopted. In the final round the result will be that C is selected, which is an equally clear-cut, although different, result.

Again, it may be decided that simple voting does not allow for different intensities of preference to be expressed. For example, some group members may be almost indifferent between two alternatives, but strongly prefer either to the third. A method of taking this into account would be to give a number of points for each individual to allocate to each alternative, so that he could indicate his relative preference more accurately. This could produce a result in which alternative B is selected.

It can be seen that although a decision rule can be chosen that avoids the intransitive nature of the group's preference function preventing a decision from being made, different decision rules will produce different results. In this particular example, any alternative may be selected, depending solely upon the decision rule used. The choice problem is only resolved if there is agreement on the decision rule to be used to resolve the conflict; the selection of such an accepted decision rule is itself a problem of group choice! Recognition of this underlying feature of social life may help to illuminate commonly observed group decision-making processes. Suppose the alternatives facing our Board of Directors represent mutually exclusive capital investment opportunities. They will convene a Board meeting at which the issue will be resolved (let us say) by a straight vote, the project receiving most votes being accepted. What will happen? Commonly a process of 'sounding out' occurs, in which each member attempts to discover how each other member will vote. To the extent that this is successful and accurate, it becomes apparent to some people that their most favoured alternative is not going to be accepted. In the above example the 2 people favouring alternative *B* will become aware both that *B* will not win the vote and also that *A*, their least favoured alternative, is likely to. What can they do? Most easily, they may choose to engage in 'strategic voting' by switching their vote to their second preference, alternative *C*. Then alternative *C* will obtain 5 votes to alternative *A*'s 4 votes. By this manoeuvre the outcome will be more to the strategic voters' liking than if they had voted simply for their first preference.

However, before the meeting the four members who prefer *A* most and *C* least realize what may happen. They react by lobbying the strategic voters and offering to vote for *B*. As this is the strategists' first preference, they accept, and a coalition that will carry *B* is formed. The three members who dislike *B* most now react by contracting the four members who have defected from *A* and offer to vote for *A*; a combination that will yield 7 votes for *A*. To avoid this occurrence, the strategic voters re-assert themselves, and so on, in theory for ever and in practice until the moment the vote is actually taken.

The lack of agreement on *aims* produces a situation in which participants come to some agreement on *means*. The process by which this is achieved is essentially one of political compromise, in which each person bargains to achieve the best possible outcome, in the circumstances, for his own aims. However, the group coheres as a group if, and only if, each individual perceives that he can best achieve his own aims by co-operating in the group activity. If this condition is not met, then he will attempt to find another group that serves his purposes better, or go it alone. In this much oversimplified example we have considered only one decision taken at one point in time. In real life, the situation will be complicated by political trade-offs between otherwise unrelated decisions (the 'support me on this and I'll vote with you on that' syndrome) and by the definition of the alternatives under consideration. All of these considerations give some indication of the reasons why straightforward economic or operational research approaches to business decision making, which essentially attempt to programme previously non-programmed decisions, run into problems. It may not be possible to agree upon an overall objective function to be optimized, or even to produce a list of alternative strategies that will be agreed by all participants. Much managerial resistance to quantitative models of this type may be explained by the fact that managers realize that once such items are specified, the decision process becomes programmed with little scope for their discretion or the negotiation of political trade-offs.

The feasible region of activity

Although we have considered a situation in which individual objectives conflict to such an extent that it is meaningless to talk of a group objective, this is something of an extreme case. Most organizations will have some common ground on which all participants can agree, and all will have ground on which some participants can agree. Most participants in business organizations will agree that the overall return to shareholders is a guiding objective, or at the very least, a crucial constraint. We have also seen that it may be easier for participants to reach agreement upon actions to be taken (i.e., means) than it is for them to agree upon objectives (i.e., ends). We may thus represent the possibilities open to an organization by a diagram in an activity space. Each point in this activity space (Fig. 1.3) represents a set of activities that the organization might undertake. Within this space, the set of activities that each interest group considers acceptable to it can be represented by means of a set boundary: activity

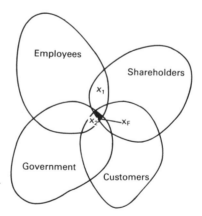

Fig. 1.3   Feasible activity space for an organization. X_1 represents a set of activities acceptable both to shareholders and employees, but not to customers or the government (e.g., high prices); X_2 represents a set acceptable to all but shareholders (e.g., low price, high wage); only X_F is feasible for satisfying all interest groups.

points within the set boundary are acceptable, whereas those outside are unacceptable. Such a set boundary may be drawn for each individual or, if groups of individuals have largely common interests, more simply for each group. The intersection of any two sets represents those activities acceptable to both groups involved. In this way, it can seem that the feasible activity space for the organization as a whole is the intersection of the sets of all the interest groups involved (Lowe and Chua, 1983).

It should be noted that this feasible region is shown as being relatively small, for it is suggested that in many circumstances it is either small or non-existent. This is mainly because not all points within each group's set of acceptable alternatives are equally acceptable. The set boundaries may perhaps best be interpreted in a similar way to contour lines; as the standard of acceptability for each group is raised so the corresponding set shrinks in size. For example, if market conditions are such that the feasible region is large, groups will revise their standards of acceptability so that it shrinks, and the benefits are allocated in some way between participants. Extreme examples of such a re-allocation of benefits can be seen:

1. In the UK coal mining industry following the large oil price rises in 1973/74. Most of the additional revenue gained by raising prices to customers up to the new market level for energy was paid to the coal miners in the form of increased wages.
2. In Rolls-Royce, following the financial collapse of the company in 1970/71. Although many of the activities of the company continued as before with much the same workforce, the cost of the collapse was borne almost exclusively by the shareholders and to some extent the major customer, Lockheed, who had to renegotiate a major contract.
3. In the pocket calculator market, where many companies invested considerable sums of money in developing microchip technology. Over-supply and low production costs (as compared with high development costs) caused a rapid price drop, which benefited customers but caused many firms (e.g., Rockwell) to withdraw from the market.
4. The collapse of the print unions at Wapping, London, when the introduction of new technology was used to eliminate the power of a small group of employees who previously had control over the newspaper production process.

The control task of management may be viewed as maintaining the activities of the organization within the feasible region determined by the intersecting acceptable sets of the organizational participants.

Such a view has several corollaries. Firstly, feasibility is seen as being a more basic concept than optimality; for optimality implies a shared objective, whereas feasibility concentrates on identifying activities acceptable to all. This is not to suggest that each interest group does not seek to improve its own position, but rather that fundamental conflicts within the organization make overall organizational optimality an elusive concept. Secondly, control can be viewed as being oriented to the implementation of agreed sets of actions, rather than as the pursuit of generalized organizational objectives. Finally, because each interest group pursues its own aims, and co-operates with others only to the extent that co-operative activity is necessary to those aims, each environmental change will lead to changes in the expectations of each interest group and a consequent change in their acceptable activity set. The feasible region for the organization will thus change frequently and have a tendency to disappear, whereas negotiations take place to identify an acceptable compromise. The management control task can be seen as identifying possible feasible regions of activity and attempting to keep the organization within them.

It can be seen that under conditions of change, both in the environment and in the changing behaviours of organizational participants, the concept of organizational control is somewhat elusive. This is partly because the system being controlled has not been closely defined but merely labelled 'the organization'. But does 'the organization' include its customers and suppliers or even its employees and shareholders? Certainly members of each of these groups change constantly, yet we still tend to regard the organization as being the same. Even when the membership of a whole such group is replaced at a stroke, many features of the original organization still persist. It is not proposed to lay down a precise (but essentially arbitrary) definition of what constitutes 'the organization' for this will differ according to the purpose of the analysis being undertaken; suffice it to note that the design of a control system must incorporate such a judgement. Many of the problems that arise in the use of management control systems can be traced back to this ambiguity in the specification of the system being controlled.

A typology of organizations

Fortunately, the conflicts of interest described in this section are not as severe in some organizations as in others, and in all organizations there are periods during which participants agree to work within a negotiated framework, accepting that certain activities require to be carried out for the common benefit. Formally designed management control systems based on accounting information are of most value at such times; when there is conflict within the organization it is less sensible to talk of an *organizational* control system, although the exercise of power by sectional interest groups is of paramount importance (Pfeffer, 1981).

Etzioni (1961) has developed a typology of organizations that provides an insight into this issue. He identifies three different types of power used in organizations (normative, remunerative and coercive) and three different kinds of personal involvement (moral, calculative and alienative). He argues that there is a natural tendency for three combinations of types of power used and type of involvement found to go together, and thus defines 3 major kinds of organization: *normative*, using normative power and obtaining moral involvement, *utilitarian*, using remunerative power and obtaining calculative involvement and *coercive*, using coercive power and obtaining alienative involvement.

In the normative organization, the issues discussed above cause no great problem because organizational members are morally committed to the aims of the organization. The organizational objectives may be viewed as, in some ways, the sum of very similar individual objectives. When conflict arises, it can generally be dealt with by appealing to the underlying shared aims of all organizational members. Examples of such organizations might be churches and religious orders, charities, political parties and crusade armies. At the other end of the spectrum, control is relatively straightforward in coercive organizations, where some members are kept within the organization against their will by coercion. Here a dominant group, with the ability to impose its will on other participants, effectively determines organizational action. The organizational goal is, for most intents and purposes, the goal of this dominant group. Examples of such organizations might be prisons, slave camps and conscript armies.

It is in utilitarian (or instrumental) organizations that the issue of objectives is most ambiguous. In such organizations, bargains are struck on the basis that individuals will undertake certain commitments to advance organizational purposes in return for negotiated rewards. The organization offers inducements to elicit contributions from individuals (Barnard, 1938). There are not necessarily any agreed goals; rather the participants have agreed on a set of contracts to ensure that activities are carried out that are acceptable to all parties involved. In utilitarian organizations, control is primarily a matter of ensuring that contracts are carried out, and of renegotiating their content whenever necessary. Examples of utilitarian organiza tions would include most industrial enterprises and mercenary armies. It is of note that although some contracts may be precise, legal definitions specifying the exact exchange agreed, others are much more open-ended. In particular, the contracts by which people are employed most usually specify only attendance requirements rather than details of the work to be performed and the manner in which it is to be done. This allows the organization a greater degree of flexibility in its actions, but it is hardly surprising that the continual interpretation of conditions and requirements of employment is the most frequent source of conflict between interest groups in the economic scene.

Although it is arguable that the dominant type of business organization is the utilitarian, there is little doubt that the point on the spectrum of normative, through utilitarian to coercive types of organization, occupied can differ considerably both from organization to organization, and by hierarchical level within the organization. Some organizations stress normative involvement with the aims of dominant participants (e.g., some of the Quaker-founded chocolate firms, professional partnerships, such as chartered accountants, and firms with high-technology products, such as computers, all lay stress on moral involvement), although it may be thought that when such involvement is codified into manuals of dress and behaviour, as in some accounting firms, the involvement is more coercive than moral! Other organizations tend towards the coercive end of the spectrum, when one group of participants, usually employees or customers, are relatively powerless in comparison with another participant (e.g., the traditional 'tally-man' and other doorstep credit traders; employers in declining industries having elderly workforces processing non-transferable skills). Whatever the tendency of the organizations as a whole, higher-ranking employees are likely to be involved in a more normative manner and lower-ranking employees in a more coercive manner, reflecting the relative power base of each group as well as other social and cultural factors. It is difficult to imagine the finance director of the Ford Motor Company uttering the sentiment expressed by a Ford assembly line worker noted by Beynon (1973):

I wouldn't touch the bloody things (Ford cars): not with what I see going on in that plant.

It has been argued that, although the exercise of control requires the existence of objectives as a standard of comparison, the typical business enterprise does not have clear-cut organizational objectives. This is because the various participants connected with the organization each have their own disparate objectives and possess comparable amounts of power with which to achieve their aims. Even if there is agreement on an overall objective, such as the maximization of shareholder wealth, the decomposition of this overall objective into sub-goals for different parts of the organization can be problematical. The organization coheres only when each group perceives that it can gain by co-operating with other groups in common activities that will assist each to attain their own goals. The dominant mode of organization is thus the utilitarian or instrumental mode where remunerative power attracts predominantly calculative involvement. Control in such organizations is based upon agreement on *means* rather than agreement on *ends*. Formal controls are likely to be of more use during periods of agreement on activities, and of less use during periods during which extensive renegotiation of the inducement – contribution balance is being carried out. One task of the management control system may be seen as assisting the organization to identify a feasible set of activities that will provide acceptable inducements to all participants and ensuring that such activities are carried out.

Effectiveness, efficiency and economy

In the previous section a model of a controlled process was developed, and in this section a major problem in applying the model to organizational control has been discussed, namely the nature of organizational objectives. It has been shown that control is a meaningful concept only where an end or an objective exists, and that great care is needed in defining an organizational objective, as distinct from an objective of an interest group connected with the organization. Even in the restricted context of a business enterprise having participants interested solely in their own economic welfare, the interests of different groups are conflicting. Shareholders are interested in the return on their investment, employees in their wages, customers and suppliers in obtaining an advantageous price, and the local community in having a healthy local economy.

However, despite such conflicts, there is also likely to be some basic level of agreement. It is usually in the interests of all involved that the firm continues to exist as an entity; to achieve this agreements are reached, implicitly or explicitly, on wages and prices in relation to a production plan for at least a limited period. During this period of apparent consensus, organizational control is a relatively straightforward concept involving the execution of agreed plans. When the longer term is considered, the concept of control becomes increasingly problematic when the adaptation of the organization to environmental changes cannot be achieved without adverse effects on one or more interest groups. For example, investment in new technology may imply a reduction in employment opportunities; protection of employment may result in higher prices and lower profits; technological change may require employees to have increased levels of skill, and so on. The process by which such conflicts are resolved is essentially political, involving negotiation between parties of differing power profiles, and the eventual decisions reached will be more favourable to some than others. In such a system, where conflicts of interest prevail, the concept of organizational control is more nebulous, although the eventual outcome of the negotiation can be regarded as a new, if short-run, plan of agreed activities.

Before progressing towards defining some measures of organizational effectiveness, there are several other aspects of control in organizations that it may be helpful to elucidate. First, there is the useful distinction made by Drucker (1964a) between 'control' and 'controls'. According to Drucker, 'controls' are a means that lead towards the objective of overall 'control'. However, he warns that such overall control may not be attained by a proliferation of controls. That is, an organization littered with rules and procedures for many possible eventualities may be less likely to be successful because it becomes so concerned with detail that it does not see much greater changes that threaten its long-term future. Thus 'control' is more than a matter of generating 'controls'; it involves a continual monitoring of the position of the enterprise as a whole.

It is also useful to note that any control action generally has adverse immediate effects on some individuals or groups. Thus the imposition of parking controls adversely affects those who habitually park all day in the street, even though it may improve the welfare of other motorists by removing congestion. Tighter credit control implies that some customers will have to pay their bills sooner than they otherwise would; improved stock control may lead to greater fluctuations in the production demanded of the factory. In general, although a control action may serve the good of the overall organization, some participants are likely to be adversely affected (for, if not, by acting in their own selfish interest the overall good would be seen to ensue, and the control action would be unnecessary). Thus control actions are often seen as unpleasant and unpopular, by some participants at least. This does not imply that the actions are unnecessary, but rather that they inevitably imply a re-distribution of benefits. For example a new manufacturing process may require a smaller workforce, yet offer improved wages and increased job security for those who remain. The implementation of control actions by managers may thus be a complex process, involving the resolution of conflict between groups who will be affected in different ways.

Finally, the distinctions between effectiveness, efficiency and economy require examination, as they are a continual source of confusion and lack of clarity. *Effectiveness* is concerned with the attainment of objectives; an action is effective to the extent that it achieves what it was intended to achieve. *Efficiency* is concerned with achieving a given result with a minimum use of resources. *Economy* is a much more restricted concept, used predominantly in the public sector. It refers only to the containment of costs without regard to the results achieved; however it is an important concept for those organizations which have to live within strict constraints such as rigid cash limits. An action may thus be effective, but inefficient in that the result could have been achieved more economically. It is not really sensible to describe an action as efficient if it is ineffective, although it might be efficient in the limited sense that it produced the actual outcome economically. An economical action may be cheap but possibly ineffective. These terms, effectiveness, efficiency and economy tend to be used very loosely by many writers, for example in discussing business efficiency. It must be stressed that in order to measure efficiency it is pre-supposed that an activity is effective. That is, efficiency is ill defined unless the objectives of activities are first clarified. Thus a lower cost of production is not evidence of productive efficiency, unless the goods produced were those required and the cost measured includes all resources used in the productive process. In the subsequent discussion, the terms *effectiveness*, *efficiency* and *economy* will be used as defined here.

A further difficulty with the notions of effectiveness and efficiency, but particularly with the latter, is that they are relative terms, not absolutes. Thus for an action that is largely effective, in that it produces nearly the effect expected or desired, there is no pre-defined scale on which effectiveness can be measured. For example, is a business that generates £80 profit when it wished to generate £100 more or less effective than one which generates £49 when it attempted to generate £50? Efficiency is an even more tenuous concept, because its measurement implies that we have a means of determining the minimum resources necessary to produce a given effect. Whereas this may be possible in the physical sciences, such as thermodynamics, where we have models of optimal behaviour, it is less feasible in connection with economic activity. The measurement of effectiveness requires a means of predicting what would have occurred in the absence of an action; the measurement of efficiency requires a means of predicting the resources that would have been used by the optimal effective action. The notions thus tend to be ambiguous, not because actual outcomes and actual resources used cannot be measured, but rather because it is difficult to find a valid standard with which actual performance can be compared.

The root of the difficulty lies in the imprecision of available predictive models of organizational performance. Not only are we usually ignorant of optimal methods of attaining desired ends, we are often ignorant of possible methods. Thus, as was argued previously, managers are as concerned with feasibility and effectiveness as they are with the fine-tuning of optimality and efficiency. There are typically five major standards available against which performance can be compared:

1. the performance of the same organization in previous time periods;
2. the performance of similar organizations;
3. estimates of expected performance made by the organization *ex ante*;
4. an estimate of what might have been achieved made by the organization *ex post*;
5. the performance necessary to achieve certain defined goals or objectives.

These standards will be considered in greater detail later, but suffice it to note for the present that they all have inherent defects in the absence of adequate predictive models. Comparison of performance over time periods involves the implicit assumption that external conditions have been constant over time; to adjust for the effect of such conditions requires a model of how performance is affected by environmental circumstances. Comparison with similar organizations, even if over a period of time, assumes that all face identical conditions and begin from equally advantageous starting conditions. A standard set *ex ante*, such as a budget, requires a predictive model of the organization and its interaction with a forecast environment; deviations from budget may represent deficiencies in the budget standard as much as ineffective or inefficient performance. *Ex post* standards obviate the need for environmental forecasts, but still require an optimal model of performance from which they can be derived. (Amey, 1969). Target standards give a clear indication of what is desirable, but assessment of what is feasible requires the first two standards of comparison to be used. Thus the assessment of organizational performance requires both the ability to measure actual outcomes and a predictive model to generate an appropriate standard of comparison.

Practical methods of assessing organizational performance usually involve the examination of trends in measure of performance over a period of time. This is a useful pragmatic procedure, but is of limited usefulness in a changing environment; a reduced current performance may still represent a valiant response to changed circumstances. Nevertheless, the use of a complete battery of trends, involving all five of the standards of comparison outlined above, can provide a means of making an informed judgement about the relative efficiency and effectiveness of an organization. The provision of such information with appropriate comparisons highlighted is a useful exercise that can be undertaken by the management accountant. Budgets are also an important control device as they represent a quantitative statement of a proposed plan of action against which subsequent performance can be monitored and controlled. The process of budgeting generally involves an iterative cycle which moves between targets of desirable performance and estimates of feasible performance until there is hopefully convergence to a plan which is both feasible and acceptable. Budgetary control is perhaps the most widely used accounting control technique and will be examined in detail in Chapter 7, but we will first consider some general problems in performance measurement.

Performance measures

A vital part of the control process, and one with which accounting is particularly concerned, is the measurement of actual performance so that it may be compared with what is desired, expected or hoped for. However, it is important to stress that performance measurement is but one stage in the overall control process; it is also necessary to set standards, and to take appropriate action to ensure that such standards are attained. Accounting has been particularly concerned with the standard-setting and performance measurement, but less involved with the development of predictive models of performance and with the generation of apt control actions. This bias has more to do with the capabilities of accounting systems and the traditional role of management accountants than it has with the relative importance of each stage. Each condition for control is necessary; none individually is sufficient. The term 'performance' in the context of organizational behaviour is highly ambiguous. Indeed its frequent use suggests that it may more often be used to avoid precise definition of what is meant. The reader is recommended to try to substitute a synonym of a more precise nature whenever the term is encountered; the difficulty experienced in so doing will be a good indication of the lack of clarity often concealed by its use.

In order to measure organizational performance, it is first necessary to discover what the organization is attempting to achieve. That is, organizational performance is closely connected with the ideas of organizational effectiveness and efficiency which are discussed at greater length in the next section. As organizational objectives are multiple, partially conflicting and subject to change over time, appropriate measures of performance will have similar characteristics. The multiple nature of objectives can generate an obsessive cycle of behaviour as illustrated by Ridgway (1956). A single performance measure is initially used, but is seen as increasingly inadequate as a representation of overall performance. Other measures are therefore added and a battery of performance indicators used. However as these measures represent partially conflicting objectives, there is pressure from members for the organization to specify the trade-offs between them. This leads to the generation of a composite performance measure that is constructed by weighting the multiple measures and combining them into a single overall measure. However, even if the composite measure initially represents an acceptable approximation, the relative priority of goals will change over time and other goals will be added, so that the composite measure will become subject to the same pressures as the original single performance measure. Thus a cycle tends to develop, involving firstly the elaboration of multiple measures of performance and then their integration into a single composite measure that is eventually elaborated once again.

Although there is a literature on organizational effectiveness (see Steers, 1977, for a compact survey and Lowe and Chua, 1983, for its connection with management control) it is often less than helpful to the designer of performance measures as it tends to avoid discussion of the fundamental issues, but concentrates instead on measuring and correlating empirical data on many dimensions having little theoretical rationale. One piece of work that gives evidence of the competing interests of the various groups associated with an organization is that by Pickle and Friedlander (1967). They correlated measures of satisfaction of the various interest groups across a sample of 97 business firms to examine how the satisfaction of one interest group was related to the satisfaction of others. Their results indicated that, although correlations were generally positive, they were all fairly low. It may be inferred that the satisfaction of any one group implies little for the satisfaction of another group, and that their interests may sometimes conflict.

Although work in this area has demonstrated clearly the conflicting nature of many objectives and, in particular, the conflict between long-run and short-run performance on virtually every dimension, it provides little information of practical use to those concerned with the management of organizations. It is, however, of interest to list some of the dimensions of performance that have been considered:

Survival
Profit
Earnings per share
Return on investment (total or shareholders)
Volume of sales
Growth (in sales, number of employees, capital employed or profit)
Efficiency
Productivity (i.e., output per unit of some input)
Market position
Product quality
Product leadership
Employee attitudes
Employee morale and job satisfaction
Accident rates
Absenteeism and labour turnover
Posture (i.e., ability to adapt to changing circumstances)
Social responsibility

This selection of effectiveness measures clearly indicates that most refer primarily to the interests of a single group rather than to the well-being of the organization as a whole. For example, earnings per share is relevant mainly to shareholders; sales volume and growth may be seen as serving managerial interests; product quality is of interest to the customer; job satisfaction to the employee and social responsibility to the community at large. Perhaps the only overall measures in the list are survival, which is a very minimal and often difficult-to-measure concept (e.g., did a company like Rolls-Royce which went into liquidation but continued to trade having the same employees and customers, but different owners, survive?), and profit (in the sense that profit measures the surplus left after other claims have been met). Which of the other measures are relevant will vary from company to company and from time to time. One example of a listing of key result areas is that produced by the General Electric Company (USA) which identified eight main indicators of its effectiveness:

1. profitability
2. market position
3. productivity
4. product leadership
5. personnel development
6. employee attitudes
7. public responsibility
8. balance between long-run and short-run goals.

It can be seen that financial measures of performance serve two distinct purposes. Firstly, they measure the return given to the providers of finance as an interest group in their own right, but additionally some financial results provide a measure of the overall viability of the enterprise as a whole. Thus the generation of profit can be seen both as a benefit accruing to investors, but also, in comparison with some standard rate of return (e.g., a 'fair' profit; a normal market return) as indication of the health of the enterprise. This distinction needs to be kept clearly in mind in view of the emotive reactions that seem to be brought out by discussion of company profitability, ranging from the view that 'all profit represents the exploitation of the working classes' to the view that 'profit is essential for the well-being of the country'. It is of interest to note that proposals for developing inflation-adjusted accounts have required the distinction to be made between capital maintenance (in real terms), and the maintenance of productive capacity. The 'going concern' concept of accounting can thus be seen to be ambiguous about the precise definition of what is the essential core of the enterprise that constitutes a standard for assessment of improvement or deterioration.

THE ROLE OF ACCOUNTING INFORMATION IN CONTROL

Accounting information is an important control tool within the organization because it provides one of the few quantitative, integrative mechanisms that are available. Although accounting information in no way reflects the totality of activities that take place within the organization and in its interaction with the wider environment, it does provide information on one dimension of such activity. Because the information is expressed in common monetary terms, it can be aggregated across all organizational units and combined into successively more aggregate measures of performance. In such a manner, it provides a vehicle for discussing ways of integrating organizational activities.

However, there is a danger inherent in its use. Because it is often the only quantitative measure of the activities of a wide variety of disparate units, it can become treated as if it represented the only important aspect of organizational activity. This tendency has often been re-inforced by the dominant position of the owner who is primarily concerned with his financial return, but it must be recognized that the other aspects of performance previously listed are equally, if not more, important and will indeed ultimately affect the accounting measures adversely if not given appropriate attention.

A similar effect can often be noted at lower hierarchical levels in the organization. Because accounting information is, of necessity, often used at senior levels as the basis for decision making and control, its importance tends to be exaggerated at junior levels, where alternative information may be available. For example, although production cost may be an appropriate control variable for a manager responsible for several different plants, physical production figures together with quality control and reliability indices may be more appropriate at plant level.

It is also necessary to distinguish between the use of accounting information in financial control and its use in organizational control. Financial control is concerned with the regulation of the flow of money through the enterprise and, in particular, with ensuring that cash is always available to pay debts when they fall due. This is self-evidently vital for the survival of the enterprise, but nevertheless finance represents only one function amongst many others, such as production, marketing and industrial relations. Organizational control, on the other hand, is primarily concerned with the overall integration of all functional activities into a viable whole. Although organizational control will require accounting information, the information required will be more extensive than that used purely for financial control. For example, whereas the financial control function will examine the impact of a proposed capital investment on future cash flows and profitability, and will require information on marketing and industrial relations to make financial predictions, organizational control is concerned with the impact of the investment on all aspects of the business. Although financial considerations are of fundamental importance, and although monetary measures may represent the only quantitative tool available for combining disparate effects, nevertheless the central thrust of information provided for organizational control is to provide an assessment of overall impact on various relevant dimensions. Organizational control is thus a wider concept than financial control, and the information required to enable it to be effective is correspondingly broader.

The major part of this book is concerned with the provision of accounting information to aid the process of overall organizational control. It must be remembered that although such accounting information is an important aid to such overall control, it is by no means sufficient. The process of ensuring that an organization adapts itself to the circumstances in which it finds itself in appropriate ways requires various skills, not least the generation of apt courses of action in response to adverse conditions. It has often been remarked, for example in relation to capital investment appraisal (King, 1975) that accountants have been over-concerned with the evaluation stage to the exclusion of concern with the generation of a short-list of good candidates for consideration. It is a truism that even a perfect system of evaluation can do no better than select the best of whatever alternatives are presented to it. Thus the provision of good accounting information is only a necessary, not a sufficient, condition for effective organizational control. Nevertheless, it is believed that the absence of such information or, perhaps worse, the provision of inadequate or misleading information, is a powerful disadvantage to effective organizational functioning, and that attention to the provision of appropriate accounting information is of vital importance.

EXERCISES

1. Explain the decision process you followed in making an important decision in the past which has now taken effect (e.g., the choice of a course of study and the university to attend; the choice of your present job). Then explain the same process in relation to a decision you are currently faced with and which you have not yet resolved (e.g., the choice of a career; the possibility of changing jobs).
   How do the two processes differ? Does your analysis illuminate the role of objectives in decision making?
2. Explain how totally utilitarian organizations can behave as if they were pursuing an agreed goal, giving some business examples.
3. A company is considering changing the price charged for one of its products. What information, both qualitative and quantitative, do you think it requires in order to evaluate whether or not this would be a desirable course of action? Having changed the price, what information does it require to evaluate whether it has taken the right decision, and how could this information actually be collected?
4. How does a system go 'out of control'? Analyse three systems with which you are familiar, including at least one social system (i.e., involving several people) and one business system, in terms of the control model developed in this chapter. Explicitly identify the predictive model used for control and where it is located in your system. How might learning occur from the experience of going out of control?
5. 'Doing things wrong is a necessary pre-condition for learning'. To what extent is this statement true? Analyse its implications for:
   (a) the design of a production control system
   (b) the design of a university course.
6. Design a set of controls that could be used to evaluate how well each of the following people were performing their jobs adequately:

    (a) a production worker on a car assembly line

    (b) a double-glazing salesman allocated a particular town as his territory

    (c) a research and development scientist in a pharmaceutical company

    (d) a managing director of a chain of retail shops.

7. Design a system to control student learning on a degree course. Explicitly identify:

    (a) objectives, including possible conflicts

    (b) measures of performance to be used

    (c) the predictive model to be used

    (d) available control actions.

    Would you like to be controlled by the system you have designed? If not, can you design a better one?

8. How would you set about discovering what the goals of a specific organization are?

9. Why is it usually easier for a group of people to agree upon a plan of action than it is for them to agree on objectives? Give some counter-examples, and relate your answer to Earl and Hopwood's (1981) analysis.

10. Analyse the goals and performance measures used in any group of which you are a member (e.g., a tutorial group; a sports club; or an organization which employs you). How well do the performance measures relate to the group goals, and what problems do any mis-matches engender?

2

The design of organizations

SUMMARY

This chapter is concerned with the ways in which organizational structure can act as a means of influencing and controlling the behaviour of the individuals who work within it. This is the subject matter of organizational theory, so the first part of the chapter reviews its development. It is found that no coherent overall theory of organizational design exists, rather organizational theory consists of a series of different yet related insights which have emerged over a period of several decades.

Early theories of organization were universal in nature, attempting to discover the optimal way in which affairs were to be organized. More modern theories have tended to be contingent, attempting to relate their prescriptions to more specifically defined circumstances. Organizations have also come to be seen as an amalgam of both rationally designed elements, consciously designed to achieve certain goals, and naturally occurring elements which can arise in an unexpected and unintended manner. Most recently, theories which stress the socially created nature of organizations and their role in sustaining patterns of power and domination have come to the fore. Here it is argued that all these theories have their own insights to offer, but that none of them is sufficient or totally encompassing.

Central to the use of organizational structure as a control device is the assignment of authority and responsibility to individuals within the organization, and the holding of them accountable for the achievement of specific tasks or objectives. Information is a central component of such an accountability cycle, and its availability influences the types of control that can be used, a theme which is further developed in Chapter 4.

Accounting information is an important subset of more general management information. The design of accounting information systems (AIS) is evidently influenced by organizational design, so it is not surprising that theories of AIS design have developed in parallel with organizational theory. Since 1975, the so-called contingency theory of management accounting has become the main focus of attention. This theory has concentrated on identifying the main features of an organization and its environment which affect AIS design. Although it is still emerging, features of both an organization's context and its internal structure and control arrangements have been found to have a substantial impact upon AIS design. But it is unlikely that any theory of this type will be able to explain all aspects of control systems design. The reaction of people against those aspects of control which negatively impinge upon them will ensure that the design of control systems will remain a developing social process within organizations. However, the theories that we do have at least allow us to begin to understand certain aspects of this on-going social process.

INTRODUCTION

Organizations consist of people, and organizational control is ultimately concerned with the control of the behaviour of individual people. Organizational structure is a potent form of control because, by arranging people in a hierarchy with defined patterns of authority and responsibility, a great deal of their behaviour can be influenced and even pre-determined. Further, within the structure of organizations many different processes of control also operate, ranging from procedures for personnel selection and recruitment to the rewards and sanctions that are applied in evaluating individual performance.

But it is not sufficient to consider organizations solely as an aggregate of individuals, for individual behaviour is heavily conditioned by the social and cultural context in which it occurs. It is therefore possible to talk of organizational behaviour as being qualitatively different from individual behaviour, and theories of organization have developed that have little to say about individual behaviour. Both individual and organizational approaches have their own distinctive contributions to make; in this chapter we will consider theories relating to the design of organizational structure and discuss theories of individual motivation and behaviour in Chapter 3.

THE HISTORICAL DEVELOPMENT OF ORGANIZATION THEORY

As organizations have increased in size, theorists have increasingly speculated about how they should be managed. It is arguable that organization theory dates back at least to Biblical times insofar as the administration of nation states and their armies are concerned, but it was only in the 19th century that organizations other than the State or Church attained sufficient size for their administration to appear problematic. Over the past 100 years there have been various approaches to the study of the organization of large numbers of people put forward; these will be briefly reviewed in this section, but first some general trends will be noted.

Many early theories of organization were universal in nature; that is, they specified the best way in which a particular task could be organized regardless of other circumstances. More modern theories are usually contingent; that is, they relate particular prescriptions about what should be done to other features of the organization and its environment. Secondly, earlier theories tended towards treating organizations implicitly as closed systems, operating in isolation from other organizations and society more generally. The problems engendered by such an implicit assumption became recognized during the 1950s and were overcome by the development of open systems approaches that explicitly model the connections between an organization and its wider environment. Finally, there has always been a tension between approaches that treat organizations as designed artefacts constructed to achieve defined purposes and approaches that consider them to be naturally occurring phenomena, displaying rationality and purpose to only a limited extent. Some characteristics of these two perspectives are given in Table 2.1. However, despite the dichotomous nature of this presentation, it needs to be recognized that human economic organizations display both sets of characteristics. They are designed to achieve certain defined purposes and yet develop in ways that are unplanned and unexpected. Purposes become displaced and parts of an organization can show great resistance to planned changes. Theories of organization that fail to consider this dual aspect of organizational activity are inevitably deficient.

Scott (1981) has suggested that the development of organization theory during this century can be viewed as a progression from rational to natural models, firstly within a closed systems perspective and more recently within an open systems perspective. But we have stated that organizations are both rational and natural and Thompson (1967) has argued that organizations display the characteristics of both open and closed systems in that they strive for rationality (closure) in the face of uncertainty (openness). Thus each stage in the development of organization theory has the potential to teach us something about the functioning of organizations, but no single theory yet has a monopoly of understanding. Boland and Pondy (1983) suggest that the study of accounting in organizations is particularly pertinent because accounting can also be viewed as both a natural and a rational process. Organization theory appears to be at a point where it is able to recognize these conflicting tendencies within

Table 2.1 Two views of organizations (Scapens, Otley and Lister, 1984)

	The organization as a designed artefact	The organization as a natural phenomenon
Basic question asked	How can organizational effectiveness best be achieved?	How may organizational behaviour best be explained?
Existence of goals	Organizational goals exist, although they may be multiple, conflicting and sometimes displaced.	Goals are an inappropriate concept; organizational behaviour is best explained in terms of power and interaction processes.
Control	Control is concerned with the overall guidance of the organization in pursuit of its goals, minimally survival, i.e., with the size of the 'cake'	Control is concerned with the exercise of power and the influence exerted by one person or group over others, i.e., with the distribution of the 'cake'
Typical theories	Classical management theory Contingency theories Sociological structural-functionalism Stress on formal organization and organizational design	Open systems theory Decision-making theories Sociological action theories Stress on informal organization and unanticipated consequences
Orientation	Normative	Descriptive
Role of management control	A rational and neutral set of procedures to ensure overall organizational effectiveness	A tool of one interest group used to enable them to dominate other groups

itself; however an integrated theory incorporating both natural and rational processes has yet to emerge.

It is not possible within the confines of this chapter to adequately survey the development of organization theory; only brief attention can be given to a few of the important highlights. Fortunately there are many good texts available for the interested reader, and particularly recommended are Kast and Rosenzweig (1974), Khandwalla (1977), Mintzberg (1979) and Pfeffer (1982). There is also a brief summary in the linking material of Chenhall *et al.*'s (1981) book of readings on the organizational context of management accounting, which is of especial value because it links organization theory with developments in management accounting research. Some more recent theories, particularly those stemming from critical theory and labour process theories are well illustrated by some of the contributions in Chua *et al.* (1989). In addition, Macintosh (1985) contains several chapters which review the connections between organization theory and the design of accounting and other management information systems.

Many of the early writers on organization were practising managers or military men who sought solutions to the practical problems they faced, and who became concerned to communicate their findings to a wider audience. Their perspective is thus managerial in nature and it is notable that several of their number were active management consultants. Thus early work has a tendency to prescribe solutions, whereas more recent work is more reflective in nature. We will first outline classical management theories, then move on to consider systems theory, and briefly conclude with descriptions of the decision-making and critical theory approaches. Finally, the role of organizational structure as a control device and the development of the contingency theories of organization will be reviewed.

Classical management theory

There are three main strands of development that can be identified under the general banner of classical management theory, namely scientific management, administrative theory and industrial psychology, all of which have their counterparts in present-day management practice. The common feature of all classical approaches to organizational design is that they attempt to derive universal prescriptions that indicate the best way to structure and manage an organization.

(a) Scientific management
The scientific management movement is inextricably linked with the name of F.W. Taylor, who rose from being a labourer to the position

of chief engineer of a large US steel works. In his work as a gang boss, Taylor became frustrated by the inefficiencies that he saw as resulting from management by pressure. Such pressure, he believed, was a consequence of management's ignorance of what constituted a proper day's work, so he therefore began to develop the work study techniques for which he has become famous. His underlying philosophy was that, for every job, there is 'one best way' of performing it, and that this can be discovered by detailed observation and analysis. Having defined the optimum method of task performance, a worker fitted to the type of work involved was selected (by scientific selection techniques), trained to follow this method exactly, and rewarded by incentive payments for reaching the pre-determined standards. The task of management was to plan and to provide the proper conditions for work; the worker's job was to do exactly as he was told. The golden rule of scientific management emerged as: 'Get the situation right, and the appropriate human behaviour and organizational performance will follow'.

Taylor thus developed methods of efficient performance for well specified tasks that could be precisely analysed (i.e., where a well defined means–end relationship could be uncovered). Labour was just that; a means of accomplishing mechanical tasks in which thinking was deliberately discouraged, and the effect of a person's feelings minimized by the use of economic incentives. It gives a little of the flavour of Taylor's work to note that two of the tasks he is most famous for studying are the shovelling of coke and iron ore, and the loading and unloading of pig iron into railway wagons. He published an account of his techniques, but a better insight into his underlying philosophy and orientation may be found in his testimony to a Congressional committee of inquiry set up to investigate labour troubles caused by the application of his methods (Taylor, 1947).

Before dismissing his approach as a hangover from 19th century forms of social organization, it is important to recognize that its variants persist today in techniques of work measurement and payment schemes, in organization and methods (O & M) analysis, in much of the practice of operational research, and, most significantly, in standard costing and management accounting. Much management accounting practice is based on the assumption that budgets and standards for human and organizational performance can be set in a more or less objective and scientifically verifiable manner. To some extent this may be true for well understood tasks, although even here the fact that one is dealing with human beings rather than machines sets limits to what can be achieved. For less well understood tasks, particularly those at senior levels of management, this assumption can be seriously misleading. It is notable that the effects of standard setting have been an early topic of behavioural accounting research, indicating the unease felt by researchers at the sweeping assumptions made in the standard costing literature.

(b) Administrative theory

The second strand of development was that of administrative theory. The thrust of this school of thought was similar to that of scientific management, but was applied to administrative rather than physical work, in that it sought to discover the best way to structure organizational activities for the effective accomplishment of organizational objectives. Stemming from the work of Fayol (1949, but originally published in French in 1914), writers such as Follett (1924), Gulick (1937), Barnard (1938) and Urwick (1947) concerned themselves with formulating principles of effective management practice and particularly issues of organizational structure and leadership style. Popular principles such as 'one man, one boss', 'responsibility should equal authority', 'no manager should have more than six direct subordinates', all derive from the work of this school. It also contains strong military overtones, Urwick in particular having served in the British Army, and a great deal of its terminology is consonant with military metaphors: for example, 'line and staff' organization, 'lines of command' and, more recently terms such as 'marketing offensive' stem from this background.

The common use of such metaphors may lead us into believing that the military model of organization, suited to a unique task and often behind the times even in its own speciality, is appropriate to the circumstances faced by a modern industrial, commercial or public enterprise (Weick, 1979). When the metaphors are stated as baldly as this, one is unlikely to be misled, but they are often only implicit. Similarly the assumption often made by administrative theorists that, regardless of the task, there is one best way of organizing for it, should also be viewed critically. Again, however, the work of administrative theorists forms the basis of much management accounting practice, particularly in the area of responsibility accounting. The implicit assumptions of the management accounting textbook tend to be those of the classical management theorists and to have a similar universalist claim, namely that there is one best way to set up a management accounting system, regardless of its organizational context. The practising management accountant seems to know better, for much of his time is taken up with adapting general-purpose accounting systems to meet the particular needs of his own organization.

(c) Industrial psychology

Industrial psychology, the third major strand, is notable in that it has been anxious to show that it is not solely identified with managerial interests, but that it also has a concern with individual welfare. Although there was suspicion even in the 1920s that industrial psychology was merely Taylorism under another name, Lupton (1971) points out that it has always been founded on sound psychology, and has sought both to increase a worker's output and his personal satisfaction by easing his difficulties rather than by pushing him from behind. Nevertheless in its studies of the causes and effects of fatigue, the need for rest breaks, the effect of hours of work and so on, it has much in common with scientific management. However it uses a much more sophisticated model of man which is behavioural rather than mechanical; its weakness is that it has tended to be concerned primarily with individuals or small groups, rather than with organizations as a whole. Its importance is that it was the forerunner of the human relations movement.

The human relations movement stems from the pioneering work of Mayo (1933) in the well known Hawthorne studies. These studies began from a scientific management or industrial psychological stance, and investigated the effects of social and working conditions, as well as individual factors, upon worker productivity. The results have been interpreted as showing the importance of the social context of work on human behaviour. For example, in one series of studies the level of illumination was altered to ascertain what the best lighting conditions were for optimal productivity. However as the lighting was turned down, productivity continued to improve until it was so low the workers could barely see what they were doing. This result was eventually explained in terms of the social situation; for the first time workers perceived that someone was interested in their job and how they performed. They thus responded with increased effort and performance, which completely masked any effect of changes in illumination. The term 'Hawthorne effect' has become part of sociological jargon, to indicate the way in which people respond when an interest is taken in their work, improving performance, but invalidating experimental results.

However it must also be noted that these findings have been subjected to massive and largely justified criticism, well documented in Burrell and Morgan (1979). Not only were the social conditions changed by the presence of social scientists, but changes were also simultaneously made to the wage payment system by the introduction of various incentive payment schemes. But the Hawthorne studies are important not for their substantive results, but rather for their effect in stimulating interest in the social environment of work, in the effect of group norms on worker behaviour and on the needs and aspirations of individuals in the work situation. More recent contributions in this tradition have been made by authors such as

Maslow (1954), Herzberg *et al.* (1959), Likert (1961), McGregor (1960) and Argyris (1964). This tradition of work is also significant for management accountants, as it formed the underlying theory on which some of the earliest behavioural accounting research rested. For example, Stedry (1960) conducted an experiment designed to indicate the optimum level of difficulty for budget standards. He concluded that a moderately difficult standard, perceived by the budgetee as 'tight, yet attainable', motivated the best performance, although it should again be noted that his experimental design was deficient in several respects (Otley, 1977).

Although a wide variety of approaches is represented by the work summarized here, a common underlying feature is that it follows a universalistic approach in seeking the 'best way' to organize, to manage or to motivate. As such, it forms a foundation of much management accounting practice until quite recently. However, organization theory underwent a substantial change in emphasis in the mid-1950s, when the systems approach established itself as a popular tool for studying organizations, although its impact on the study of management accounting was delayed until around 1975. But in practice, management accountants have adapted their techniques, mainly by trial and error, for a much longer period.

SYSTEMS APPROACHES

The central feature of the open systems approach is that it seeks to study the activities of an organization by reference to the context of the wider environment in which it is set. The basic premise for understanding organizational behaviour is that the organization is profoundly affected by, and dependent upon, its environment, and that its ultimate survival is determined by the degree to which it is able to adapt and accommodate itself to environmental contingencies. Initially, the chain of causation was seen as running solely from the environment to the organization, essentially determining what the most effective adaptive response should be; later the interaction was seen as two-way, with the organization influencing its environment, as well as vice-versa.

A major development was the recognition that the work situation involves both social and technological factors, with overall task performance being influenced by both these factors and by their interaction. The earliest and best known study of this kind was conducted by Trist and Bamforth (1951), under the auspices of the Tavistock Institute, into the effects of the introduction of the long-wall system of coal-getting in some British coal mines. This partly mechanized system replaced a traditional manual method and involved a complete re-organization of both work and social arrangements in a mine; the expected technological benefits were much reduced by the social frictions the new system engendered. A new approach to job design, the socio-technical systems approach, was developed, which recognized the importance of both elements in organizational functioning, and was to be a major influence for the following 30 years.

As this work developed the concept of the organization as a social system was to increase in importance. Initially much work used an organic analogy: the organization was viewed as a living organism that was open to its environment and that survived by the exchange of materials and information with its environment, a model from level 4 or 5 of Boulding's hierarchy. The total organization was broken down into sub-systems, each of which had a different primary task (its function) to perform. The role of theory was to guide organizational design in integrating the activities of these differentiated sub-systems to attain a satisfactory overall result, minimally the survival of the organization. Work in this tradition includes Rice's (1958) study of an Indian textile plant, Katz and Kahn's (1966) now classic study of the social psychology of organizations and Lawrence and Lorsch's (1967b) analysis of the interaction between an organization and its environment. The major issue with regard to this work is the pre-eminence that it gives to the total organization and its survival over its parts and the individuals who comprise it. It is essentially a form of sociological structural functionalism and subject to the usual criticisms of that position (see Silverman, 1970, for a comprehensive and understandable discussion). However the systems approach has also been popular in the past two decades outside of organization theory, and has been applied to management, notably by Beer (1972, 1975) and has attracted accounting researchers as a potentially useful conceptual tool (Amey, 1979; Ansari, 1977, 1979). Nevertheless, it is notable for the dearth of applicable results that it has produced, arguably because of the mismatch between the assumptions of the theoretical models used and the nature of human organizations (see Otley, 1983, for a review of the contribution of cybernetics and general systems theory to the study of management control).

The study of the impact of the environment on the organization led to one major change in the thrust of organizational research. Whereas nearly all previous work had been universalist in approach, seeking the one best organizational solution, much of the work conducted in the late 1950s and early 1960s noted that particular forms of organization were best suited to particular environmental conditions, and laid the foundation for the development of *contingency* theories. Lawrence and Lorsch's (1967b) study suggested that dif-

ferent organizational principles were appropriate in different environmental circumstances and, indeed, within different parts of the
organization. Burns and Stalker (1961) had already noted the appropriateness of mechanistic (i.e., formal, bureaucratic) and organismic
(i.e., less formal and more flexible) forms of organization to stable
and dynamic technological environments, respectively; to adapt successfully in a rapidly changing environment required a more fluid
and flexible form of organization than the classical bureaucracy. A
study by Woodward (1958, 1965), designed to lend empirical support
to classical management theory, had found it necessary to recommend different principles of management depending upon the nature
of the production process (i.e., unit, batch, mass or process production); classical design prescriptions, such as a fixed span of control,
were found to be dependent upon the technology being used. Chandler
(1962) had discovered a link between the corporate strategy selected
by a firm and the organizational structure appropriate to its effective
implementation; growth by means of diversification was best achieved
with a multidivisional organizational structure. All these results
indicate that there is no single form of organization that is best in
all circumstances. Many factors, both external and internal to the
organization impact on the choice of an appropriate organizational
structure.

But it is important to recognize that although the contingency
framework is a means of reconciling the results of a growing body
of empirical evidence, there is little underlying consensus on its
theoretical foundations. In its present state, the contingency theory of
organizations may best be described (Burrell and Morgan, 1979) as:

> a loosely organized set of propositions which in principle are committed to
> an open systems view of organization, which are committed to some form
> of multi-variate analysis of the relationship between key organizational
> variables as a basis for organizational analysis, and which endorse the view
> that there are no universally valid rules of organization and management.

The extent of the theoretical confusion can begin to be seen when
the major contingencies that are believed to affect organizational
design are examined. These include the nature of the production
technology employed, the stability of the product – market environment, whether product markets are homogeneous or heterogeneous
in nature, and the organization's competitive strategy. When more
recent empirical studies are considered, almost any factor that seems
to explain some of the variation in observed organizational arrangements appears to have been seized upon by some researcher. The
most complete empirical studies are perhaps those of the Aston group

(Pugh and Hickson, 1976) where variables, such as origin and history, size, ownership and control, charter, technology, location, resources and interdependence with other organizations, have been used to characterize the organization's context. The results of this type of work have been somewhat disappointing, in that it has been primarily cross-sectional in nature with only quite low correlations being found, and connections with any underlying theory have been tenuous.

However the contingency approach is of considerable importance for management accounting researchers, since it has dominated behavioural management accounting research from about 1975, although Khandwalla's (1972) work is an early example. This work is described later and is reviewed in Otley (1980), and more fully in Otley and Wilkinson (1988); at this point it is sufficient to note that the contingency framework seems to have been uncritically accepted by management accounting researchers at the time when it was being seriously criticized in the organization theory literature (see, for example, Wood, 1979; Schreyögg, 1980; Cooper, 1981). Nevertheless, despite problems in conducting research using this approach, its underlying premise is sound: the design of organizational structure is an important mechanism for achieving organizational control, and different structures are appropriate in different circumstances.

Decision-making approaches

A third major stream of work in the analysis of how organizations work studies organizational information flows and decision-making processes. This approach can be traced back to Barnard (1938) (whose work is notable in that it combines elements of administrative theory, the human relations approach, systems approaches and decision making) and has been heavily influenced by Simon (1957) and the associated Carnegie school. The determining factor of organizational functioning is suggested to be the limited rationality and information-processing abilities of the human beings that make it up.

Because individuals have limited powers of understanding and can deal with only very small amounts of information at a time, they inevitably display limited rationality. Thus, when faced with a problem, they tend to search for solutions only until the first acceptable solution is found, rather than continuing to search until the best solution is discovered. Such behaviour is known as 'satisficing', where search is terminated on finding a satisfactory rather than an optimal solution. Further, the problem of being faced by a set of multiple goals that conflict with each other, is also solved in a simple manner. At any one time, a particular goal is seen as being of prime importance, and action is taken to try to attain it. As time progresses other, neglected, goals become relatively more important, and attention is then devoted to them in turn. This 'sequential attention' to goals is a means of avoiding computing trade-offs between mutually conflicting goals.

The behaviour of decision makers who pay sequential attention to goals and who satisfice rather than maximize has been described as 'muddling through' (Lindblom, 1959) and is perhaps a more accurate description of actual behaviour in organizations than the rational decision maker of economic models. Economists may argue that satisficing is equivalent to optimizing in the face of costs of information search and analysis, although estimation of these costs can be difficult. It may be better to begin from this reality and attempt to design organizational structures and procedures that are intended to improve the quality of actual decision making, rather than attempting to implement totally rational procedures that assume unlimited information and an unlimited capacity to process it.

A useful collection of work in this tradition can be found in March and Olsen (1976) where a 'garbage can' model of decision making is developed to explain decisions in terms of the relatively random interaction of problems, solutions, participants and choice opportunities. This model views organizational life as a continual stream of problems that interact with an independent stream of possible solutions in an almost random manner. A given solution is chosen because it happens to be available and perceived at the time at which a problem emerges. This extreme and almost anarchic view of decision making nevertheless provides an important contrast to more rational models. Decision making in organizations displays some rationality, but such rationality is by no means perfect. These theories go a long way towards making sense of descriptive studies of managerial activities (see Chapter 4), which are difficult to incorporate within other approaches. Indeed, work by organization theorists such as Weick (1979) has a closer fit with this school of thought than other, more traditional, organizational theory.

The tradition represented by the decision-making approach is particularly important to management accounting researchers for, despite the oft-proclaimed cliché that management accounting is about providing information for management decision making, the underlying theoretical approach has derived solely from economics where rational models are pre-eminent. Many of the implementation problems faced by improved quantitative techniques in management accounting become explicable when human decision making processes are more fully understood. Work in the decision making tradition, therefore, provides a valuable counter-balance to the more value-laden approaches that have already been discussed.

Critical theory

Whereas decision-making approaches have tended to focus on the individual level of analysis, critical approaches adopt a sociological perspective, although both approaches are concerned to avoid accepting the values implicit in much managerially oriented work. However, critical theory is much more concerned to uncover and elaborate the structure of values and power relationships which underlie any system of social control. Thus, the emphasis in the critical literature is on the exercise of power and dominance, using the techniques of management control, and it tends to interpret control as the methods used by one group to impose its wishes on others. Thus, in Burrell and Morgan's (1979) terms, critical theory is categorized as radical and subjective in its orientation.

Critical theorists would argue that social knowledge is *inseparably* bound up with cognitive interests that have *unavoidable* political conditions and consequences (Willmott, 1989). Thus, the social scientist seeking to understand organizational phenomena should try to penetrate the illusion of social 'facts' and focus upon the nexus of political interests which serve to create such 'facts'. As Knights and Willmott (1982) argue, critical analysis does not attempt to generate more refined predictive models of a depoliticized object-world, nor does it seek to improve the functioning of existing, oppressive institutions. Instead it assigns to reason a partisan position in facilitating emancipation from social relations and ideologies that involve or legitimize socially unnecessary suffering. Thus, critical theorists would maintain that, in seeking to maintain and reproduce a capitalist world economy, managerial action is preoccupied with easing and containing their dysfunctions by introducing or reviving ever more sophisticated, insidious and coercive forms of technocratic control. From this point of view, an appreciation of how, within the labour process, for example, capital continues to sustain and extend its expropriation of control over the means of production would be central to an analysis of managerial control. Some insightful examples of this type of analysis can be found in Knights and Willmott (1986).

Although this approach is in its infancy as far as the study of accounting and managerial control systems is concerned, it represents an important strand which draws attention to the role of interests and values in the control process. Thus, control is not an abstract phenomenon which can be scientifically applied to certain objective circumstances. Rather the very act of control itself defines some of the circumstances which surround it. Management control is not necessarily exercised in the pursuit of some accepted organizational objective, but it may be the mechanism by which one group exercises its dominance over another. However, important though this point is, the critical literature gives little guidance (as yet, at least) in the design of control systems intended to serve emancipatory rather than coercive purposes; it seeks only to point out and explore the wider web of connections within which a control system is embedded. Here our focus is on the design of control systems to serve specific purposes, and the remainder of this chapter will be devoted to aspects of the design of organizational structures and accounting information systems which will help achieve those purposes.

ORGANIZATIONAL DESIGN AS A CONTROL DEVICE

As is apparent from the previous discussion, the structure adopted by an organization is itself an important control device. By adopting a particular structure certain kinds of contact and relationship will be encouraged, but others will be discouraged. A contingency approach to the design of control systems suggests that the inter-relationships between organizational structure, management controls, accounting information and other organizational controls, such as personnel selection and training must be considered (Hopper and Berry, 1983). As pointed out by Otley (1980) all these control techniques interact significantly with each other and form a (more or less well integrated) package. Different forms of organizational structure will require different types of accounting information to be provided to enable them to function effectively.

Decentralization

An important element in organizational structure is the degree to which decision making is decentralized. Whereas a small organization can operate effectively in a highly centralized manner, in larger organizations centralized decision making can lead to inefficiencies in both the timeliness and quality of decisions and control actions. Decentralization refers to the extent to which decisions are taken by subordinate managers rather than senior managers. It is thus evident that all organizations are decentralized to some extent; what matters is the degree of decentralization operated.

In a highly centralized organization most decisions of any importance are taken centrally with middle managers being constrained by various rules, procedures and policies that govern what they are able to do. The result is a uniform set of practices being

applied to all situations faced. Examples of highly centralized organizations would include the Department of Health and Social Security,
the major High Street banks and retail store chains such as Marks
and Spencer. Little or no discretion is given to local managers as to
how they should operate; their major responsibility is to run their
unit in accordance with set procedures.

As an organization decentralizes it gives various kinds of decision
making power to lower managers. Bank managers may have authority
to grant loans within certain limits; a store manager may be able to
select the merchandise he stocks from that available, although he
may not have the authority to buy in other lines; he may also select
the staff he employs, but probably only on the company's standard
terms and salary scales. Greater decentralization may allow local
managers almost complete autonomy in how they operate, subject
only to profitability and investment constraints. At the extreme, we
have loose associations of independent companies that cooperate in
marketing (e.g., estate agents) or purchasing (e.g., SPAR retail shops).
There is thus no single overall measure of decentralization; moderate
degrees of decentralization can be achieved in different ways by
delegating different decision making powers.

The degree of decentralization chosen reflects the choice made by
an organization between the advantages of coordinated decision
making from the centre and those of rapid and informed decision
making at the periphery. This will depend on the nature of the
environment in which the organization operates, but even in a given
environment there may be no clear optimal structure, for each possible solution has its own particular advantages and disadvantages.

Divisionalization

One popular form of decentralization is divisionalization. A divisionalized organization delegates a great deal of decision making
authority from central senior managers to their immediate subordinates. The manager of a division is given substantial authority
over how he operates the division in his charge, in many ways being
equivalent to the chief executive of a subsidiary company, held responsible primarily for achieving financial performance targets.
Even so, he may still be required to operate within centrally determined policies, such as those relating to terms and conditions of
personnel employment, standard administrative and accounting
procedures and public relations policies. Also, he is not usually
permitted to make capital investment decisions involving more than
relatively trivial sums of money; these powers are reserved by central
management (Tomkins, 1973). It should be noted that the fact that a

company is divisionalized does not indicate the degree to which it is decentralized at other levels. Individual divisions may themselves be highly centralized or they may decentralize certain decision making powers; at the extreme they may themselves be divisionalized, although this would be unusual.

Why do organizations structure themselves in a divisionalized manner when it is evident that any form of decentralization creates considerable problems of integration and coordination? The major argument in favour of divisionalization is based on the speed and quality of decision making. Local managers are better informed than central managers about their organization, its product markets and the environment it faces, and are thus in the best position to take decisions affecting its future. By being closer to the situation they are able to make better decisions and to make them more speedily without having recourse to head office. Further, central managers have limitations on their information processing ability, like all other human beings; a policy of divisionalization saves them from being overloaded by short-term and detailed matters and allows them to concentrate on longer term planning and overall strategy and control. Finally, divisionalization allows future general managers to be trained. In a centralized company, no internal candidate will have had general management experience and promoting a functional manager to be chief executive, regardless of the quality of his functional experience, can be a hazardous move. A divisionalized company has a pool of divisional general managers, with track records, who are potential candidates for the job.

However divisionalization brings with it its own disadvantages. Most importantly, joint activities that require cooperation and co-ordination between divisions may be jeopardized as divisions now see themselves as quasi-independent companies in competition with each other. There may also be expensive duplication of staff, and some facilities that are now provided in several divisions instead of centrally. Divisional managers may follow their own objectives and strategies rather than those laid down by central company management. Finally, senior management have to learn that they have a new role in the divisionalized structure, where they concentrate upon overall strategy and control without becoming too involved in the day-to-day management of divisions. Such a 'hands-off' approach may not come easily to a chief executive previously used to a centralized approach.

Divisionalization also requires a different and more extensive formal information system. If divisional managers are to be given autonomy subject only to overall financial and output targets, a formal information system must be devised that monitors and provides feedback information on their actual achievement (Solomons, 1965). Selecting appropriate performance indicators and monitoring their achievement is a skilled task, from both a technical and a behavioural viewpoint, and is extensively explored in Part Three. It can be seen that divisionalization is not to be undertaken lightly. If a centralized structure can be made to work effectively, it is an efficient form of organization, perhaps best exemplified by the High Street banks and retail chains. Only when centralized structures show severe signs of strain is divisionalization an appropriate solution.

In summary, it can be argued that divisionalization is the worst possible solution to the problems of complex organizations, except for any other that has yet been suggested! As a centralized organization gets larger and more complex, its decision making and control procedures tend to break down because of information overload. Senior managers spend more and more time becoming submerged in day-to-day operating decisions to the neglect of longer-term planning and strategy. They work harder and harder to keep up; if no action is taken the organization may disintegrate because of centralized information overload. By contrast, the divisionalization organization has built-in structural inefficiencies; it is less efficient at dealing with problems of inter-dependence, coordination and integration. However senior management will be aware of this in-built inefficiency and can take steps to minimize its effects by careful monitoring and oversight. Their prime tasks are overall planning and control, and the integration of divisional activities into a coherent whole. Thus in a very large organization, divisionalization can represent an important form of control, requiring its own specific type of management information system for its effective operation.

The choice of organizational design

A more comprehensive theoretical basis for organizational design that includes the design of social processes within an organization as well as its structure has been put forward by Galbraith (1977), based on the decision making approach of the Carnegie School. Managers are seen as having three major choices to make. Firstly, there is the choice of domain involving the determination of strategy and the setting of goals; secondly, there is the choice of organizational structure; thirdly, there is the design of the social processes that affect the integration of the individual into the organization. These two latter choices are the principal means of coordinating activities, with the precise form of coordination used being dependent upon the degree of uncertainty confronting senior management. The greater the level of uncertainty, the more information must be processed, creating a situation of overload upon management, who must resolve this by reducing the number of exceptions referred to them.

For Galbraith, managing exceptions is the fundamental managerial activity. A manager's initial response will be to move from personalized, central control to a form of control exercised through a hierarchy of authority. Subsequent responses will include instituting rules and procedures, using staff specialists for planning, and narrowing the spans of control. When these possibilities are exhausted managers have two choices. Firstly, the information to be processed can be reduced by environmental management, creating slack resources or by recombining units from a functional grouping to a task-oriented grouping by the creation of self-contained tasks. Alternatively, the organization's capacity to process information can be increased by either improving the vertical information system, or by creating lateral relationships by implementing joint decision-making processes, using task forces or designing matrix structures. Galbraith provides a useful reminder that investing in an accounting information system is but one method of achieving organizational control.

A similar explanation of how and why controls may vary from organization to organization is given by Mintzberg (1979). He suggests that there are five major types of control mechanisms associated with five different organizational forms (see Table 2.2).

Both Galbraith and Mintzberg indicate how, as uncertainty increases, techniques of management control shift from behaviour control, first by personal means and then by impersonal means reinforced by hierarchical supervision, to short-run output control with centralized coordination, and subsequently to long-run output control with decentralized coordination. Finally, the uncertainty may be so great that output goals can no longer be set and the major form of control shifts to control over inputs, especially personnel training and selection.

It can be seen that the choice of appropriate controls is influenced by the nature of the environment faced by the organization, as well

Table 2.2 Organizational forms and control mechanisms

Organizational form	*Prime control mechanism*
1 Simple structure	Direct supervision
2 Machine bureaucracy	Standardization of work processes
3 Professional bureaucracy	Standardization of skills
4 Divisionalized form	Standardization of outputs
5 Adhocracy	Mutual adjustment

as its chosen strategy and technology, but remains a matter of managerial choice. The design of control systems involves juggling with several interdependent variables that include the type of information system used, the form of organizational structure adopted, the personnel selection and training techniques selected and the reward and incentive systems developed. The design of each sub-system will affect the other sub-systems. For example, in adhocracies, the organic structures with their laterally based information and decision making processes can be exceedingly stressful and require organizational members who have considerable commitment as well as specific technical and social skills. To reduce personal stress and role ambiguity, reward systems in these organizations need to stress intrinsic and social rewards rather than focusing on immediate output (Hopper and Berry, 1983).

Organizational design is thus an important control device open to managerial choice and decision, and includes both the choice of an organizational structure and the selection of appropriate matching information systems and other control systems. The design of an appropriate management accounting system is dependent upon the choices that have been made in these other areas.

THE CONTINGENCY THEORY OF MANAGEMENT ACCOUNTING

The development of contingency theories of organization structure in the mid-sixties was paralleled by their applications to management accounting in the mid-seventies. The contingency approach to management accounting is based on the premise that there is no universally appropriate accounting system applicable to all organizations in all circumstances. Rather a contingency theory attempts to identify specific aspects of an accounting system that are associated with certain defined circumstances and to demonstrate an appropriate matching.

Such an idea is not new, for it has been implicitly recognized by practising management accountants for many years. What contingency theorists have done is to try to identify the specific features of an organization's context that impact on particular features of accounting system design. Three major classes of contingent factor have been identified; the environment, organizational structure and technology. Relevant features of an organization's environment affecting accounting system design that have been suggested include its degree of predictability, the degree of competition faced in the market place, the number of different product – markets faced, and the degree of hostility exhibited. Structural features suggested in-

clude size, interdependence, decentralization and resource availability; technological factors include the nature of the production
process, its degree of routineness, how well means – end relationships are understood and the amount of task variety. A summary of
the variables included in the main early empirical studies is outlined
in Table 2.3.

Despite the identification of such a wide range of potentially influential factors, little substantive evidence has been obtained of
their effect on management accounting system design. Most empirical
studies have assumed a simple linear model with contingent variables
influencing accounting system design only by way of organizational
design. However this approach appears unnecessarily limited, for
organizational structure is but one control mechanism, and it is more
fruitful to consider all aspects of the organizational control package
together (Otley, 1980). These would include its accounting system,
management information system, organizational design, reward and
incentive system, and other control arrangements. In addition, it
may be expected that corporate aims and strategy would play a
crucial role in the design of other parts of the control package.

Each part of the overall control package will interact with other
parts as organizational design and accounting system design are
interdependent. This view was expressed long ago by Horngren
(1962) and also echoes the sentiments often expressed by industrial
managers who indicate that the particular form of accounting system
used by their company is intended to cope with known weaknesses
in organizational design. Other companies use particular forms of
organization and operating procedures (typically highly centralized
procedures) to avoid the expense of running complex accounting
systems. Reward and incentive systems can be used where organizational structure and accounting performance measurement impact
on individuals only weakly, such as the common practice of giving
salesmen fairly low base salaries but high rates of commission (interestingly usually based on sales revenue rather than profit or contribution margin). Finally, the selection and training of personnel is
an important control mechanism by which individuals who are
thought to fit in well with the control practices of the organization
are selected in preference to those who might otherwise disrupt the
system.

In the remainder of this chapter, we shall outline some of the major
studies conducted in the contingency theory tradition. These will be
categorized depending on whether their major focus has been on the
effects of environmental uncertainty, technology, size, strategy or
culture. However, it must be emphasized that most of the connections suggested are only tentative, and that a considerable amount of

Table 2.3 Variables included in studies of structural features (adapted from Otley, 1980)

Study	Contingent variables	Organizational design	Type of accounting information system	Organizational effectiveness
Bruns and Waterhouse (1975)	Organizational context (origin, size, technology, dependence)	Structuring of activities Concentration of authority	Control system complexity and perceived control leading to budget-related behaviour; interpersonal and administrative control strategies	
Daft and MacIntosh (1978)	Technology (task variety; search procedures)		IS Style (amount, focus and use of data)	
Dermer (1977)	Organizational objectives Technology Managerial style	Decentralization Differentiation	Choice of AIS or MCS techniques	
Gordon and Miller (1976)	Environment (dynamism, heterogeneity and hostility)	Decentralization Bureaucratization Resource availability	Technical characteristics of accounting IS	
Hayes (1977)	Environmental factors Inter-dependency factors Internal factors		Appropriate performance evaluation techniques	Departmental effectiveness
Khandwalla (1972)	Type of competition faced		Sophistication of accounting controls	
Piper (1978)	Task complexity (product range and diversity variability between units)	Decentralization of decision making	Financial control structure (e.g., use of financial planning models; frequency of reports)	
Waterhouse and Tiessen (1978)	Environmental predictability Technological routineness	Nature of sub-units– operational or managerial	Management accounting system design	

empirical research requires to be undertaken before confident pre-scription is possible.

Environment

It is perhaps self-evident that the nature of an AIS will be affected by the external environment, for the purpose of a control system is to assist an organization to adapt to the environment which it faces. However, it must be emphasized that formal control systems are only one of many mechanisms that may be used to assist in attaining overall control.

Khandwalla (1972) was one of the first accounting researchers to examine the effect of the external environment on management control practices. He concluded that the sophistication of an AIS was influenced by the intensity of the competition faced by the firm. More-over, different types of competition, for example, price, marketing or product competition, had very different impacts upon the uses made of accounting information in manufacturing firms.

A similar conclusion was reached by Otley (1978), who studied the effects of different environments faced by unit managers within a single firm. Senior managers were found to use budget information in quite different ways in 'tough' environments compared to 'liberal' environments. Whereas a rigid style of performance evaluation that emphasized the attainment of budget targets was effective in a liberal environment, a more flexible style was required in a tough environment.

In a seminal theoretical paper, Gordon and Miller (1976) identify three main environmental characteristics, hypothesized to affect control systems, namely dynamism, heterogeneity and hostility. A high level of dynamism, or rate of change, will require frequent control reports incorporating both financial and non-financial infor-mation, and which emphasize forecasts rather than past actual results; heterogeneity, or the number of different product markets served, will lead to a decentralized control system with quasi-independent responsibility centres; in the face of severe competition or market hostility, a more sophisticated AIS is required, again in-corporating non-financial information about critical threats.

Waterhouse and Tiessen (1978) see the environment as having two important dimensions that affect AIS design: the simple – complex and the static – dynamic. These are very similar to the dimensions identified by Thompson (1967) in his analysis of the effect of environ-ment on organizational structure. Other accounting researchers have taken up these ideas and they can be seen in studies such as that of Hayes (1977). Thus the contingency theory of organizational structure can be seen to have had a profound impact on the approach taken by accounting researchers.

Amigioni (1978) developed a different framework in which he assesses the appropriateness of different accounting control tools, ranging from financial accounting and ratio analysis through financial simulation models and responsibility accounting to strategic planning devices. He identifies two major contingent variables, namely the degree of structural complexity of the enterprise and the degree of turbulence in its environment. Whereas increasing structural complexity leads to the *addition* of new accounting tools to those already in use, environmental discontinuity will often require the *replacement* of tools which have become obsolete, by new ones.

Gordon and Narayanan (1984) hypothesized a tripartite association between perceived environmental uncertainty, organic forms of organizational structure and the use of external, non-financial and *ex-ante* information for control purposes. Their analysis showed strong correlations between these three variables, but after controlling for the effect of uncertainty, information systems and structure were not significantly related to each other. This supports the view that both structure and control systems are dependent upon the state of the environment rather than control systems being determined by structure.

Another study which focused on environmental uncertainty and also considered performance outcomes was that of Govindarajan (1984). He found no direct connection between evaluative styles, reward systems and effectiveness until the mediating effect of uncertainty was considered. Under conditions of high uncertainty, a correlation between more subjective methods of evaluating performance and effectiveness emerged, again supporting the contention that effective controls are contingent upon environmental circumstances.

Environmental 'stress', 'restrictiveness' and 'aggressiveness' have also been referenced by researchers. All of these aspects of the organization's environment involve factors such as the availability of opportunities and the extent to which the firm is manipulated or controlled by other organizations such as competitors, suppliers, customers and government bodies (Khandwalla, 1977; Pfeffer, 1981). It can be argued that the existence of powerful interest groups in the organization's environment increases the level of uncertainty it faces. Similarly, a high degree of heterogeneity or other forms of complexity may also increase uncertainty at the centre, if only through inadequacies in information processing. Thus the major factor underlying control systems design that has been identified appears to be environmental unpredictability in its various guises (Otley, 1980).

The considerable body of work conducted by organization theorists on the effect of unpredictability on organizational and information systems design, summarized in such work as Galbraith (1977), Mintzberg (1979) and Pfeffer (1982) has yet to be fully incorporated into accounting and control systems research.

Technology

One of the longest-established relationships between a contingent variable and control systems design has been its connection with production technology. Woodward's (1958) work which linked different structural arrangements with particular types of workflows has been paralleled by AIS design. It has long been recognized by accountants that the nature of the production process determines the amount of cost allocation rather than cost apportionment that can take place. The level of accuracy that is possible in costing unit and small-batch production cannot be carried over into process production because the bulk of costs are incurred jointly by a mix of final products. There is thus a technological constraint on AIS design due to product inter-dependence.

Production technology has an important effect on the type of control information that can be provided, and recent work has indicated other aspects of technology that impact on the information that should be provided to aid effective control. For example, Piper (1978) demonstrates that the complexity of the task faced by an organization is relevant to defining an appropriate financial control structure. In his study of four retail organizations, task complexity (defined by the range of products sold, the diversity of the range, seasonal variations and variations in the type of outlet) affected the financial control structure adopted via the intervening variable of organizational structure.

Technology is specifically introduced as a major contingent variable for effective AIS design by Daft and Macintosh (1978). Following Perrow (1967), two dimensions of technology were studied (the number of exceptions that arise in the production process and the search procedures used to resolve such exceptions) which correlated highly with measures of information systems style (i.e., the amount, focus and use made of data), although it should be noted that no attempt was made to assess effectiveness. More recent work by Merchant (1984) has indicated a positive association between the degree of automation in the production process and the formality of budget systems use. Finally, Merchant (1985c) has found some weak evidence to suggest that the propensity of production managers to create budgetary slack is inversely related to the degree of predictability of the production process.

Waterhouse and Tiessen's (1978) definition of technology again follows that of Perrow (1967), but it is reduced to the single dimension of organizational routineness. Organizational sub-units are seen as having predominantly operational functions (defined similarly to Anthony's (1965) operational control) or managerial functions (which include both Anthony's management control and some of his strategic planning activities). It is suggested that managerial functions can be best understood by focusing on environmental variables, whereas the structure and processes of operating units will be more directly related to technological variables.

The AIS is thus viewed as one type of control mechanism which is primarily dependent upon the control needs of each organizational sub-unit. The definition of a sub-unit is dependent upon organizational structure which, in turn, is contingent upon both environment and technology. However, the evidence linking technological, organizational and managerial variables with overall effectiveness is still weak, and even the definition of the variables involved is often vague.

Size

Organizational size is an important variable affecting both structure and other control arrangements which has figured extensively in the work of both organization theorists and economists. For example, Williamson (1970) has argued that as an organization grows, it will initially organize on a functional basis. However, increased growth by means of diversification and the consequent exposure to more diverse product-market environments prompts the re-organization of activities into semi-autonomous divisions. This allows the AIS to be used to measure and compare divisional performance using similar accounting measures to those used to measure overall firm performace.

More recently, Merchant (1981) focused on the differences found in corporate-level budgeting systems. His results showed that in larger organizations, where there was greater diversity and decentralization of decision making, there was greater participation in budgeting despite less personal interaction between managers, and a general attitude that meeting the budget was important to managers' career progression. Perhaps the most significant finding was that performance was highest in the larger firms when an administrative approach to budgeting was used, in contrast to smaller firms where the best performance was associated with a more personal approach. This supports the contingency notion of the need for a fit between size and the way in which a budget system is operated, and it is consistent with the findings of Bruns and Waterhouse (1975).

This study was extended to the departmental level by Merchant (1984). Here size, functional differentiation and the degree of automation in the production process all led to greater formality in the budgeting process. Performance was again higher in those departments where the expected fit between context and budget use was found than where it was absent. However, performance was negatively correlated with the requirement to explain budget variances. This led Merchant to suggest that performance should perhaps be considered as an independent variable affecting style of budget use, rather than *vice versa*, as previously suggested by Otley (1978). This possibility will be considered further in the subsequent section on budgetary style.

Merchant's work clearly suggests a contingency relationship between size and budgetary system characteristics at both the corporate and departmental level. It should be noted, however, that departmental size is to some extent controllable by the organization in its determination of organizational structure.

Further evidence of the impact of size on control techniques can be found in Jones' (1985) study of the role of management accounting systems following merger or take-over. Differences in control practices that existed in small, medium and large companies prior to merger or take-over almost entirely disappeared afterwards as the new subsidiary was required to conform to the practices laid down by the acquiring company. It may be that pressures for conformity to corporate control systems limit the ability of subsidiary companies to design and operate the control systems best suited to their individual environments. If so, attention needs to be paid to the alternative control arrangements that are put into place to replace them. With the tendency towards corporatism in many areas of economic activity, where ownership is concentrated into fewer large corporations, more complex information handling systems will be required to cope with the increasing levels of complexity and diversity.

Strategy

Consideration of corporate strategy has, rather surprisingly, not been prominent in studies of control systems design, despite Dermer's (1977) argument that differences in corporate strategies should logically lead to differences in planning and control systems design. Chandler (1962) demonstrated a link between corporate strategy and organizational structure, but this has not been carried through to the design of other control mechanisms until recently.

Govindarajan and Gupta (1985) examined the relationship between business strategy, style of evaluation and effectiveness. Strategy was measured along a spectrum ranging from 'pure harvest' to 'pure build', the former being characterized by a high market share and the maximization of earnings and cash flow, while the latter represented a mission to increase market share in high growth markets, often resulting in poor short-term profits and net cash outflows. They found that when greater reliance was placed on long-run criteria of evaluation, and managerial bonuses were determined by subjective (non-formula) methods, effectiveness was enhanced for 'build' strategies but diminished for 'harvest' strategies. However, the relationship between reliance on short-run criteria in bonus determination and effectiveness was virtually independent of business unit strategy.

Merchant (1985a) used a similar method of categorizing strategy, but his findings do not support those of Govindarjan and Gupta, in that he found strong evidence that spending decisions in conditions of rapid growth were *more* constrained by short-term criteria such as monthly income targets. Such a relationship seems highly plausible, as resources are often in short supply during periods of rapid growth, and it may be that the studies are not, in fact, inconsistent. It may be quite possible to attempt to manage resources very carefully in conditions of rapid growth while, at the same time, attempting to increase market share in a competitive environment.

The effect of strategy on control systems design is therefore still unclear. In the short-term a strategy can be seen as a response to an environment, but in the longer term the environment is itself determined by strategic decisions about the markets and environments in which the firm wishes to operate. Studies of control systems need to specify clearly the time-span of the controls which they examine. Variables, such as structure and strategy which can be considered as given in the design of short-term controls, themselves become responses when a longer perspective is taken.

Culture

Flamholtz (1983) has developed a schematic model of an organizational core control system consisting of four elements (planning, operations, measurement and evaluation – reward systems) located within the framework of an overall organizational control system which includes factors such as organizational structure, dominant organizational culture and values, and it is all set within an external environment. He argues that the process of exercising control is much more complex than traditional management accounting theory suggests, and that accounting controls must be viewed as a part of a more comprehensive control system. He also warned of the dangers of ignoring organizational culture in control systems design; control systems which are inconsistent with an organization's value system are likely to create resistance and to produce motivations aimed at defeating the purposes of the core control system.

Another piece of work which recognizes the importance of both organizational culture and power relationships within organizations is that of Markus and Pfeffer (1983). They, too, argue that the language and symbols of control systems and the goal assumptions incorporated within them must correspond to the dominant organizational culture, otherwise the controls may engender sufficient resistance to cause them to fail. The introduction of new control systems that alter existing power relationships may be thwarted by those who consider their position to be threatened by the new system. These conclusions were substantiated by evidence from a number of case histories of the introduction on computerized accounting and control systems which were unsuccessful, despite their technical sophistication.

The idea that control systems are dependent upon power relationships *within* organizations can be extended to the view that they are also dependent upon power relationships *between* the organization and its environment. Pfeffer and Salancik (1978) have developed a resource dependence framework that attempts to explore the impact of important resource dependencies upon organizational strategy and control.

Work on the impact of culture upon control systems design is evidently at a very early stage, but it is of evident importance. Perhaps the most effective control processes are those which operate by generating a corporate culture that is supportive of organizational aims, objectives and methods of working, and which is consistent with the demands of the environment in which the organization operates.

CONCLUSIONS

The contingency theories outlined in this chapter are not based on sufficient evidence to provide a firm basis for prescription. Many factors have been suggested that evidently impact strongly upon organizational functioning, but their precise effect and relative importance have yet to be elucidated. In particular, the impact of specific combinations of controls, used in conjunction, has yet to be investigated in detail. However, the contingency framework of control systems design, in conjunction with the organizational design literature that preceded it, provides valuable guidance in conceptualizing importance issues in accounting information systems design. The latter part of this book uses the contingency framework to structure consideration of the impact of various factors upon accounting information systems' design and use.

EXERCISES

1. Choose any large organization with which you are familiar (e.g., a company you have worked for, the university at which you study, the bank you use). What insights do the various theories of organization outlined in this chapter give you into the way your chosen organization functions? To what extent do different approaches give different insights?

2. Compare and contrast the strategies chosen by the different chain stores that operate in your town. To what extent do you think that the way in which they operate (e.g., the way customers are treated, the range of merchandise offered, etc.) is affected by their overall strategy?

3. Do theories of management, developed to explain how business organizations operate, apply to other types of organization? How applicable are they to the management of
   (a) hospitals (also compare the UK with the USA)
   (b) universities
   (c) postal services and telecommunications
   (d) local government?

4. Compare and contrast military organizations with business organizations, paying particular attention to the different operating requirements and the different environments faced by each.

5. Outline the main tenets of the contingency theory of organizational structure and the contingency theory of management accounting. What are their similarities and differences?

6. In many service industries (such as hotels, restaurants, airlines and railways) time is a critical resource. For example, an unoccupied room or seat can never be resold. How do you think that this affects the organization and control of lower-level staff who deal directly with potential customers (such as receptionists and booking clerks)?

7. Choose an organization that faces a very high level of uncertainty in relation to some part of its activities (e.g., a manufacturer of fashion clothes). What alternative ways of coping with the uncertainty might it develop? How could it choose between alternative control strategies?

8. Explain what you understand by the terms 'decentralization' and 'divisionalization', clearly indicating the difference between them. What are the major accounting problems that have to be over-

come in constructing a profit-based measure of performance for a division of a multidivisional company?

9. Outline the role played by accounting information in an overall system of management control. Explain how the contingency theory of management accounting can be used to provide guide-lines for effective management control systems' design and operation.

3

Individual motivation and incentives

SUMMARY

A major aim of a management control system is to induce individuals to behave in ways which contribute to overall organizational performance. An important element of the control process is therefore concerned with how and why individuals are motivated to act. In this chapter, we shall consider two major classes of motivational theory, namely content and process theories, and apply them in the context of accounting control.

Central to effective motivation is the link between incentives (i.e., rewards and/or penalties) and those aspects of behaviour that it is wished to encourage. There seems to be little difficulty in providing incentives that will encourage behaviours designed to gain them; the major problem lies in ensuring that achievement of the required measures of performance is done in the desired manner. That is, it is devising adequate systems of performance measurement that is crucial to linking performance with rewards.

INTRODUCTION

What is it that induces an individual to behave in ways that are to the advantage of the organization rather than solely in his own narrow self-interest? The quick answer is that an organization sets up a system of incentives (rewards and penalties) that represent an attempt to align individual self-interest and organizational objectives. Evidently the design of such an incentive structure is a complex and difficult task, and it is never totally accomplished. Nevertheless most large organizations, by using many different types of incentives and controls, manage to encourage a great deal of such functional behaviour. However the crucial moment when the incentive system impacts upon the individual is when he has to decide on a course of action.

We will take a utilitarian stance and regard individuals as being basically indifferent to the aims and objectives of the organization, but acting solely in their own best interest as they perceive it. This is evidently an oversimplification, for it ignores both normative and coercive influences. Normative influences are probably significant at senior management levels, if only because of a social norm that requires senior managers to put on a public face of acting in the organization's best interests. But, at all levels, organizations develop their own cultures that exert a social influence on individual behaviour whether for good or ill. Coercive influences may come into play at lower levels where the organization can be significantly more powerful than the individual and even collectives of individuals such as trades unions (for example, where an organization is the only employer for workers whose skills are highly specific). Nevertheless a utilitarian model will be at least partially applicable even in these circumstances, and can thus provide insight over a considerable range of motivational situations.

However, although business enterprises in the UK and USA probably assume a utilitarian model of man as the norm, and attempt to construct systems of rewards and incentives to encourage their employees to produce appropriate outputs, this may be an inefficient method of operation. An alternative approach would be to attempt to develop a more normative culture that encourages employees to identify with the enterprise; appropriate behaviour would follow from the underlying concern for the well-being of the organization. Such approaches have been suggested as one of the reasons for success of Japanese industry (Wilkinson, 1983), and have been adapted for Western culture by writers such as Ouchi (1981). The observant reader will note the emergence of some of these normative features in the discussion of the basically utilitarian models of motivation that follows.

THEORIES OF MOTIVATION

The development of motivational theory shows certain parallels with the development of organizational theory. Initially, general theories were posited that claimed to explain individual behaviour with little reference to the context in which it occurred. But the trend in the development of theories of motivation has been a movement away from the identification of specific factors that were believed to be associated with high degrees of motivation in most individuals, towards more general formulations that allow different people to be motivated in different ways. That is, modern theories recognize that individuals differ in the values they place on particular outcomes and are thus likely to be motivated differently by specific rewards.

However the gain in generality has been balanced by a loss of specificity; older theories gave specific guidance in fairly practical terms whereas the newer theories provide only a framework that has to be applied anew for each fresh situation.

It also needs to be observed that motivation is only one factor involved in obtaining satisfactory individual performance. Performance is a function of both motivation and ability; and ability itself can be further subdivided into intrinsic aptitude and training and experience. In symbolic terms:

$$\text{Ability} = f(\text{Aptitude} \times [\text{Training} + \text{Experience}])$$
$$\text{Performance} = f(\text{Motivation} \times \text{Ability})$$

Thus it may be that managers seeking to improve their subordinates' performance should be as concerned with personnel selection (the matching of aptitudes with task requirements) and with education and training as with increasing their motivation to work. Nevertheless, an understanding of the factors that influence individual motivation is important in designing and evaluating systems of incentives that are intended to lead to effective task performance, and it is to these theories of motivation that we now turn.

Content theories

One of the most general theories of human motivation is that put forward by Maslow (1954). Maslow characterizes human beings as wanting animals having a hierarchy of needs ranging from basic physiological needs (food, drink, shelter, etc.), through security and safety needs, social needs, needs for esteem, to needs for self-expression and fulfilment by the exercise of one's own abilities.

These needs are ranked in a hierarchy, as shown in Fig. 3.1, to indicate that the lower needs are more basic and require to be satisfied first. In crude terms, self-actualization does not act as a motivator to a starving man, but food does. Thus Maslow suggests that:

1. lower needs must be satisfied before higher needs can have a motivational impact;
2. a need that is largely satisfied does not act as a motivator.

The inner triangle in Fig. 3.1 indicates a typical pattern of need satisfaction, with lower order needs largely satisfied but higher order needs largely unfulfilled. The best point of attack, according to Maslow, is the tip of the inner triangle, i.e., needs that are recognized but unfulfilled.

However, despite the simplicity of this framework, it is not easy to

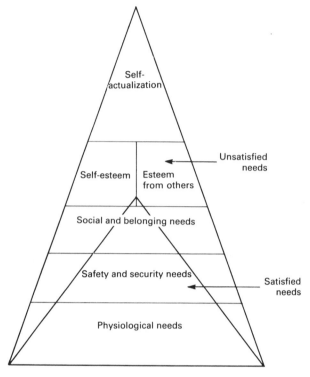

Fig. 3.1   Maslow's hierarchy of needs.

place specific incentives within it. For example, is the provision of a company car for private use satisfying safety, social or esteem needs, for it may be seen solely as a means of transport or as a status symbol. Similarly, a monetary incentive could be used to satisfy an even wider spectrum of needs from the purely physiological to aiding in a process of self-actualization. Nevertheless, the framework does alert us to the range of human needs and various ways in which specific incentives can operate, particularly amongst people in different cultures and in different social classes and income groups.

Unfortunately, Maslow's complete framework has not stood up to rigorous empirical testing, and summaries of prior research together with original studies that use more adequate experimental design than previous work can be found in Hall and Nougaim (1968) and Lawler and Suttle (1972). However, a two-step theory has found some support in the literature; this accepts that lower level needs dominate until largely satisfied, but does not attempt to predict which higher level needs will predominate once the basic level of satisfaction has been attained. Individuals, even within English-speaking Western society, evidently differ widely in their goals and aspirations.

An approach that can be seen as a more specific application of Maslow's general theory in the context of US employees has been developed by Herzberg *et al.* (1959). He began by asking a large number of managers and employees about specific incidents in their jobs that had made them feel particularly good or bad. He found that the basic causes of these incidents could be categorized into two groups; those that contributed towards satisfaction and those that contributed to dissatisfaction. Although the dissatisfying (or hygiene) factors could reduce performance if they were not up to standard, unlike the satisfying factors they could not positively motivate improved performance. The basic causes found in each group included those shown in Table 3.1.

Herzberg was thus able to argue that time and money spent on improving hygiene factors could at best only stop employees from becoming dissatisfied. To motivate them positively required attention to the motivating factors. An added attraction to his approach was that the motivating factors were (superficially, at least) cheap! A pat on the back and the giving of responsibility costs nothing; improving working conditions can be very expensive. Over the past 25 years Herzberg has been a highly successful consultant in the USA, advising many companies about the application of his ideas.

Few theories have received more attention than two-factor theory, and it has served a useful purpose in focusing attention on job content. But more recent studies have failed to establish that two independent factors corresponding to motivators and hygiene factors exist (Campbell *et al.*, 1970). There is a close connection between Herzberg's approach and Maslow's theory. In modern Western society most basic needs are well satisfied, and Herzberg's hygiene factors generally refer to these basic needs and their absence can thus cause dissatisfaction. The motivating factors, however, refer to higher needs such as the need for esteem and self-fulfilment. Thus Herz-

Table 3.1 Factors improving or reducing performance

Dissatisfiers (hygiene factors)	Satisfiers (motivating factors)
Competent supervision	Achievement
Policy and administration	Recognition
Working conditions	Responsibility
Money	Advancement

berg's work can be seen as an application of Maslow's general theory in the context of a particular society. Both provide a general approach that identifies an important factor that had previously been neglected; neither provide a robust theoretical framework that has withstood rigorous testing.

In particular, the role of money, categorized by Herzberg as a hygiene factor, requires further comment. An examination of Herzberg's data on which he based his categorization indicates that money is referred to both as a cause for satisfaction and for dissatisfaction on an almost equal number of occasions, unlike most other influences that have a clear majority of references in just one category. It is fairly clear that money is a general incentive that can have differing effects and it is perhaps particularly important as an indicator of status. One only has to observe the acrimonious effect that very small differences in salary can have on personal relationships to understand the reasons why salary policy is an item of highly confidential information in many companies. Further, the social circumstances in which money is received also affects its motivational impact, as indicated by the following example.

A factory on the East coast of Britain employed girls to gut fish before a canning process. It was a hard and unpleasant task, and to improve motivation the company introduced an incentive scheme. The effect was mixed; some girls, generally the older ones, responded well and increased their output, but the new scheme had little effect on other girls. In seeking the cause for the lack of motivational effect, an academic researcher eventually stumbled across the home arrangements common in the locality. Young girls, when starting work, were expected to hand over their pay packets, unopened, to their mother and receive a fixed allowance from it. As they became older the system changed; they made a fixed contribution for their keep to their mother and kept the residual amount themselves. The effect of factors quite outside of the workplace is thus clearly apparent!

An interesting perspective on the effect of the mechanisms used by a manager to motivate his subordinates is provided by McGregor (1960). He distinguished between two contrasting sets of assumptions managers could hold. Managers holding the first set, called Theory X, sought to motivate subordinates on the assumption that people were generally lazy, lacked ambition, like to be led and told what to do and were motivated by personal economic concerns. Such assumptions lead to the development of tight, impersonal managerial controls over behaviour, reinforced by punitive sanctions, often of a monetary kind. However the use of such controls is likely to encourage behaviour aimed at avoiding their effect and to set up a cycle of controls and counter-controls, resulting in poor personal relationships and a deterioration in overall performance. The alternative set of assumptions, Theory Y, suggest that people enjoy work, wish to do well and are motivated by self-control and self-development. Here control is achieved by tapping people's enthusiasms, giving them tasks that use their talents, and involving them in deciding what is to be done.

It is probably best to leave the reader to decide which set of assumptions best fits the particular situation being considered, but it is interesting to note that both styles are self-perpetuating. If you treat people as if they cannot be trusted and require coercion to make them work, you will probably find that you are right. However if you make the Theory Y assumptions, you may well find that people respond well to being treated in this way and that your faith in them is justified. However, by way of caveat, it is probably also true that those who have had long experience of being treated as if Theory X is correct will be highly suspicious of any alternative approach; Theory Y is not something that can be introduced overnight. Further, Ouchi (1981), in putting forward his Theory Z, has suggested that even Theory Y is too utilitarian in its approach, and that the best form of motivation will occur in an organizational culture that stresses normative involvement with organizational goals.

There have been other general theories of motivation that focus on particular aspects of the work situation. Equity theory notes that we have a tendency to compare ourselves with other similar people; if we perceive ourselves to be under-rewarded in comparison with them, we will tend to reduce the effort we put into our work and become dissatisfied. Conversely if we feel that we are over-rewarded, not only do we tend to increase our effort, but may also feel insecure if we fear that this inequity may be noticed and rectified. A complementary theory, goal theory, suggests that the crucial factor in motivation is the goal that we set for ourselves. The more demanding the goal, provided that we accept it for ourselves, the better our performance is likely to be. As we succeed, we tend to raise our sights and set more demanding goals; if we fail, we tend to reduce the standards we set for ourselves.

All these theories have elements of wisdom within them, but they tend to select just a few aspects of the total work situation and concentrate solely on them. Any content theory also tends to be specific to a particular social setting and culture, whether factory, regional or national. Nevertheless these theories do suggest specific lines of action that might fruitfully be developed in the design of incentive systems to motivate improved performance. Their weakness is that they do not provide a general framework from which to analyse their likely effect in a given situation. Such a framework is provided by process theories which we now examine.

Process theories

The trend in the development of theories of motivation has been a movement away from the identification of specific factors (such as pay, working conditions and self-fulfilment) towards more general formulations that allow for different people to be motivated in different ways. That is, modern theories recognize that individuals differ in the values that they attach to different aspects of a job, and may thus be motivated differently by the same incentives. The cultural assumptions of a manager can lead him to define a situation in a way completely at variance to the way it is seen by his subordinates. This is graphically illustrated in the then Chairman of the National Coal Board's questioning of a mineworker (Robens, 1972). When the miner was asked why he only turned up for four shifts each week (implicitly, instead of a full five), his considered response was that he could not live adequately on the wages obtained from working only three shifts!

The central concept of modern motivation theory is that of activation. People find different events involving and stimulating to different extents, but the level of activation can be considered to be roughly determined by the multiplicative effect of three factors (Burgoyne, 1975), namely:

Activation = Uncertainty about the outcome of the event × Importance of the outcome of the event × Ability to influence the outcome of the event

Activation, the amount of psychological energy a person has available to deal with a given situation or event, is thus seen to increase to the extent that an outcome is not certain to occur, to the extent that the person concerned feels that the outcome is important to him, and to the extent that he believes he is able to influence the outcome. The relationship is shown as multiplicative not to imply any great deal of mathematical precision in the model, but merely to suggest that the absence of any one factor will remove activation. Thus if outcomes are certain, or if the outcome is of no concern to the person or if he believes he can exert no influence over it, little activation will result. In a managerial situation, this model suggests that a high degree of activation will occur to the extent that a manager is uncertain as to whether he will be able to meet his objectives (i.e., they represent challenging targets), that he attaches great importance to objective achievement (e.g., he believes he will be rewarded) and that he perceives that he is able to significantly influence his operations to ensure that his objectives are achieved.

However, it is important not to confuse activation with motivation. Whereas low levels of activation may be considered undesirable and represent the tedium of a boring task, equally there is likely to be a maximum amount of psychological energy that can be constructively used in a situation. When activation exceeds this maximum amount, the excess will result in destructive consequences, and this is the condition of 'stress'. Aside from its personal consequences, stress also causes a decrease in effective task performance, and very high levels of activation are therefore to be avoided. There is thus an optimal amount of activation that yields the most effective task performance. Deviations from this optimal level, in either direction, result in a decrease in performance.

The above framework is evidently a much simplified version of real life, but it provides a structure for thinking about motivation. In particular, a manager is concerned with pursuing many activities simultaneously. Stress in this situation is probably not caused by any single activity, but rather by the cumulative effect of all interacting activities over a period of time. Nevertheless, it is important to recognize that setting demanding targets, and emphasizing their importance in circumstances where a manager has relatively little control over outcomes, can lead to stressful levels of activation. If this occurs, various coping mechanisms, such as avoidance and defensive strategies, are likely to be invoked with unfortunate results for the organization and the manager. In particular, managers may attempt to discover methods of meeting targets by engaging in manipulative and dysfunctional activities, which once established are difficult to eradicate.

Expectancy theory
A more complete formulation of the variables that interact to produce motivation, which is in accord with the ideas of activation discussed above, is provided by the expectancy theory of motivation (Lawler, 1973). This suggests that motivation is influenced by both the value attached to an outcome by an individual (known as the valence of the outcome) and the likelihood that it will occur. Two likelihoods are important. Firstly, there is the likelihood that effort will in fact produce the desired performance (symbolically, $E \rightarrow P$); secondly, there is the likelihood that this level of performance will lead to desired outcomes and rewards ($P \rightarrow O$). There are several versions of expectancy theory, but one that has been used extensively in an accounting context is that expounded by Ronen and Livingstone (1975) based on Lawler's work. They hypothesize that:

$$\text{Motivation} = IV_b + P_1(IV_a + \sum_i P_{2i} EV_i)$$

where IV_a is the intrinsic valence associated with successful task performance, IV_b is the intrinsic valence associated with goal-directed behaviour, EV_i are the extrinsic valences associated with extrinsic rewards contingent on work-goal accomplishment, P_1 is the expectancy that goal-directed behaviour will accomplish the work goal $(E \rightarrow P)$, and P_{2i} are the expectancies that work-goal accomplishment will lead to reward $(P \rightarrow O)$. In this model, the summation and multiplication signs should be treated as symbolic rather than precise; what is being suggested is that the motivation to perform a particular act comprises three components that can be summed in order to measure total motivation, and that the act selected will be that for which the total motivation is the highest.

The first component is the intrinsic valence of the behaviour involved in performing the act; some managers work hard because they gain satisfaction from the very act of working hard in comparison with other alternatives (and at the extreme may become workoholics). More commonly, because a high level of effort may be tiring and provide less immediate gratification than other alternatives, this component may be negative and predispose the manager to do other things. Thus, managers may spend too much time doing what they enjoy and too little doing what is most important.

The second component involves the intrinsic valence of successfully accomplishing a work goal, and the feelings of satisfaction and self-fulfilment this engenders. However, motivation to work hard is mediated by P_1, the probability that working hard will lead to successful task accomplishment (i.e., the probability that $E \rightarrow P$). Motivation will be reduced if it is thought unlikely that the effort expended will produce the desired results.

The final component is the extrinsic valence of all the rewards such as status and esteem from others to monetary rewards. These are mediated by P_1 as before, and now additionally by P_{2i}, the likelihood that successful task performance will lead to the sought-after reward (i.e., the probability that $P \rightarrow O$). This latter expression is summed over all the extrinsic rewards involved. Here, the manager is motivated to work hard so as to perform successfully a task that will lead to him receiving extrinsic rewards that he values highly.

As an example, it is instructive once again to consider McGregor's two models of man, Theory X and Theory Y. In the Theory X model, work is held to be unpleasant and to be avoided where possible; IV_b is thus assumed to be negative. Further, as little or no value is attached to successful task performance, IV_a is effectively zero. Extrinsic rewards must therefore be provided in order to overcome the inherent negative motivations for working, for example by incentive payment schemes. Additionally, punishments might be devised for failing to work hard enough, so as to ensure that working hard is the least unpleasant option open to the manager. Thus in Theory X the stress is placed on extrinsic rewards and punishments designed to overcome the assumed propensity of individuals to avoid working.

By contrast, Theory Y assumes that some aspects of working are felt to be desirable and suggests that by re-structuring the work situation positive aspects can be enhanced and negative aspects reduced. That is, IV_b can be positive, or at worst zero, and IV_a positive because of the status, esteem and self-actualization needs that it can fulfil. Because of the positive motivation assumed to be derived from these factors, extrinsic rewards serve a more minor function, acting as fine tuning to increase the already positive motivation further.

It can be seen from this example that expectancy theory provides a more general framework encompassing earlier theories. However, it achieves its generality by not being specific about what features of the task environment will have positive motivational impact; these must be investigated by the user of the theory in each particular set of circumstances.

THE USE OF ACCOUNTING CONTROLS

Expectancy theories of motivation have been applied to accounting control by several researchers. Ronen and Livingstone (1975) have argued that previous accounting studies on budgetary motivation and the generally accepted principles of responsibility accounting are consistent with the expectancy model. They demonstrate that five behavioural assumptions made by accountants in designing budgetary systems can plausibly be argued to be consistent with the expectancy model. These are:

1. budget standards should be reasonably attainable;
2. managers should participate in budget development;
3. managers should use the principle of management by exception;
4. managers should be held responsible only for that over which they have reasonable control;
5. dimensions of performance that cannot be captured in monetary measurements should be excluded from budgetary control.

Although the above work is entirely theoretical, an experimental evaluation of the relevance of expectancy theory to budgetary control has been conducted by Rockness (1977). This study found that:

1. A budget that was difficult to achieve (previously attained one-third of the time) resulted in better performance than a budget of medium difficulty (previously attained one-half of the time), although budget satisfaction was slightly less.

2. A predictable reward structure produced better performance and higher levels of satisfaction than when the same total monetary rewards were distributed in a less predictable manner.
3. Formal feedback on results led to only a slight improvement in performance, although it was associated with a significant improvement in satisfaction.

Overall, these results are supportive of the expectancy theory model, and both pieces of work add credibility to using the expectancy framework in developing models of budgetary motivations. However, it should be noted that the model fared less well when it was used to predict the performance of audit staff members by Ferris (1977). In this professional environment, several expectancy models were found to be weak at predicting audit staff performance (although this result may be a consequence of using peer evaluation of job performance), but they were useful at predicting job satisfaction.

The expectancy theory of motivation indicates that, of themselves, accounting controls have little, if any, motivational impact. The only source of positive motivation is the intrinsic satisfaction that may be gained from actually attaining a pre-set budget target. The major motivational impact lies in the extrinsic rewards, such as salary bonuses, enhanced promotion prospects or status that are associated with target attainment. Although earlier studies have been reported as describing the effect of budget targets *per se* (e.g., Stedry, 1960; Hofstede, 1968), these almost invariably confound the effects of extrinsic rewards with the effect of the budget target itself, in much the same way as popular accounts of the Hawthorne experiments neglect to mention the confounding effects of the differential feedback of information that was involved and changes in the payment system that were made. Further, given that important consequences are usually associated with budget attainment or non-attainment, a crucial variable is the way in which senior managers treat budget variances, a factor that will be further studied in Chapter 6.

Further, the appropriate managerial use of an accounting control system will be affected by the knowledge that is available about means – end relationships in the process being managed and the ability of the accounting system to measure process outputs. Ouchi (1979) has identified three types of control mechanisms: behaviour controls that monitor what a manager is doing; output controls that monitor what is produced or achieved; and input controls that monitor what resources are used. However, output controls are valid only to the extent to which desired outputs can be validly measured; behaviour controls are useful only to the extent that behaviours that will produce desired outcomes are known; and input controls are always inadequate, even if they represent all that is available when outputs cannot be measured and desirable behaviours are not known. It is important to recognize that methods of accounting control can be used in ways that overlap all of these categories. Accounting controls are usually input controls as they measure the use of resources; they are output controls when outputs are measured and valued as in the construction of budgets for profit centres; they are behaviour controls to the extent that the plan they respresent and the amounts allocated to each account heading constrain a manager to achieve his results in one defined manner, rather than giving him greater freedom of choice. It is necessary to tailor the control system and the way in which it is operated to the circumstances of the organization in which it is being used.

THE DESIGN OF REWARD SYSTEMS

One of the principal means senior managers use to motivate their subordinates towards effective performance is to link organizational rewards ·to the level of performance achieved. For example, shop-floor workers may be paid by piece-rate or have an incentive bonus scheme, salesmen may be paid commission on sales and managers may receive bonuses based on the profitability of their unit. But the rewards need not be monetary, and can involve status and prestige, increased responsibility and job interest, and job satisfaction more generally. For example, several chains of retail stores have competitions whereby the stores that attain certain targets are awarded trophies to be displayed (status) together with small monetary bonuses for each member of staff. This example also illustrates the point that rewards need not be exclusively individual, but given on the basis of group performance, although the larger the group involved the less likely it is than each individual will believe that his own efforts will have a significant impact.

A simple representation of the general approach to the design of reward systems is developed by Hopwood (1974) and is shown in Fig. 3.2. In the absence of any system for relating individual efforts to organizational rewards, the aspects of behaviour that individuals are likely to concentrate on in fulfillment of their personal goals (B) do not, in general, correspond with those necessary for achieving organizational purposes (A). However it is possible to modify individual behaviour by establishing measures of behaviour (C) that will be rewarded. The existence of the rewards will motivate individuals now to do some of the activities included in the measurement process (C) which they previously did not do.

In an ideal system, the measured behaviours (C) would be defined

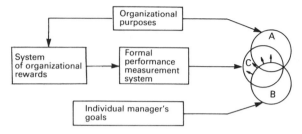

A – behaviour necessary to achieve organizational purposes
B – behaviour actually engaged in by individual manager
C – behaviour formally measured by control systems

Fig. 3.2   The measurement – reward process with imperfect measurement. A, behaviour necessary to achieve organization purposes; B, behaviour actually engaged in by individual manager; C, behaviour formally measured by control systems. (From Hopwood, 1974.)

by, and completely included in, the area of necessary behaviours (A), and cover as large a part of A as possible. In practice however it proves difficult to construct measures for all desirable behaviour (so C does not completely cover A), and those measures that are used do not perfectly represent what is required (so that C includes an area outside of A). To the extent that individuals desire the rewards offered by the organization, their actual behaviour (B) will be modified to include more of C (i.e., behaviour measured and subsequently rewarded) and, to the extent that C coincides with A, more of A (i.e., organizationally desired behaviour). That is, the existence of a particular performance measure together with appropriate rewards will motivate actions that improve the measure, but which will improve organizational performance only to the extent that the measure accurately represents what is organizationally desirable.

This framework focuses attention on both the construction of measures of performance and the specification of rewards and incentives based on them. Although the introduction of incentive payment schemes generally increases productivity, there is a continuing problem regarding the setting of appropriate standards of production. For example, in one city, ratepayers were disturbed to discover that, following the introduction of an incentive scheme, dustmen were finishing work at lunchtime having completed their daily quota. Although they were completing more work than had previously been done in a full day under the old system, early clocking-off made abuse of the new system apparent, and there were also complaints about the quality of work done.

Measurement of work output is also a problem, as there are usually several different criteria of performance that have to be simultaneously met (e.g., quantity and quality, short term and long term) and most measures cannot satisfactorily encompass all necessary aspects. Increasingly, tasks are becoming more interdependent, with the work of one person being highly dependent on that of his colleagues. Further, incentives very often fail to motivate in the way that was expected when they were installed. Individuals attempt to gain a degree of personal control; they 'fiddle' schemes in ingenious ways and, when some important tasks are not explicitly rewarded, these are neglected in favour of tasks that are rewarded. In seeking social esteem from their colleagues, people develop informal rules or norms concerning appropriate levels of performance, often well below those technically achievable.

The design of reward schemes based on performance is evidently a complex and difficult task. It is probably most straightforward at shop floor level, but even there no simple answers exist. The idea of a fit between the method of payment for shop floor workers and such features as the job time cycle, work flow arrangements, labour market conditions and social factors has been developed by Lupton and Gowler (1969) to provide a procedure for selecting the most appropriate wage payment system from those available. Even at this level, the method is not without its problems, and these increase as one ascends the managerial hierarchy.

At managerial levels, budgets are often used as standards for performance evaluation, and performance is monitored by accounting measures. An enormous amount of attention has been paid to the dysfunctional consequences that result from the inappropriate use of accounting measures in performance evaluation. Initially the focus was on the harmful effects of such practices on individuals, characterized by Argyris's (1952) book *The Impact of Budgets on People*. More recently, the focus has changed to consider the consequences to the organization, as in Schiff and Lewin's (1970) article, 'The impact of people on budgets'. Yet surprisingly little consideration has been given to studying the precise causes of such practices and how they might be avoided. This aspect of accounting information use deserves a more detailed consideration, and is pursued in Chapter 7.

The construction of suitable incentive payment and other reward systems requires the design of appropriate measures of performance. Any management control system depends crucially on measures of performance that will be fed-back to those involved and upon which their subsequent actions will be based. If there is one message from the literature on performance measurement, it is that no satisfactory measure of overall performance exists; all measures are, to a greater or lesser extent, imperfect. The danger to be avoided is that of motivating managers to turn in good measures of performance by the use of suitable reward systems. There is little doubt that good measures will be obtained, but they will probably not be obtained in the desired manner.

CONCLUSIONS

The past 15 years have seen a move away from universal theories of motivation towards more conditional theories, such as the expectancy approach. As might be expected, the conclusions of expectancy theory do not differ much from previous findings in the specific circumstances where they were derived. However, the advantage of the expectancy approach is that it alerts us to the circumstances that can affect the validity of commonsense relationships. Thus different 'models of man' held by senior managers, different types of managerial tasks, and different amounts of unpredictability in the internal and external environment are likely to moderate the applicability of such assumed relationships. Accounting control methods thus become one element in an overall organizational strategy for motivation and control; their use and importance will vary according to circumstances.

Nevertheless there is one seemingly universal result that runs through many studies. If significantly valued rewards (such as enhanced promotion prospects, salary bonuses or status) are attached to the successful attainment of performance targets, it is likely that managers will be highly motivated to attain such targets, and that many managers will report performance at or near the target levels (Argyris, 1952). However, it is also likely that such reports of good performance will have been achieved in various ways, many of which may be considered as less than desirable. For example, the target itself may have been adjusted initially, possibly by the manager taking advantage of the opportunities allowed by participation in the target-setting process, to be relatively easily attainable.

This strategy is likely to occur particularly when the degree of complexity and uncertainty in the task itself are such that senior managers have little independent knowledge by which they can validate the estimates of their subordinates. Further, the target may be achieved by the subordinate manager taking undesirable actions to ensure that the reported accounting figures are acceptable at the expense of long-run good performance. The accounting literature is replete with examples of how summary performance measures such as profit and return on investment can be increased by undesirable actions. Finally, the performance report can be enhanced by direct manipulation of the reported accounting figures, by such actions as adjusting the timing of reports, charging items to incorrect accounts and otherwise falsifying reported information. Thus managers may resort to activities that have been categorized as smoothing, biasing, focusing, gaming, filtering and falsifying information in order to improve the outcome to suit their own, rather than organizational, purposes (Birnberg *et al.*, 1983).

Thus, to the degree that the accounting measurements involved in the operation of a control system are imperfect measures of performance, too great a stress on target attainment is likely to provoke a wide range of undesirable side effects. Traditional theories of motivation and control seem most valid in situations where means – end relationships are well understood (i.e., programmable tasks) and where results are accurately measurable. Unfortunately, it is precisely in such situations that techniques of accounting control are largely redundant, and can be replaced by alternative, more direct, means of motivation and control. In more usual situations, the art of control involves balancing the rewards attached to successful target attainment with the potentially destructive side effects they may engender. The expectancy models of motivation provide a framework for assessing the effects of the former; the user of accounting control must also be alert for signs that he has been too successful by monitoring the latter. It is necessary to tailor the design of an accounting control system, and the way in which it is operated, to the particular characteristics of the organization in which it is implemented. Such a conclusion will not surprise the practitioner; however, it is encouraging that academic frameworks are being developed that provide a basis for making such choices in a more coherent manner. More specific attention to the design of performance – related reward systems will be given in Chapter 10.

EXERCISES

1. What incentives would encourage you to work harder? Could you design a reward system that would encourage you to devote more effort towards organizational goal attainment?
2. The relationship between work effort and actual attainment is conditioned by factors external to the control of either the individual or the organization. What is the effect of the state of affairs on the design of reward systems?
3. To what extent does Herzberg's two-factor approach to motivation accord with your own experience?
4. What effect do you think cultural factors, whether specific to the workplace, locality, ethnic group or nationality, have on appropriate methods of motivation?
5. What implicit theories of motivation seem to be inherent in the way in which the educational institution you attended treated you

as a student? What motivates you to contribute (or not contribute) in a tutorial class? What changes could be made that would improve your level of motivation?

6. Use the expectancy theory of motivation to analyse the amount of effort you put into various aspects of your work. Suggest changes that would encourage you to work harder and check what effect such changes would have on your colleagues.

7. How can you ensure that the targets you, as a future manager, set your subordinates are sufficiently challenging to motivate high performance, yet not so difficult as to discourage them from attempting to attain them?

8. Find out how a professional accounting firm organizes its auditing activities, and how it attempts to motivate and control its staff. What theories of organization and motivation do you think lie behind the way it operates?

9. Elegant Electronics compensates its salesmen according to the following scheme. A salesman's remuneration comprises three components:
   (a) a basic salary of £200 per month,
   (b) a sales commission amounting to 1% of gross sales, and
   (c) a bonus amounting to 5% of all gross sales made in excess of a budget target.

The budget target was initially set in July at £40 000 for all salesmen, but is revised monthly on the basis of actual sales made in the previous month plus a 10% increase.

On reviewing the scheme after 6 months' operation it is noticed that two salesmen selling the same products in different areas have the following sales records:

	Simon Smooth (£)	Percival Plodder (£)
July	20 000	40 000
August	50 000	46 000
September	30 000	36 000
October	60 000	42 000
November	20 000	38 000
December	60 000	48 000

   (a) Calculate the total remuneration for Simon Smooth and for Percival Plodder.
   (b) Evaluate the compensation system, and suggest any changes you would recommend to improve it.

From: Certified Diploma in Accounting and Finance, Paper 2, Pilot papers 1980.

4

The management of
business enterprises

SUMMARY

The focus of this text is on the provision of information that will assist managers to guide their organizations in appropriate directions. Previous chapters have reviewed the nature of the control process and have outlined current theories of individual motivation and organizational structure. We now turn to the nature of the management task itself and the provision of management information. Firstly, the function of management is investigated to determine what management is and what purposes it serves. Next, the context of management is reviewed, and the circumstances and ethos in which managers operate outlined. Finally, the role of information in the management process is considered, with an emphasis on how it is gathered, processed and used.

Although much of the material presented here is applicable to many types of organization, we will progressively narrow our concern to the management of economic organizations in the private sector, that is, business enterprises. This is not to deny the importance of management in the public sector or in organizations that seek to serve non-economic ends, but there is not space here to discuss the wider issues raised in accounting for the control of these other types of organization. (See Pendlebury, 1989, for some examples of the management accounting issues in the public sector.)

THE FUNCTION OF MANAGEMENT

Management has been described as the profession of control (Beer, 1959). What Stafford Beer intended to convey by this definition is that the essential function and purpose of having managers in an organization is to ensure that all the activities undertaken contribute towards the attainment of overall aims or objectives. The essence of managerial work is that it seeks to monitor and control individual activities and to coordinate them in such a way that overall purposes are achieved.

In a large organization, this task needs to take place at many levels. First-line supervisors or foremen are managers to the extent that they allocate resources to the production process, and monitor and regulate its on-going activity. In addition, they may engage in non-managerial activities when, for example, they replenish stocks of raw materials or operate machinery themselves. Above them may be managers concerned solely with a single product or factory; then those concerned with specific product ranges or geographical areas, until finally we reach top management concerned with the activities of the whole enterprise. Even then, in a large international corporation there may be further tiers in the managerial hierarchy with holding companies owning other trading companies and an international headquarters involved in coordinating world-wide operations. But at each of these levels there is work that is uniquely managerial in nature; such work is concerned with the overall integration, coordination and control of otherwise disparate and differentiated activities.

Such managerial responsibility for effective integration, coordination and control need not reside in a single person, although in practice it usually does. A team of individuals, each concerned with their own specialist activities, may act together in a managerial role to coordinate the results of their work into a coherent set of outcomes. For example, in the British National Health Service, the overall management of a District Health Authority was, until 1984, the responsibility of a District Management Team consisting of representatives of consultant doctors, nurses, ancillary staff, logistical service providers and finance staff, with no single manager having overall authority. But the exercise of overall control in this way is extremely time-consuming and has the potential to be ineffective, so is usually restricted to situations having particularly severe problems of integration. It is significant that in 1984 Health Authorities were instructed to appoint General Managers to take overall responsibility for the management of a District, although it remains to be seen how effective this change of structure will prove to be.

The identification of underlying similarities in managerial work at all levels does not imply that differences do not exist, for they surely do. The nature of the tasks being managed, the context in which they take place, the background and culture of the people being managed, and the wider economic environment all have their impact on the nature of the managerial task, how it is carried out, and the way in which information is gathered and used. In general, the higher he rises in the managerial hierarchy, the more a manager is concerned with external events and circumstances, the more dependent he is on formal sources of information (particularly accounting information) to monitor organizational performance and the longer is the time horizon on which he operates.

Indeed, one well known management researcher (Jacques, 1961) has suggested that the single most important measure of the responsibility borne by a manager is his time span of discretion. This is defined as the time that will elapse before the effects of a marginally sub-standard decision will become apparent. It can vary from a few hours for a production foreman who fails to balance his production line effectively to several years for a chief executive who makes a poor strategic choice. In order to substantiate his claim that time span of discretion is a measure of managerial responsibility, Jacques has compiled charts that demonstrate that it has a consistent relationship with salary (and has further argued that it could be used as a means of establishing equitable payment schemes, but without marked success!).

We must finally distinguish between the function or purpose of management (i.e., the overall integration and control of diverse activities) and the activities of managers as an interest group in their own right. No-one would deny that managers are an interest group in the same way as other employees and other interest groups such as shareholders, suppliers, customers and government who were identified in Chapter 1. As such managers may well take actions designed to further their own personal or sectional interests (although it may be necessary, for purposes of analysis, to divide managers into subgroups depending upon their level in the hierarchy) and their social and educational background (e.g., foremen may be unionized, whereas senior managers rarely are, except insofar as one may view professional associations, such as the British Institute of Management and the Institute of Directors in this light). But such activities do not define the *raison d'être* of management any more than union activities define the function of production employees (i.e., to manufacture products).

However, although the function of management is to exercise overall control, managers have a uniquely powerful position from which they can also promote their own welfare. Being supplied with information about overall activities and having the authority to take decisions designed to achieve overall objectives places them in a position of considerable power and influence. In practice, it may not be possible to distinguish between actions taken primarily to advance particular managerial interests and actions taken primarily to achieve overall organizational goals. For example, senior managers' opposition to a take-over bid may reflect their belief that the company would be better to remain in its current ownership, or it may follow from their belief that their own jobs would be in jeopardy if the bid succeeded. But although it may be difficult to make the distinction in practice, it is conceptually important to distinguish between the function of managerial activity itself and actions taken by managers acting from self-interest.

Managers have the responsibility for each of the major dimensions of control identified in Chapter 1. They are concerned with the setting of aims and objectives, and the development of strategies for their part of the organization, within the general guidelines and objectives set for them by their superiors. In particular, they will develop plans of action that are both feasible in terms of their acceptability to their subordinates, and likely to be acceptable in terms of what they will achieve for their superiors. Having developed such a plan, activities will be monitored to check that they are contributing to the plan in the way anticipated; where deviations occur, corrective action will follow. Such control activities require information, much of which will be gathered in informal ways, but some of which will be routed through the formal management information system. Further, in real life, much feedback information necessary for adequate control may be absent or imperfect; here managers have to rely on their own predictive model of the situation being controlled. As Vickers (1967) elegantly puts it:

in the management of human organizations, feedback is often absent, ambiguous or uninformative and (the cybernetic concept of control) points to the complementary processes of mental simulation which enable management to function in such conditions

The process of mental simulation referred to is essentially that of attempting to predict the likely outcomes of particular courses of action. Managers thus have their own predictive models of individual and organizational behaviour that they use to guide their actions, so as to obtain overall results in line with their objectives.

However, both Vickers and others, such as Morgan (1979), have argued that organizations do not seek goals as such, but rather attempt to avoid undesirable states occurring (e.g., commercial firms do not seek to maximize profit, but perhaps seek to avoid bankruptcy, strikes and government intervention). If one takes this idea of error-avoidance seriously, then it is possible to interpret most managerial decision making and control activities as being primarily motivated by the desire to avoid potentially undesirable consequences. In short, a satisficing theory of decision making is adopted in which courses of action are selected on the basis that they are predicted to have the smallest likelihood of negative consequences.

Whatever view of the management process is taken, it is still possible to interpret managerial activity as being fundamentally concerned with control, although the nature and time scale of that activity may differ considerably at different levels of management. But we now need to turn from abstract considerations of the function of management, to more concrete descriptions of the context in which managerial activity takes place.

THE CONTEXT OF MANAGEMENT

Although a voluminous literature on the practice of management exists, it is surprising how few studies of what managers actually do have been conducted. As the way in which managers operate in their everyday work is likely to have a profound impact upon the effectiveness of alternative methods of control, it is important to consider the context and content of managerial work.

The nature of managerial work

One major study of how managers actually go about their tasks was conducted by Mintzberg (1973) and focused on chief executives, although it is probable that many of the findings will be applicable to lower levels of management with only slight modification. The life of a senior executive was found to be characterized by the unrelenting pace at which his working day was conducted. A great quantity of work was processed at a high rate of activity, and no single item of business was allowed to take up more than a short time. Work activities were characterized by their brevity, fragmentation and variety; items would be raised with the manager, considered and action decided upon. Before one item had been fully considered, another would arise, the chief executive being interrupted by the telephone or by another manager. Each new item appeared to require his urgent attention or decision.

The typical amount of time spent on a single matter was between 5 and 10 minutes. Even during this brief time the manager might be interrupted and have to decide what priority he should give to the item causing the interruption. In this context, it is not surprising that oral communication dominated. Only matters that forced themselves on the manager's attention by personal communication tended to be considered; written reports and letters took a secondary place, until the manager found time to read them, probably away from his office (either while travelling or at home). Most managers also initiated action by means of issuing oral instructions; few wrote letters except in response to correspondence they had received. The written word was pushed into the background by the more urgent demands of the spoken word.

The manager's day was structured around scheduled meetings with other people, both internal and external to the organization, but interrupted by unscheduled contacts to deal with more immediate and pressing issues. Typically, external contacts involved a third to a half of a senior manager's time; discussions with subordinates another third to a half, and contact with his immediate superior less than a tenth. The manager is thus involved with processing a very great deal of current information, much of it obtained from personal spoken contact with others inside and outside the organization. Many of his instructions to subordinates also involved their discovering further relevant information, often within a tight time deadline.

The result of this hectic pace of work is that a manager's attention tends to be devoted to the current, urgent problem rather than to longer-term, although no less vital, issues. Formal control information, such as budget variance analyses, does not force itself on the manager's attention unless he has a specific interest in a particular point and asks for information about it. Rather, formal information provides the backdrop against which the action takes place. It provides the essential background knowledge that keeps the managers own predictive model up-to-date, but rarely provides the primary motivation for action. Control is exercised in a more direct manner. As Mintzberg (1973) himself pithily summarizes his work:

Managers prefer issues that are current, specific and *ad hoc*. As a result there is virtually no science in managerial work. The management scientist has done little to change this. He is unable to understand work that has never been adequately described and has poor access to a manager's information, most of which is never documented.

Managers thus operate in a complex and imperfectly understood manner, attempting to adapt organizational activities to match a complex, uncertain and changing environment. In such a context there is an inevitable tendency to be drawn into 'fire-fighting' activities to solve urgent current problems rather than to spend time reflecting upon longer-term strategy. Indeed it may be quite proper for time to be spent in this way, as an organization that does not survive today cannot implement its carefully thought-out plans for tomorrow. However, proper consideration of longer-term issues requires that scheduled time is made available for that purpose to ensure that discussion is not invariably deferred owing to short-term considerations. Formally provided management information is perhaps more relevant to the discussion of long-term policy than to day-to-day operating decisions.

Organizational culture

Another perspective on managerial work is provided by Handy (1978) who describes four different organizational cultures; namely, club, role, task and existential. The club culture is typified by a reliance upon people and the informal relationships that exist between them. It is perhaps most often found in small entrepreneurial organizations, although it also occurs in financial institutions and in start-up situations of many sorts. There is little formal structure and individuals are given a high degree of autonomy in making decisions; the culture depends upon trust and personal contact. Although open to abuse, this method of management can be very effective in the right circumstances, particularly where speedy decisions based on subjective judgements are required.

The role culture is that typified by the large bureaucracy in which jobs and responsibilities are precisely defined. Such a culture is efficient when life is relatively stable and predictable, but runs into problems when faced by environmental changes. By contrast, a task culture concentrates on the solution of new problems. The culture operates by defining a problem, allocating appropriate resources of men, machines and money and then allowing a solution to emerge. Because the task is non-programmed and unpredictable, great reliance has to be placed on the skills and motivation of those assigned to undertake it. Performance is judged primarily by results, and such a culture is perhaps most common in high-technology industries, such as aerospace and computers. However, it is an expensive culture that may disintegrate in times of economic recession when resources are restricted. Finally, the existential culture assumes that the organization exists to help the individual achieve his purposes, rather than vice versa. Professional partnerships of doctors, accountants or artists may operate in this way; universities are perhaps the largest institutions of this type. Existential organizations have to be managed primarily by consent rather than by the exercise of formal authority.

But most organizations have an amalgam of all four cultures, with different aspects of each being prominent in different parts of the organization. Even universities have role cultures in their administrative functions, task cultures in their research units and perhaps a club culture in their higher levels of management. The vital point is to recognize that each culture has its virtues and weaknesses in performing different tasks; different parts of the organization seem to require different cultures. Each culture also has its own appropriate control techniques. In a club culture personal controls predominate, whereas a role culture tends to use formal procedures and accounting controls. A task culture focuses attention upon results and output, whereas the existential culture stresses the need for agreement and is more democratic in nature. The relative importance of accounting techniques in the management control of parts of organizations with different cultures will evidently vary. We will concentrate mainly on role cultures because these predominate in most large organizations and it is in such cultures that accounting controls are of greatest importance. But it must be remembered that such techniques are less appropriate in other cultures.

The political dimension

It can be argued (Willmott, 1984) that much of the literature on managerial work systematically neglects the political dimension, and that a more politically sensitive management theory is required. Mintzberg's analysis is essentially descriptive, but takes for granted (and maybe thus conceals) its underlying presuppositions. In fact, by concentrating on the content of managerial work, it removes the 'how' and 'why' of such work from its historical and organizational context.

To some extent, these defects are overcome in Kotter's (1982) study of the work of general managers, which connects managerial responsibilities with the formation and maintenance of a network of relationships; Kotter reveals how managers,

> ... tried to make others feel legitimately obliged to them by doing favours or by stressing their formal relationships. They acted in ways to encourage others to identify with them. They carefully nurtured their professional reputations in the eyes of others. They even manoeuvred to make others feel that they were particularly dependent on the general managers for resources, or career advancement or support.

Managers also used symbolic methods, such as meetings, architecture, language, stories about the organization, time and space, to communicate messages indirectly. In pointing out these features of managerial activity, he provides a corrective to images which portray managerial work as the performance of functions and roles abstracted from the political aspects of organizational life.

However, this approach is unusual in the management literature. Willmott (1984) suggests that there is little appreciation of institutional politics in most accounts of managerial work. Yet management *is* a political activity, in that it is intimately concerned with the exercise of power. The idea of control contains both the thread of informational and feedback processes inextricably linked with the thread of the exercise of power to implement selected actions. The image of managerial work that reflects a 'boundedly rational' view of organization has been challenged by 'pluralist' and 'political economy' perspectives which both conceptualize organization in terms of conflicts of interest.

From a pluralist perspective, the nature of managerial work is shaped by political forces, including the self-interest of managerial sub-units within the organization. As Sayles (1979) points out: 'Only naïve managers assume that budgets get allocated and key decisions are made solely on the basis of rational decision-making.' This pluralist approach is well illustrated in Pettigrew's (1973) study of the politics of organizational decision making, in which he argues that the power of any group within an organization is directly related to its structural access to the resources needed to secure compliance with its demands. One major resource in this process is information itself, and the design, operation and control of management information is a key issue in management control.

However, the pluralist approach tends to take for granted the institutional arrangements that exist and, therefore, is inclined not to explain the distribution of power that is observed in practice. By contrast, the political economy approach tries to reveal how organizational structures are designed to secure and advance the interests of a ruling managerial class. From this 'radical' perspective, managerial work is seen as involving the development, application and maintenance of the social and material technologies capable of preserving the prevailing structure of production relations (Edwards, 1975). Even though managers may see themselves as safeguarding the interests of all stakeholders in the organization, the radical political economy perspective sees them as constrained and guided by 'rules of the game' that systematically favour the interests of capital against those of labour.

There is not space here to explore further these competing, or perhaps largely complementary, approaches to the study of managerial work. Suffice it to say, that the exercise of power is an important component of managerial activity and that the study of the sources and legitimacy of such power is an important area for research. To focus on management control as being a purely technical activity which acts only in the interests of the total organization (however these are defined) would be misleading. Organizations consist of individuals and groups with competing aims and objectives, and the power relationships that exist undoubtedly affect the distribution of benefits of those individuals. Nevertheless, it is also important to recognize that the continued survival and prosperity of an organization can lead to increasing benefits to all concerned, and that political in-fighting can become more concerned with the distribution of the cake than with its total size. Management control is a central organizational process that has an important political dimension.

THE ROLE OF ACCOUNTING INFORMATION IN MANAGEMENT CONTROL

Strategic planning, management control and operational control

Another analysis of managerial activity, specifically relating to accounting, has been developed by Anthony (1965, 1988). He categorized managerial decision making and control activities into three major types, namely strategic planning, management control and operational control and argued that most managers would be primarily concerned with only one type of activity. As the nature of the control process is very different in each case, it is important that a manager's task is correctly identified. Strategic planning was defined as being concerned with the setting and changing of overall corporate strategies and objectives; management control involved monitoring activities and taking action to assure that resources were being effectively and efficiently used in accomplishing organizational objectives; operational control was concerned with carrying out specific tasks on a day-to-day basis. Some dimensions of each of these activities are shown in Table 4.1.

Table 4.1   Dimensions of management control

	Strategic planning	*Management control*	*Task or operational control*
Focus	One aspect at a time	Whole organization	Single task
Persons involved	Top management, staff specialists	Top management, line managers	First-line supervisors
Nature of information	Tailor-made External Predictive	Integrated Mainly internal More historical	Tailor-made Internal Real-time
Type of cost	Committed	Managed	Engineered
Time horizon	Years	Months	Days
Source academic discipline	Economics	Social psychology	Physical science and technology

Management control is thus seen as the mediating activity between strategic planning (the setting of objectives) and task control (the carrying out of specific tasks). It is integrative because it involves the whole organization and is concerned with the effective management of the interrelationships between disparate parts. Unlike strategic planning and operational control, management control is an essentially routine affair, reporting on the performance of all aspects of an organization's activity on a regular basis, so that all areas are systematically reviewed. Defined in this way, the major tool for achieving management control is thus seen to be management accounting information. Such information is collected in a standard manner from all parts of an organization; because it is in quantitative (monetary) form it can easily be aggregated into summaries for higher levels of management; it is routinely collected and disseminated. More recent research into the behavioural aspects of management accounting generally, and budgetary control in particular, fit neatly into this viewpoint as emphasizing the essentially social, psychological and motivational aspects of control.

There is no doubt that management accounting is an important tool of management control, as more widely defined, perhaps taking Sizer's (1979) definition as a starting point, i.e.:

Control is concerned not with correcting past mistakes, but directing future activities. Thus management control consists, in part, of inducing people in an organization to do certain things and to refrain from doing others.

The reality of management also gives a superficial justification for the idea that accounting information is the basis of management control (Machin, 1983). First, whenever an organization has a controllership function, it seems invariably to be staffed by accountants. Secondly, the principal overall control system in most organizations is the budget. Nevertheless, the appropriateness of budgetary control in the areas of committed and engineered costs overshadows its relative ineffectiveness in the area of managed cost.

It would be erroneous to assume that management accounting is the only, or even the major, means of management control. Anthony's (1965) categorization assumes away too many problems. Strategic planning cannot be divorced from control, for effective control involves changing plans and objectives. Nor can operational control be kept separate from management control for its technological complexities impinge directly on the control process. The all-important linkages between the three sets of activities are neglected in Anthony's work (see Puxty, 1985, for a fuller critique), leading to an overemphasis on accounting controls.

As Machin argues, Anthony had himself specified social psychology as the major source discipline for the study of management control, and it is perhaps surprising that he continued to hope that accounting would continue to dominate. The publication of Anthony's framework can be seen as the high point of accounting domination of management control systems and Machin sees it as inevitable that mainstream work in management control would swing away from the study solely of accounting systems. Although this text is primarily concerned with accounting for management control, it cannot be overemphasized that accounting is just one technique that is available to assist in the control process, not the totality of that process. The wider range of available controls is examined in Chapter 5.

The use of management accounting information

Management accounting concentrates its attention on those aspects of control which are regular, and which depend on formally provided information about activities that are measurable in quantitative terms. These are vital aspects of the control process, but the description of the context of management outlined in the previous section clearly indicates that it is only part of that process, and probably a background part. Informally derived information, often non-quantified and obtained sporadically, is at least as important.

Such arguments may indicate the limited importance of management accounting information that has been shown to exist in a number of studies of the central activities of middle managers. One series of such studies (Dew and Gee, 1973) was conducted on middle managers in manufacturing firms, and focused on their use of budgetary control information. This was categorized into full use, limited use (where managers used at least some of the information) and no use. The results (shown in Table 4.2) indicate only a small minority of managers made extensive use of the budgetary information provided to them; the vital pre-condition for use of budget infor-

Table 4.2 Use made of budget information (adapted from Dew and Gee, 1973)

No. of managers who made:	Total	Participation	Consultation	Neither
Full use of their budget	12	10	1	1
Limited use of their budget	35	20	8	7
No use of their budget	38	4	6	28
Totals	85	34	15	36

Table 4.3 Perceived purpose of cost information (adapted from Dew and Gee, 1973)

Percentages of managers who thought purpose of cost information was:	*Senior managers*	*Middle managers*
To measure personal efficiency	4	41
To measure efficiency of operations	4	15
To act as a control tool for managers	87	24
To assist in product costing	4	17
Don't know	2	3
Number of managers in sample	54	406

mation appeared to be participation (or minimally, consultation) in budget preparation. Managers who were not consulted at the preparation stage were highly unlikely to use the information produced, whereas those who participated were likely to make at least limited use of it. Thus many middle managers evidently perceive the accounting information they receive as being irrelevant to their needs, in part owing to their lack of involvement in its production. However, participation appears to be a necessary, but not sufficient, condition for accounting information to be seen as relevant.

Further light may be thrown on the issue by considering the response of a larger sample of middle and senior managers as to how they saw the primary purpose of cost accounting reports (shown in Table 4.3). Although the vast majority of senior managers involved stated that they saw the information as a control tool for middle managers to use themselves, more than half the middle managers concerned perceived it as being used to measure their efficiency (either their personal efficiency or the efficiency of the operations under their command). There is thus a serious difference of opinion as to the purpose of control information: senior managers see it as being useful to subordinates in controlling their own activities, whereas their subordinates see it as a mechanism of control over themselves. Possibly both are right, although it is our belief that the senior managers were being somewhat simplistic in stating their beliefs – or maybe they considered that as they didn't find the information very useful themselves, it must be useful to their subordinates! Unfortunately Dew and Gee did not go on to discover what other information was actually used by the managers they studied.

Impediments to the use of management information

Some of the reasons for the widespread lack of use of formally provided management information that some empirical studies have observed, are explored in a report written by Mintzberg (1975) for the US National Association of Accountants and The Society of Industrial Accountants of Canada. He identified three main areas of concern: formal *versus* informal information; organizational problems; and individual cognitive problems.

Formal and informal information systems are contrasted to identify why managers often favour the latter, and four basic weaknesses of formal management information system are highlighted, namely:

1. The formal information system is too limited in that it is weak on providing external information, and tends to ignore non-quantitative and non-economic information. For example, formal systems rarely report information on why sales were lost, but only on how many sales were made.
2. Formal systems tend to reduce overload by aggregating data; as a result much of the information produced is too general for the manager who requires specific and tangible detail. Details of one order reported as being unsatisfactory may be of more use than an aggregate figure of the number of complaints received.
3. Much formal information arrives too late to be of use; many managers need to act on rumours and grapevine information that arrive ahead of events, rather than reports that arrive after they have happened.
4. Some formal information is unreliable; often quantitative surrogates used for important, but essentially qualitative, information distort the message being conveyed.

A second set of problems arise from the fact that information is used in an organizational context. Specifically noted are:

5. Organizational objectives are often rigid and dysfunctional and may encourage the manager to use inappropriate information. The literature on performance measurement (see later) is replete with examples of managers who met the targets they were set (e.g., production output, return on investment, etc.) with harmful consequences to their organization.
6. The power structure and political situation within the organization may cause the manager to ignore or distort information related to overall effectiveness. Budgetary bias and mis-reporting occur frequently in practice.
7. The nature of his work drives the manager to favour verbal channels and neglect documented sources for his information.

Finally, individual cognitive limitations and personality factors can also affect information use:

8. The manager has cognitive limitations that restrict the amount of information he can consider in complex decision processes. Important information may be hidden in a mass of data.
9. The brain systematically filters information in line with pre-determined patterns of experience. Cyert *et al.* (1961) found that people extrapolated the same basic data differently depending upon whether it was labelled 'costs' or 'revenues'. Costs were overestimated and revenues underestimated, perhaps owing to conservatism or knowledge of the impact of errors in estimation.
10. Psychological failures and threats further impede the brain's openness to information. In particular, managers may tend to filter out negative information once they have committed themselves to a particular course of action.

All the preceding factors are considered as impediments to the use of management information: of all available information the formal system captures only a subset; of what is captured, the manager receives only part; of what he chooses to use, the brain absorbs only a small part; and of what the brain absorbs only a yet smaller part is relevant and accurate. Given all these impediments, perhaps the surprising result is that managers ever are able to exercise effective control! In view of the problems identified, Mintzberg (1975) makes several recommendations, of which the more important are:

1. Managers need broad-based formal information systems, in large part independence of the computer (because it is argued it is not well suited to handling qualitative, behavioural, external, speculative and current information – perhaps more modern knowledge-based systems can be devised to handle such data).
2. The information system needs to contain the intelligent filtering systems, more sophisticated than mere aggregation, to avoid the problems of information overload.
3. Appropriate channels of communication, geared to the manager's pattern of activity, need to be used.
4. The information system should have a capability for in-depth search and encourage the use of multiple, possibly conflicting sources of information. The manager needs different points of view and contrary opinions to counter his own mental prejudices.

Informal information systems

Our discussion has so far involved only formal management accounting and information systems. Yet the adequate functioning of organizations seems also to depend upon the extensive use of informal information networks by managers (Preston, 1986). There are several reasons for this state of affairs. Firstly, for many control purposes, timely information is essential; this may be most easily obtained by direct observation or word of mouth, rather than by reliance on a formal, possibly computerized, system. Secondly, formal information may be fragmented and incomplete in serving the purposes for which it is required; informal information may be necessary to complement it. Thirdly, the formal information system may provide only bland, 'agreed' information, rather than the variety of partially conflicting evidence more representative of real life. Points of view and opinions can be as important to effective control as 'hard facts'. Finally, and probably most important, information is itself a source of power, thus it is managed and traded as a resource within organizations.

This process of informing and being informed is central to our perceptions of social reality. Arrangements for giving and receiving information form an important part of the fabric of social life. Preston (1986) presents a range of evidence concerning how managers obtain, interpret and share information relevant to their jobs. In many cases, he observed the construction and maintenance of private information systems designed to preserve a manager's control, power or influence over particular activities. In other cases, he observed the strategic use of misinformation to serve the same purposes. Further, the information that was supplied to the formal system sometimes bore only a fleeting resemblance to reality. (The issue of bias and manipulation in information systems will be further considered in Chapter 7.) Preston concludes:

These processes (of interaction, observation and keeping personal records) are intrinsic to the construction of reality and of making sense of the social and physical world. Despite attempts to design more timely, detailed and accurate information systems, I believe managers will continue to talk to each other, observe events, and keep personal records of those events they regard as important. Furthermore, these processes are important to the operation of an organization. The process of informing therefore has implications for the design and implementation of formal documented information systems.

Informal information systems are often referred to in pejorative terms such as 'grapevines', 'black books' and 'gossip'. But there is considerable evidence that these informal processes are highly valued by managers and are intrinsic to many of their activities. It has been suggested that they should be included in formal management information systems design, although the conflict between rational, designed information systems and essentially emergent social processes (Foucault, 1975) may preclude such a step. Nevertheless, it is important to remember that formal information systems form any one part of the control information flows in an organization, and that informal information is equally, if not more, important.

The design of management accounting systems

Considerations such as the above begin to allow us to specify the conditions under which traditional management accounting systems are likely to be most useful in management control. They would suggest that the ideal conditions for effective budgetary control include a stable operating environment, a clear-cut organizational hierarchy with well specified responsibility centres (preferably profit centres so that both inputs and outputs can be measured), clear definition of what is controllable by a manager and a minimum of interdependence with other parts of the organization. It might well be argued that if such conditions existed, then the need for budgetary control would be minimal! However, in practice, external environments are changing, often rapidly; responsibilities are necessarily not clearly defined, but overlap; many organizational units are at best cost centres; what is controllable shades imperceptibly into what is not. Finally, parts of organizations tend to be highly interdependent with each other. Budgetary control is evidently an imperfect control tool in such circumstances. It is not surprising that it often does not work perfectly; nevertheless it is still, despite its imperfections, an important tool of control as evidenced by its widespread use.

The dilemma found by those wishing to implement effective budgetary control systems is well encapsulated by Hofstede (1968). He found that where budgetary control systems were used extensively as a means of performance evaluation, typically in the USA, they engendered all kinds of harmful side effects and were associated with many negative feelings on the part of managers. By contrast in Europe, budgetary control was not associated with such negative feelings, mainly because it was not extensively used. His recommendation was that managers should treat budgetary control somewhat less than totally seriously, as a 'game', and he lists several pages of detailed methods by which such an approach could be implemented. Hopwood (1972) also suggests that it is the way in which senior managers actually use budget systems, rather than the systems themselves, that determine their effectiveness. The consequences of these conclusions will be further developed in Part Two, but it is evident that the internal and external conditions in which an organization operates will have a profouond effect on the type of control mechanisms that are most appropriate.

This conclusion is consistent with the contingency theory of management accounting outlined at the end of Chapter 2. Differences in the external environments faced by organizations and differences in their internal structure will make different accounting and management information systems appropriate. For example, Gordon and Miller (1976) identify three environmental characteristics (dynamism, heterogeneity and hostility) and several organizational characteristics that they hypothesize will affect information systems. The greater the environmental dynamism (or rate of change), the greater the need for external, non-financial information reported at more frequent intervals. Thus a chain of fashion boutiques may gather market intelligence by sending employees to leading discos and clubs to observe the latest fashion trends. The greater the heterogeneity of the product market (i.e., the variety of product lines sold in different market sectors) the more internal departmentalization and compartmentalization is likely to follow, with the information system being similarly dis-aggregated. Finally, the more hostile and competitive the market place, the more likely it is the organization will develop tight systems of cost control that it monitors frequently. On the organizational front, strategies of differentiation and decentralization will need to be coupled with methods of integrating the diversified package of activities being managed.

CONCLUSIONS

In this chapter we have undertaken a wide-ranging review of some aspects of the management of business enterprises. We have argued that the central function of senior management is control; control of both the overall strategy of the organizational unit for which they are responsible, and control of its actual performance. The context in which they exercise this function is often hectic, for having overall responsibility for the viability of a unit is a wide-ranging and complex task. Further, different parts of an organization may have different cultures, each appropriate to its own needs but requiring different control mechanisms to regulate it.

Traditional management accounting information is only partially successful as a control device. It has to be used in different ways in different circumstances and can never be the sole means of management control. However it serves a vital role in large organizations particularly where role cultures are appropriate. Organizational structure is also an important mechanism of control, and the divisional form of structure is particularly prevalent in large, diversified organizations. This structural form has its own management information requirements, which will be considered more fully in Part

Three. However, it is important to recognize that accounting control systems exist within all organizations and thus reflect some major underlying issues of organizational life.

Wildavsky (1975) has identified three basic facts of organizational life, each of which is reflected in the exercise of budgetary control. Firstly, resources are scarce, so it is necessary for there to be a careful and considered determination of how, where and when they should be used. In most budget systems, the roles of the advocate, who wishes to use resources, and the guardian, who wishes to conserve them, become institutionalized. Secondly, objectives differ from person to person, and the resulting conflicts require resolution. This leads to processes of bargaining and negotiation around what is included in plans and budgetary estimates. Thirdly, there is the underlying complexity of the situation being managed, so that those who are responsible for integrating the activities of diverse parts of the organization are partly ignorant of the nature and value of those activities. This tends to lead to an incremental approach to decision making, where only small changes are made to previous patterns of activity, and the use of simple procedures such as the application of uniform cuts to budgeted expenditures. Finally, the existence of uncertainty, where the relationship between causes and effects is not well understood, tends to exacerbate the problems arising from these three facts of organizational life as it increases the scope for political bargaining rather than rational planning.

The implication for the designer of accounting information systems is clear. He must be aware of the organizational and environmental situation in which he is designing his system, and of its interrelationships with other mechanisms of integration and control. He must also be responsive to the political processes in which accounting information plays a role, for the accounting system will inevitably be moulded by such pressures. And he must recognize that accounting system design is but a means to an end; the more effective integration of all aspects of organizational activity towards desired ends.

If we have succeeded in conveying some small part of the complexity of the process of organizational control, then this chapter has achieved its purpose. The ultimate criterion by which any accounting control system should be assessed is behavioural; that is, how does it affect what managers and their subordinates actually do and how do such activities fit into overall plans. Both the way in which accounting controls are used, as well as their technical design, will affect the response of people to those controls. Firstly, accounting controls represent just one of the integrative control mechanisms that play a part in organizational adaptation and control. The formal information system is, however, only one component of the total information flows in an organization, and formal information can be distorted by the political processes that are part of any human activity.

In the final chapter of this Part, we shall take an avowedly managerialist stance towards the design of formal control systems. We consider the range of formal controls that are available to managers and also the relative effectiveness of each type of control in different circumstances. In this way, we shall develop some practical prescriptions for the design and use of formal accounting and other controls.

EXERCISES

1. The management control systems framework has been criticized on the grounds that all managerial activity (e.g., planning, decision making, intelligence gathering) is seen as control activity. To what extent do you consider all managerial activities are essentially control based? What aspects of managerial work do you think can be more fruitfully analysed from other points of view?

2. It has been observed that managers make little use of many quantitative techniques that have been recommended to them. Why do you think this is? What, if anything, should be done about it?

3. Although the pattern of hectic activity observed by Mintzberg is generally agreed to be a true reflection of a typical senior manager's life, it has been argued that it is a sign of a poorly organized manager. A more competent manager should arrange his work activities in a better way. Do you agree, and what do you think the manager should do to be more effective?

4. The lack of use of accounting information by managers clearly displays their ignorance and lack of confidence in this area. Most managers admit to a poor understanding of how to interpret financial information; what is needed is better training in the use and interpretation of accounting information. Do you agree? What would you wish to include in a course on using accounting information for (a) production managers (b) marketing managers?

5. Choose a small business with which you are familiar and outline the major features of an information system for it that is designed in accordance with Mintzberg's recommendations.

6. Classify some organizations you have dealt with in terms of their dominant culture. What effects did this culture have on the effectiveness of their operations?

7. The most influential controls in an organization are often the least obvious. For example, personnel selection and training can have an impact far more pervasive than that of any information system. Examine the range of controls operated by some organizations with which you are familiar (including non-economic organizations, such as universities) that explain why they behave in the manner you observe.

8. As a manager rises in the organizational hierarchy it is said that he knows less and less about more and more. To what extent do you think this statement is true, and what are the implications for management control?

9. Define management control, and justify why you consider your definition to be an improvement on others that have been advanced.

10. As a manager becomes more senior, it appears that he needs to rely more on formal information yet that his style of life encourages him to use it less. How would you explain this apparent paradox?

11. What insights into the role of information in management control do the different perspectives outlined in the chapter give? To what extent do you consider them to be complementary or competing?

12. If informal information systems are so pervasive, why do organizations need formal information and control systems?

13. A group of senior managers from the Exacta Electronics Company had recently attended a seminar on the application of organizational theory to management control systems design. They meet a week later to discuss whether changes should be made in their own management control system. Part of the discussion was as follows:

    Accountant: I quite agree that we need a better system. What we have was quite adequate when we were a small concern, supplying electrical parts to large manufacturers; but now we have grown much larger and design our own sophisticated electronic products.

    Marketing Manager: Not only have the products changed, but so has the market. A product that didn't exist yesterday can be obsolete by tomorrow. We must have up-to-date information so that we can adapt quickly to market changes and competitor's strategies.

    R and D Manager: Our existing system is far too rigid. In the past it might have been possible to estimate how much it would cost to develop a new product, but it isn't possible now. Trying to hold me accountable to a budget made months ago is ridiculous.

Sometimes I'll spend twice as much because of technical snags; sometimes only half as much because it all works out with no problems.

Production Manager: That's as may be, but a vital part of our business is ensuring that our production runs are efficient and cheap. Once a product has been designed we must make it quickly and cheaply so as to fill the orders that have been received. If we don't maintain close control here, our profit margin disappears.

Accountant: That's quite right. The heavy development costs can only be recouped by selling a large number of efficiently manufactured products. But although close budgeting control is needed in the factory, it doesn't seem to work in R and D and Marketing. What sort of system can I design that will be suitable for everybody?

Required:

Outline the control problems faced by each manager and suggest how the content of the seminar might be relevant to designing a management control system for the whole company.

From: Certified Diploma in Accounting and Finance, Paper 2, June 1983.

5

Controls in business organizations

SUMMARY

The previous four chapters have outlined the general background against which the activity of management control takes place. In this chapter, a more managerially oriented stance is taken in outlining and evaluating the various control options that are available to senior managers. Accounting-based controls are thus set in the context of the wider range of controls that are available to management.

Paradoxically, the first control decision that needs to be considered is control avoidance; that is, can a potential control problem be side-stepped by using alternative organizational arrangements such as automation, centralization, risk-sharing or even ceasing to be involved in a particular type of activity? Having defined the domain in which controls will operate, a selection between the use of results controls, action controls and personnel controls needs to be made, each of which have their own advantages and disadvantages.

The final decision that needs to be made is how tightly the chosen controls should be operated. It is argued that tight controls should be restricted to those areas of activity that are critical to organizational survival and success. The choices of an appropriate mix of controls and the tightness with which they should be operated is a key managerial decision.

THE NEED FOR CONTROLS

The different tasks managers perform can be classified and studied in many alternative ways. For example, *functional* classifications distinguish marketing, production and finance, whereas *resource* classifications distinguish people, money, machines and information. Each of these classifications has been the focus of many management books and academic courses. The control function of management appears when using a *process* classification such as that of Anthony (1965, 1988) that distinguishes objective setting, strategy formulation and control. Control is thus the final stage of the management process. It includes the steps managers take to ensure that organizational strategies are implemented, or, if conditions warrant, that strategies are modified. (This definition and the discussion that follows are taken from Merchant, 1982, 1985.) Management control is thus fundamentally concerned with ensuring that appropriate actions are taken to implement overall organizational plans, and with monitoring the effectiveness of such action and plans.

Since management involves directing the activities of others, a major portion of the control function involves influencing the behaviour of subordinates. Managers must take steps to ensure that people connected with the organization, particularly employees, do what needs to be done to achieve the organization's aims and objectives. If all employees always did what was best for the organization, a control system, and even the activity of management itself, would be unnecessary. But obviously, individuals are not always willing or able to act in the best interests of an organization. Consequently, control systems which include combinations of individual devices we shall call controls, are necessary to guard against undesirable actions and to encourage desirable actions.

People may fail to act in an organization's best interest for any of three basic reasons. The first is lack of direction: people do not always understand what is expected of them. The second is lack of motivation: some people who know what is expected of them are not interested in behaving appropriately because their individual incentives are not adequate to motivate them to perform. The third is lack of abilities, either abilities innate to all human beings or abilities specific to a particular person. Some people fail in their jobs because the jobs are not designed properly; the jobs may be so complex or so demanding that no human being could expect to succeed in them. Other people fail because they lack some abilities, experiences or information that are necessary for them to perform adequately in the jobs to which they are assigned.

If management fails to implement a system of control to protect the organization against the effects of these problems, people on whom the organization relies may behave inappropriately. As a consequence, severe repercussions may result. The minimum adverse consequence will be diminished performance or, at least, a higher risk of poor performance. At the extreme, if performance is not controlled in one or more critical performance areas, the outcome could be organizational failure.

By definition, the goal of every control system is good control. This can be taken to mean that an informed person can be reasonably confident that no major, unpleasant surprises will occur. An out-of-control situation is then one where there is a high probability of forthcoming poor performance, despite a reasonable operating strategy. However, good control is not synonymous with perfect control. Perfect control, which would mean a complete assurance that all individuals on whom the organization must rely will always act as the organization wishes, is not a realistic objective. It is rarely possible to implement controls so well designed that they guarantee appropriate behaviour by all involved. Even if this were possible, it might not be cost-effective because the costs of the controls might exceed the benefits of the high degree of control obtained. Further, people may react against such comprehensive control of their activities. Control, then, is probabilistic. Managers improve control by increasing the probability that people will act in the organization's best interest. But behavioural problems can still occur, even those organizations with good control systems.

ACHIEVING GOOD CONTROL

Good control is usually achieved in a composite manner. Managers can firstly attempt to avoid some behavioural problems; they can then attempt to protect the organization against the remaining problems by implementing one or more different types of control. Methods of control problem avoidance and the categories of control that can be used are outlined below.

Control problem-avoidance

Managers can avoid some control problems by trying to eliminate the risk of undesired behaviours or by ensuring that such risks are passed on to an external party. One avoidance possibility is *automation*. Computers, robots and other means of automation reduce the organization's exposure to control problems because machines can be set to perform more consistently than human beings. Machines do not become bored, nor do they show any inclination to follow their own desires rather than pursuing organizational goals. However, automation is not always feasible, and it can be an expensive and inflexible option.

Centralization is a second avoidance possibility. Top-level managers usually reserve some important decisions to themselves. Control is then not a problem in those areas because only a small group of people are involved. However, in a large and complex organization, only a limited number of decisions can be centralized before information overload reduces the effectiveness of such a strategy.

Risk-sharing with an outside entity is a third possibility. For example, companies bond employees in sensitive positions with an insurance company to protect themselves against the risk of financial loss. In so doing, they reduce the potential harm that can befall the company if an employee behaves inappropriately. Other risk-sharing arrangements can involve joint production or marketing arrangements, or franchising.

Finally, some control problems can be avoided through *elimination* of an entity or operation. Managers without the means to control certain activities, perhaps because they do not understand the processes involved well enough, can eliminate the associated control problems by divesting themselves of the activity, and restricting their operations to activities they are confident can be properly controlled.

If management cannot avoid the control problems caused by relying on other individuals, or if they choose not to avoid them, they must then address these problems by implementing one or more controls. The large number of different types of control that are available can be usefully classified into three main categories, according to the object of control; that is, whether control is exercised over results, actions or personnel.

Results controls

Control can often be effected by focusing on results. Results controls come in only one basic form, that of results accountability. To implement results control, managers must:

1. define the dimensions along which results are desired (e.g., quality, efficiency) and set standards of performance;
2. measure performance on these dimensions and compare it with the pre-set standards;
3. provide rewards for the desired results so as to encourage the behaviours that lead to those results.

Management accounting techniques, such as budgetary control, to the extent that they measure outputs as well as inputs, are an important form of results control. Results controls thus use the basic feedback control model, described in Chapter 1. But even though results controls involve historical measurement, feedback and reward, they are future-oriented. The promises of future rewards (or penalties) are designed to motivate people to behave appropriately in the future.

Action controls

Action controls are a second form of control. They aim to ensure that individuals perform certain actions that are known to be desirable, or that they do not perform actions that are undesirable. Action controls exist in three major forms. *Behavioural constraints* provide a preventative form of action control by making some undesirable behaviours impossible, or at least difficult. These constraints include both physical constraints, such as locks, personnel identification systems and passwords, and administrative constraints, such as segregation of duties which make it difficult for one person to carry out improper acts. *Pre-action review* involves observing the work of others before the activity is complete and making corrections if necessary. Common examples are formal planning reviews, approvals on capital expenditure proposals and direct supervision of manufacturing activities. *Action-accountability controls* are similar to results-accountability controls. They require:

1. defining the limits of acceptable behaviours – e.g., in the form of work rules, policies and procedures, and codes of conduct;
2. tracking the behaviours that employees engage in;
3. punishing deviations from the defined limits.

These controls help employees understand what is expected of them and motivate them to behave as expected. However, they also require a detailed knowledge of appropriate actions on the part of senior management. They can also be seen as unnecessarily limiting and constraining by employees.

Personnel controls

Finally, there is personnel control; in using personnel controls, managers are trying to derive control benefits from either or both of two basic forces. The first is individual self-control, a naturally present force that pushes most people to want to do a good job, at least most of the time. The second force is social control, a pressure exerted by workgroups on those who deviate from group norms and values.

Managers can tap and encourage one of these basic forces in a number of ways. They can upgrade the capabilities or reliability of personnel in key positions by improving selection and placement policies. They can institute training programmes. They can improve communications to help individuals understand their roles better and can provide the resources that people need to perform their jobs well. They can encourage peer control by establishing cohesive workgroups with shared goals. And they can build a strong corporate culture that increases employees' identification with corporate goals and values. All of these steps increase the probability that employees will behave as the organization wishes, so they are properly identified as improving the organization's control system.

FEASIBILITY CONSTRAINTS ON THE CHOICE OF CONTROLS

Not all of the control tools described above can be used in every situation. Although managers are sometimes able to choose from among all the control types described above, in certain circumstances choice is much more constrained. Personnel controls are the most adaptable to a broad range of situations. To some extent, all organizations rely on their employees to guide and motivate themselves, and this self-control can be increased with some care in recruitment, placement and training. For example, even in prisons, where administrators are faced with a distinct lack of goal congruence and where few control options are available other than physical constraints, inmates are screened, so that those considered unreliable are not assigned to high-risk positions such as one allowing access to a machine shop.

The factor which most constrains the use of action controls is the availability of knowledge as to what actions are desirable. While it may be easy to define precisely desired behaviours for assembly-line employees, definition of desired behaviours for middle managers cannot be as precise. Indeed, the very nature of managerial work suggests that it cannot be controlled in this way. Action tracking is also necessary for use of action accountability controls, but with rare exceptions if the desired actions can be defined, they can be tracked, such as through direct observation or the work of internal auditors, although there are circumstances where this is difficult. For example, the very different work of a coal miner and a travelling salesman are both difficult to track because neither's behaviour is easily observable.

Two factors constrain the use of results controls. One is the ability to measure the desired results effectively. Ideally, measures should be:

1. *congruent* with the results that are truly desired;
2. *precise*, not determined only by crude estimations;
3. *objective*, free of bias;
4. *timely*;
5. *understandable*.

While ideal measures are rarely available, reasonable surrogates often can be found or developed. For example, ratings from 'secret shoppers' or customer surveys are sometimes used as measures of customer service in retail establishments.

Significant difficulty in achieving any of these five measurement qualities, however, can lead to failure of results controls. A second condition necessary for results control to work is that the person whose behaviours are being controlled must have some influence over the results measures. Monitoring results that are totally uncontrollable provides neither motivation nor information about the effectiveness of the actions that were taken.

CONTROL SYSTEM DESIGN

When managers design control systems, they adapt combinations of the feasible controls – personnel, action and results controls – to the demands of the situations being controlled, or they decide to avoid the behavioural problems that they cannot control. Proper adaptation of the controls requires accurate knowledge of the potential control problems and the advantages and disadvantages of each of the feasible control types.

The first step in designing a control system is to identify the control problems that exist. A control problem exists where it is determined that desired actions may not be taken. For each problem, it is useful to know whether it is caused by lack of direction, motivational problems or personal limitations. The analysis of the causes of the potential control problems is useful because the control types are not equally effective at addressing each of the control problems. Results controls, for example, do not help solve personal limitation problems, and training does not solve motivational problems. Table 5.1 provides a summary of the control problems addressed by each of the different types of control.

In most situations, managers can design their control systems by choosing from among multiple forms of control which are both feasible and potentially effective. Their choices should depend on the advantages and disadvantages of the control forms. A logical place to start the control-adaptation process is to think about how effective personnel controls will be by themselves. As described above, personnel controls are feasible in virtually all organizational settings. In addition, personnel controls have relatively few harmful side-effects and relatively low out-of-pocket costs. Except in rare circumstances, such as in a small, family-run company, however, personnel controls are not adequate by themselves. Many companies have learned this lesson painfully.

For example, Burrough (1985) described the sorry case of Mitchell Energy and Development Corporation, one of the largest independent oil companies in the USA. The company failed to develop a tight control system to catch kickbacks from suppliers because it had a long-standing 'tradition of trust' with its employees. An anonymous

Table 5.1   Control types and the behavioural problems they address

CONTROL TYPES	BEHAVIOURAL PROBLEMS		
	Lack of direction	*Lack of motivation*	*Lack of abilities*
Results:			
Results accountability	X	X	
Actions:			
Behavioural constraints		X	
Pre-action reviews	X	X	X
Action accountability	X	X	X
Personnel:			
Selection and placement	X	X	X
Training	X		X
Provision of necessary resources			X
Group-based rewards	X	X	
Build corporate culture	X	X	

caller, however, informed them that several of their superintendents and managers had been receiving large kickbacks for many years. The company's lawyer lamented, 'We trusted the employees. We thought everyone would be too proud of the company to do something like that'.

Because the personnel controls are rarely sufficient by themselves, managers must usually implement some action and/or results controls. Their choices should depend on the distinct advantages and disadvantages each of these types of control have.

ADVANTAGES AND DISADVANTAGES OF DIFFERENT CONTROLS

Advantages of action controls

One advantage of action controls is that they provide a direct link between the control and the object ultimately being controlled – that is, actions. Thus they direct managerial attention to the actions being used within the firm, and debates and conflicts that arise are then focused on the right questions – the desired actions and those that are probable or possible.

Secondly, action-accountability controls, in particular, tend to lead to documentation of the accumulation of knowledge about effective organizational practices. The documents (for example, policies and procedures manuals) are an efficient way to transfer knowledge to the people who are performing the actions. They also act as a form of organizational memory; the knowledge is not lost if key employees leave the organization.

Thirdly, action controls are an efficient way to aid organizational coordination. Policies and procedures increase the predictability of actions and reduce the amount of inter-organizational information flows required to achieve a coordinated effort. Pre-action reviews provide an efficient way to direct information flows to people who need to be informed (Galbraith, 1977).

Finally, the effects of some action controls, particularly physical or administrative constraints and pre-action reviews, are more immediate – they can prevent even the first occurrence of undesirable actions. Thus, where it is essential that a good (or bad) action is taken (or is not taken) on the first occasion, a situation is encountered, for example, when a major decision is being made, where these forms of action control should probably be used.

Disadvantages of action controls

Action controls, however, have a number of significant disadvantages. First, it is easy to focus action controls on actions that are easy to define and monitor but that are of relatively little importance. Even an extensive set of action controls may not have much effect on the performance of an organization's critical activities. There is sometimes a tendency of organizations to concentrate on controlling what can easily be controlled to the neglect of important areas where control is difficult.

Secondly, most forms of action controls discourage creativity, innovation and responsiveness to change. People learn to follow the rules and gradually begin to depend on them. They tend to resist change, and they cease to think how their actions could be improved. Indeed, a perverse delight may be taken in implementing rules that are clearly inappropriate in a particular situation.

Thirdly, where the actions being controlled require professional judgement, action controls are costly. The evaluations of actions taken must be done by individuals who are as well or more qualified than those who are taking the actions. Such people are highly skilled and typically not motivated to perform these review or audit functions, and their time is expensive.

Finally, most people are not content to work under an extensive set of action controls for an extended period of time. Action controls constrain behaviour and people who want to be independent and creative in their jobs may leave to find other jobs that allow greater opportunity for achievement and self-actualization.

Advantages of results controls

Results controls also have several significant advantages and disadvantages. One advantage is that results controls can influence people's behaviour, even though they are allowed significant autonomy. High autonomy usually yields greater employee commitment and motivation because higher-level personal needs (e.g., for self-actualization) are activated. It also allows room for individuals to exercise their creativity and idiosyncratic styles of behaviour. And it can provide on-the-job training by allowing people to make choices and learn from their mistakes and successes.

Another advantage is feasibility. Results controls can provide effective control, even where knowledge is to what actions are desirable is lacking. For most professional and managerial roles, such information is often less than complete. A final advantage of results controls is that they are often inexpensive. Performance measures are typically collected for other purposes such as financial or tax reporting, or strategy formulation. If these measures can be used or easily adapted for results control use, the incremental expense of the control can be relatively small.

Disadvantages of results controls

Results controls, however, have two major disadvantages. Firstly, if the measures used provide poor indicators of whether good actions have been taken, severe problems are likely. Indicators are poor because the measures fail to meet one or more of the qualities of good measures – e.g., congruence, precision, objectivity, timeliness or understandability – or because the results were significantly influenced by factors over which the person involved had little control. Each measurement failure causes its own problems. For example, if congruence is lacking, people will actually be motivated to act in ways that are not in the organization's best interests. If precision is lacking, managers will alter their judgements (for example, about accounting reserves) to make their performance reports look better. Often it is difficult even to recognize that one or more of these problems exist. For example, many managers focus on short-term accounting earnings without considering how meaningful such earnings are as an indication of the long-term performance of their unit.

A second problem, described in Barrett and Fraser (1977) and Merchant and Manzoni (1989), is that results targets are often asked to perform several important but competing control functions. For motivational purposes, it may be best for targets to be challenging, that is, achievable but having a less than a 50% chance of achievement. But results targets are also used for planning and communication purposes. The targets are often treated as commitments and passed among the various sub-units in an organization, so that each knows what to expect from the others. For this purpose, the targets should be a best guess or maybe even slightly conservative estimates to ensure that they are achieved. Obviously, one set of targets cannot serve both motivation and planning purposes optimally; one (or both) must be sacrificed if results controls are used.

CRITICAL SUCCESS FACTORS

Perhaps the most important consideration in designing a control system is to maintain 'tight' control over an organization's critical success factors. Managers can identify the critical factors in terms of the key actions that must be performed to yield the highest probability of success or the key results that determine success or failure. The term 'tight' control is used to refer to mechanisms which ensure a high probability that people will act as the organization wishes. Thus, tight control over the critical success factors in an organization usually provides benefits that are greater than the costs of the controls and the possibilities of harmful side-effects that are often coincident with tight control.

The designs of the results and action controls can be altered to be tighter or looser. Results controls can be made tighter if:

1. the measures of performance are improved in terms of congruence, precision, objectivity, timeliness and understandability;
2. the goals are described in more specific terms, such as a 35% return on assets, rather than a vague 'good profitability';
3. the goals are defined for shorter increments of time such as for a month rather than a year;
4. the rewards (or penalties) associated with good (or bad) results are made more significant.

Action-accountability controls can be made tighter in the same ways as results controls – e.g., improved action tracking, more specific action definitions, and more significant rewards and penalties. The tightness of the behavioural constraints varies, on average, directly with the cost of the protection. Pre-action reviews are tighter if the reviews are more detailed, more frequent and performed by more knowledgeable persons.

Control also tends to be tighter if managers use all the feasible forms of control. Multiple forms of controls reinforce one another and address a broader set of control problems. They also provide possibilities for learning, in particular, how actions or certain personnel characteristics are related to results, so that one or more of the controls can be improved at a later time. However, the use of tight controls engenders potentially harmful side-effects. Therefore, it appears wise to restrict the use of such controls to as few truly critical areas as possible, and to use looser and more general controls, giving greater freedom and flexibility, where possible. The choice of an appropriate mix of controls is a matter of considerable managerial judgement, and one which seems to be subject to amendment and change as the consequences of previous control judgements become apparent.

The underlying aim of whatever combination of controls is adopted centres on the concept of behaviour congruence. Results, action and personnel controls are established to encourage desirable behaviour and to guard against undesirable behaviour taken by organization members. These controls serve to operationalize behaviour congruence. To gain agreement between managers to take actions at a particular point in time to maintain or expand the feasible region of the organization's strategy is extremely difficult. The parts of the organization that they manage may be subject to different environmental, strategic and political factors; their professional training and experience may be markedly different; their personal ambitions and management styles may vary dramatically. While all may agree a corporate goal of maximizing shareholders' wealth, each may have a different perspective on how to accomplish this. Attempting to decompose the corporate goal into complete, well-specified sub-goals to which individual managers are committed may prove impossible, and carries the danger that managers will blindly attain the sub-goal regardless of adverse effects elsewhere in the firm or in future time periods.

Specific results, action and personnel controls can, on the other hand, be invoked and emphasized to provide managers with specific guidance relative to an agreed course of action. Take, for example, the agreement between corporate and several divisional managers to tender for a major development site.

Results controls may require:

1. That each part of the tender is prepared by a manager who would be able to influence significantly that part of the contract if accepted.
2. That each part of the tender is prepared in:

   (a) a 'jargon-free' manner;
   (b) using consistent standards of estimation, and
   (c) submitted within a specific time horizon.
3. That the total tender is reviewed or uplifted in price to provide a sufficient return for the shareholders.

Action controls may be required:

1. To ensure consistent application of any corporate conventions or rules governing tender submissions.
2. To identify accounting rules and ensure their consistent application by each manager responsible for a part of the tender preparation.
3. To identify personnel whose past performance suggests they are capable of undertaking this work efficiently.

Personnel controls may be required:

1. To identify qualified personnel who are:
   (a) able to work conscientiously alone, and
   (b) able to contribute and co-operate with a large team of tender preparers.
2. To identify a manager – corporate or divisional – who can provide the necessary leadership and encouragement to bring the tender in on time at an acceptable price.

Different controls, or aspects of forms of control, may be emphasized in light of past experience. For example, late submissions may suggest detailed result control on timeliness; inadequate actual returns may suggest an action controls emphasis; poor implementation of past tenders may suggest that personnel controls are inadequate when identifying the appropriate estimator and executor of a part of a tender.

The possibility of changing the point of emphasis of these controls provides greater flexibility than adherence to an incomplete sub-goal can offer. While the goal of maximizing shareholder wealth is accepted, the application of results, action and personnel controls suggests that behaviour rather than goal congruence is the overall aim of the control system. Behaviour-congruent controls are therefore not only aimed at ensuring that agreement, when appropriate, is reached and results accurately measured, but also that managers capable of significantly influencing that agreement are properly identified and motivated.

CONCLUSIONS

This chapter has provided an introduction to the subject of control in organizations. It has described the goals of control systems, the devices managers use to maintain control over organizations and some of the main factors that managers should consider in making their control system design choices.

Control is a complex subject because the benefits and costs of controls depend on how people react to those controls, and predicting human behaviour is a far from exact science. The study and evaluation of control systems is also complicated by the probabilistic nature of controls. Managers must balance the expected costs of inadequate control against costs of implementing stricter controls of their side-effects. Thus the existence of behavioural problems does not necessarily mean that a control system is flawed. Poor outcomes may mean no more than that the organization has been unlucky.

Despite these complexities and uncertainties, managers must not ignore the control function of management. Good control is essential for long-term organizational success. They must also recognize that control is fundamentally a behavioural issue: the task is to influence employees to behave in desirable ways. They must recognize too that they need to maintain tight control over those few activities that are critical to the success of their entity, while allowing more flexibility in less crucial areas. The flexibility that results, action and personnel controls offer to influence managerial behaviour suggests that development of control systems consistent with behaviour congruence is a practical and worthwhile aim.

EXERCISES

1. What is the difference between the 'control' and 'strategy implementation' functions of management?
2. The feasibility constraints on the choice of controls should usually not be considered as absolute. Often each of the control types can be placed at a point on a continuum varying from 'totally sufficient' to 'totally useless'. What questions should managers ask to determine where on the continuum to place each of the types of controls – action, results and personnel controls – in their situation?
3. It has been said that all controls are action controls, they simply vary in the degree of specificity of the desired actions. Do you agree or disagree with this statement?
4. It has been said that results controls should be used wherever they are feasible because, after all, the primary organizational purpose is to generate results. Do you agree or disagree with this statement?

5. This chapter describes maintenance of tight control over each entity's critical success factors as being important. Yet a criticism of some organizational control systems is that they are stifling because they are too tight. How can you reconcile these two statements?

6. How can managers identify their critical success factors? If it is considered necessary to maintain tight control over the critical success factors, should control feasibility affect the identification of the factors? That is, should the factors be identified in terms that can be easily controlled?

Part Two

Accounting for Programmed Activities

Most accounting control techniques are designed on the basis of an underlying assumption that the activities being controlled are programmable. A programmable activity is one where the relationships that exist between the inputs to a process and the resulting outputs from that process are well understood; given knowledge of the inputs, the outputs can be predicted. Thus, in terms of the control model outlined in Chapter 1, a programmable activity is one for which an adequate predictive model exists and desired actions are known. For example, a routine production process, where knowledge of the amounts of labour, materials and machine time available allows production to be accurately predicted, can be considered to be programmable. Such a process can be optimized in terms of the output and product mix that will yield the maximum financial return, provided that certain technical information about production capabilities and accounting information about resource costs and output revenues is available.

Management accounting techniques are generally constructed on the assumption that the situation in which they will be used is essentially programmable, but in practice the techniques are used in a much wider variety of circumstances. In this section we give a brief resumé of current management accounting techniques, outline some of their assumptions and limitations, and describe ways in which they behave when used in situations that do not completely accord with these implicit assumptions. We assume that the reader is familiar with, or is currently studying, basic cost and management accounting techniques, such as systems of cost collection and accumulation, cost analysis, product costing, cost allocation methods, responsibility accounting and transfer pricing. No attempt is made to present the technical basis of such procedures; good cost and management accounting texts are available and the interested reader is referred to these (e.g., Amey and Egginton, 1973; Bierman and

Dyckman, 1976; Arnold and Hope, 1983; Horngren and Foster, 1987; Drury, 1988; Kaplan and Atkinson, 1989).

The major assumptions made in the typical management accounting system are that the external environment is relatively stable and predictable, that individuals behave in a quite predictable and mechanistic way, that the data entered into the accounting system is accurate and reliable and that centralized decision making is operative. Obviously, these conditions are never fully met; here in Part Two we consider the applicability and usefulness of traditional accounting techniques when these conditions are reasonably closely satisfied, and in Part Three we consider the consequences for the techniques as departures from these assumptions occur.

In Chapter 6 a brief resumé of the role of accounting information in decision making is given, with particular attention being paid to the underlying assumptions that are made and the limitations these impose upon the use of accounting data. Many decision-making applications are particularly suited to implementation on a computer precisely because they are 'programmable' (in both senses of the term), and linear programming is used to illustrate both the strengths and the limitations of these techniques. Chapter 7 moves on to consider the use of accounting techniques in business planning and control. The main focus is on systems of budgetary control, both because these are widely used in practice and because they have been extensively studied by accounting researchers. Study of such systems graphically illustrates the problems that can arise when information that is intended for use in decision making is also used for control purposes.

Of course, decision making, planning and control are not mutually exclusive activities. Decisions are the output of planning and control processes; planning is itself a form of future control; control must involve the setting of objectives, the making of plans designed to achieve them and the implementation of decisions to attain them. It is indeed the interplay of these various aspects of organizational activity that makes the design of appropriate accounting information systems such an important, fascinating and difficult task.

6

Accounting for decision making

SUMMARY

A major function of management accounting information is to support managerial decision making, for a main criterion for rational decision making in business organizations is the maximization of financial benefits. However, the estimation of financial costs and benefits involves the combination of historical data with subjective estimates concerning future events.

This chapter reviews the accounting techniques used in both short- and long-term decision-making to illustrate that they are based on a few, powerfully simplifying assumptions. A linear programming approach is used to elucidate these assumptions and to indicate how many issues in management accounting, including transfer pricing, can be modelled using this technique. The linear programming model also illustrates the role of optimization techniques in management accounting. However, when the assumptions required to operationalize optimizing models become too heroic, the management accountant has to fall back on to simulation models, of which financial planning models are the most widely used.

INTRODUCTION

Management accounting is often defined (Arnold and Hope, 1983, p. 3) as being concerned with the provision of information to those responsible for managing businesses and other economic organizations to help them in making decisions about the future of the organization and in controlling the implementation of the decisions they make.

Indeed, many management texts define the task of management itself in terms of decision making, for decisions are the only obvious output of managerial activity.

Strictly, decision making is only one aspect of the wider process of management control; objectives need to be defined before rational decisions can be made, the need to make a decision has to be brought to a manager's attention and, once made, the decision has to be implemented and its implementation monitored. Nevertheless, decision making is a vital aspect of the overall control process involving the identification of alternative courses of action, the prediction of their likely effects and the selection of the best alternative.

Traditional textbook approaches to decision making emphasize the evaluation of alternatives, but have little to say about the first, and perhaps most important stage of decision making (King, 1975; Harrison, 1975). The identification of alternative possibilities is a vital first step and one involving creative and innovative thought. Subsequent steps aimed at discovering the optimum course of action can deal only with those possibilities previously identified; if an alternative is not suggested, no formal decision-making process can ensure that it is considered. The second stage, the prediction of outcomes that will follow from each alternative, has also received rather sparse treatment. Apart from discussion of the application of statistical forecasting techniques, the prediction of the consequences of actions is assumed to be possible, but the process by which this is achieved is left vague. We have noted in Chapter 1 that at the heart of every control system there is a predictive model and this model is central to effective decision making. Before a choice between alternatives can be made, their likely outcomes must be predicted and values attributed to each aspect of them.

It is the process of attaching values to predicted outcomes and choosing between them that has been the focus of attention of economic theory and, thus, management accounting. Economic theory has settled on 'profit maximization' as the fundamental objective guiding the activity of business firms; accounting has followed this lead although, being more aware of the practical problems of measuring profit, it has operationalized this concept in various ways; the more modern approaches have suggested the maximization of the present value of future cash flows as a suitable operational surrogate for profit maximization. We shall necessarily eventually have to take a more complex approach, involving multiple criteria, but the objective of present value maximization will serve as an initial criterion of choice.

Accounting texts usually distinguish between long-term and short-term decisions. Long-term decisions are those where the time value of money becomes significant and decision making techniques based on the maximization of the net present value of expected future cash flows are recommended. Short-term decisions are those that can be altered within a time span where the effect of the time value of money can be neglected (say, up to a time horizon of one year). Such short-term decisions would often include output, product mix, inventory level and pricing decisions, whereas long-term decisions usually involve capital investment.

SHORT-TERM DECISIONS

The central accounting concept necessary for evaluating short-term decisions is that of variable cost. Variable cost items are defined as those costs that change in (direct) proportion to output, in contrast to fixed costs that remain constant over a range of different output levels. Traditionally, cost items such as materials and direct labour have been considered variable (despite the impact of trades unions and recent employment security legislation); cost items such as rent, rates, depreciation and many administrative costs are considered fixed. Most cost and management accounting texts go into considerable detail with regard to how fixed and variable costs should be estimated, and how the distinction can be made more sophisticated by defining step-function fixed costs and by defining several variable cost rates, each operating at different output levels. In such ways, accounting data can be used to operationalize the economic idea of marginal analysis.

However, the distinction between fixed and variable costs depends crucially upon the time horizon of the decision being considered. In the short-term nearly all costs (with the possible exception of re-saleable material inventories) are fixed; in the long term, all costs become variable, as is shown in Fig. 6.1.

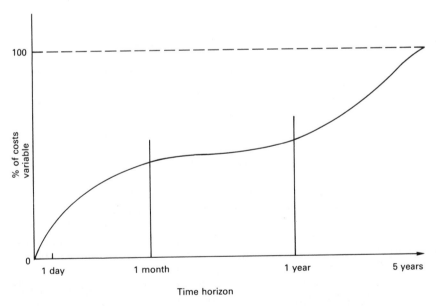

Fig. 6.1 Categorization of costs, with respect to time horizon.

Thus, a particular split between fixed and variable costs is valid only for one particular time horizon of decision. Although it is reasonable to analyse costs in this way to assist in making a particular decision having a defined time horizon, it is not possible to produce general purpose accounting statements applicable to all decisions, although this is what so-called 'contribution' accounting systems purport to do. Such statements are valid only for the particular time horizon for which they are constructed, although it is perhaps possible to argue that most costs do not change category for time horizons between about 1 month and 1 year. To the extent that this is true, it is possible to construct general-purpose accounting statements that contain information valid for all decisions having a time horizon in this range.

A major problem in cost analysis is in the allocation of joint costs to particular products. If a decision concerning the best level of output of a specific product is being considered, it is necessary to define the fixed and variable costs relating to that product. However, some costs are joint to several products (perhaps because the products are made using the same facilities); how should these joint costs be allocated to products, if at all? The issue can be illustrated by means of a simple example.

A small factory makes just two products, a standard and de luxe model of a table lamp. The sole difference between the two products is the material from which they are made; the standard model being fabricated from steel and the de luxe model from brass. Every other aspect of their production is identical, each machine in the factory being able to process both products. For convenience, however, the brass lamps are made in one corner of the factory floor adjacent to the stock of brass tubing.

An accounting statement for the two products is set out in Table 6.1. Some 900 units per week of the standard model are produced and sold to wholesalers at £15 each; only 100 units of the de luxe model are produced, and sold at £30 each. The variable costs (here assumed to include direct labour and direct materials) of producing the standard model amount to £14 per unit; the de luxe model requires more expensive materials resulting in a variable cost of £20 per unit. Fixed factory costs include items such as the factory rent (rented on a 1-year lease), depreciation on machinery and the works manager's salary. In order to produce a statement of product profitability, the accountant has allocated these fixed costs on the most reasonable basis he can ascertain, namely relative production units, as it seems that the de luxe product does indeed use 10% of the available capacity in contrast to the 90% used by the standard product. It should be noted that, although reasonable, any allocation is essentially arbitrary;

although there is perhaps more working capital tied up in the inventories of brass, we shall assume that this allocation is, in fact, appropriate. What information does this accounting statement contain?

Firstly, it is evident that production of both products should continue, at least in the short-run. Both products generate a positive contribution, and to discontinue either would reduce the total profit, turning it into a loss. This would occur because the fixed costs of £1200 per week would continue to be incurred.

Secondly, it is noted that the standard product is shown as incurring a loss of £180 per week. However it has already been decided that it would not be sensible to cease its production forthwith. Should a loss-making product really continue to be produced? In the long-run (defined as the time after which fixed costs can be avoided) the standard product should indeed be discontinued, although in the short-run it should not, unless the capacity thus released can be used in other, more profitable, ways.

Thirdly, the statement sets out a suitable format for considering the likely impact of changes, such as cost reduction programmes, new pricing policies or the acceptance of penalties for buying-out of the lease. The individual product profit and loss figures may be interpreted as the results that would be obtained were each product to be produced independently, in a factory geared to the appropriate volume of production. Thus, in this case, were it possible to lease a factory 10% of the size, using 10% of the machinery and paying only 10% of the works manager's salary, then it would be possible to produce only the de luxe model and earn an increased profit of £880 per week.

The format may also be used to evaluate the effect of changes in pricing policy, provided it is possible to estimate the changes in sales that will result from a given price change. Pricing policy is dealt with in accounting texts, but primarily from the point of view of supplying cost information relevant to pricing decisions (see Arnold, 1973, for a fuller discussion). But it is also necessary to produce forecasts of the likely relationship that exists between price and demand (i.e., the economist's demand curve). Although often illustrated in textbooks by the use of a mathematical formula, in practice it is usual for numerical estimates to exist only for a limited set of possible prices. The amount of *a priori* analysis that can be conducted is therefore limited; nevertheless pricing is a vital decision, and one that can be explored more extensively using the financial planning models discussed in the next section, provided the necessary market data is available.

The figures for accounting profit given in Table 6.1 thus have to be interpreted with a great deal of care. Although the contribution figures are relevant to the short-run and the profit figures relevant to

Table 6.1 Long- and short-term decisions

Product	Output (units)	Price	Unit variable cost Direct labour	Unit variable cost Direct materials	Total	Unit contribution	Total contribution	Fixed costs	Profit/ (loss)
Standard	900	£15	£10	£4	£14	£1	£900	£1080	£(180)
De luxe	100	£30	£10	£10	£20	£10	£1000	£120	£880
Total							£1900	£1200	£700

the long-run, the profit figures require more extensive assumptions to be made in their construction. Many of these assumptions represent arbitrary, although hopefully reasonable, allocations of lump-sum costs between products. However, carefully carried out such allocations can yield figures that have an important information content in directing attention to critical issues. In this case the message is clear; think of ways of using the capacity currently occupied by the loss-making standard product in more profitable ways. This may involve consideration of changing the pricing policy (how many of the standard product would be sold if the price were raised to £18?); of substituting the de luxe for the standard product (if 200 de luxe units could be sold at £26, should production of the standard model be cut back?); or of using the capacity for a completely new product.

Many companies do not provide statements such as that given in Table 6.1 on a routine basis, relying solely on full-cost statements that show only revenue, total cost and profit, in part owing to the difficulty of establishing reliable variable cost data. Where only profit figures are reported it is very easy for managers to fall into the trap of treating them as being valid for all decision making purposes, regardless of the impact of changes in volume of output. It is all too common to see a senior manager run his finger down a list of product profit figures and demand instant action whenever he encounters a product shown as making a loss.

Both the full-cost and the variable-cost statements contain valuable information that, if interpreted correctly, can give guidance to the decision maker. But both are based on assumptions about relationships between costs and activity. These assumptions are most obviously made in constructing the full cost statement, but there are also assumptions made in the variable-cost statement. Have the variable costs been correctly computed? Over what range is the linear relationship valid? Would the direct labour cost really be saved if production were reduced? Indeed, the analysis that is required to be performed before accurate variable costing statements can be constructed has caused many companies not to produce them on a regular basis. Where profit figures alone represent the major summary measure of product performance, it is even more vital to exercise care so as not to interpret them in inappropriate ways. All short-run decisions require information on short-run cost changes represented by variable costs; if these are not routinely collected and presented, they will require to be estimated on an *ad hoc* basis for day-to-day decision making.

Thus, most cost accounting techniques can be seen as providing a calculative mechanism by which the financial impact of alternative courses of action can be assessed. Evidently, these techniques require to be backed up by underlying predictive models, which often rely on information obtained from those directly involved in managing the production and marketing functions. For example, what will be the effect on labour requirements it production methods are altered? What change in sales can be expected if a product price is changed? How will the installation of new equipment affect productivity and costs?

Although the resultant cost accounting analysis appears to be firmly based on rationally derived figures that are objectively verifiable, this is misleading to the extent that it incorporates estimates and subjective judgements. Indeed, insofar as it includes information provided by managers who may be directly affected by the outcome of the decision, the analysis may be biased by the provision of estimates slanted to support a particular point of view. Perhaps the most important point to remember is that the question 'How much does it cost?' is not adequately specified, and cannot be answered without a great deal of additional information. For example, is production being increased or decreased? And over what time span? Are we considering how to make use of slack capacity or increasing capacity? What effects will changes made here have on other products or departments?, etc.

Routine cost accounting attempts to provide general-purpose information to assist in evaluating a wide variety of different decisions. Inevitably, it fails in that task because it represents an impossible target. However, what it can provide is basic data from which useful estimates can be derived using assumptions, skill and judgement in combining this data with other information. The user of accounting information of this kind needs to be aware of the assumptions and subjective judgements that lie behing the apparently hard numbers.

LONG-TERM DECISIONS

Long-term decisions generally appear to raise fewer accounting problems than short-term decisions, although they are more difficult in other respects, raising such issues as corporate strategy and the collection of information about the future state of the environment. The relative ease of the accounting process is primarily because information for such decisions is collected specifically with a particular decision in mind, rather than being extracted from general-purpose accounting reports. Analysed in accounting texts under the heading of capital investment decision making, it now appears generally accepted that the maximization of the net present value of expected future cash flows is an appropriate criterion for evaluation. There are several unresolved problems, such as how risk and uncertainty should be assessed and incorporated into the analysis, and how the discount rate used in the evaluation should be arrived at, but these are not specifically accounting issues and will not be discussed here (but see texts such as Brealey and Myers, 1988; Lumby, 1984).

More relevant to our purpose is the observation that many firms appear to use a combination of measures to evaluate capital investments, including payback period (both discounted and absolute), accounting rate of return on investment, net present value (NPV) and internal rate of return. The likely reason for the use of several criteria is that firms are attempting to satisfy multiple objectives (or constraints). Thus an investment with a positive NPV may still be thought inappropriate if the cash inflows will not occur for several years, and the payback period would clearly indicate this potential disadvantage. But a potentially more serious problem occurs when managers' performance is not evaluated using NPV criteria.

The most commonly used summary performance figure for profit or investment centres is the accounting rate of return earned on investment (Scapens *et al.*, 1982). This would typically be calculated using a figure of profit before tax (and possibly before central HQ expenses) divided by the net book value of assets employed. It has been frequently pointed out (see, e.g., Kaplan, 1982) that such an accounting rate of return bears little relationship to NPV. A project with poor or even negative accounting returns in its early years may still have an acceptable NPV; conversely a project that has an unacceptable NPV might generate good accounting returns in its early years. Moreover, NPV evaluation is properly carried out on an after-tax basis, as taxation is a relevant cash flow, but management performance is almost invariably assessed on the basis of pre-tax figures because it is difficult to associate overall tax liabilities with particular segments of the business.

This distinction between the criterion used to evaluate capital investments and the measures used to evaluate subsequent performance can lead to managers biasing the estimates entered into the NPV calculations. A manager keen to show good short-term results may wish for a project that has good accounting returns in its initial years to be undertaken, despite its probable negative NPV, and thus be motivated to be optimistic about its likely cash flows in later years. Conversely, he may not wish to undertake a viable project having positive NPV because it has poor returns in early years; in this case, he may merely neglect to put it forward for formal evaluation.

This problem occurs because of the difference between the criterion used for decision making and the measure used for evaluation. One possible conclusion might be that managers should not be evaluated on the basis of accounting returns but on actual cash flows compared with those originally budgeted (Emmanuel and Otley, 1976). However, at this stage, it will suffice to point out the problem; methods of resolving it will be discussed at some length in Part Three. The central problem in evaluating long-term decisions is that actual results occur only after a considerable period of time. The feed-back information necessary to control the decision making process is only available long after the decisions have been taken; learning in this type of situation is necessarily a slow process.

This also makes capital investment decisions a fruitful area for bias and manipulation. Estimates are invariably subjective judgements of outcomes over a considerable future period and are, therefore, difficult to validate. In addition, the acquisition of the substantial assets that can follow the acceptance of a capital investment proposal may carry with it a range of other benefits to the managers involved. This is the reason for the very stringent capital investment appraisal procedures generally used, and for such decision making being reserved to the very highest levels of management.

FINANCIAL PLANNING

The decisions considered in the previous sections have related to individual parts of the enterprise and, in particular, to individual products or projects. We now turn to consider overall decisions that relate to the coordination of the overall situation in either a part or the whole of an enterprise, particularly in terms of financial planning. Finance is a major business function on a par with other functions such as production, marketing, research and development, and personnel. It is necessary for financial managers to have information about the plans of the outer major functions so that finance can be provided when necessary, but without unnecessary waste of financial resources.

The major integrative tool used in this process is the budget. A budget may be defined as 'a plan showing how resources are to be acquired and used over a specified time interval' (Moore and Jaedicke, 1980). Its use is not limited to financial planning, as pointed out by Horngren (1981):

A budget is a quantitative expression of a plan of action and an aid to co-ordination and implementation. In most cases, the budget is the best practical approximation to a formal model of the whole organization: its objective, its inputs and its outputs.

However we shall defer consideration of the wider use of budgets as a tool of overall management control until the next chapter, and confine ourselves here to the use of budgets for financial planning.

The three main areas in which a budget can assist financial planning relate to profitability, liquidity and asset structure, all of which are relevant to the determination of overall financial structure (Edey, 1966). Profitability is of evident importance for it forms the substance of external financial information disclosure. Reported profits are likely to affect share price movements, to the extent they are not already anticipated, if only because the underlying cash flows and expected future cash flows are not public knowledge. Liquidity is a short-term constraint, but a vital one nevertheless, for the consequences of running out of cash tend to be short, sharp and nasty. Asset structure is a longer-term issue, but one that must be considered when the overall financial structure of the enterprise is being planned. Budget statements in each of these three areas exactly match the equivalent reports of actual results, but using forecast and estimated figures rather than actuals. Thus budgeted profit and loss accounts, cash flow statements and balance sheets may be constructed, so that the financial outcomes of any set of plans can be predicted and assessed.

Although budgeting is normally presented in accounting textbooks as an iterative technique whereby unacceptable outcomes are altered by revising the plans on which they are based, in practice the sheer time and tedium involved in budget re-calculation generally leads to a very limited number of alternatives being considered. However the advent of computerization and, in particular, interactive terminals and microcomputers, has now produced a situation where a great deal of useful exploration can be conducted using a budget model. Spreadsheet programs, or the more sophisticated financial planning models now available, enable the consequences of many plans to be quickly assessed once the basic budget model of the enterprise has been developed.

At the technical level, the process is straightforward if complex, and a good guide to the process is contained in Sherwood (1983). Budgeted financial statements are produced in exactly the same way as actual financial statements, but based on estimated data rather than actual data. Given these estimates and a computerized financial planning package it is possible to program a simple budget model in a few hours and even a relatively complex model for a quite sizeable organization can be constructed in a few man-months. (The student is encouraged to gain experience in this process by attempting the questions given at the end of this chapter, which are quite feasible on a microcomputer with a suitable spreadsheet program.) The major difficulty lies in estimating the relationships that exist between variables. For example, what proportion of production costs of a product are variable? At what point do overtime rates become payable? What are the capacity limitations on the plant? What is the relationship between price and sales? And so on. A great deal of detailed work generally has to be done, even where standard cost and variable cost systems are currently implemented.

The financial planning packages are generally set up in a way that helps to cope with this problem. Most can have many prior years of historical data entered into them, and allow the planner to analyse relationships that seem to have existed in the past, and to project these as forecasts into the future. Nevertheless, the provision of accurate predictions of future consequences is a demanding and time-consuming task, but one on which the validity of the budget model totally depends. Inevitably, some estimates will come from the line managers directly concerned, as they are often in the best position to predict what is likely to happen. This is quite reasonable procedure, but can prove to be dangerous if these estimates are subsequently altered by the planner, without making any necessary consequential changes, because knowledge of these may exist only in the mind of the manager, not having been incorporated into the formal model.

There is no doubt that computer-based financial planning packages provide a powerful tool capable of enabling financial managers to explore the consequences of a much wider range of plans than was possible in the past, and thus to arrive at better plans, if only because of the greater number of alternatives considered. But it must always be remembered that a model (especially a computerized model) is only as good as the assumptions about relationships on which it is based. The role of the accountant in providing managers with financial models of their operations, so that they can jointly explore the consequences of alternative possibilities is likely to be increasingly important in future.

ASSUMPTIONS OF MANAGEMENT ACCOUNTING

A quick scan of the main management accounting textbooks provides a quite remarkable consensus as to the major decisions that management accounting is considered able to assist. Scapens' (1984) survey indicates that decisions such as cost classification (into fixed and variable), cost – volume – profit decisions, product-mix decisions, inventory and working-capital decisions, pricing decisions and capital-investment decisions dominate, together with discussions of transfer pricing and performance evaluation in divisionalized organizations. Essentially such problems are simplified for the purposes of analysis, so as to eliminate uncertainty (perhaps to be brought back at a later stage in the guise of statistical probability) and to deal only with situations where complete information exists. Whether these de-cisions are ones with which the practising accountant is primarily concerned is not well known, owing to a paucity of research studies, but it is open to considerable doubt.

However, on the basis of these simplifications, various techniques have been developed, of which the most powerful is linear program-ming (LP). LP is essentially an optimizing technique for situations characterized by limited resources (and certainty). It subsumes many of the major management accounting techniques and most accounting rules (e.g., maximize the contribution per unit of limiting resource) can be derived from its models. It has also been applied to the prob-lem of pricing goods and services transferred internally between one part of a company and another. Good summaries of application of LP techniques to accounting problems can be found in Mepham (1980) and in Bierman and Dyckman (1976). The LP model therefore provides a means of summarizing many different accounting models, and can be used to expose their common weaknesses and limitations. We will therefore embark upon an extended example, the Jayfax Company, to illustrate these points.

Initially, we shall consider only the production problem of one division of the Jayfax Company that sells finished goods directly to the final customers. Here the use of the LP model will enable us to derive the well-known cost accounting rule that the optimum use of resources can be obtained by maximizing the contribution yielded by a limiting resource, and also to extend it to the case where several resources prove to be limiting factors.

This example will then be extended to include a production division that sells its product only internally, but which is evaluated as a profit centre. In order to accomplish this, it is necessary for a price to be attached to the products that are transferred internally from one division to another (the so-called transfer price). This analysis antic-ipates much of the material dealt with in Part Three, where the con-trol of divisionalized organizations is explicitly considered; however, the technical analysis follows directly from the LP approach presented here, so it is most conveniently dealt with at this point. The reader may wish to skim this material now and return to it after studying Chapter 11.

The use of the LP approach will highlight a number of the major assumptions made in most accounting models. It requires a single objective function to operate (e.g., the maximization of contribution); costs must be accurately categorized into fixed and variable elements for the decision at hand; it is a deterministic technique that allows the incorporation of uncertainty only with difficulty; and it is generally applied as a single-period model, although multi-period analysis is possible. Finally, it is essentially a mechanism for centralized decision making, despite some claims that have been made for it.

The Jayfax Company

The Jayfax Company has two divisions, Alpha and Beta. As the Alpha division produces only intermediate products (A_1 and A_2) used in the manufacture of Beta's final products (B_1 and B_2) we will firstly consider only the Beta division and treat the cost of products A_1 and A_2 as given. The product flows are shown in Fig. 6.2.

Beta Division
The major constraints on the Beta division are the availability of machine time on the two machines (Y and Z) needed to convert the intermediate A products into the final B products. The times necessary to do this, the variable costs of the conversion process and the machine availabilities are shown in Table 6.2. In addition the material

Fig. 6.2   Product flows in the Jaymax Company.

Table 6.2   Beta Division production constraints

Production of one unit of	Time required on machine Y	Z	Variable cost to B
B_1	1 hr	1 hr	£2
B_2	1 hr	2 hr	£3
Machine availability	300 hr/wk	400 hr/wk	

Table 6.3   Beta Division input requirements

Production of one unit of	Input requirements of A_1	A_2	Total input cost*
B_1	2 units	3 units	£17
B_2	1 unit	2 units	£10

* Initially assumed to be £4 per unit of A_1 and £3 per unit of A_2

Table 6.4 Beta Division revenues and contribution

Sales of one unit of	Sales revenue	Input cost	Additional variable cost	Contribution margin
B_1	£26	£17	£2	£7
B_2	£23	£10	£3	£10

Table 6.5 Contribution analysis for Beta Division

Product	Contribution per unit	Time on each machine		Contribution per machine-hour	
		Y	Z	Y	Z
B_1	£7	1 hr	1 hr	£7	£7
B_2	£10	1 hr	2 hr	£10	£5

requirements of A_1 and A_2 in the production of B_1 and B_2 are given in Table 6.3, together with the total material input cost for each unit of B_1 and B_2 made. Finally the sales revenues gained from the sales of Beta division are shown in Table 6.4.

The decision problem facing the company is one of maximizing its total contribution, by selecting the optimum product mix. It might initially go about this by calculating the contribution it obtains from the use of each hour of scarce resource (machine time). The results of such an analysis are shown in Table 6.5. This indicates that as far as machine Y is concerned, it is more profitable to produce B_2 because this will yield £10/hr; however the situation with regard to machine Z is reversed, because it is more profitable to produce product B_1. Evidently it is necessary to strike a balance between these conflicting demands and produce some of both B_1 and B_2. The LP approach allows such a problem to be formulated and solved.

Suppose that b_1 units of B_1 and b_2 units of B_2 are produced. The decision problem can then be formulated as:

$$\text{Maximize} \qquad £7\, b_1 + £10 b_2$$

subject to the following constraints:

$$\text{Machine } Y \text{ usage} \quad b_1 + b_2 \leq 300 \text{ hr}$$
$$\text{Machine } Z \text{ usage} \quad b_1 + 2b_2 \leq 400 \text{ hr}$$

The first line indicates that the total contribution obtained from selling b_1 units of B_1 and b_2 units of B_2 is to be maximized; the two machine constraints measure the total time this amount of production will take and ensure that it is limited to the time actually available.

A problem as simple as this, with just two variables, can be solved graphically, as shown in Fig. 6.3, although computer-based techniques are available for any size of problem. This graph indicates that the maximum contribution can be obtained (by moving the equi-contribution line as far to the north-east as it will go) by producing 200 units of b_1 and 100 units of b_2. Such a solution uses both machines to capacity and results in a total contribution of £2400. This is clearly in excess of any single-product solution, for a maximum of 300 units of B_1 could be produced, yielding a contribution of £2100 *or* 200 units of B_2, yielding a contribution of £2000.

The simple accounting rule can in fact be used to obtain this solution. From initially producing nothing, B_2 has the best unit contribution, so we first choose to produce as many units of B_2 as possible; at a production of 200 units of B_2 the machine Z constraint becomes binding. In this situation B_1 has a better contribution per machine hour than B_2 (on machine Z) so we move along the machine Z constraint, substituting B_1 for B_2 until the machine Y constraint is reached. Here, Table 6.5 shows that the two constraints yield opposing recommendations, which indicates that the optimal mix has been obtained. Indeed this procedure is precisely that used by the well-known Simplex method for solving an LP. Suffice it to say, however, that computer techniques exist that will generate the optimum solution to any LP problem.

Note that, in order to arrive at this solution, it is necessary to have variable cost and revenue information, and also technical information relating to the machine constraints, all of which were assumed to be certain and accurately known. The problem would have become too complex to solve if it had been necessary to estimate a relationship

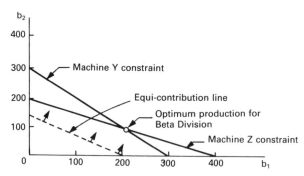

Fig. 6.3 Graphical representation of Beta's production problem.

between sales volume and sales revenue. As it stands, the results can only be checked to see if they appear to be reasonable; if not, new revenue figures would have to be inserted appropriate to the calculated optimal production figures, and the LP re-run to ascertain if the optimal plan remains the same.

Alpha and Beta divisions

The example can now be extended by assuming that A_1 and A_2 are manufactured by the Alpha division of Jayfax, and transferred internally to the Beta division. It is further assumed that there is no external market for the intermediate products (A_1 and A_2) so that Alpha manufactures only what Beta requires, namely a_1 units of A_1 and a_2 units of A_2. The additional data about Division Alpha is given in Table 6.6. The new decision problem facing the total company can now be formulated as:

Table 6.6 Alpha Division production constraints

Production of one unit of	Time required on machine W	X	Variable cost to Alpha
A_1	1 hr	3 hr	£4
A_2	2 hr	1 hr	£3
Machine availability	2000 hr	2000 hr	

$$\text{Maximize} \quad -4a_1 - 3a_2 + 24b_1 + 20b_2$$

subject to the following constraints:

Machine W	$a_1 + 2a_2$		$\leqslant 2000$
Machine X	$3a_1 + a_2$		$\leqslant 2000$
Machine Y		$b_1 + b_2$	$\leqslant 300$
Machine Z		$b_1 + 2b_2$	$\leqslant 400$
Link A_1	$-a_1$	$+ 2b_1 + b_2$	$\leqslant 0$
Link A_2	$- a_2$	$+ 3b_1 + 2b_2$	$\leqslant 0$

Note that the contribution function now separates the costs of A_1 and A_2 from those of B_1 and B_2. The machine constraints for Division Alpha are exactly similar to those for Division Beta. In addition, linking constraints are necessary to ensure that enough A_1 and A_2 are produced to permit these required quantities of B_1 and B_2 to be manufactured. *In this particular case,* by making the linking constraints equalities (which a moment's thought will indicate as optimal) the problem can be reduced to two variables by substitution, as shown below, and thus allow a graphical solution. This is done purely for illustrative purposes; a real problem would be solved using a suitable LP package on a computer:

$$
\begin{array}{lll}
\text{Maximize} & 7b_1 + 10b_2 & \text{subject to} \\
\text{Machine } W & 8b_1 + 5b_2 \leqslant 2000 \\
\text{Machine } X & 9b_1 + 5b_2 \leqslant 2000 \\
\text{Machine } Y & b_1 + b_2 \leqslant 300 \\
\text{Machine } Z & b_1 + 2b_2 \leqslant 400
\end{array}
$$

This is illustrated in Fig. 6.5. Note constraint X dominated constraint W, giving the solution:

$$
\begin{aligned}
a_1 &= 430.8 \\
a_2 &= 707.7 \\
b_1 &= 153.8 \\
b_2 &= 123.1 \quad \text{Total contribution} = \pounds2307.7
\end{aligned}
$$

This is a lower contribution than was previously calculated for the Beta Division alone because, there are now additional capacity constraints on the availability of A_1 and A_2. Additional information generated by an LP package would include the shadow prices associated with each binding constraint (i.e., the amount it would be worth paying to have an additional hour of machine time, or unit of other constraint). The shadow prices are:

Machine W constraint		Slack by 153.8 hr
Machine X constraint		$\pounds0.308$/hr
Machine Y constraint		Slack by 23.1 hr
Machine Z constraint		$\pounds4.231$/hr
Link	A_1 constraint	$\pounds4.923$ per unit
	A_2 constraint	$\pounds3.308$ per unit

The firm should thus be willing to pay up to $\pounds0.308$ for an extra hour on machine X and $\pounds4.231$ for an extra hour on machine Z.

If values are attributed to the goods produced by using the relationship (Mepham, 1980):

Value = Variable cost of production + opportunity cost of using the scarce resource

an unsurprising conclusion is reached, namely that:

$$
\begin{aligned}
\text{Value of } A_1 &= 4 + 1 \times 0 + 3 \times 0.308 = \pounds4.924 \\
A_2 &= 3 + 2 \times 0 + 1 \times 0.308 = \pounds3.308 \\
B_1 &= 2 + (2 \times 4.924 + 3 \times 3.308) + 1 \times 4.231 = \pounds26.00 \\
B_2 &= 3 + (1 \times 4.924 + 2 \times 3.308) + 2 \times 4.231 = \pounds23.00
\end{aligned}
$$

i.e., the value of those products having only an internal market is the shadow price associated with their linking constraints, whereas the value of those products for which an external market exists is their market price. Contribution may thus be attributed to divisions by assigning values to their *scarce* resources only:

$$\text{Alpha Division} \quad 2000 \text{ hr} \times £0.308 = £\ 616.$$
$$\text{Beta Division} \quad 400 \text{ hr} \times £4.231 = £1692.4$$
$$\overline{£2308.4}$$

which divides the overall company profit into that attributable to each division (subject only to slight rounding errors).

Although this procedure has been recommended to avoid many of the motivational problems associated with other methods of setting transfer prices (dealt with in detail in Part Three), it still does not succeed for the division is rewarded only for scarce resources in this single-period model. Thus a division that planned to have enough capacity to meet all the demands likely to be made upon it, with a little slack to meet unforeseen contingencies, would be penalized by being allocated no contribution above its own variable costs of production. Because the model is essentially a single-period one, it cannot take this effect into account. Further, knowledge of transfer prices alone does not indicate to a division what it ought to do. The overall optimum would not be selected by the Beta Division whatever its contribution function, except by chance; further information is necessary.

External markets for the intermediate product and transfer pricing

Although we have restricted ourselves to the case in which the Alpha Division supplies only the Beta Division, there is no technical difficulty in extending the analysis to include the case where an external market exists for the intermediate products. Thus, if quantities a_{1e} and a_{2e} of products A_1 and A_2 can be sold externally at prices P_1 and P_2, in addition to the quantities a_{1i} and a_{2i} sold internally, the new LP formulation becomes:

Maximize
$$-4a_{1i} + (-4 + P_1)a_{1e} - 3a_{2i} + (-3 + P_2)a_{2e} + 24b_1 + 20b_2$$

subject to the following constraints:

Machine W
$$a_{1i} + \qquad a_{1e} + 2a_{2i} + \qquad 2a_{2e} \qquad\qquad \leqslant 2000$$
Machine X
$$3a_{1i} + \qquad 3a_{1e} + \ a_{2i} + \qquad a_{2e} \qquad\qquad \leqslant 2000$$
Machine Y
$$b_1 + \quad b_2 \leqslant\ 300$$

Machine Z

$$b_1 + 2b_2 \leqslant 400$$

Link A_1

$\quad -a_{1i} - \qquad\qquad a_{1e} \qquad\qquad\qquad + 2b_1 + \quad b_2 \leqslant \quad 0$

Link A_2

$\qquad\qquad\qquad - a_{2i} - \qquad\qquad a_{2e} + 3b_1 + 2b_2 \leqslant \quad 0$

It has further been suggested that the LP formulation of the transfer pricing problem enables decentralization to be combined with over-all optimal decision making in the following way (see Solomons, 1965, and Mepham, 1980, for a fuller discussion). The LP formulation breaks down into three major components, as shown in Fig. 6.4.

The suggestion is that each division solves its own LP (neglecting the corporate linking constraints) and sends its solution to HQ. HQ then puts these prices into its contribution function, solves the LP consisting solely of the linking constraints and its own objective function, and revises the transfer prices sent to divisions. The process is iterated, as shown below, until an overall optimum is reached:

1. divisions solve divisional LPs;
2. solutions sent to HQ;
3. HQ sends out new transfer prices;
4. when optimum is reached, divisions informed of quantities to produce.

Note that step 4 is necessary because knowledge of the transfer prices alone does not give divisions enough information to calculate optimum production quantities, as is illustrated below.

In the original example, the problem would be formulated as follows:

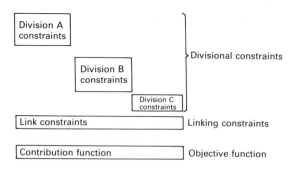

Fig. 6.4 Constraints in LP formulation.

Alpha Division's problem

$$\text{Maximize} \qquad (-4 + P_1).a_1 + (-3 + P_2).a_2$$
$$\text{Machine } W \qquad a_1 + 2a_2 \leqslant 2000$$
$$\text{Machine } X \qquad 3a_1 + a_2 \leqslant 2000$$

where P_1 and P_2 are the transfer prices for A_1 and A_2. Note that substituting the shadow transfer prices of £4.924 for A_1 and £3.308 for A_2 gives the contribution function a slope of exactly 3 and an optimal solution anywhere on the machine X constraint.

Beta Division's problem

$$\text{Maximize} \qquad (24 - 2P_1 - 3P_2).b_1 + (20 - P_1 - 2P_2).b_2$$
$$\text{Machine } Y \qquad b_1 + b_2 \leqslant 300$$
$$\text{Machine } Z \qquad b_1 + 2b_2 \leqslant 400$$

Again, substituting the shadow transfer prices given an optimal solution anywhere on the machine Z constraint. Thus the overall optimum lies at the intersection of the X and Z constraints, but this information has to be conveyed to the divisions by HQ as illustrated in Fig. 6.5.

Such a procedure is technically feasible, and it can be shown mathematically that it will eventually lead to the optimal solution being formed. Indeed the decomposition method, as it is known, was originally developed to solve linear programming problems that were too large to fit into the computers available (see Baumol and Fabian, 1964). But it cannot seriously be suggested that it allows decentralized decision making, because the divisions, having re-planned several times on the basis of different sets of transfer prices being supplied by the HQ, and arriving at their own optimum

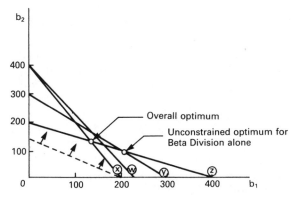

Fig. 6.5 Graphical representation of overall LP.

plan, also have to be instructed as to the quantities of each product they shall produce. Although these quantities will be consistent with the final optimum plan (for the final contribution function will be parallel to a divisional constraint, allowing a variety of production possibilities), the whole process must appear highly constrained (Godfrey, 1971). Why not submit the divisional constraints to HQ and let HQ inform the divisions of the required production plan?

Thus the LP approach assumes centralized decision making, a precise analytical relationship between costs and volume, and well-defined technical relationships between variables, in much the same way as the more specific accounting models developed in textbooks. This is not to deny the usefulness of the model in exploring possibilities and understanding the implications of various policies. By way of example, a question at the end of the chapter asks you to explore the implications of changing a constraint and of permitting an intermediate product to be sold in an external market. Discussion of the transfer pricing problem is continued in Chapter 11.

THE ROLE OF MANAGEMENT ACCOUNTING IN DECISION MAKING

We have spent some time considering financial planning models and linear programming formulations of the use of scarce resources because together they provide an overview of most management accounting techniques. Other specific models from economics and operational research are used in the accounting literature (e.g., economic order quantities, job-shop scheduling), but these two approaches indicate the two major classes of model used, namely simulation models and optimization models.

For an optimization model to be effective, it is necessary to be able to specify both an objective function and the relationships that exist between the variables used in the model. Thus in the LP formulation it is necessary to derive both the contribution function (requiring cost estimation) and the machine capacity constraints (requiring technical information). Within their assumptions, optimization models are highly effective, although more is often learnt from the process of building the model than from the optimization itself (Tomlinson, 1981). Neither are the models quite as restrictive as is sometimes supposed; LP can be extended so that non-linear objective functions and fuzzy constraints can be incorporated, and multi-period models can be constructed. Nevertheless, there is usually a point when necessary realism can no longer be incorporated into the structure of an optimization model.

It is at this stage that simulation models take over. Such models incorporate those relationships that can be framed in precise mathematical terms, but allow the exercise of managerial judgement to explore the likely consequences of various alternative assumptions about the state of the real world. Spreadsheet financial planning models provide a good example of this, in that known cost/volume relationships can be built-in and the accounting structure fixed (e.g., profit equals revenue *less* variable costs *less* fixed costs) although unknown relationships are omitted (e.g., the relationship between price and demand). These latter variables can then be entered in numerical form to explore the effects of various alternative assumptions. Even a measure of uncertainty, in the form of statistical probability distributions, can be incorporated, and simulation methods used to build up a statistical distribution of likely outcomes (see Hertz, 1964, for an early application of these techniques to capital budgeting).

In most cases it is the estimation techniques used to provide data for the models, rather than the models themselves, that provide the most severe limitation on their practical applicability. For example, in capital budgeting, accountants have spent considerable time developing discounting techniques and the NPV model, but very little on studying the process of estimating the cash flows to be used in the model. Again, the concept of variable cost and its application to different decisions has been well studied; in this case, methods of variable cost estimation have also been considered, but these may be more applicable to the industrial scene of the past rather than the present. To what extent do we know what costs are variable in the capital-intensive and unionized factory of today? Academic accountants, in particular, need to devote more effort to understanding specific management accounting problems that exist in practice, rather than inventing ever more sophisticated analyses of over-simplified 'problems' (Kaplan, 1984).

Most management accounting techniques assume the underlying processes being studied are programmable, in the sense that we possess a predictive model capable of accurately forecasting outputs given a knowledge of inputs. In practice this is only partially true. Relationships are not completely stable over time, uncertainty is a key feature of the business environment, and organizations consist of human beings as well as machines. The traditional accounting treatment of decision making has assumed a stable and predictable environment, a clear organizational objective, and relationships that do not alter over time. The same assumptions have been made, although to a lesser extent, in accounting for control which is examined in the next chapter; here human relationships within organizations have forced themselves on to the accountant's attention. But the textbook wisdom applies mainly to the stable, centralized firm of classical economics and organizational theory. The practical applicability of methods derived on the basis of such assumptions, and the consequences of using them in other circumstances will form the basis of Part Three.

EXERCISES

1. Note: although this exercise ideally requires a computerized spreadsheet, it is possible to complete it manually.

   Pygmalion Products manufactures and sells two products, *A* and *B*, which are both made in the same factory using the same machinery. At present *A* is the main product, but sales of *A* are declining slowly and it is hoped to build up sales of *B* to compensate for the lost sales of *A*.

   At the end of December the Managing Director calls upon you, as Chief Accountant, to forecast what the likely outcome of present trends will be. You note that December sales of *A* were 5000 unit and have been undergoing a cumulative decline of 3% per month (i.e., each month's sales are 3% less than the previous month); the selling price is £10 per unit. December sales of *B* were 1000 units, but have been growing at 12% per month (cumulatively). The list price of B is £20 per unit, but an introductory discount of 10% has been offered, valid until the end of March next year. At these prices you expect the steady 3% decline of *A*'s sales and the 12% growth in *B*'s sales to continue for the next year.

   Details of the standard unit production costs are given below and are expected to be valid throughout the coming year:

	A	*B*
Direct labour cost	£2	£ 3
Raw material cost	£4	£10
Variable factory overhead	£1	£ 1

   Fixed factory overhead amounts to £13 000 per month (of which £3000 per month is depreciation) and is allocated to products *pro rata* to their total direct labour costs. Selling and distribution costs comprise a fixed cost of £500 per month for product *A* and £1000 per month for product *B* and a variable cost of £0.50 per units sold for both products.

   Inventory is valued at the standard variable cost of production, and at the end of December will amount to 2000 units of product *A* and 1000 units of product *B*. The company has decided that it would be wise to maintain month-end stocks at a half of the following month's expected sales for product *A* and the whole of the following month's expected sales for product *B*.

All goods are sold on credit. For product *A*, 50% of debts are collected in the month following sale and 48% in the subsequent month. The remaining 2% prove to be not collectable. For product *B*, the corresponding figures are 20% after one month, 75% after two months and 5% uncollectable. All costs are paid in cash during the month in which they are incurred, except for raw materials, which are paid for one month in advance of their use in production, owing to the need to maintain adequate raw material stocks.

Required:
(a) Using a financial planning package, produce statements for the Managing Director for next year, clearly showing:
   (i)   the monthly profit for the company, and for each product individually, using a variable costing format.
   (ii) cash flow forecasts for the same period.
   (iii) annual totals for the above figures (NB, although only a calendar year's figures are required to be presented, you will find it useful to extend your spreadsheet by two months at the beginning and end of the period).
(b) Repeat the exercise twice for each of the two sets of assumptions:
   (i) sales of *A* will decline at 5% per month (cumulatively) during next year (although at only 3% in this December). Sales of *B* will grow at only 10% per month (cumulatively) during next year (although at 12% this December).
   (ii) sales of *A* and *B* remain at their December levels indefinitely.
(c) Comment on your results, numerically reconciling the profit and loss figures with cash flow figures, and assess their implications for the company.
(d) Suppose the company is owned by a holding company and that the Managing Director has been instructed to maximize his profit while exercising firm control over cash. What are the behavioural implications of the situation you have analysed here?

2. Taking the LP formulation of the transfer pricing problem of the Jayfax Company as your starting point, analyse the effect of having an additional constraint that limits the total production of A_2 to 600 units. What should the new transfer prices be, and how would the allocation of profits to each division be affected? Further, suppose that A_2 can be sold to an external market at a price of:

(a) £3
(b) £6
(c) £9

How does the optimal solution change, and what should the internal transfer prices be?

3. Division A of Incorrigible Dysfunctionals Limited is the only source of supply for an intermediate product that is converted by Division B into its final saleable form. Most of A's costs are fixed. At an output of 1000 units per day its total costs amount to £550 per day and increase by £100 for each additional 1000 units made. Division A judges that its own results will be optimized if it sets its price at 40p a unit, and it acts accordingly.

   Division B incurs additional costs in converting the intermediate product supplied by A into a finished product. These costs amount to £1250 per day at an output of 1000 units and increase by £250 for each additional 1000 units made. On the revenue side, increased sales require a reduction in price and an increase in sales promotion. Its sales forecast is:

Sales (units)	Net revenue per 1000 units
1000	£1750
2000	£1325
3000	£1100
4000	£ 925
5000	£ 800
6000	£ 667

Required:

(a) Prepare a schedule comparing B's costs (including its purchases from A), revenues and net income at various levels of output.

(b) What is B's optimum output, and what results does this imply for A and the company as a whole?

(c) Suppose the company abandons its divisionalized structure. Instead of being two profit centres, A and B are combined into a single profit centre with responsibility for the complete production and marketing of the product. Prepare a schedule as in (a) and find the optimal output.

(d) Why does (c) differ from (b)? How would you adjust the transfer price system to ensure that corporate optimality is attained when A and B are maintained as separate profit centres?

4. Microchip Manufacturers Ltd, have recently developed a micro-processor that will enable them to market a new computer chess-playing game. Development costs were in excess of £200 000, but the new product is thought to be significantly better than other currently available games. The game considered to be its nearest competitor sells at a wholesale price of £128. If the new game were to be offered at a similar price the Marketing Department believe about 1000 units would be sold over the next 2 years, after which it would become obsolete. However, past experience has indicated that demand would be quadrupled each time the price was cut by one half. Substantial price reductions seem possible as the variable cost of production and distribution amounts to approximately £16 per unit. The contribution analysis given in Table 6.7 indicates that a price of £32 would yield the highest contribution, although it is thought that the small sales at the highest prices would occur in a very short period following the introduction of the product.

Required:

Develop a pricing policy for this product to cover all stages of its life from initial introduction to its eventual obsolescence, indicating the contribution you would expect from each stage.

From: Certified Diploma in Accounting and Finance, Paper 2, December 1981.

Table 6.7

Price (wholesale) (£)	Estimated Market for Microchip ('000s)	Unit contribution (£)	Total contribution (£'000)
128	1	112	112
64	4	48	192
48	7.1	32	228
40	10.25	24	246
36	12.6	20	253
32	16	16	256
28	20.9	12	250
24	28.5	8	228
20	41	4	164
16	64	0	0

5. Megacorp plc is a large multidivisional company operating primarily within the UK. One of its divisions, Aira, operates a small production plant solely devoted to the manufacture of three materials, Ingots, Jars and Knuts. All the output of the plant is

transferred to a factory operated by the Blackside division of Megacorp plc where the three products are used as the major raw materials in the production of two products, Lemons and Mavericks. These products are then sold externally.

In the Aira division's production plant, three main production operations are carried out, namely Forging, Grinding and Heating. These take place using different types of equipment, each of limited capacity. To produce one unit of each of the three products requires different amounts of time in the three processes, as follows:

	Forging	Grinding	Heating
	Time required in hours for each production process		
To make one unit of			
Ingots	5	1	2
Jars	1	2	2
Knuts	1	3	2
Daily availability (hours)	810	605	630

Conversion of Ingots, Jars and Knuts into Lemons and Mavericks also requires three processes, Rolling, Stirring and Turning. To make a Lemon requires one Ingot, two Jars and two Knuts; a Maverick requires three Ingots, two Jars and one Knut. The processing times and availabilities are as follows:

	Rolling	Stirring	Turning
	Time required in hours for each production process		
To make one			
Lemon	4	1	2
Maverick	1	4	1
Daily availability (hours)	160	160	90

The raw materials used in the production of Ingots, Jars and Knuts are otherwise worthless by-products from other production processes in Megacorp plc, but each production process in both the Aira and the Blackside divisions has a variable cost of £1 per hour to operate. The current market price of Lemons is £47 each, and Mavericks £56 each.

Required:

1. Formulate the overall production problem of the two divisions as a linear program designed to maximize the total contribution to profit of the two divisions combined (6 marks).
2. The LP solution indicates that only Grinding and Heating are limiting resources. Grinding has a shadow (i.e., dual) price per

hour of 62.5p and Heating 31.25p. The optimum daily production is 30 Lemons and 27.5 Mavericks. Using these shadow prices:

(a) calculate transfer prices for Ingots, Jars and Knuts (3 marks).

(b) calculate the total contribution the production plan generates for each division (2 marks).

3. Describe how divisional profits would be affected if the Aira division provided extra capacity, so that limiting resources now existed only in the Blackside division (4 marks).

4. Discuss the practical problems and possible advantages of Megacorp plc implementing a market price based system of transfer pricing rather than a system based on shadow prices (10 marks).

(25 marks)

From: ICAEW, PEII, Management Accounting, July 1988.

6. The Argent Company, which makes and sells a single product, is preparing a budget for the next three months. Because of possible seasonal fluctuations in sales, the company normally keeps finished stock at a level equal to 150% of the budgeted unit sales for the following month.

The budgeted costs and selling price for the product are as follows:

Selling price	£25 per unit
Raw material cost	£4 per unit
Direct labour cost	£5 per unit
Variable production overhead cost	£2 per unit
Fixed production overhead cost	£9000 per month
Selling and administration	
sales commission	£2 per unit sold
fixed costs	£6000 per month

The factory can normally produce up to 2000 units per month, but it is possible to increase production by 25% by leasing an extra machine at a cost of £2000 per month and working overtime, which is paid at double the normal rate. The fixed production overheads include a depreciation charge on existing machinery. This machinery cost £240 000 new, and is being depreciated on a straight-line basis over its expected 5-year life. Finished goods stock is valued on an absorption cost basis, using the weighted average method. At the end of July 1988, finished stock was expected to amount to 2500 units valued at £35 300.

Raw material is paid for 1 month after delivery and sufficient is kept in stock to cover one month's budgeted production. The

finished goods are sold on credit with 20% of debts being collected in the month of sale. 78% in the following month, and the
remaining 2% being bad debts. All other costs are paid for in the
month they are incurred, except for sales commission which is
paid in the following month.

Expected unit sales for July 1988 and the following five months
are:

July 1988	1100
August 1988	1500
September 1988	1800
October 1988	1900
November 1988	2000
December 1988	2500

The managing director realizes that substantial overtime may be
needed in November 1988 to meet the December demand and is
concerned that this may lead to hidden costs or other adverse
effects on the business.

Required:

1. Prepare a budgeted profit and loss account, with supporting
   schedules, for the period 1 August to 31 October 1988 (10
   marks).
2. Calculate the budgeted cash flow for the same period and
   reconcile the net cash flow and profit figures for the quarter
   (6 marks).
3. Write a short report to the managing director outlining the
   likely impact on profit and the business generally from the
   level of overtime working expected. Suggest alternative
   operating strategies which would reduce the level of overtime
   working and improve business performance (9 marks).

(25 marks)

NB: Make all calculations to the nearest pound.

From: ICAEW, PEII, Managing Accounting, July 1988.

7. A small company producing a single product estimates that it
   will sell the following amounts of its product in the next few
   months:

Month	*Estimated sales (units)*
January	900
February	1800
March	1200
April	600

It wishes to construct a profit budget for the first 3 months of the
new year and has made the following estimates:

(a) The product will sell at an ex-factory price of £12 per unit.
(b) Variable production costs comprise:

direct labour	£1.50 per unit
direct materials	£2.75 per unit
variable overhead	£0.75 per unit.

(c) Fixed costs are:

production fixed costs	£8000 per month
selling and administration	£1500 per month.

The production fixed costs include £3000 per month depreciation on machinery and other fixed assets.
(d) The finished goods inventory at the end of December amounts to 200 units, valued at £10 each. Finished goods inventory is valued on an average actual-cost basis.

Required:
(a) Compute, the budgeted profit for January, February and March, presenting your workings in the form of a neat schedule.
(b) Compute the net cash flow for March, assuming that 40% of debtors pay after 1 month and the remainder after 2 months, and that all other cash costs are paid by the end of each month.
(c) Prepare a brief report for management explaining the differences in budgeted profit each month, and also the difference between the March cash flow and profit figures. Would you have preferred to have valued inventory on a different basis?

8. The Caradoc Company has two divisions. The Argent Division makes three products (A1, A2 and A3) which are transferred to the Belvoir Division. The Belvoir Division uses Argent's products as raw materials which it converts into two different final products (B1 and B2). Production and cost information for the two Divisions is given below.

Argent Division Production Data

Production of one unit of:	Machine requirements (hrs) Machine L	M	N	Variable cost of production
A1	1	1	1	£4
A2	2	3	1	£7
A3	1	2	3	£9
Machine availability (hrs)	480	715	640	

Belvoir Division Production Data

Production of one unit of:	Input requirement			Machine requirement (hrs)	
	A1	*A2*	*A3*	*X*	*Y*
B1	3	2	1	5	4
B2	1	2	3	3	6
Machine availability (hrs)				270	300

Belvoir Division Costs and Revenues

Sales of one unit of:	Sales revenue	Additional variable processing costs incurred in Belvoir Division
B1	£50	£7
B2	£60	£9

Required:
(a) The Caradoc Company wishes to make the maximum possible contribution. Formulate its decision problem as a linear programme, clearly indicating the interpretation of the variables you use.
(b) How would your formulation need to be amended if the intermediate products could be sold in an external market, as well as being transferred internally?
(c) The optimal solution to the Caradoc Company's problem is for it to produce 45 units of product B1 and 15 units of B2. The limiting constraints prove to be the utilization of machines L and Y, which are given the following shadow prices:

> Machine L   £0.375 per hr
> Machine Y   £1.000 per hr

Derive appropriate transfer prices for the intermediate products A1, A2 and A3, and calculate the profit that would be made by each division.
(d) What are the limitations of this method of setting transfer prices?

9. Accounting models are generally static and generate solutions that are assumed to be valid for an indefinite period of time. However, the world faced by the manager is continually changing. How do you think that this restricts the usefulness of accounting models, and how could they be made more useful?

10. What are the dangers inherent in using general-purpose accounting data for various different decisions? How might these be overcome?
11. How would you expect an accounting information system in a manufacturing company to differ from that found in a service industry?
12. 'Financial planning is constrained more by the need to estimate parameters to be used in a model than by the form of the relationships between variables that have to be assumed'. Discuss.

7

Budgetary planning and control

SUMMARY

Budgetary planning and control is the most visible use of accounting information in the management control process. By setting standards of performance and providing feedback by means of variance reports, the accountant supplies much of the fundamental information required for overall planning and control.

However, budgetary information serves a variety of potentially conflicting purposes within an organization. Budget standards may be set as motivational targets or as best estimates of expected outcomes. Reported actual results compared with those budget standards may be used as a means of evaluating the performance of managers or the units for which they are responsible. Thus budgetary figures are subject to a variety of pressures for bias and manipulation.

These problems become most severe in conditions of high uncertainty and when there is a great deal of inter-dependence between organizational sub-units; yet these are the circumstances in which the budgetary system is most needed. The way in which managers use the admittedly imperfect accounting information with which they are provided is crucial to effective control. Thus, although accounting information has a vital role to play, it has to be used in a manner that takes account of its imperfections and limitations.

INTRODUCTION

It has been suggested that accounting information serves three major functions (Simon *et al.*, 1954): attention directing, problem solving and scorecard keeping. The attention-directing function serves primarily to make a manager aware of a deviation from a previously determined plan, but once the 'alarm bell' has been rung other information is sought in order to decide what action should be taken. A budgetary-control system serves this function by setting budgetary standards, collecting actual cost and revenue information and reporting accounting variances on a routine and regular basis. It thus forms part, but only part, of a management control system, for analysing alternative courses of action by interrogation of a predictive model and the implementation of a chosen action are conducted using a great deal of non-accounting information.

The problem-solving function of accounting information is, by contrast, one-off rather than regular. It arises when a particular problem is identified and various alternative courses of action are proposed to handle it. Accounting information is used to assist in evaluating the economic consequences of the various courses of action proposed. Although routinely collected accounting information may act as a database, the analysis is *ad hoc* as it is aimed at predicting what the future costs and benefits are likely to be. The result is often a special report, prepared by an accounting analyst, quite separately for each problem. This use of accounting for decision making has already been discussed in Chapter 6.

The scorecard or performance-evaluation function of accounting information is concerned with monitoring the performance of individual managers or business units. It is similar to the attention-directing function, but focuses on the overall performance of a manager, or of the unit under his command, relative to the objectives and targets that have been set. This use of accounting information is a particularly critical one, for managers who are aware that their performance is being monitored will be motivated to act in ways that will be reported favourably by the information system, even when such behaviour may be inappropriate from a longer-term or organizational standpoint.

Despite having to serve these different functions, most accounting information systems are constructed from a unified set of accounts, with the same basic information being presented in different ways to serve the different purposes. The problems of using a single universal system for multiple purposes are graphically illustrated in the literature on budgetary planning and control systems (Otley, 1977).

Nearly all organizations of any size have some sort of system of budgetary planning and control, even if it is used solely for financial planning and control rather than overall management control. The basic techniques of constructing budgets have been outlined in Chapter 6, and the technical processes involved raise relatively few problems. However, once a budget has been constructed for, say, financial planning, it tends to be used for other purposes for which it may be less well suited. Indeed, the other uses to which it is put may adversely affect its usefulness for financial planning. In this section we will review some of the purposes for which budgets can be used, the assumptions upon which such uses rest, and the interactions between different uses that can occur.

MULTIPLE FUNCTIONS OF BUDGETS

Budgets can act in different roles in organizations. Some possible roles involve budgets being used as:

1. a system of authorization;
2. a means of forecasting and planning;
3. a channel of communication and coordination;
4. a motivational device;
5. a means of performance evaluation and control, as well as providing a basis for decision making.

The budget may serve as a formal authorization to a manager to spend a given amount of money on specific activities. This is most commonly found with respect to discretionary expenditure (e.g., advertising, R & D) and capital expenditure where final approval of the budget indicates authorization to spend the money. It may also be applied to operating budgets, but normally in a less rigid manner, as overspending may well be preferable to the cessation of production that an absolute expenditure limit might imply. However, the authors have observed a manager close the material issue stores towards the end of the month to control expenditure, and Argyris (1952) details many other unfortunate side-effects of over-strict budgetary control. Such a system of authorization must be evaluated in terms of the responsibility structure adopted by the organization. What is appropriate for a highly centralized organization operating in a stable and predictable environment is likely to be dysfunctional in an industry characterized by rapid changes in technology and customer requirements.

The second function served by most budgets is that of forecasting and planning. Forecasting refers to the prediction of events over which the organization has little or no control; planning is the attempt to shape the future by altering those factors that are controllable in the light of available forecasts. All budgets thus incorporate forecasts (e.g., of general economic factors, such as inflation rates, of competitors' policies and reactions, and of technological and efficiency changes) and a major use of computerized financial planning models lies in testing the robustness of plans to possible inaccuracies in these forecasts. However, given a set of forecasts, the budget model is then able to operate in an optimizing role, attempting to ascertain which plan of action will result in the greatest benefits to the organization. The accountant may see financial planning as the major purpose of the budgeting system, enabling him to make predictions of profit, cash flow and asset structure, and thus to take the necessary decisions regarding the provision of finance. Other managers may see such financial consequences as constraints imposed upon them and regard the budgetary system solely as a means of communicating such information, rather than as a more generally useful planning tool.

Evidently budgets are an important channel of communicating certain types of information that will enable managers in different parts of the organization to coordinate their activities more efficiently. However, in a highly centralized organization the budget may be of only minor importance in this respect, as there will be many other channels of communication that will indicate the necessary information more directly (e.g., required production of different products, capital investment in plant and machinery, and sales targets). But in a decentralized organization, the budget may serve as a major tool of coordination, as indicated in the transfer pricing example in Chapter 6. In this way budgets can aid in the process of organizational integration both formally, by aggregating relevant information for successive levels in the hierarchy, and informally, by creating greater visibility within the organization. Overall, control is aided when individuals cooperate and make adjustments in their activities to assist what is required in other parts of the organization.

Budgets often serve as a means of motivating managers to strive towards the achievement of organizational objectives. They do this by acting as an external standard that may be accepted by a manager as his own target (i.e., 'internalized'), thus providing a motivational target. Further, extrinsic rewards and penalties may also be attached to budget achievement (e.g., bonuses, performance awards) to increase its motivational effect further. Unfortunately, using budget targets as motivational devices was found in practice to be associated with undue pressure on subordinates, inefficiency, aggression towards the budget system and conflicts between managers (Argyris, 1952). However, as Hofstede (1968) has pointed out, budgets only motivate significantly if they represent challenging targets that have a risk that they will not be met. Thus, if budget variances are always treated as a sign that somebody is at fault rather than as a sign of a healthy system, it is likely budgets will soon be met, but will cease to act as motivational targets. The motivational role of budgets is thus likely to conflict with other roles, particularly forecasting and planning.

Finally, budgets can serve as a standard against which managerial performance is evaluated. The budget often represents the only available quantitative reference point against which performance can be assessed. A danger in this situation is that performance relative to budget can become the dominant measure of overall performance, yet the budget itself represents only an imperfect standard. Both budget and actual information can be manipulated by managers, as will be seen in later sections. A strong stress on budget attainment is likely to lead to budgets that are met, but at the expense of worse long-run performance together with various harmful side effects. Nevertheless, properly used, budgets can be a vital tool in monitoring and controlling managerial and business unit performance. However, if budgets are used for performance evaluation, this use is likely to dominate the budget preparation process and restrict the usefulness of the budget for other functions, particularly financial planning.

By outlining some of the roles that can be served by budgets, it is not intended to suggest that a single budget will necessarily serve all these functions in any particular organization. But it should be borne in mind that most budget systems do serve several purposes, and that these purposes may well conflict with each other. For example, a budget target intended to motivate high levels of performance will probably be set at a higher level of difficulty than it is expected will be achieved. The budget estimate is thus of little use as a forecast for financial planning purposes. Indeed some organizations formally recognize such a difference, calling it a 'planning variance'. On the other hand, budgets that will be used to assess performance may well be set at a lower level of difficulty by managers who know they will be evaluated against the budget standard. Such possibilities will be further discussed in subsequent sections; for the present it is sufficient to note that budgets generally serve multiple and partially conflicting purposes. The budgetary system pervades many areas of organizational activity and is open to a wide range of powerful pressures. It cannot be expected that a single set of budget estimates will serve all the functions demanded of it equally well. Part of the art of designing an effective budgetary system is to select those purposes for which reliable budgetary information is essential and to protect the system against those influences that tend to subvert its effectiveness in these chosen areas.

It can thus be seen that information based on budget estimates, as well as normal accounting information concerning actual costs and revenues, is relevant to all three major functions identified by Simon *et al.* (1954). This is most evident in the attention-directing and performance-evaluation functions, where a budget standard is used as the basis of comparison with actual results. However, budgetary information is also used in problem solving because relevant information for decision making must refer to the future. Past actuals are useful only as a basis for making future predictions, and the budget, together with the production plans and standard costs on which it is based, often forms a convenient source of relevant information. Because of the widespread use of budget data, it is important to identify the basis on which it is prepared and the possible distortions that can affect it.

THE BASIS OF BUDGET PREPARATION

The technical process of budget preparation is straightforward, if complex, and is well covered in most management accounting texts (see Arnold and Hope, 1983, for a brief summary and Edey, 1966, for a classic and fuller exposition). However, it will be helpful to clarify several assumptions necessarily made in the process.

Firstly the process of budget preparation follows the organizational pattern of authority and responsibility. Overall budgets are built up from budgets for individual responsibility centres as defined by the organizational hierarchy. Typically the managers of these responsibility centres will have some influence over the content of the budget, although the degree of influence can vary dramatically from organization to organization, and even in different parts of the same organization. But at least some consultation is usual, and fuller participation up to almost total responsibility for the preparation of their own budget (within certain corporate constraints) occurs in many organizations. It is thus evident that the figure that is entered into a budget is the result of a discussion or bargaining process between a manager and his immediate superior, with a budget accountant possibly acting as an intermediary, in which the relative degree of influence of the two parties can vary considerably. The lesser degree of formal power and authority of the subordinate manager, relative to his superior, is often more than compensated for by his greater degree of knowledge and understanding of the operation of the unit under his control.

Secondly, the organizational structure will determine whether responsibility centres will be treated as cost, revenue, profit or investment centres for the purposes of budgetary control, although some limited degree of discretion is possible. It is normally suggested that managers should be held responsible only for those costs and revenues over which they exert significant influence. Responsibility centres are usually either cost or profit centres. A manager in charge of a cost centre is responsible for performing defined activities (outputs) within a defined (input) cost budget. However, monetary values are not assigned to the outputs he produces and his effectiveness (as distinct from his efficiency) is assessed without the aid of accounting data. By contrast, the manager of a profit centre is held responsible both for costs (inputs) and revenues (outputs) resulting in an overall profit (or contribution) figure. An investment centre manager is additionally held responsible for the cost of capital employed. The advantages of such an arrangement are evident; in particular both effectiveness and efficiency can be assessed by reference to accounting data. In practice, the undoubted advantages of profit centres had led to their creation, even when the manager has only minimal influence over his reported revenues (sometimes termed 'pseudo profit centres').

It may appear that the structure of organizational responsibilities determines the form of the budgetary control system, and indeed this is formally the case. However the reverse effect should not be overlooked. Organizations may adapt their responsibility structure so as to attempt to gain the advantages of profit or investment centre control. However this requires giving subordinate managers a greater degree of authority and autonomy as well as raising several accounting issues such as the setting of internal prices for goods and services transferred between responsibility centres. The consequences of having such decentralized and possibly divisionalized forms of organizational structure are explored in Part Three; for the moment it is sufficient to note the assumption that a manager has control over those aspects of his responsibility centre for which he is held accountable.

Thirdly, budget preparation for production activities is based directly upon standard costing. Although it may be possible to set an aggregate budget for a responsibility centre without a formal standard costing system, the *ad hoc* work involved makes it highly desirable that standard costing is implemented. A standard cost is a predetermined cost for the production of a unit of product (which may further be deemed to earn as a standard price); the cost budget is the aggregate of all such standard costs, multiplied by planned production volumes (and possibly supplemented by lump sum costs not attributed to individual products). Again the technical process is straightforward, although it involves a very considerable amount of detailed work. The fundamental problem involved relates to how the standards are derived.

There are basically two methods of determining standard costs. The first method involves the analysis of historical data; the standard cost then represents what has been achieved in the past, adjusted for expected changes in efficiency and external economic factors (such as wage and material cost inflation). The second method involves work measurement designed to assess scientifically the appropriate labour and material content of each product and to cost it accordingly; the standard cost here represents a carefully assessed standard of attainment based on work study measurements. It is arguable that there is a third method, namely the setting of target costs that will enable the company to compete effectively in the market. However, it is still necessary to assess the feasibility of attaining such targets. Although the second method appears to have significant advantages it requires a great deal of painstaking work and may not possess the degree of accuracy initially expected. Work study is firmly in the Taylorian Scientific Management tradition (see Chapter 2), and it is usual for timings to be made only with the prior knowledge of the worker involved. Further, as such timings often form the basis of a wage payment scheme with a productivity bonus, it is in the workers' interest to exaggerate the time required to perform an operation. Of course, work study officers are well aware of such problems, but the process tends to lose its supposed scientific exactness and revert to a process of bargaining in which both sides appear well matched. The authors well recollect a slow motion ballet that was performed by local dustmen outside their office windows. The strange performance only became explicable when a young man with a clip-board and stop watch was observed in one corner. The following week he was absent and the dustbins were once more emptied at their usual speed!

Finally it should be noted that budgets for profit centres require estimates of product prices and quantities to be sold. However price setting, even in conditions of low uncertainty, requires information about market demands and production costs (certainly variable costs, and in the longer-term arguably 'full costs') and the process can become circular, i.e., price affects quantities sold, and thus quantities produced, which in turn influences costs. Costs themselves then have an influence on the optimal pricing policy. Care needs to be taken to ensure that the assumptions made about the relationship between price and demand in constructing a budget are properly related to real market conditions and are not just arbitrary formulae used for convenience.

MANAGERIAL USE OF BUDGETARY INFORMATION

Despite the issues raised above, budget preparation is a fairly straightforward process. The critical problems arise out of how managers use the information provided by the budget system, and how the effects of such use feedback on the information that is entered into the budget. The three major areas of potential conflict that we have identified occur when budgetary data is used as a forecast of future events, when budgetary standards are used as motivational targets and when actuals are compared with standards as a means of evaluating managerial and unit performance. We will consider the use of budget information for each of these purposes in turn, and progressively review the interaction between the different use.

Budgets as forecasts

The overall corporate budget may be used by managers in different parts of an organization as a forecast of what is likely to happen else-where as a basis for their own planning and decision making. The question thus arises: how accurate are the budget estimates as fore-casts of actual outcomes? The answer to this question is likely to be of particular concern to the financial director as he seeks to arrange the provision of finance in efficient manner.

There have been numerous experiments concerned with assessing the forecasting abilities of individuals, one of which studied the effect of the label attached to figures of past performance when making estimates of future outcomes (Cyert *et al.*, 1961). Subjects who were told that a given set of past actuals represented past sales tended to forecast a lower figure than subjects who were told they represented past costs. It appears that people always consider the decision for which the information is sought and bias their estimates with regard to the likely consequences of error. In this experiment, it seems to have been perceived that less harm is done when forecasts of sales and costs are conservative, and profit is thus understand, than vice-versa.

More generally it has been argued that managers see it as being in their own interest to set easier rather than more difficult budgets for themselves and thus incorporate 'slack' into their budget estimates (Schiff and Lewin, 1970). There is also some evidence that slack is built up during good years and converted into reported profits in poor years (Williamson, 1964). However there is also evidence that managers operating in tough environments may bias their estimates in the opposite direction and set themselves budgets that are unlikely to be achieved (Otley, 1978); the gains from promising good per-formance appear to outweigh the consequences of subsequently not attaining it, perhaps illustrating sequential attention to those goals currently felt to be important.

The most complete analysis of the incorporation of bias into budget estimates is given in a study of the sales budgeting process of a chain of retail shops (Lowe and Shaw, 1968). Three major causes of ob-served bias were put forward:

1. The reward system of the company, which involved salary, incre-ments, bonuses and promotions based on performance relative to budget.

2. The influence of past company history, which had evolved an implicit belief that sales would continue to grow.
3. The insecurity of some managers, who, because of their recent poor performance, felt obliged to promise better performance in future.

All three causes of bias identified involved rational economic behaviour on the part of the managers concerned. In the first case, slack would be incorporated into the budget in order to make the budget easier to attain in the future. In the second and third cases, optimistic budgets would be submitted in the hope that these would gain current approval, even at the risk of future disappointment. Thus the amount and direction of bias a manager may incorporate into his budget estimate may vary considerably in either direction; budgets used for other purposes are unlikely to be good estimates of actual outcomes.

There is also evidence that individuals in uncertain situations find it difficult to estimate the expected value of an outcome, even when it is in their own best interest to do so (Peterson and Miller, 1964) although they fare somewhat better at estimating most likely outcomes. Expected and most likely values differ when underlying distributions are skew, so the suggestion by Turvey (1979) that distributions of cost and revenue are likely to be skew is of some importance. Certainly it would appear more straightforward to estimate a most likely outcome, which is a well defined event, rather than an expected value, which is merely a weighted average of all possible outcomes. In another study many managers stated they estimated at the most likely outcome, rather than the mean (Otley, 1978), and the standard estimation procedures in many operational research techniques involve most likely rather than mean estimates for similar reasons.

The consequences of submitting non-mean estimates, whether unintentionally or deliberately, may be severe, particularly when estimates are aggregated at successive levels in the organizational hierarchy. Otley and Berry (1979) have demonstrated that estimates that are only slightly optimistic at unit level (30% chance of achievement) become highly optimistic when 9 such units are aggregated together at the next level in the hierarchy (6% chance of achievement). They argue that some procedure is necessary at each level of aggregation to remove any such excessive optimism that can be detected. Although such a procedure would produce a set of output budget estimates at the unit level that add up to more than the total output budget for the next hierarchical level, such a system might well be preferable to basing corporate policy on unrealistic assumptions. In general, the budget process requires to be tailored to fit the characteristics of the situation in which it has to operate, and estimates should be adjusted at each level in the hierarchy to give the required chance of attainment. It may well be appropriate to have optimistic targets for motivational purposes at lower levels, but to require accurate estimates at corporate level to enable planning to be carried out effectively.

The bias in estimates we have described might be part of a general tendency on the part of managers to distort the information they pass to their superiors in a consistent manner, so that the superior is less well informed about unfavourable items (Read, 1962). This may be a deliberate policy on the part of an ambitious manager who hopes to be promoted before the true situation becomes apparent; or it might be unintentional, as when a manager begins by reporting favourable items and is interrupted before reaching the unfavourable. The opportunity for bias is constrained by the ability of the senior manager to make is own independent predictions of likely outcomes. To this extent, improved predictive models and better statistical forecasting techniques can reduce the area in which bias can occur, but counter-bias by senior managers is likely only to be of limited effectiveness.

The problem lies in both the detection and correction of inaccuracies. Detection is difficult because errors can be in either direction and caused by unexpected changes in external circumstances, by poor forecasting models or by deliberate intention. Even when bias is detected, it may be unwise to alter budget estimates because of the potential adverse motivational effect on the subordinate, although private adjustments may be made. Indeed, it seems likely that 'black books' (i.e., private budget estimates) are as an important part of budgetary procedures in many organizations as are the formal systems.

Thus, although accurate budgets are desirable for planning purposes, particularly at senior levels in the organizational hierarchy, there are substantial problems in aggregating subordinates' estimates to arrive at such forecasts. It may be that better accuracy at the corporate level is attained by using forecasting models unrelated to the normal budget process (i.e., private forecasting models developed by senior staff advisors); indeed many corporate financial planning models seem to be constructed and used in this way. If budget estimates do not represent accurate forecasts, there is an evident danger in using them in other decision making processes, such as pricing policy and the evaluation of capital-investment proposals.

Budgets as targets

The existence of a budget standard can act as a target to be aimed for. There is substantial evidence from psychological studies that having a defined, quantitative target results in better performance than when no such target is stated (Tosi, 1975). Further, the more difficult and demanding the target set, the better the resulting performance, although targets thought to be unattainable are counter-productive.

Specific targets produce better performance than vague exhortations to 'do your best'. In one study on goal-setting (Meyer, Kay and French, 1965) where performance requirements were translated into specific goals 65 per cent showed subsequent improvement in contrast to only 27 per cent of those which were left non-specific. However, it is important to note that although difficult goals can easily be *assigned* to people they are not necessarily *accepted* by them. If people decide that a goal is impossible to attain, they are likely to give up and turn in results that are worse than if a less demanding goal had been set. An industrial study on goal-setting (Stedry and Kay, 1966) found that difficult goals produced either very good or very bad results compared with goals of normal difficulty, with the poor results occurring particularly when several difficult goals were set at the same time. Another study concerned with the evaluation of a system of management by objectives (Carroll and Tosi, 1973) found that difficult goals led to reduced effort on the part of those managers who were less mature and experienced and who had less self-assurance.

The psychological evidence therefore suggests that the best results will be obtained by setting the most difficult goals that will be accepted by managers and thus 'internalized' and accepted as their own personal objectives. However, it is important that managers successfully attain their targets sufficiently often to give positive reinforcement and to prevent them from falling into a cycle of failure. A budget has a very strong potential for motivation as it represents a definite, quantitative goal, but the standards it incorporates need to be accepted by those involved before their existence will motivate better performance. The level of difficulty that will be accepted is likely to vary significantly from person to person and may bear little resemblance to the 'tight, yet attainable' accounting adage. Formally agreed budget goals will be more effective than implicit self-set goals only when the formal goals were set at a more demanding level than the self-set goals and when the formal goals are accepted by the manager involved (Locke, 1968).

These findings are in close agreement with the predictions of the expectancy theory of motivation. Motivation is increased as the joint product of the valence attached to successful task performance (i.e., budget achievement) and the perceived probability that extra effort will in fact result in success. Once it is thought that extra effort will not be successful, the motivational impact vanishes. The expectancy model also leads us to examine the rewards that are attached to successful task performance, a topic that has been neglected in many motivational studies which purport to describe the effect of budget targets *per se*. In fact, the effect of the budget target itself is almost invariably confounded with the effects of extrinsic rewards.

These results also indicate the importance of participation in budget-setting. Managers who are actively involved in the process of setting their own budget are much more likely to accept the standards incorporated into it. Nevertheless, there are also dangers inherent in participative budgeting. Some managers may use the opportunity given by participation to reduce the standards demanded of them and to bias the estimates they submit. Thus participation is no universal panacea; it is an essential part of effective budgetary control, but needs to be used with care and understanding.

Most of the studies referred to above have been experimental. More reliable evidence on the effects of budget targets in a real organizational context can be obtained from field studies, although only a handful of these exist. One major such study was conducted in a European context by Hofstede (1968). Hofstede was concerned to discover the conditions under which budgets could be used to promote positive attitudes in managing task performance. Previous US-based studies had indicated that although managers saw budgets as being highly relevant, the use of budgets also invoked negative attitudes such as undue pressure, conflict between managers and manipulation of accounting data. European experience, although less well documented, suggested that more positive attitudes to budgets were prevalent but that these existed only because operating managers generally regarded budgets as irrelevant. Hofstede's study therefore set out to try to find the conditions under which budgets could have a high degree of relevance to managers, and thus act as an important motivational device, yet also not have counter-productive side-effects associated with them. His conclusions concerning budget difficulty were:

1. Budgets have no motivational effect unless they are accepted by the managers involved as their own personal target.
2. Up to the point where the budget target is no longer accepted, the more demanding the budget target, then the better are the results achieved.

3. Demanding budgets are also seen as more relevant than less difficult targets, but negative attitudes result if they are seen as *too* difficult.
4. Acceptance of budgets is facilitated when good upward communication exists. The use of departmental meetings was found helpful in encouraging managers to accept budget targets.
5. Managers' reactions to budget targets were affected both by their own personality (some managers intensely disliked budgets that they thought they would not achieve) and by more general cultural and organizational norms.

An important implication of these findings is that the budget level which motivates the best performance is one that is somewhat more demanding than the level of performance that will actually be achieved. However, a budget that is likely to be achieved will motivate only a lower level of performance, as shown in Fig. 7.1. The budget level that most usually motivates the optimum results (a challenging target accepted by the manager) is in excess of the average performance actually attained by that manager. But if it is reduced to a less demanding level, actual performance also decreases.

There is thus a conflict between the planning and control uses of

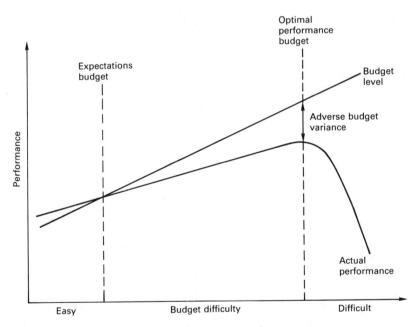

Fig. 7.1   The effect of budget difficulty on performance.

the budget. To motivate the best possible level of actual performance the budget must be set at a level above that which will, on average, be attained. Adverse budget variances will thus be generated, but these are a sign that the budget system is working as intended. A budget that is always achieved with no adverse variances indicates that the standards are too loose to motivate the best possible results. To obtain the desired motivational effects from an appropriately set budget target thus requires that adverse budget variances are treated appropriately; small adverse variances are a healthy sign and should not be treated as something to be avoided.

The attitude of senior managers to adverse budget variances is thus crucial to the successful operation of a truly motivating budget system. If junior managers are strongly criticized whenever their performance is even slightly below budget, there is little doubt that less adverse variances will be reported; but the means by which this is achieved will be less than desirable and overall performance is likely to be reduced rather than increased. A further implication of using budgets for motivational purposes is that they become unsuitable for planning purposes. Financial planning requires the best possible estimates of what is likely to occur. Motivational budgets will generally give a more optimistic picture of the future and will require to be amended before being used for planning purposes.

The central problem in setting motivational targets is therefore to ensure that they are accepted by the manager to whom they are given. An important method of ensuring that the budget is accepted by the subordinate manager is allowing him to participate in the budget-setting process. There is a great deal of literature on participation, but it appears to reduce to three major arguments for suggesting that participation may improve performance (Hofstede, 1968):

1. Participation on budget-setting will help ensure that the budget is accepted by the subordinate and thus act as a motivational target.
2. Participation will lead to improved communication and thus to better and more relevant budget standards.
3. Participation in budget-setting will decrease the likelihood of information distortion and manipulation.

The first two arguments are straightforward, but the final one is based on the premise that participation will both remove the motivation for bias and allow the senior manager to detect it more easily. This may be true, but participation also allows the junior manager a greater degree of opportunity to bias estimates if he so desires. It is also the case that participation may be viewed less enthusiastically in different cultures and by individuals of certain personality types. Brownell (1981) found that the link between participation and performance was dependent upon the personality of the manager involved. Managers who felt that they had a significant degree of control over their destiny exhibited the expected relationship, but for those who felt their destiny was controlled by luck, chance or fate, budgetary participation resulted in poorer performance. Participation is therefore not a universal panacea, but can be selectively useful in helping promote commitment to organizational goals. It is perhaps most useful in decentralized organizations for those tasks that are well defined and highly structured (Bruns and Waterhouse, 1975). Participation has a positive motivational effect only with managers who are confident of their ability to cope with and control the many factors that influence their performance; to the extent they lack such confidence, participation probably only increases their feelings of stress and tension due to uncertainty.

Budgets as standards for performance evaluation

The expectancy theory of motivation makes it clear that budgets, of themselves, have little motivational impact. The only source of positive motivation lies in the intrinsic satisfaction that can be gained from attaining a pre-set target. Rather the major motivational potential of budgets lies in the rewards, such as salary bonuses, incentives and enhanced promotion prospects and status that are seen to follow from budget attainment. The reward structure associated with budget attainment is one of the most potent motivational devices available to senior management. Such rewards may be explicitly conditional on meeting the budget and take a monetary form (e.g., a salesman who receives a bonus when he attains his quota), they may be implicit and of a longer-term nature (e.g., a manager who believes his future promotion depends partly on his budget record), or of a social and diffuse nature (e.g., a manager who perceives his status to depend on his relative ranking against other managers).

When budgets are used as standards for performance evaluation, rewards are connected directly with budget achievement. The problems of designing and operating a successful budgetary control system largely devolve into constructing an appropriate set of performance measures that when achieved, result in desired organizational performance. There is usually no difficulty in persuading managers to achieve the specified results; what is difficult is ensuring they achieve them in the intended manner!

The development of performance measures for parts of an organization involves the following major issues:

1. Organizational purposes are complex and cannot easily be condensed into single integrated measures of overall performance.
2. Many tasks are interdependent and require cooperation between managers; thus a performance measure for any individual manager is bound to be inadequate.
3. The essence of much managerial work is such that it requires the exercise of judgement and cannot be precisely specified in advance.
4. Many important aspects of performance (e.g., quality, service, maintenance of morale) cannot be adequately measured in quantitative terms.
5. Management takes place in a complex and uncertain environment; it may therefore be inappropriate to reward achievement alone, as effort may also be deserving of recognition.

The difficulties involved in specifying and rewarding appropriate managerial *behaviour* have led to a concentration on monitoring and rewarding *performance*, despite the above problems. The measures of performance most often used involve accounting information and use budgets as the standard against which results are monitored. Thus, not only are there problems in defining the dimensions of performance to be pursued, but the setting of the level of performance expected on each dimension may also be problematic, particularly in industries subject to rapid environmental change.

If the rewards attached to good performance are such that they will motivate managers to work hard to attain them, it is also likely that the budget standard will come under considerable pressure. Further, the accounting information itself may be manipulated to give the impression of improved performance where this, in fact, has not been achieved. Finally, and most seriously, actual behaviour may be affected so that desired results may be reported, despite the fact that these may have been achieved in undesirable ways.

Perhaps the best documented example of such behaviour in the accounting literature is the use of return on investment (ROI) as an overall measure of performance, which can lead to the retention of depreciated assets beyond their economic life (Dearden, 1962a). Because the accounting system places little value on the old assets, quite a modest profit can inflate the ROI to a high value. Further, using fully depreciated assets will result in no depreciation charge being levied against current profit, since the cost of the asset has already been charged against the profit of previous periods. A manager obtaining a high ROI in this way may well not wish to relace his old assets because it would depress his reported performance. Further, consider an organization that wishes to attain a 20% ROI and evaluates divisional managers by monitoring their actual ROI. A manager currently averaging a return in excess of 20% will not be motivated to accept projects having a return less than his present average, although still in excess of 20%. Conversely a manager with an average return below 20% may attempt to take on investments with a return below 20%, but in excess of his current average. There have been a number of more recent studies on the effect various characteristics of budgetary control systems have on managerial performance which have yielded broadly similar conclusions, although it should be noted that they have all been conducted in the USA. One study by Kenis (1979) found that:

1. Both the clarity of budget-goals and participation in budget-setting were positively associated with job satisfaction, as was the provision of feedback information on budget achievement. Goal clarity and participation were also shown to contribute to higher levels of motivation to meet budgets and with actual budget achievement. In particular, the findings indicate that most managers react well to having budget goals spelt out as clearly and unambiguously as possible.
2. The idea of a 'tight yet attainable' budget standard appeared to lead to the best actual performance.
3. Participation in budget-setting tended to improve the degree to which budgets were met but was unrelated to other measures of overall job performance.

This last finding illustrates the problems that exist in assuming that managers who meet their budget are, in fact, performing well. It may solely be that they have obtained a relatively easy budget standard or that they are taking actions that enable them to meet their budgets to the detriment of longer-term performance. Other studies, such as those by Ivancevich (1976), Milani (1975) and Steers (1976), have found only relatively insignificant connections between budgetary characteristics and job performance.

A further study by Merchant (1981) has been conducted at an organizational level of analysis; he found that:

1. Firms which were large, diversified in their activities and decentralized tended to operate a control strategy that could be described as administrative rather than personal in orientation. This involved greater stress on formal control techniques such as

budgeting. In these firms lower-level managers tended to participate more in budgeting and greater stress was laid on the use, development and achievement of budget targets.
2. Participation in budget-setting and the emphasis placed on budget achievement by senior managers were both important factors affecting attitudes towards the budget system and the motivation of junior managers to meet the budget.
3. The contingency theory notion of a 'fit' between organizational characteristics and its environmental context, and the use made of budgets (as indicated in (a), above) was supported, in that performance was higher where such a 'fit' was found to exist than where it was not.

These studies also have implications for the way in which budgetary standards are set. Standards can be derived from basically three sources; past experience of the same operation, what is currently being achieved elsewhere or what is necessary in order to achieve other goals. Standards derived from all three sources can be problematic from a motivational standpoint.

Historical standards based on past experience reflect only what has already been achieved; although suitable for planning purposes, they generally require to be modified if they are to act as a motivational target. Standards derived from similar activities being undertaken elsewhere, whether in other parts of the same organization or by competitors, are generally most suited for motivational purposes. The danger in their use is that they may not be perceived as relevant by those to whom they are given. Apparently minor differences in circumstances can cause this type of evidence to be seen as irrelevant by operating managers. Standards based on what is necessary to achieve overall company objectives, although likely to represent challenging targets, suffer from the problem that they may be seen as unrealistic, particularly if the manager to whom they are given was not party to the process of setting those overall objectives.

Nevertheless, all three sources of information are valuable in the process of setting budgets that are sufficiently challenging to have a motivational impact yet are accepted by those who work under them as being an attainable target. Such a balance cannot be struck without the active involvement of each individual manager, for some will prefer easier targets yet over-achieve, whereas others will accept very difficult goals, even if they do not always manage to attain them. Budget-setting can never be reduced to a purely mechanical or technical process; it must be tailored to individual human needs and personalities.

Despite these imperfections, accounting measurement procedures are used and recognized to be valuable in a wide variety of organizations. Managers seem to use imperfect accounting measures in more complex ways than is commonly suggested in accounting texts. The study of the effective use of budgetary information in the evaluation of managerial performance demands empirical work to be conducted in organizations. Such studies are unfortunately rare, and only guarded conclusions can be drawn, but it is worthwhile to review two such studies here.

In his pioneering study, Hopwood (1972) observed cost centre managers to adopt three different styles of using budget and actual cost information in the evaluation of managerial performance. These were described as:

1. A Budget-Constrained Style in which, despite the many problems in using accounting data as a comprehensive measure of managerial performance, the manager's performance is evaluated rigidly on the basis of his ability to meet the short-term budget.
2. A Profit-Conscious Style in which a manager's performance is evaluated on the basis of his ability to improve the general effectiveness of his unit's operations, with budgetary information being used in a careful and flexible manner, often supplemented with other information.
3. A Non-Accounting Style in which budgetary data played a relatively unimportant part in the evaluation of managerial performance.

The three styles of evaluation are thus distinguished by the way in which extrinsic rewards are associated with budget achievement. In the rigid (budget-constrained) style there is a clear-cut relationship; not achieving budget targets results in punishment, whereas achievement results in rewards. In the flexible (profit-conscious) style, the relationship depends on other factors; given good reasons for overspending, non-attainment of the budget can still result in rewards, whereas the attainment of budget targets in undesirable ways may result in punishment. In the non-accounting style, the budget is relatively unimportant because rewards and punishments are not directly associated with its attainment.

By studying an organization that was ill suited to the rigid application of budgetary measures of performance because the cost centres involved were highly interdependent and because long-term performance could be traded against short-term results, Hopwood observed various undesirable consequences of rigid methods of performance evaluation. For example, managers evaluated under this style reported very high levels of job-related stress and tension, poor relationships with both their colleagues and superiors, and they exhibited a tendency to manipulate the accounting information that formed their budget reports (either by mis-reporting or by actually taking undesirable actions that improved the accounting measures). This study contains ample evidence that the association of extrinsic rewards with budgetary achievement is a powerful means of motivating managers; unfortunately it also shows that the actions thus motivated may often be in the direction of adjustments to the reports of performance rather than towards the performance itself.

Some of the undesirable effects reported by Hopwood can be attributed to a poorly designed system. For example, he reports instances of the manipulation of a repair and maintenance budget that occurred under the rigid evaluative style that are evidently due to an emphasis on meeting an inappropriate budget. However, to the extent that all accounting performance measures are imperfect to some degree, his findings indicate in a graphic manner some of the unfortunate side effects of an inflexible use of budgetary information.

A subsequent study by Otley (1978) repeated some of Hopwood's work in the setting of independent profit centres where it was thought that the budgetary information would represent a much more adequate measure of managerial performance. Here there was little impact of style of budget use on job-related tension or on information manipulation. In this situation, rigid performance evaluation based on budget achievement appeared to be an effective management style, although it still led to an emphasis on the short term at the expense of the long term. This was explained in terms of the expectancy theory of motivation by noting that, although rigid evaluative styles increase both the extrinsic valence of meeting the budget (by attaching valued rewards) and the probability of an outcome (budget achievement) leading to a reward, this effect could be mediated by associated changes in the probability that goal-directed behaviour would result in budget achievement. When a rigid style of evaluation is also associated with highly supportive behaviour by senior managers and their staff, so that high effort is more likely to be followed by high achievement, overall motivation is enhanced. But this result is contingent upon the budget being a good standard of performance in the sense that budget attainment signifies good performance. If there are methods of achieving the budget that do not represent good performance then a high stress on budget attainment is likely to motivate undesirable behaviour.

More recently, Hirst (1981) has sought to place these results in a wider context by noting that accounting standards of performance will be a less complete description of adequate job performance in conditions of high uncertainty. He argues that a medium to high reliance on accounting performance measures will minimize the incidence of dysfunctional behaviour in situations of low task uncertainty, whereas only a medium to low reliance on accounting data is appropriate in conditions of high uncertainty. A later study by Govindarajan (1984) also suggests that managers are likely to be evaluated in a more subjective manner if their unit faces a high degree of uncertainty. It is significant that the observed style of performance evaluation adopted was regarded as resulting from environmental conditions rather than from individual personality traits. This study clearly supports Hirst's conclusion that high reliance on accounting measures of performance under conditions of uncertainty is likely to prejudice effective performance.

The central finding of these studies relevant to the impact of accounting control is two-fold. First, it is the way in which accounting information is used by managers and the rewards that are made contingent upon budget attainment that are critical in determining the impact of the control system. Secondly, the effect of high reliance on budgetary measures of performance is contingent upon circumstances such as the degree of knowledge we have about how managerial behaviour contributes towards successful performance (often low) and also the uncertainty that exists in the external environment of the organization. When faced with internal and external uncertainty of this sort, what may be required is a reward system that is supportive of innovation and which avoids penalizing occasional failure, for only then will managers feel able to devote their efforts towards achieving success rather than avoiding failure.

In addition to the situational factors discussed above, it has also been suggested that a variety of individual personality factors affect how managers use accounting information. In particular, cognitive style and locus of control have been used to explain differences in the way information is perceived and processed.

Cognitive style is that aspect of personality that is concerned with the way in which a person structures and processes information obtained from a wider environment (Doctor and Hamilton, 1973). One conceptual scheme differentiates people as being either field-dependent (low analytic) or field-independent (high analytic) according to their ability to pick out information from its context. Thus a high-analytic person will approach a problem by selecting information from its context on the basis of some conceptual model of the situation; a low-analytic person will tend to see the situation more holistically and be more influenced by the context in which the information is embedded. Benbasat and Dexter (1979) conducted an experiment using a business simulation that indicated cognitive style influenced profit performance, decision time and accounting report request behaviour. It appeared that structured-aggregated accounting information (e.g., income statements, balance sheets, cost reports and funds flow statements) were well suited to high-analytic types; after all, such statements are essentially models which allow a complicated situation to be structured. By contrast, this type of information appeared to act as a hindrance to low-analytic types who performed better when provided with disaggregated raw data.

This style provides some evidence to suggest that aspects of personality such as cognitive style can be important factors in determining the appropriate type of accounting information to provide to managers. Indeed, it has been suggested that accounting system designers should provide information to decision makers in a format that is compatible with their cognitive style (Macintosh, 1985). However, other results have been less clear-cut. For example, Otley and Dias (1982) found that cognitive style had no discernible effect on information use, although such null results may be a consequence of the fact that most managers tend to be high-analytic types, and that the sample selected did not show sufficient variation.

Another personality variable that has been studied is locus of control, or the degree to which people accept personal responsibility for what happens to them. People with an external locus of control tend to see events as being unrelated to their own behaviour and thus beyond their personal control: those with an internal locus believe that they have a substantial influence over their destiny. An experiment conducted by Brownell (1981) investigated the interaction of locus of control with participation in budget-setting. This confirmed the expected interaction; those with an internal locus of control performed best and learnt most quickly when allowed to participate in budget-setting. By contrast, those with an external locus did best when targets were set for them, without participation. These results suggest that people who find themselves working under conditions which complement their personality learn faster, and consequently perform better, than when there is a mis-match.

THE ROLE OF ACCOUNTING INFORMATION IN PLANNING AND CONTROL

We have seen that accounting information can serve various organizational purposes, which conflict to a certain extent. The degree of conflict is least when we are dealing with an organization having a clearly defined responsibility structure where individual managers are in charge of activities that are largely independent of each other. Estimation also becomes less problematic when dealing with routine, well understood activities in a fairly stable or, at least, predictable world. However, in such circumstances, there is considerably less need to rely on accounting information to plan, control or evaluate performance; other measures can equally well be used. We most need to rely on accounting measures precisely in those circumstances when these assumptions are not well met, i.e., in organizations having less well defined responsibility structures, with a high degree of mutual interdependence and operating in non-routine ways in a world whose future state is difficult to predict.

Here accounting information becomes more difficult to produce and interpret, conflicts between its various uses become apparent and managers need to make use of this information in more sophisticated ways. The required change in underlying assumptions is parallel to that in the movement from classical (Taylorian) management theory to modern organizational theory; the vastly different behavioural assumptions of 'traditional' management accounting and those required by modern organizational theory are well set out by Caplan (1966) and extended by McRae (1971). These changed assumptions are particularly relevant in a world where commercial organizations are tending to become bigger and more complex, where technological change is proceeding at a rapid rate, and where the external environment is increasingly less predictable. However, despite the problems in interpreting and using such accounting information, it is still produced. Interdependence between operating units can be handled in accounting terms, either by cost allocation or by transfer pricing. A spectrum of alternative treatments can be observed in practice ranging from non-allocation, through various forms of cost apportionment and negotiation, to systems based on charges for actual usage. These latter systems may be based on transfer prices, defined as a monetary value placed on the transfer of goods and services from one unit to another in the same company. In theory and practice, transfer prices can be attached to the movement of goods or services under all three forms of inter-dependence, and the cost allocation methods of apportionment, negotiation or actual usage each have counterparts in transfer pricing.

Both cost allocation and transfer pricing represent mechanisms which allow accounting statements to be drawn up for operating units *as if* they were independent profit centres. In some cases, this may not cause too great a degree of distortion. Where the bulk of an operating unit's trade is external to the company, and where internally provided goods and services are provided at market rates (or a close approximation thereto), no particular problems arise. However, where a substantial proportion of trade is conducted internally, and where reliable market prices do not exist, the accounting statements that can be produced lose their significance. But they do so in an insidious manner that cannot be detected from the accounting report.

Essentially, the operating unit moves from being a true profit centre to being a pseudo-profit centre. The form of the accounting statement is unchanged, but its meaning is dramatically altered. From being a fair representation of the performance of the unit as an independent entity, it becomes an accounting fiction that includes large sums allocated or transferred on an essentially arbitrary basis (Thomas, 1971). Such a change in meaning is particularly dangerous because the *form* of the accounting statement does not change: the pseudo-profit centre appears to be identical to a normal profit centre. But the meaning of the figures has altered drastically, and they may contain little of economic substance.

There is a great pressure to create profit centres for accounting control, because a true profit centre can be controlled in a very straightforward manner. Provided a balance between costs and revenues is maintained such that adequate profits are being earned, little attention needs to be paid to the details of internal operation. These can be left to the manager of the operating unit, and his/her performance evaluated against budgeted profit targets. But this ease of control generates a pressure to categorize as many units as possible as profit centres, even when this requires the allocation of large items of cost and the extensive use of transfer prices unrelated to market prices. Here the profit centre is transformed into a pseudo-profit centre and the apparent exercise of control becomes an illusion, unless it is clearly realized that attention must be focused only on what is actually controllable.

One has only to consider the car firm whose production and assembly units were apparently profitable, but whose marketing division made a substantial loss to realize the dangers involved. There was a great temptation to conclude that the problems lay in marketing, but this was not so, the main problems being a combination of poor quality and high production costs. This did not show in the accounting reports because parts were transferred between units at the full cost of production. It was only when the total cost of finished vehicles proved to be in excess of the price that could be obtained for them in the market place that the true loss became apparent. And even then it appeared in the accounts of the wrong division!

This is a good example of the danger of attempting to use accounting information beyond the limits of its validity. If operating units are interdependent, no amount of accounting allocation will allow them to be controlled as if they were independent. Cost control is still possible, and should be used in conjunction with cost budgets, but the use of profit centres becomes highly suspect. Interdependence requires a high degree of coordination, and to pretend that decentralized control can be exercised *via* accounting reports is fallacious.

There have been a number of attempts to produce accounting reports that try to distinguish between managerial and unit performance, with managers being held responsible only for those factors deemed to be within their control (Solomons, 1965; Amey and Egginton, 1973). However, although these reports isolate one important factor (i.e., degree of control), they do not make any attempt to assess the impact of other features of the external and internal environment which may affect performance. Further, it may be argued that it is part of the manager's job to anticipate and react to the so-called uncontrollable factors. For even if certain factors cannot be controlled, it is possible they can be predicted and steps taken to guard against the adverse consequences. Finally, even where the factors could not be predicted, perhaps it would be regarded as part of the manager's duty to prepare his/her units, so that it could respond flexibly to whatever situation developed.

Thus traditional ideas of responsibility accounting have only a limited applicability. There is undoubtedly an element of wisdom in ensuring that managers are not held responsible for the poor performance of one of their colleagues, but there are also circumstances where no clear dividing line can be constructed and the attempt to specify a precise division of responsibilities may be counterproductive. In addition, the vagaries of the external environment may be better viewed as an enemy that requires to be outsmarted rather than as an uncontrollable factor that is outside the manager's competence to affect.

Evidently accounting information has only a partial role to play in the process of overall organizational control, and must be supplemented by other information systems. We are not yet quite at the stage where 'accountants submit monthly reports to managers, so that the managers can check that the accountants know what is going on' (we first heard this remark from Dr Tony Berry). However, accounting information does require to be used carefully by managers, who need to have an understanding of what it is, and is not, capable of doing. Most important, accounting serves as a language in which the performance of many disparate parts of a business can be aggregated to present an overall picture. Money still represents the only quantitative measure of overall performance that is available to a diversified organization.

The two major problems in the accounting information itself relate to data collection and information disaggregation. The crucial part of most management accounting systems is when data is initially entered into the system. Most of the reported examples of the manipulation of accounting information occur at this point. For example, Hopwood (1972) reports managers who charged materials to incorrect accounts, who switched spending between accounts and who incorporated bias into their budget estimates. Yetton (1976) shows how the manipulation of time cards led to improved bonuses in the short term, but also to misleading accounting information used for pricing purposes that was detrimental to the longer-term prospects of the company. Once the basic data is in the system, it is less likely to be corrupted, although Otley (1976) cites the case of expenditure on a large item of equipment being charged in monthly instalments (contrary to the accounting manual), owing to pressure from a line manager on a cost accountant.

Data disaggregation is the second major problem, where the accountant allocates a cost or revenue between several responsibility centres (or over several time periods) to serve some particular purpose. For example, managers may be charged for the provision of certain central services (e.g., computing) or depreciation may be charged on capital equipment rather than it being expensed in the period of acquisition. Although the method of allocation may be reasonable for a particular purpose (though it should be noted that allocation is always arbitrary), it is generally unsuitable for the other purposes for which the information is used. Thus managers may be led, for example, to continue to use old, fully depreciated assets rather than replacing them with new, because reported profit figures are better for the less economic alternative.

All this implies that, although accounting information has an important role to play, it has to be used in a way that takes account of its limitations. By far the most crucial use of accounting information is in performance evaluation, because this impinges most directly upon line managers in a position to influence both the information gathered and the actions that are taken as a result. As any accounting system is an imperfect tool, it is the way in which senior managers make use of the information that will determine the response of others in the organization. It is thus important that both accounting system designers and senior managers are aware of both the technical limitations of accounting measurement procedures and the likely effects of the way in which managers use accounting information.

Further, it is possible that the lack of use of accounting information is as serious a problem as its mis-use, particularly at middle-management level (Dew and Gee, 1973). Line managers will ignore formally produced accounting information when they perceive it to be of little relevance to their tasks and they will develop alternative sources of information that are of more value to them. Here the responsibility lies with the accounting systems designer to develop a deeper understanding of the information requirements of specific tasks so as to be able to provide more appropriate information.

In the following chapters we turn to face these issues of how accounting information can be appropriately provided and used where the traditional underlying assumptions of management accounting are not met. In particular, we consider the role of accounting information where inter-dependencies between parts of the organization are significant and when uncertainty is such that predictions become unreliable. There are no simple solutions; we seek to explore how accounting information might most effectively be used in controlling the activities of real-world organizations.

EXERCISES

1. Explain the different reasons why a manager might submit a budget estimate that is biased. What might a senior manager do in order to detect and correct such biased information?
2. It has been suggested that modern methods of statistical forecasting can almost totally eliminate the problem of budgetary bias. Do you agree?
3. Outline the contribution that the techniques of work measurement and standard costing can make to budgetary control. To what extent are control budgets suitable for planning purposes?
4. 'The conditions under which budgetary control is most effective are precisely those under which it is of least value'. Specify the conditions that you think make for effective budgetary control, and evaluate the above statement.
5. Ten managers, each operating identical factories, submit production budgets that are optimistic, such that each has a 25% chance of attainment. How likely is it that the total production budget for all ten factories will be achieved? (Hint: assume the probability distribution of a production budget follows a Normal distribution).
6. What kinds of management accounting information are most suitable for serving each of the three major functions of attention directing, problem solving and performance evaluation?
7. As Budget Accountant you have been asked to investigate a division of your company where the managers usually fail to attain their budget targets. By contrast, managers in other divisions are normally successful at meeting their budgets. What information would you try to discover and what actions might you recommend on the basis of the answers you receive?
8. Give some examples of how a manager might achieve his budget by methods that are harmful to the organization. How would you guard against such practices occurring?

9. The Mammoth Manufacturing Company had introduced a budgetary control system in January 1982. In October 1982 senior managers were reviewing the past nine month's results before beginning work on the 1983 budget, and the following conversation ensued:

Accountant: Our results look very disappointing; we have missed our budget estimates in every one of the past nine months. Revenues have been less than expected and costs have exceeded budget estimates, so our profit is way below budget.

Production Manager: That's right, but our results aren't that bad. In fact, they're slightly better than the same period in 1981. Considering the economic situation, we've done quite well to hold costs at these levels.

Marketing Manager: The sales force have performed exceptionally well, too. Our best man has beaten his quota target six months out of nine; that's rare even in good times.

Accountant: That's as may be, but neither of you have met your original budget estimates. I use those figures to plan our capital requirements. In March, I negotiated a loan to cover our estimated operating requirements over the summer because of the sales growth you forecast. In fact we didn't need the money because the growth was much smaller than budgeted. The result is that we have paid high interest rates to raise unused capital.

Marketing Manager: But you can't expect salesmen to meet their quotas every month. I set those quotas to be a demanding target, to motivate the people out on the road to aim high. The average salesman meets his quota maybe one month in three; if it was lower he just would not work as hard.

Production Manager: It's the same in the factory. My output and cost standards are based on a week in which everything goes right, and that happens only once a month. Most weeks something goes wrong and we don't achieve our target. But the target is important; it shows what can be done if only we can get everything right.

Accountant: That may be all right for you people, but I can't work like that. What would our bankers say if I promised to repay a loan in June, but found that I couldn't and had to delay until August? You can't run a business on hopes; the budget must be an accurate estimate of what is expected to happen, not a daydream of what might happen if all went well.

Required:

Outline the different functions of the budget system as seen by each manager and carefully explain how these different views might be reconciled in constructing the budget for 1983.

From: Certified Diploma in Accounting and Finance, Paper 2, December 1982.

10. In the face of poor operating results, the Chief Executive of a multidivisional manufacturing company called a meeting of his divisional managers. At the meeting he exhorted them to improve the profitability of their divisions during the coming year and announced that he would hold each manager rigorously accountable for improved performance at the year end. However, in line with company policy, each manager was given the freedom to act as he thought best for his own circumstances.

At the end of the year the results for two of the divisions gave the Chief Executive cause for concern. The summary results are given in Table 7.1, with the previous year's performance shown in brackets:

Table 7.1

	Division A	Division B
Net operating profit	£100 000 (£50 000)	£50 000 (£75 000)
Capital employed	£1 600 000 (£1 000 000)	£300 000 (£500 000)
Return on capital employed	$6\frac{1}{4}$% (5%)	$16\frac{2}{3}$% (15%)

On requesting a brief explanation of their results, he received the following comments from the two managers:

Manager A: The introduction of new machinery and production facilities during the year has enabled the division to double its operating profit. Despite the increased level of investment, the return on capital employed has been considerably increased, indicating a marked improvement in overall operating efficiency. Plans for a further modernization programme are in hand and continued improvement may be confidently expected.

Manager B: The year has seen a most successful programme involving the identification and phasing out of activities having a below average return on investment. By selling off these less profitable activities it has proved possible to increase return on investment from the already good level of 15% to a level approaching 17%. Further rationalization of this nature is planned for the coming year and a target return of 20% has been set.

Required:

(a) By assuming that the company's cost of capital is 10%, carefully explain whether you consider the Chief Executive's concern is justified.

(b) What steps would you advise the Chief Executive to take to improve the accountability arrangements in future?

From: Certified Diploma in Accounting and Finance, Paper 2, June 1982.

Part Three

Accounting for Non-Programmed Activities

Our concern is to evaluate the contribution of the accounting information system (AIS) to effective management control in the decentralized, multidivisional firm. The reason for this focus stems from a recognition that the incidence of non-programmed decisions is greater in those firms that have these characteristics. We shall argue that companies adopt different strategies to avoid uncertainty and that one of these, namely diversification, results in the enlarged firm facing various dynamic and unstable product market environments. In order to absorb this uncertainty, the multidivisional structure develops that allows lower-level managers greater discretion in decision taking. However, the decisions they are then required to make, although limited to a specific product market, take place under conditions of uncertainty. The outcomes of actions taken cannot be predicted with accuracy, and a good deal of judgement, innovation and intuition is required of lower-level managers.

Chapter 8 expands this discussion to examine the planning needs of divisional managers to take effective non-programmed decisions. The design of the AIS contingent upon the incidence of non-programmed decisions is developed and, in particular, the appropriateness of participation and relevant feed-forward controls is highlighted. In Chapter 9, the impact of the conventional AIS to provide feedback controls, especially in the form of accounting performance measures, is examined. The accuracy, completeness and neutrality of such measures are questioned in situations where non-programmed decisions occur. Recognizing the presence of information asymmetry within the multidivisional firm leads us to conclude that the conventional AIS may actually encourage opportunistic behaviour by lower-level managers. The combination of environmental uncertainty, information asymmetry and imperfect accounting measures suggests that optimal decision making is an empty concept. Instead the AIS should be concerned with the promotion of behaviour congruence, where managers are encouraged to agree feasible actions. Alternative accounting performance measures and styles of evaluation are investigated to discover their compatibility with the behaviour congruence criterion.

The creation of incentive schemes may mitigate or promote opportunistic behaviour by managers. In Chapter 10, the forms of reward and the relationship with results are examined. Empirical evidence indicates the present popularity and growing significance of incentive schemes, hence their potential to influence managerial behaviour.

The needs of the AIS to cope with complexity and unpredictability are our concern in Chapters 11 and 12. The first of these examines the accounting treatments of inter-dependence and the vexed problem of transfer pricing is encountered. The conditions underlying the true transfer pricing problem in multidivisional companies are uncovered and the theoretically acceptable solutions using relevant costs are criticized. Essentially, the solutions depend on the provision of complete, unbiased information that results in re-centralized decision making. A transfer pricing system that is adaptive to changing external environments and changing internal responses is required without undermining the divisional management's authority. A suggestion is made for a fair and neutral transfer pricing system to be incorporated in the AIS.

In Chapter 13, we concentrate on the capital-investment decision in the decentralized, multidivisional firm and examine the divisional management's influence over certain stages of the capital-budgeting process. Acknowledging that information asymmetry exists because the investment decision is essentially non-programmed requires that the AIS does not motivate divisional management to pursue short-term, profit-performance measures at the expense of taking decisions that are in the firm's best interests. Hence alternative measures of profit to give managers guidance consistent with discounted cash flow techniques are analysed. Also the possibility of evaluating managerial performance in terms of cash flow accounting is considered. Finally, the appropriateness of an AIS that uses multiple performance measures is assessed in terms of promoting effective management control.

8

Planning and control in a complex and uncertain world

SUMMARY

This chapter argues that as companies grow to avoid environmental uncertainty, they subsequently become more complex to manage. By diversifying, the enlarged company encounters the combined problem of operating in an increased number of distinct, dynamic product and geographical markets where top management ability to identify and monitor constantly changing factors which effect success is limited. Hence the judgement, intuition and skill of lower level managers is required.

We concentrate on the multidivisional structure because it is most likely that divisional managers will undertake non-programmed decision making. While control loss associated with communication and coordination may be diminished by adoption of this structure, the problem of opportunistic behaviour may become more pronounced. Decentralization implies a greater involvement of divisional general managers in setting plans and participation but there is also a greater emphasis on performance measurement of the distinct and separate divisions. The accounting information system should promote behaviour congruence by not encouraging managers to abuse participation by intentionally over- or under-estimating forecasts. In the complexity of the multidivisional structure, results, actions and personnel controls may not always give consistent recommendations for a behaviour congruent accounting information system.

INTRODUCTION

In previous chapters, we have argued that traditional management accounting techniques are most suited for programmed decision making because of the implicit assumptions that are built-in to their models. Although conditions of absolute certainty, environmental stability, predictability of human behaviour and centralization of decision making are never found, traditional accounting techniques work best in situations where such assumptions are largely satisfied. It is now time to consider the design of appropriate forms of accounting information systems in a complex and uncertain world, where such assumptions hold to a much lesser extent and where decision making, therefore, becomes less programmed.

This chapter has two main sections. In the first section, a theoretical framework for non-programmed decision making is developed. The underlying causes for non-programmed decision making in organizations are uncovered, and the organizational responses that these conditions generate are examined. Two fundamental reasons for non-programmed decision making are exposed, namely the existence of uncertainty and the complexity and diversity of organizational activities. Organizations may respond to uncertainty by attempting to avoid it, and may handle complexity and diversity by adapting their organizational structure. This section concludes by comparing the characteristics of unitary and multidivisional organizational structures. The second section examines the different requirements for accounting information systems in these circumstances, in particular, in organizations adopting a multidivisional structure. For example, whereas managers in unitary organizations may be relatively little involved in planning and other feed-forward control activities, managers in multidivisional organizations are necessarily required to participate in planning to a much greater extent. The chapter concludes by identifying the planning needs of multidivisional organizations and the appropriate forms of accounting information systems needed to support them.

A THEORETICAL FRAMEWORK FOR NON-PROGRAMMED DECISION MAKING

The task of explaining the incidence of non-programmed decisions in large, complex, economic organizations is hampered by the absence of a universally accepted theory that describes why economic activities are organized in a particular way. Why, for example, among companies making the same product, do we find some that process raw material inputs to make the product, others that merely assemble the product and still others that not only make and assemble the final product, but also distribute and market it as well?

There are at least three frameworks that attempt to explain these differences and each carries its own implications for the design of the accounting information system. These are the information evaluation approach, the organizational failures framework and contingency theory. Each framework offers insights into why economic activities become organized in a particular way, and although we have stated previously that we shall follow a contingency approach, this does not exclude using insights from other theoretical frameworks.

The information evaluation approach, as presented by Demski (1972, 1980) and Demski and Feltham (1978), provides a rigorous analysis that can be used to evaluate different information systems. An information system is regarded as a source of messages that will effect the decision maker's assessment of the likelihood of various possible states of nature (Itami, 1977). The value of an information system is measured by the expected increase in utility from having the system over not having it. However, the mathematical rigour of the analysis confines its application to highly simplified decision settings. Further, because the relevant variables, parameters and relationships must be unambiguously specified, the way the organization has chosen to organize its activities must be known, so that the alternative actions and their probability distributions can be clearly defined. It must also be possible to define the utility function of the decision maker, who is assumed to be rational in an economic sense. Hence, although the information evaluation approach can measure the value of accounting information, it presumes that the structure of that organizational context is known in considerable detail. At present, it seems that this approach is more useful in its application to programmed rather than to non-programmed decisions.

The organizational failures framework stems from the work of Coase (1937), and is concerned with explaining why some economic transactions are conducted in markets but others are conducted in hierarchies or firms (Williamson, 1975). Transaction costs form the major focus of this theory, and the search for transactional efficiency involves considering the characteristics of exchange transactions along the dimensions shown in Table 8.1.

Recurring, complex and uncertain exchanges that involve substantial investment may be more efficiently undertaken when internal organization replaces market transactions. The efficiency of a trans-

Table 8.1 Characteristics of transactions (after Spicer and Van Ballew, 1983)

Standardized	⟨------⟩	Non-standardized
Non-idiosyncratic	⟨------⟩	Idiosyncratic
One time or occasional	⟨------⟩	Recurring
Trivial investment in human or physical capital	⟨------⟩	Substantial investment in human or physical capital
Little uncertainty	⟨------⟩	Significant uncertainty

action conducted within the firm depends on the employment relation within the company (i.e., how the behaviour of managers is governed or constrained), how the economic activities are sub-divided and how the accounting information system is structured. The theory assumes that decision makers are rational, self-interested individuals who possess varying amounts of relevant information about operations undertaken in uncertain or complex settings. Decision makers may therefore indulge in opportunistic behaviour that causes the potential benefits of conducting transactions internally to be reduced. The accounting information system serves the important purpose of helping to ensure that internal transactions are conducted efficiently.

Contingency theory explains how an appropriate accounting information system can be designed to match the organization structure, technology and environment of the firm. The focus of attention is the overall firm rather than transaction costs. Whereas the organizational failures framework seeks an optimal mechanism to ensure efficient transactions, contingency theorists have been content with the notion of merely improving organizational effectiveness. The precise meaning of organizational effectiveness is a fundamental problem (Steers, 1975; Otley 1983), but as we have argued in Chapter 1, the accounting information system has a role to play in maintaining decision makers' commitment to the feasible region of intersecting, acceptable sets of actions. Feasibility is not synonymous with optimality, for it does not assume that objectives are shared or even placed in order of priority, but only that some agreement to implement a set of actions exists. However, as environmental changes occur, participants' views about what is an acceptable activity set will also change. Renegotiation will have to take place in order to identify a new feasible region and to maintain the commitment of organizational participants.

An analysis of this aim of identifying possible feasible regions of activity and attempting to keep the organization within them is offered by Thomas (1980b). He argues that in the absence of agreed objectives, managers should be encouraged to propose actions that they are willing to take and that are consistent with top management's desires. In other words, *behaviour congruence* (i.e., an agreed set of actions) replaces *goal congruence* (i.e., an agreed set of goals) as a guiding principle. If top management emphasizes profit measures when evaluating unit performance, behaviour congruence can effectively replace goal congruence. If top management emphasizes transactional efficiency, then the idea of behaviour congruence is consistent with the organizational failures framework. Although behaviour congruence is only a general guideline, it has some specific, positive characteristics.

First, it emphasizes the necessity of matching organizational structure and its AIS, so that decision makers are actively encouraged to implement actions that are beneficial to the overall organization. Secondly, it makes it clear that incentives for promoting self-interest must be constrained by organizational controls and that the AIS therefore plays a fundamental role in the control process. At the very least, a behaviour congruent AIS should not provide incentives for managers to implement organizationally undesirable actions.

Examples of behaviour promoted by inappropriate incentive systems include:

1. Decision makers failing to propose capital investment projects that involve other parts of the organization because the cost allocation or transfer pricing system is not under their control.
2. Pressures to record expenses inaccurately to different cost headings or different time periods, so that targets are met, but which make the accounting information misleading.
3. The attainment of a planned profit target by generating sales with uncreditworthy purchasers.

In each example, recorded profit may be maintained or even increased but only at the expense of actions that will cause problems in the future. Hence, behaviour congruence is a broader concept than goal congruence, which is usually dominated by ideas of profit maximization, and as such it provides a means of operationalizing the notion of organizational effectiveness. Behaviour congruence may also be seen as encompassing some of the aspects of transactional efficiency. Where the organizational failures framework emphasizes reducing transactional inefficiencies, the idea of behaviour congruence is concerned with curtailing opportunistic behaviour, but not to the extent of finding an optimal solution. In other words, it is a satisficing rather than an optimizing concept.

There are several other similarities between the contingency and organizational failures frameworks. Both are positive theories; both acknowledge that decision makers are self-interested; and, to varying degrees, both frameworks recognize that organizational design and the design of accounting information systems are influenced by the external environment. Spicer and Van Ballew (1983, p. 93) conclude that 'in a number of ways the organizational failures framework can be viewed as capturing the essence of contingency models of organization while at the same time giving explicit attention to the dynamic decision making and exchange process taking place within and between firms'. In particular, it can be seen that the characteristics of transactions, organizational structure, the employment relation and the accounting information system's 'goodness of fit' with these variables influence the economic performance of the firm.

Environmental uncertainty

Earlier we have argued that certainty is an essential assumption that underpins the effective use of many management accounting techniques. The results of actions can be accurately predicted because key variables are identified and their inter-relationships are known. Centralization operates efficiently in a stable environment, exhibiting relative certainty. Lower-level managers merely execute decisions involving well-defined, structured and repetitive tasks, thereby making human behaviour more predictable (March and Simon, 1958). In a programmed situation, the AIS contributes to the creation of routines and standardized operating procedures, provides an acceptable means of observing and measuring the inputs and outputs of the organization's activities and gives useful information for control purposes. How justified is such a use of the AIS in more realistic situations?

In the real world, there are very few product or service markets that do not experience some degree of turbulence, competitive hostility and restrictiveness. Technological advances, whether in the field of production processes, distribution and marketing or raw material extraction, tend to be occurring at an accelerating rate. Increasingly, domestic markets are affected by the policies of external governments and agencies as well as by home economic and fiscal changes. New, potentially important factors must be evaluated and their relationship with existing circumstances assessed. Therefore, it appears likely that decision makers in most economic organizations will face an increasing number of non-programmed decisions. Situations where the outcomes of actions taken can only be guessed at, and where past experience is of limited usefulness, are increasingly common. Here planning models are likely to become less formal and more intuitive and the need for judgement becomes of paramount importance. It is the contention of contingency theory that the greater the environmental uncertainty the firm is exposed to, the more non-programmed decisions will be necessary (Khandwalla, 1977).

Uncertainty avoidance
One of the distinguishing features of economic organizations in the second half of this century is their size. One explanation for their growth is that it is undertaken to reduce or to avoid environmental uncertainty. Chandler (1962, 1977), Johnson (1980) and other researchers interested in business history have also shown that grow-

ing firms benefit from matching their organization structures and AIS with their business strategies.

Horizontal integration (i.e., the merger of firms in the same line of business) may safeguard the profitable survival of the enlarged firm by conferring a more dominant market position. Uncertainty associated with competition is avoided by increasing market concentration. Alternatively, a strategy of growth via vertical integration (i.e., the merger of firms involved in successive stages of the production and marketing process) can overcome the uncertainty in securing distribution channels for the firm's outputs and ensure the availability of scarce inputs. Economies of scale, market power and other economic aspects of synergy also explain growth by these strategies.

A different strategy of uncertainty avoidance is offered by diversified growth. Take-overs or mergers into activities that are unrelated to current operations reduce the dependence of a firm on a single market, product line, technology or industry. The combination of diverse activities, each subject to differing economic and cyclical trends, market competition and technological advances, offers the enlarged firm the opportunity to earn a more stable overall return. Diversification may therefore have some benefits in reducing earnings and cash flow volatility. Growth by means of diversification allows risk-pooling, but does not usually lead to economies of scale in production or marketing.

In each form of growth, the firm attempts to avoid uncertainty by limiting the impact of adverse environmental changes. Alternative reasons for growth such as to provide promotion opportunities for employees and to justify increased compensation for top management who subsequently preside over enlarged companies cannot be dismissed. However, the growth strategies as outlined here may be distinguished by the number of environments that the enlarged firm subsequently has to respond to. In order for the benefits to be realized, an appropriate organization structure and AIS is needed that is compatible with the chosen strategy.

Growth and organization structure
The use of strategies to avoid uncertainty necessitates that firms organize their internal activities, so that environmental uncertainty is identified and monitored. Contingency theory offers several insights into the way a firm's structure adjusts to environmental change. It is no less important for the diversified firm to recognize the different environments in which it operates than it is for the vertically integrated firm to acknowledge the technological differences in the various production processes. The changes in the purchasing, manu-

facturing and marketing sub-environments of the horizontally integrated firm must be monitored because failure to adapt in one function will affect the entire firm's survival.

Williamson argues that as an organization grows in size, it will naturally organize on a functional basis (1970). Centralization and line and staff organization enable functionally organized firms to achieve economies of specialization and scale. These organizational changes are accompanied by the introduction of formal accounting routines for planning capital investment and for monitoring the overall financial performance of the firm and its diverse departments (Caves, 1980). However, with increased growth via diversification, the functional structure can be overwhelmed by the difficulties of coordinating internal transactions of increasing complexity and volume. Exposure to an increasing number of product and/or geographical market environments prompts the re-organization of internal activities into divisions. These divisions are differentiated by the distinct markets they serve and the varying uncertainty that those markets exhibit. The AIS can now be used to measure divisional performance in terms compatible with overall performance. Further, top management can be freed from responsibility for day-to-day operations in order to concentrate on strategic planning.

Many researchers have attempted to trace the sequence of changes in structure as an organization grows. Wrigley (1970), Williamson (1970), Rumelt (1974) and Williamson and Bhargava (1972) have all contributed classification schemes of organizational development, and one such scheme is shown in Table 8.2.

Stage I represents the owner-managed firm with a single product or product line that is distributed via one channel or set of channels to a particular market. With increasing volume, task specialization is merited, and the organization evolves to the unitary form in Stage II.

Table 8.2   Organizational development (after Scott, 1971)

Characteristic	Stage I	Stage II Unitary	Stage III Multidivisional	Stage IV Free-form
Product line	Single	Single	Multiple	Multiple
Distribution	Single	Single	Multiple	Multiple
Organization structure	Little/no formal structure	Function-based and integrated	Product market based and quasi-autonomous	Product market based and largely autonomous

Here the tasks and activities tend to become increasingly differentiated, but the need to integrate activities in order to serve the single market remains of paramount importance. The transition to the multidivisional form in Stage III reflects a new transactional relationship between activities. The organizational units now have considerable independence and serve separate markets. The focus is upon separate product market activities whose integration on a day-to-day basis is not essential to the survival of the total organization. The free-form organization of Stage IV recognizes the separate product markets as distinct businesses, and top management acts as a holding company. The organizational sub-units operate independently and determine their own strategies, subject to some loose accountability to the centre.

For the purposes of our analysis, we shall concentrate on the unitary and multidivisional forms of organizational structure. The classification is a simplification, and any given organization will not necessarily fit neatly into a category. For example, a single division within a multidivisional organization may exhibit a specialized unitary structure. However, the distinction provides an initial insight into the conditions where non-programmed decisions are most likely to occur.

A division in a diversified firm will require a complete set of functions to serve its chosen product market. Lawrence and Lorsch (1967a) show that uncertainty affects not only the degree of differentiation in the firm's divisions, but also the structure of those divisions and the character of the devices used to integrate them. A division may be subject to rapid changes in its product market and also in its technology. For example, a firm that has activities in book, magazine and newspaper publishing may distinguish at least three product markets on the grounds that the consumers are different, the technologies are different and the speed of reaction required to respond to changes in the separate markets is different. The book division may be facing increased competition because of product innovation by a competitor such as the inclusion of computer software packages with books. The magazine division may be widening the existing distribution channels by introducing new points of sale at supermarket check-outs. The newspaper division may be experimenting with new printing technologies that change job specifications and manning requirements. In each division, a different key variable is currently recognized and new and different challenges will no doubt emerge in the future. The multidivisional organization acknowledges that these differences are important, but at the cost of allowing differences in orientations, goals, attitudes and beliefs to develop between the separate divisions. Hence the adoption or development of a multidivisional structure is a response to the recognition of uncertainty in distinct product market environments. The more accelerated the changes in these environments, the greater becomes the need to develop means of absorbing the uncertainty created.

Uncertainty absorption

Contingency theorists argue that organizational structure is designed to match environmental uncertainty. Organizational sub-units face different combinations of environments. Perrow (1970) categorizes this differentiation along the dimensions of variability and the need to search for solutions. When tasks are uniform or repetitive and the actions needed to attain particular outcomes are known, then it is not necessary to search for further information. On the other hand, when tasks are variable and there are several alternative actions that may be taken, additional information is essential.

Top management is unlikely to be able to provide all the additional information needed. The task of collecting data on all potentially critical variables in all the divisions' environments is immense and top management may not even be able to recognize the key variables for which data require to be collected. If the multidivisional structure has developed to match the uncertainty in different environments, it is unlikely that top management possesses the best predictive model for each environment. The best models are likely to be those held by the divisional managers who constantly interact with their own specific product markets. For example, consider the launch of a new book by our hypothetical book division. The divisional manager may believe that each new book has a different market and that different advertising and marketing campaigns are appropriate. He may isolate the topical nature or content of the book, the reputation of the author, the timing of the launch and competitors' offerings as key variables affecting advertising expenditure and choice of media. There is a need for future-oriented, external information that is regularly updated before the implementation of the decision. It is unrealistic to expect that top management could process this amount of information in a timely fashion, and it is even more unlikely that such centrally generated information would remain relevant, because top management is too distant from the changing environments.

To absorb the recognized uncertainty associated with several environments, top management may consciously delegate decision-making authority to lower-level managers. The degree of decentralization will vary between firms and even within firms, but in all instances it will stem from a twofold pressure. The first pressure results from the company's growth strategy of operating in distinct product markets. The second pressure results from a conscious acknowledgement that top management cannot recognize and monitor the constantly changing variables that effect success in these distinct product markets. The combination of these two structural assumptions gives rise to non-programmed decisions being an important feature of multidivisional, decentralized firms. Non-programmed decision making will be frequent and largely unavoidable in firms that perceive they operate in uncertain environments. This is not to say that non-programmed decisions are never present in unitary structures, but rather that the incidence of such decisions at lower management levels will be limited because the total activities of the company will be coordinated by top management.

Control loss and internal organization

In examining the impact of a high level of non-programmed decisions on the AIS, it is worth restating the reasons why the transition from a unitary to a multidivisional organization structure occurs. The fundamental distinction between the two forms of structure relates to how activities are recognized. Differentiation by function is commonly associated with the unitary structure and differentiation by product market activity characterizes the multidivisional structure. There is some evidence (Lorsch and Allen, 1973) to support the view that successful firms are those that can combine a high degree of differentiation with a necessary level of integration. Integrative devices can take various forms, such as company rules or manuals of instruction, organization hierarchy, planning contact liaison roles, taskforces and integrators who specialize in the role of coordinating activities either as individuals, departments or via a matrix form of organization (Galbraith, 1972), As the list progresses, the devices become increasingly sophisticated but the AIS is generally categorized as falling within the initial devices, that is as rules and routines incorporated within a manual and straddling the organizational hierarchy (Watson and Baumler, 1975). Our concern here is to determine the appropriate AIS for the different planning needs of multidivisional, as opposed to unitary, firms. The main reason for the transition to a multidivisional structure is essentially that of control loss, which highlights the problems of communication, coordination and opportunistic behaviour.

Communication
The functional activities within a unitary firm should be largely programmable because of its homogeneity of products and its relative stability of demand and technology. However, growth in the number of product lines or the technologies used can have a detrimental

effect on the unitary structure. Firstly, the span of control, or the number of people over whom a manager exercises formal authority, may increase. If the tasks of this increased number of people are interdependent, then the number of communication channels needed to coordinate their efforts also increases. For example, if the number of operatives who need to interact to make a product increases from 4 to 6, then the number of communication channels necessary rises from 6 to 15 (i.e., using the formula developed by Williamson, 1970, $\frac{1}{2}(M^2 - M)$, where M is the number of operatives). Alternatively, the span of control may be maintained by increasing the number of levels in the organizational hierarchy. A post of first-line supervisor may be created with three people reporting to each of two supervisors. Coordination by an individual supervisor requires only three communication channels, and the overall manager requires only two channels to coordinate the work of the two supervisors. This second alternative involves less channels and may seem more appropriate in view of the limited information-processing capabilities of individuals. Unfortunately, accommodating growth by increasing the number of levels in the organizational hierarchy causes other communication problems.

Messages are filtered as they pass through successive levels of the hierarchy. Managers may also perceive and interpret the important parts of the message differently, and information may be intentionally biased to ensure that the filtered message presents lower-level managers in a favourable light. Moreover, it may be shown that if just 10% of a message is suppressed at each of our management levels, only two-thirds of the original communication remains intact. (This is easily shown as being $(0.9)^4$, resulting in only 66% of the original message being transmitted: Monsen and Downs, 1965.)

The large unitary organization may be subject to both kinds of communication control loss due to the increase in specializations. Ultimately, each specialist function has to be coordinated with others. This requires more communication channels, and the information available to top functional managers is liable to be more biased because of the increased number of levels in the hierarchy.

Coordination
The response to growth of creating more functional activities and more hierarchical levels increases the number of complex relationships and communication patterns that will exist within the large unitary organization. Coordination of diverse functions becomes increasingly difficult because the functional goals or targets cannot be easily interrelated. Merely aggregating data within a functional activity and then across functional activities incorporates a wide

range of differences in lower-level managers' expectations and aspirations. The degree of optimism incorporated into a planning estimate is conditioned by each manager's view of the future and may vary significantly. For example, aggregating such financial estimates to form a master budget, with top management subsequently adjusting departmental estimates on a pro-rata basis, can result in significant problems, of which one is gaining the commitment of lower-level management to possibly unattainable targets (Otley and Berry, 1979). Take, for example, a situation where each of the three production plants in Sumo plc expect to produce 100 000 kg of output with a standard deviation of 20 000 kg for a given time period. If each production manager submits a budget of 115 000 kg, each can expect to attain or exceed the target about 22% of the time. (Assuming a normal distribution, 115 000 − 100 000 ÷ 20 000 = 0.75 standard deviations above the mean translated by normal distribution tables to 22.6%.)

In total, if all three managers behave in this way, the budget will be 345 000 kg. If it is assumed that each plant's output is independent of each other, and also that the total output has a normal distribution, then total expected output is 300 000 kg (3 × 100 000) with a standard deviation of 34 641 kg ($\sqrt{3}$ × 20 000). The budget of 345 000 kg is 45 000 above the mean, equivalent to 1.3 standard deviations (45 000 ÷ 34 641). This has a probability of achievement of just 9.6%. With a few production plants, the aggregation effect can be significant; the impact can be even greater when the production plants are different in size (see Table 8.3).

In this case, the standard deviations of the plant's output have been adjusted in proportion to the square root of expected output (Otley and Berry, 1979). (For plant A, the standard deviation is calculated as 50 000 ÷ 300 000 of 34 641 squared and then the square root is found.) As before, budget estimates having a 22.6% chance of attainment when aggregated have only a 13% chance of achievement in total (i.e., 338 540 − 300 000 ÷ 34 641 = 1.11 standard deviations from the mean).

Table 8.3　Aggregation of budget estimates for plants of different size

Plant	Expected output	Standard deviation	Original submission	Revised submission	Probability of attainment
A	50 000	12 393	59 295	57 095	28.5%
B	100 000	17 527	113 145	108 948	30.5%
C	150 000	21 466	166 100	159 938	32.3%
Total	300 000	34 641	338 540	325 981	22.6%

If the total is now revised such that it has a 22.6% chance of being attained, the original submissions being adjusted pro rata, the individual plant managers have different probabilities of attainment. The pro-rata adjustment takes the revised total submission over the original submission applied to the individual plant original submission (325 981 ÷ 338 540 × 59 295 for plant A).

The implication of simple aggregation of budgets is that mildly optimistic individual estimates become wildly optimistic when totalled and vice versa. Pro-rata adjustments merely compound the problem.

The subsequent translation of the physical output into budgeted financial data may cause some functional managers to reject the budget as unattainable, whereas others will be able to over-attain. This represents an operational problem of coordination, in that the functional departments are not able to follow goals or targets that are qualitatively identical to those of the organization as a whole (Zannetos, 1965).

Opportunistic behaviour
The goal-setting procedure in the large unitary organization gradually becomes unmanageable for the overall coordinator, that is top management (Hunt, 1966). Top managers typically suffer from information overload (Mintzberg, 1973) as they have both to develop strategic plans and to maintain day-to-day control over an ever-increasing variety of functional activities. Control loss owing to communication and coordination problems ultimately makes top management's role untenable. Inaccurate translations of strategic goals into operational targets result in some facilities being under-used and the intrinsic inter-dependence of some activities being overlooked.

In addition, there is the possibility that functional managers will intentionally bias information to gain a departmental advantage. The functional manager has near-exclusive responsibility for the welfare and performance of his functional activity, but only partial and ill-defined responsibility for overall corporate goals to which his contribution cannot be accurately assessed. Organizational slack therefore occurs, because top management has neither the time nor the information accurately to appraise the performance of the functional activities. Departmental managers' attempts to promote their functional self-interest may go largely undetected.

The combination of control losses caused by communication, coordination and opportunistic behaviour place a limit on efficient growth in a unitary structure. This is because the increasing complexity of coordinating functional activities reduces the accuracy of information used within the firm. Activities that could be regarded as programmable tend to become non-programmable. When uncertainty in the form of changing demand and technology occurs, the large unitary structure is unable to react quickly or effectively. The multidivisional form of organization is superior in reducing control loss of this kind.

ACCOUNTING IN A MULTIDIVISIONAL FRAMEWORK

Control loss in a multidivisional structure

Re-organizing a firm's activities into a multidivisional structure is an attempt to plan and implement strategies of diversification (Williamson, 1975). Interdependence between activities can be recognized and placed under the operational control of a divisional manager. By giving this divisional manager authority to make decisions, the number of hierarchical levels through which information is transmitted is reduced, diminishing the complexity of the control problem. The divisional manager still needs to maintain communication channels with the functional managers within his division, but this is a more confined task. The divisional manager should also receive less biased information from his limited number of subordinates for developing plans internally. Hence decentralization may be seen as a beneficial strategy for overcoming the problem of control loss.

The adoption of a multidivisional structure should mitigate the most serious aspects of the coordination problem. If divisions are identified with separate product market environments and are allocated sufficient resources to operate as semi-autonomous businesses, coordination and interdependence between divisions can be restricted. Additionally, the divisions may be given qualitative or quantitative targets expressed in the same terms as the overall company's targets. As long as the goals of the total firm can be expressed operationally, the goals of the individual divisions can be expressed in identical terms. The possibility of consistent objectives being developed within different divisions remains a problem, but the limited interdependence between divisions makes the problem less acute than that faced by top management in unitary structures.

The likelihood of the multidivisional structure effectively curbing opportunistic, self-interested behaviour is more difficult to assess. Here we shall concentrate on the effects of the structural change and later introduce principal-agent theory to explore the potentially negative features of non-programmed decision making in the multidivisional firm. One significant advantage associated with the adoption of decentralization within a multidivisional structure is that responsibilities for long-term strategy development and short-term planning are clearly distinguished.

Top management is no longer responsible for the coordination of day-to-day operations, and can devote time to formulate strategy for the firm and monitor the progress of the divisions in their respective product markets. The ultimate responsibility for changing the profile of the firm and the strategic business units that are identified within it rests with top management. Thus it is an advantage of the decentralized, multidivisional enterprise that it allows different levels of management to concentrate on those issues with which they are best placed to deal. Whether or not the multidivisional structure curbs or compounds the incentives for opportunistic behaviour by divisional managers is a matter that is best judged in relation to the AIS which the firm uses. On the surface, at least, it appears that the multidivisional structure has several advantages over the unitary form when diverse, uncertain environments are faced, but there are costs associated with such a change in organizational structure.

In order to ensure that the decision-making authority delegated to the divisional management is not misused, top management may require an increased monitoring capability. One potentially significant cost relates to the provision of head office staff advisers (Solomons, 1965, p. 13): 'However careful the organization is to avoid the duplication of authority, having head office staff personnel over-looking divisional personnel will generally lead to a more expensive administrative organization than a centralized company would need.' The proliferation of head office staff in functions such as research and development, industrial relations and legal and financial services represent incremental costs of the multidivisional structure. Further, worthwhile advice will require head office staff of a high calibre and expertise, thereby further increasing the cost.

A second implication of adopting a multidivisional structure is that lower-level managers will expect greater rewards for their increased responsibility. The departmental manager in the unitary structure is expected to execute decisions, the details of which have been clearly set out in the operating budget. The divisional manager, on the other hand, is expected to depart from the details of his operating plan to react to changed environmental circumstances in order to meet planned targets. Such managers therefore expect to share in the success of their divisions by receiving rewards for the increased responsibility they bear. Share options, cash bonuses and perquisites given as rewards permeate to a lower level of management in the multidivisional structure and increase the costs to the firm (Dearden, 1962b).

A more subtle cost may arise from the competitive atmosphere that the multidivisional structure creates. The acknowledgement that divisional managers have decision making authority gives rise to the concern that divisional performance may be improved at the expense of the total firm. Innovations in marketing, production or quality control developed in one division may not be brought to the attention of other divisions. A change in production technique in one division that might be of benefit to another division may never be publicized. There is a danger that the increased visibility of the separate divisions causes parochial attitudes and an over-competitive atmosphere to emerge. The reduced need to cooperate with other divisional managers in day-to-day operations strengthens these attitudes. The presence of incentive schemes institutionalizes and confirms the separate status of the divisions. In short, the divisional managers may take decisions that are best for their divisions regardless of the effect on the total business enterprise. Thus the occurrence of opportunistic behaviour by managers may actually be enhanced by adoption of the multidivisional structure.

The potential advantages of changing to the multidivisional structure may be lost unless divisional managers can be encouraged to take actions in the interests of the total firm. The AIS, especially in its role as a monitoring device, has the potential to affect the behaviour of divisional managers. The means of overcoming control loss in the unitary structure, namely decentralization into a multidivisional structure, causes a higher incidence of non-programmed decisions. In taking these decisions, the use of judgement and intuition by divisional managers is essential, and the use of this judgement should not be misdirected by the AIS and associated incentive schemes.

The AIS and the multidivisional structure

The multidivisional structure can suffer control loss if the AIS is inappropriately matched to the organization's situation. We will now examine the information requirements of planning in firms adopting the multidivisional structure. The employment relation of lower-level managers in the firm is presented using a principal – agent framework, and because of the incidence of non-programmed decisions at the divisional level, we will concentrate on the interface between divisional and top management.

In its present state of development, principal–agent theory (PAT) relates to a single principal and a single agent, as indicated by Kaplan (1982, p. 567): 'An agency relationship exists whenever one party (the principal) hires another party (the agent) to perform some service.' In our case, the divisional manager is hired by top management. PAT explicitly recognizes that the agent is hired to perform a task in an uncertain environment. In recognition of this, the principal delegates decision making authority to the agent, but owing to the complexity and environmental uncertainty surrounding the agent's task, the principal can only observe the agent's effort to a limited extent. Relevant information is thus unevenly distributed between the parties, and the existence of such information asymmetry means that the principal must either depend on communications from the agent or incur monitoring costs to discover whether the agent is actually performing in accordance with the principal's best interests. The agent can undertake not to make decisions that are contrary to the principal's well-being, and this can be seen as a bonding cost. An example is afforded by the case of Mr Archie McCardell, the past chief executive officer of International Harvester, who agreed to receive a minimal salary unless his firm outperformed a group of competitors. Despite the use of monitoring, PAT recognizes that a residual loss is likely. The agent may not take decisions that are wholeheartedly to the benefit of the principal. This is because the agent may not share the same preferences or beliefs as the principal or be unaware of them. Also the agent is assumed to be a rational utility maximizer who seeks financial compensation and non-pecuniary perquisites, and who prefers leisure to work. These are the parameters of the positive theory of the principal–agent relationship and the concern is to create an efficient contract which will improve the firm's efficiency.

PAT can thus be regarded as part of the organizational failures framework, attempting to minimize transaction costs, particularly those affecting the employment contract. The assumptions of PAT closely match the conditions of non-programmed decision making in the decentralized multidivisional structure. In terms of monitoring costs, the size of the head office staff serves as an example. The willingness of divisional managers to comply with an incentive scheme may be seen as a bonding cost, and the residual loss is reflected by the managers' parochial attitudes.

While top management cannot keep lower-level managers from defining problems and formulating solutions in ways that are coloured by their situational context, they can influence that context by careful attention to organizational design and the measurement/reward system employed. (Caves, 1980, p. 76)

PAT offers insight to the appropriateness of different AIS by focusing on the problems of information asymmetry. There are two sets of problems, moral hazard and adverse selection, that arise owing to information asymmetry.

One aspect of moral hazard is the misrepresentation of outcomes in circumstances where it is costly for the other party to judge outcomes. Moral hazard arises from top management's remoteness from the individual product markets, and their reliance on accounting information as a measure of the effort expended by the divisional manager. The presence of environmental uncertainty makes it extremely difficult for top management to discover whether a budget variance, say, is due to uncontrollable, external events or the failure of the divisional manager to take appropriate action. When the manager's effort cannot be directly observed, the role of the AIS is to promote optimal risk-sharing (Shavell, 1979). The moral hazard problem therefore leads to an evaluation of different performance measures in terms of their association with incentive schemes. Using normative models, Holstrum (1979) and others demonstrate that any additional information about the agent's effort can be useful, although they assume that the additional information can be provided costlessly!

Adverse selection is closely linked with moral hazard, but concentrates on pre-decision information. It is the misrepresentation of the true attributes or qualities of a task under circumstances in which it is not possible for the other party to determine the truth at low cost. That is, the effort the divisional manager expends in developing plans and the detail of the predictive model he uses can never be perfectly known by the top management. Owing to the superior information the divisional manager possesses about the operation of his division, top management can only guess at the effort required to meet a certain plan or target. Top management may have to incur considerable costs to determine whether or not the manager's information misrepresents reality either unintentionally or intentionally. Adverse selection therefore focuses on the needs of planning and, in particular, the incentives a divisional manager may have to introduce bias and budget slack.

Opportunistic behaviour of this sort represents a major challenge to the efficient operation of the multidivisional firm because the process by which inputs are transformed into outputs can only be imperfectly known or agreed by top management (Ouchi, 1977). Unfortunately, PAT to date offers no solutions to these problems, although the moral hazard aspect of information asymmetry has received the bulk of the research effort. This attempt at isolating the two aspects has led to the principal–agent relationship being analysed in a single period setting that implies that planning and control can be distinguished. At this stage, it appears that PAT offers a fairly realistic positive theory that may in time be applied to decentralized, multidivisional structures, but that the normative models and tests fail to provide any solutions for the adverse selection problems.

Participation in planning

Almost inevitably when the approaches to budgeting are outlined in the literature, planning is given emphasis (Horngren and Foster, 1987). Combined with the roles of communication and coordination, the importance of the process of budgeting is highlighted, but unfortunately, knowledge about whether an autocratic, consultative or democratic approach is taken tends to be firm specific. In practice, budgets may be set in a top-down, bottom-up and iterative manner, with each approach carrying implications for meaningful managerial participation in feed-forward controls. A traditional starting point is the sales budget which, once agreed, provides the basis for coordinating production, purchasing and other budgets. By implication, these latter budgets are therefore formulated in apparently known and stable conditions or, at least, this appears to be the premise. Lower-level managers' opinions and judgements are of limited usefulness in such circumstances. A top-down budget approach, emphasizing coordination, may appear to give these managers programmed activities. Of course, there are some functions like advertising, marketing and research and development within even the unitary firm where managers of necessity must take non-programmed decisions. But the likelihood is that most functional managers under a budget approach emphasizing coordination will find their discretion to plan independently constrained.

As a result of the high incidence of non-programmed decision taking in the decentralized, multidivisional firm, top management has to rely to a large extent on divisional managers' judgement. The involvement of divisional managers in supplying forecasts, plans and information about alternative actions is inevitable. Given some degree of participation in planning, it is essential that top management learns whether the divisional managers attempt to predict the likely outcomes of particular courses of action realistically or whether they satisfice and attempt to minimize the negative consequences of their actions. Thus adverse selection and feed-forward control are inextricably linked. As we have explained in Chapter 7, participation is really a double-edged sword. It can give rise to relevant targets being set, but it may lead to the creation of organizational slack.

The divisional manager may bias the plan by understating revenue and overstating cost expectations. Alternatively, biasing of plans may be in the opposite direction, when over-optimistic forecasts are supplied to gain top management's approval, especially if recent actual performance has been lower than expected. The planning information may also be biased by the divisional management's perception that conforming with corporate norms is important. For example, it may be expected that each division will plan for an annual sales growth of 2%. These motives for introducing bias have been detected in practice (Lowe and Shaw, 1968) but, in addition, bias can be unintentional. The fact that the divisional manager is taking non-programmed decisions means that inherent uncertainty can adversely affect the best intended of forecasts. Admitting this possibility indicates that bias can be intentional or unintentional, optimistic or pessimistic! The detection of intentional bias may test the investigatory powers of any top manager, regardless of the strength of their head office advisers. And yet, by excluding the participation of divisional management, unattainable plans may be set at a considerable administrative cost, which may fail to gain the commitment of divisional managers. On balance, some participation by divisional management in planning is essential.

In practice, Solomons (1965, p. 238) notes that: 'divisions are specifically required to develop such (long-term) objectives for their particular businesses with the help of the corporate financial staff and with the concurrence, when the objectives have been formulated, of the corporate management.'

Long-term forecasts are useful in providing guidelines within which short-term plans are to be drawn up. Although top management may provide or approve the short-term targets for the divisions, it is the divisions who provide the plan, and this accords with the need to develop an AIS that promotes behaviour congruence. This should recognize that planning is an iterative process involving both top-down and bottom-up communication. Active participation can bring together the top management's knowledge of broad issues and economy-wide uncertainties with the divisional managers' knowledge of the specific environmental and product market uncertainties (Batty, 1970).

It therefore appears that divisional managers play an important role in planning. They provide predictions of what outputs are expected to be achieved at some future time. Top management compare these predictions with what is desired at that future time and actions are sought that will minimize any differences. These actions may include top management requesting divisional management to develop alternative plans that will generate expected outcomes consistent with top management's targets. Alternatively, it may result in the top management reviewing their targets. Owing to their specialist knowledge and the significance of monitoring costs, divisional management may be able to exert considerable influence over the firm's strategies and operating plans. It is therefore essential that the AIS does not misdirect divisional managers and that it promotes the development of consensus between the managerial levels.

Feed-forward control

The ability of the multidivisional structure to improve economic performance thus relies on the existence of an appropriate AIS. Reliance on goal congruence is misplaced when diverse, environmental uncertainty combines with the multidivisional structure to create a high incidence of non-programmed decisions at lower management levels. The assumption that top management can translate objectives into realistic divisional profit or other targets is extremely dubious. Involving divisional managers in planning, however, carries the danger that they may indulge in opportunistic behaviour, and linking rewards with performance may actually encourage this, as will be discussed in a later chapter. For feed-forward control to be effective, the AIS in the multidivisional, decentralized firm needs to promote behaviour congruence.

Organizational control is the maintenance of activities in a feasible region which is determined by the intersection of the acceptable sets of actions of the organizational participants. The goals of divisional management may influence the definition of this feasible region via their involvement in the planning process. It is the divisional managers who normally possess the most detailed predictive models of the enterprise's specific activities. Their involvement in developing long-term plans and strategies appears essential, and the feed-forward mechanism provides the means whereby the enterprise's targets may be influenced. However, such participation also offers the opportunity to bias and to pursue parochial self-interest with only a limited chance of detection by top management. In order to avoid such problems, the AIS can assist in the process of gaining a consensus between the beliefs and preferences of the two management levels. Divisional management should reach agreement with top management on those activities that the organization is most effective at undertaking. A consensus may emerge as to the appropriate profile for the firm, so that it continues to operate in the best product markets or that plans to rectify any perceived imbalance are developed. The actions that top management would like to see taken need to be matched with the actions divisional management are willing to take.

The willingness of divisional managers to provide planning information that reduces the size, profitability or importance of their specific divisions may be achieved only if they are informed of how their actions will improve the overall effectiveness of the firm. Top management therefore needs to specify what future developments are envisaged and how individual divisions will contribute to these. The strategic planning responsibility of the top management remains intact, but it is the communication of these plans to divisional managers that is crucial if effective changes are to be made. Moreover, it is the assumptions incorporated in top management's plans that need to be open to questioning by divisional management.

At present, the different ways in which individual British universities are adapting to their environment provides a good example. Some universities have passed on the cash limits they have been set to faculties and departments for the latter to decide where cuts can be made. Departmental and faculty planning has usually reflected a self-preservation, 'cut them, not us' attitude. Eventually, the top management of the university is forced to invoke an across-the-board, pro-rata reduction in costs that meets the new cash limit. By this time, the departments are totally uncommitted to planning exercises and are frustrated by their ineffectiveness to make changes. Other universities have attempted to match departmental plans with a profile of a planned university that is envisaged by top management. Then a painstaking process of convincing departments that their plans need to be modified is embarked upon. But this procedure ensures that departmental heads can question the assumptions that underpin the strategy. The strategy may be altered, the departmental plans may be altered or, more likely, both will change. As a result, a consensus as to what actions are feasible can emerge and will be willingly (or begrudgingly) implemented. Future departmental planning can take place, not in a vacuum, but with an acknowledgement of the overall strategy, but a strategy that can be altered with cooperative dialogue.

To gain the greatest benefit from the participation of divisional management in the planning process, top management needs to specify the beliefs and assumptions underlying the proposed strategy. Divisional management must be able to question these assumptions in order that a consensus as to how a specific division fits in the proposed profile can be developed (Mason, 1969). Flexibility in the actions and strategies to be taken should ensure that divisional managers remain committed to the planning exercise. The possibility of altering the actions top management originally contemplated seems to offer the greatest assurance of this. Perhaps an indication of this happening is afforded by the increased number of management buy-outs. Wright and Thompson (1987) argue that divestment of unwanted divisions allows multidivisional companies in appropriate circumstances to function more effectively. Identification of viable businesses which do not fit easily within the corporate strategy may be clearly seen by divisional and top management.

Hence planning in the decentralized, multidivisional firm requires communication and matching of divisional and top management assumptions and beliefs. Specific goals for the divisions may not emerge from this procedure, but agreed actions can be determined. The number of participants influencing the process and the large number of changing environments involved supports Dyckman's (1975) argument that the assumption of explicit, clear company objectives being available is indeed heroic. Top management is concerned with the actions lower-level managers take. The planning procedure should encourage divisional managers to propose actions that they are willing to take and that are consistent with top management's desires. This emphasizes that, in the decentralized, multidivisional firm, we are more concerned with behaviour congruence than with goal congruence.

Implications for planning

The importance of divisional and top management actively communicating and questioning the assumptions by which operating and strategic plans are matched cannot be underestimated. Adoption of such a procedure carries implications for the way divisions, divisional management, the firm and top management are subsequently evaluated. This involves not only on what dimensions performance is measured, but also how the evaluation is to be used; it is our concern in the next chapter. What should be apparent is that planning in the multidivisional firm requires a democratic interaction of divisional and top managers if it is to be effective. In terms of Handy's outline of organizational cultures, introduced in Chapter 3, a move towards an existential culture is needed. The power that divisional managers have by virtue of their possession of the specific information needed to take non-programmed decisions suggests that planning by consent, rather than by authority, is needed. The information advantage that divisional management holds over top management in respect to operating activities is counter-balanced by top management's advantage in identifying strategic opportunities for growth, profitability, etc., for the firm as a whole. The move away from the role culture to the existential culture suggests that the AIS also needs to be adapted. For example, the regular checking of independent trade journals and economic forecasting agencies can provide information to moderate contentious assumptions. External scanning of the environments becomes of integral, rather than incidental, importance if challenging plans are to be based on agreed assumptions.

The involvement of divisional management in questioning the assumptions on which strategic plans are based suggests that the AIS in the multidivisional firm should be as much concerned with the effectiveness as with the efficiency of the company's plans. In Chapter 1, we stressed that to measure efficiency (or economy) it is pre-supposed that an activity is effective. In the uncertain environment surrounding the multidivisional firm, it appears essential that the AIS provides feed-forward control in order to ensure that the agreed actions are effective for both individual division's activities and the overall company's strategy. That is, that the agreed plan maintains the division within the feasible region of the firm. The increased communication and uncovering of key assumptions and variables that is envisaged by the planning procedure may serve to achieve this.

CONCLUSIONS

The growth of firms and their diversification into unrelated activities that encounter different environmental uncertainties results in the adoption of the multidivisional structure. The number of product market environments recognized by the enlarged firm renders infeasible day-to-day control by top management. Decentralization results in many non-programmed decisions being delegated to divisional managers. The explicit acknowledgement of uncertainty is reflected by information asymmetries, the most important for planning being the adverse selection problem. Control loss and opportunistic behaviour may be reduced by increasing the monitoring capabilities of top management and by developing incentive schemes for divisional managers. However, the costs of such schemes are not insignificant, and it is unlikely that they will totally eliminate opportunistic behaviour on the part of divisional managers. Therefore, the relationship developed between the divisional and top management is of great importance.

The design of an AIS that promotes participation is required if the beliefs and preferences of the different management levels are to be made mutually compatible. However, the dynamic nature of the environments interacting with the numerous participants who influence the feasible region of the enterprise's activities, makes the setting of clear objectives by top management extremely difficult. All that may be available is a strategy that will change the firm's profile over a span of time. The effectiveness of the proposed strategy depends on the attitude and commitment of divisional management, because the individual divisional manager has a superior predictive model of his product market environment. The AIS should encourage behaviour congruence and make the divisional manager aware of how his division is expected to contribute to the changes envisaged in the enterprise's profile. By having the assumptions, beliefs and preferences underpinning the strategy made explicit, divisional managers may recognize that they are able to make alterations to the strategy by disclosing the assumptions on which their own plans are made. A constructive dialogue between the management levels that concentrates on the assumptions of planned actions should promote consensus. This communication is thought to be essential in order to avoid the submission of biased plans by divisional management and the setting of irrelevant or unattainable divisional targets by top management.

The clear implication emerges that in the decentralized, multi-divisional structure, divisional managers are concerned as much with the effectiveness of their operations as with their efficiency. The effectiveness of the individual division within the agreed strategy of the overall firm must be the primary concern of the divisional manager. As a result, the design of the AIS needs to place greater emphasis on the requirements of an existential culture than of a role culture. In addition, there is a need to broaden the AIS to record the agreed key assumptions, whether expressed in quantitative or qualitative terms. The planning needs of firms in which the incidence of non-programmed decision taking is relatively high and low are shown in Table 8.4.

The table should be examined from top to bottom, indicating that the planning needs and aims of the AIS are contingent upon the

Table 8.4 A contingency framework for planning

| *Environmental uncertainty* | |
Great	**Low**
Growth into **unrelated** activities	Growth into **related** activities
Multidivisional organization structure	**Unitary** organization structure
Decentralized decision making	**Centralized** decision making
Incidence of non-programmed decisions is **high**	Incidence of non-programmed decisions is **low**
Planning requires **participation**	Planning does **not** require **participation**
Existential culture promoted	**Role** culture promoted
Aim of AIS to secure **effectiveness**	Aim of AIS to secure **efficiency**

different structural characteristics determining the incidence of non-programmed decisions. The two columns represent the extremes, and readers are reminded that a continuum of business enterprises will be represented in the intervening gap.

The low incidence of non-programmed decisions in the unitary structure suggests that the lower-level manager's tasks are set in a relatively stable, certain environment. Predictions of planned outcomes are provided as accurately by the top management as by the departmental managers. The coordination of distinct functions to serve a single or limited number of product markets suggests that only the top management will possess a complete planning model of the enterprise's activities. In these circumstances, allowing departmental managers to participate in planning may be counter-productive. Non-involvement eliminates the generation of biased targets and allows the role culture using accounting measures as formal controls to dominate. Accounting measures, such as standard costs and budget variances, appear quite appropriate to promote the efficiency of departmental activities undertaken in a stable environment, but much less appropriate for planning and control in a more uncertain environment.

EXERCISES

1. What are the structural causes of non-programmed decisions?
   Categorize the following as programmed or non-programmed decision takers, making your assumptions clear:
   (a) the local manager of a franchized fast-food restaurant.
   (b) the manager in charge of research and development in a large, decentralized company.
   (c) the manager in charge of the cold mill division, the last process in a steelmaking company.
   (d) the manager in charge of a division manufacturing and selling microcomputers.
   (e) the head of the accounting department within a large university.
   (f) the bar steward of a rugby club who is concerned about the number of helpers to employ on a regular basis.
2. What is information asymmetry?
   What are the problems that it highlights in planning?
3. The pursuit of sub-goals is a defect of the unitary structure that the multidivisional structure overcomes. Discuss.
4. 'Participation is a double-edged sword.' Clearly, explain and evaluate the significance of this statement will respect to planning in the decentralized, multidivisional structure.

5. In the context of planning, how consistent are the assumptions of the traditional AIS with the circumstances in which non-programmed decisions occur?
   What alterations, if any, would you recommend to the traditional AIS in a non-programmed situation?
6. (a) Participation in budget-setting both improves subsequent performance and avoids the problems of biased and manipulated information. Do you agree?
   (b) Nine independent operating units have the following expections of output and its variability during the coming year:

Unit	Expected output	Standard deviation
A	500	100
B	600	110
C	700	120
D	800	130
E	900	140
F	1000	150
G	1100	160
H	1200	170
ʜ	1300	180

Unit managers each submit estimates of output having a 16% chance of being exceeded. How likely is it that the total output estimate for the company will be met? (Assume the distribution of output to be Normal.)
Corporate management reduces the total estimate, so that it has a 16% chance of being exceeded by reducing each estimate pro rata. How likely is it now that each unit estimate will be met?
What are the implications for the design of budgetary systems?
   (c) Aggregation is one potential cause of control loss in large organizations. Identify other potential causes and evaluate the extent to which the multidivisional structure overcomes these problems.
7. The owner and managing director of Eaglet plc, a large, independent garage, is considering how to improve the company's management information system. The garage engages in 3 main activities: the sale of new cars under franchise, the sale of all makes of used cars and the repair and service of new, used and external customers' cars. Each activity has its own manager.

Outline the factors you would consider important in following the
alternative strategies of:

(a) a balanced dealership
(b) emphasizing new car sales
(c) emphasizing used car sales.

What are the implications under each strategy for the AIS?
8. Sennapods plc is contemplating an organizational restructuring.
   At present, the company is organized functionally, as follows:

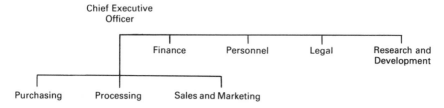

Sennapods plc has 3 main product ranges, health foods, medica-
tions for the National Health Service and agricultural fertilizers.
In terms of profitability, each of these product ranges is performing equally well and the growth prospects for each are
equally optimistic.
Required:
(a) Extend the existing functional organization to accommodate
    the product ranges. What problems of control loss may
    emerge?
(b) Devise an alternative multidivisional structure for Sennapods
    plc. Indicate the possible advantages and disadvantages of
    this structure.
(c) Under the multidivisional structure, provide justified
    arguments for a change in the management accounting
    performance measurement system highlighting the differences
    with the system likely to be used under the functionally
    organized structure.

9

Performance measurement and evaluation

SUMMARY

Financial performance measures provide quantitative and common yardsticks to evaluate achievement relative to a plan or to compare parts of the company. In that these reflect or are taken to reflect the achievement of the individual divisional manager, we can see that financial performance measures contribute to results controls, in particular.

The conventional use of profit performance measures is open to criticism in the multidivisional company. Quite apart from the variety of definitions of profit, all such measures can exhibit defects of incompleteness, inaccuracy and non-neutrality. Technical sophistications like residual income and divisional costs of capital offer some advantages but cannot in themselves ensure behaviour congruence. A wider perspective is required to examine performance measurement and evaluation in the organizational context. This recognition leads to the development of a contingency framework which includes financial performance measures and the importance of linked incentives and also personnel and monitoring devices and the style of evaluation.

INTRODUCTION

This chapter is divided into three sections. The first section outlines the conventional contribution that an AIS makes to management control. The measurement of the performance of the divisional management in practice is reviewed, and the connections between incentive schemes and accounting performance measures are examined, particularly the fundamental assumption that performance can be accurately measured by means of accounting information. In the second section, the potential defects of accounting measures of performance, namely that they are incomplete, inaccurate and non-neutral, are analysed. The repercussions of using the conventional AIS in the multidivisional company are outlined and some alternatives put forward. The third section presents alternative forms of performance measures, monitoring devices and styles of evaluation that are more appropriate to the aim of promoting behaviour congruence, and a contingency framework for performance evaluation is developed.

THE CONTRIBUTION OF THE AIS TO MANAGEMENT CONTROL

The conventional review of the contribution of the AIS to management control in divisionalized firms assumes (Gordon, 1964; Thomas, 1980b) that:

1. Divisional managers desire certain rewards that top management can give – e.g., esteem, increased perquisites, bonuses and promotion.
2. Divisional managers are led to understand that receipt of these rewards will be positively correlated with the performance of their divisions.
3. Divisional managers are left to maximize their self-interest by attaining or surpassing the performance measures set by top management.

Of fundamental importance in upholding this view is the assumption that accounting performance measures accurately reflect the decision-making capabilities of the divisional manager. A comparison of expected and actual performance highlights deviations from plans, and, with recourse to a predictive model, ways to avoid future deviations can be suggested. The accurate measurement of actual performance is important if this form of feedback control is to be effective. This form of management control assumes that accounting performance measures can help detect inefficiencies, and requires managers to be held accountable for them. Hence top management's use of accounting information for feedback control may reduce the incentives for opportunistic behaviour by divisional managers. The divisional managers' commitment to the targeted performance is motivated by the clear connection between 'good' performance and various desired rewards. It is therefore important to understand how such systems are used in practice, and we now turn to the empirical evidence to gauge the use made of the AIS in performance evaluation.

The extent of decentralization

Ideally, we would like to report empirical evidence relating to:

1. how the performance measures or targets are set.
2. how appropriate the measures are for performance evaluation.
3. how the measures are used in evaluating managers.

There is a disappointing dearth of such data, especially relating to the UK. Certainly, the US surveys suggest that divisional managers responsible for profit and investment centres are common within large companies, and Franko (1974) indicates that the trend towards such responsibility is increasing in Europe generally. Table 9.1 shows the results of four major surveys.

The definition of an investment centre adds to profit responsibility the attribute that the manager 'to some significant extent can influence the size of the investment base' (Mauriel and Anthony, 1966, p. 99). An earlier study reported by Solomons (1965) indicated that multidivisional companies divide more or less equally into those that delegate wide powers of discretion to divisional managers and those in which top management retains considerable authority. Table 9.1 may therefore include 'pseudo' profit or investment centres whose performance is expressed in profit terms, but over which the divisional manager has little control.

Ezzamel and Hilton (1980a, 1980b) investigated the degree of autonomy allowed divisional managers in 129 large UK companies and found that only limited discretion was granted in determining the methods of budgetary control and internal audit procedures. Close supervision by top management in choosing capital projects and specifying capital expenditures in the annual budget was ob-

Table 9.1   Incidence of decentralization

	Mauriel & Anthony (1966) (USA)	*Reece & Cool (1978) (USA)*	*Vancil (1979) (USA)*	*Tomkins (1973) (UK)*
Total companies contacted	3525	1000	684	200
Total response percentage	75.4%	62%	46%	32.5%
who have profit centres	20.9	21.8	13.0	40.5
who have investment centres	60.3	74.0	82.0	38.0
who have neither	18.8	4.2	5.0	21.5

served. However, divisional managers enjoyed substantial discretion in taking operating decisions relating to output, selling prices, setting credit terms, advertising and purchasing policies.

Vancil's (1979) study represents the most comprehensive analysis to date of gauging divisional autonomy. In common with the other studies, Vancil collected data by means of postal questionnaire. An initial structured questionnaire was followed by an 'autonomy' questionnaire sent to each of three 'typical' profit centre managers in companies who had responded to the structured questionnaire. Based on the responses of 291 companies to the structured questions, profit centre managers were found to have physical custody over a substantial pool of functional resources, such as research and development, distribution, sales, manufacturing and administrative services. Most notably, this authority increased substantially for managers in diversified companies in comparison with profit centre managers in unitary structured, single-business companies. The autonomy of the manager in a diversified company to make product, personnel, sourcing and other decisions is also greater than that of his counterpart in the single-business organization.

In the UK, Tomkins expanded the questionnaire used by the NICB (1961) to gauge the degree of autonomy possessed by the divisional manager. Less than half of the respondents had significant influence over capital investment, with corporate approval being required for expenditure above a fairly low limit. However, most enjoyed complete freedom in forecasting economic conditions in the division's particular industry and in setting prices, sales targets and production levels. The authority of divisional managers to arrange long-term loans and to maintain relations with banks was constrained, although their autonomy over setting credit terms, discounts and working capital ratios appeared to be greater than their counterparts in the USA, as was indicated by the earlier NICB survey.

The evidence from both sides of the Atlantic thus points to the existence of both profit and investment centres. It is debatable whether all the companies surveyed are truly divisionalized in the sense that lower-level managers not only decide how their activities will be conducted, but also what those activities are. There is evidence, however, to suggest that divisionalization is more common in companies having diversified activities than when a single, dominant or related set of activities is undertaken.

The setting of performance targets

The most common measures of performance used are the rate of return on investment (ROI) and residual income (RI), as shown in

Table 9.2   Performance measures in practice

	Mauriel & Anthony (1966)	Reece & Cool (1978)	Tomkins (1973)
ROI only	60%	65%	–
Both ROI and RI	20%	28%	65%
RI only	7%	2%	–
Other criterion	–	4%	33%
No answer	13%	1%	2%

Table 9.2. RI is defined as the net earnings less a charge for the cost of capital employed. Mauriel and Anthony (1966) asked what general criteria were used to determine the target rate or acceptable performance range for a given investment centre. The most frequent response was that the target was based on the business, industry or competitive conditions pertaining to that division. An almost equal number of companies required each division to meet a corporate rate of return. Then, in decreasing order of popularity, the past performance of the division, the corporate rate of return plus a percentage, the corporate cost of capital and future potential or budgeted profit were given as the bases of setting targets. Reece and Cool (1978) argued that a budgeted target is only developed after budgeted sales, profits and assets are approved by top management, and consequently the past performance of the division and the uniform corporate rate of return played only a minor role. In their survey, most respondents set target performance measures based on the individual division's profit potential. Only 7% expected all divisions to meet the corporate rate of return, but surprisingly almost a quarter did not set any targets. The reason for an undefined criterion or an instruction 'to do your best' may be an attempt to avoid overemphasizing the accounting performance measure and the consequences of opportunistic behaviour.

The Ezzamel and Hilton (1980a, 1980b) and the Vancil (1979) surveys do not address the question of the specific performance measure used, although Vancil indicates that the investment base is included by most companies. The tentative conclusion may be drawn from these studies that top management involvement in setting accounting performance measures or targets is rarely absent, but that the precise extent of divisional management involvement has yet to be determined.

Most companies in all these surveys seem to favour ROI as the appropriate measure of performance. It is worth noting that although

Mauriel and Anthony (1966, p. 105) found that 'the rules and pro-cedures established for guiding financial accounting or external reporting to shareholders strongly influence the methods adopted for investment centre accounting', Reece and Cool found that expenses outside the control of the divisional manager were excluded. Whether generally accepted accounting principles (GAAP) or the responsibility structure within the company form the framework on which profit is calculated is important. The former suggests an external use of the information, whereas the latter, an internal use. In several respects, both uses cannot be appropriately served by a single profit figure.

In Vancil's study, where nearly all the companies used GAAP, the two major design flaws managers perceived were:

1. a mis-match between the items over which the manager has ef-fective control and the items for which he is held accountable;
2. the arbitrary allocation of corporate overheads and the changes in accounting policy.

Most companies assign central research and development, and finance and accounting costs, to profit centres. It is also more likely that interest expense and tax will be allocated to the profit centres of diversified companies than to their counterparts in single, dominant or related activity enterprises.

Allocation in practice

The allocation problem is irrelevant if companies and managers do not use such accounting information in internal decision making. The National Association of Accountants' study (1957) contains some em-pirical evidence to suggest that companies do not. However, Baumes (1963) found that 53% of the 158 companies he studied allocated all 'central expenses' to divisions, whereas an additional 36% made partial allocations. A significant number of these companies then re-allocated the central expenses to product lines or products. The Reece and Cool survey showed that only 3% of the companies used direct costing rather than full, absorption costing. Perhaps the most pertinent evidence is contained in a British Institute of Management Survey Report (BIM, 1974). Of the 273 UK companies participating in this study, 81% charged all or part of central expenses to the divisions or subsidiaries. The main reasons given for this were that it helped to ascertain divisions' real profits (71% of respondents), that it showed the divisional manager the true cost of operating his division (67%) and that it helped with the costing and pricing of divisional products and services (50%). Of the 37% of companies that charged out only part of central costs, the most important aims were to cover the administrative costs of those central services, which would otherwise have to be provided by the divisions themselves, and to control the growth of central services.

The survey found that in almost all companies, variance analysis was carried out in respect of the central costs, and appeared to form part of the on-going budgetary control system. Not surprisingly, the charges of central costs tended to create adverse reactions in the divisions. Personal interviews with 20 subsidiaries or divisions indicated that acceptance was conditioned by the control that divisions believed they exercised over the charge and the degree to which they were held responsible for it. Also important were the extent of group identity, the size of the charge and the degree of control exercised centrally over the growth of central services.

Only 19% of the respondent companies in the BIM survey did not charge central expenses to the divisions or subsidiaries. The reasons given were either that divisional management had no control over central costs or that there was no suitable basis for allocation or apportionment. Possibly the most disturbing evidence to emerge from this study relates to the changes that occurred in company practices. From 1969 to 1974 a quarter of the companies changed their policies either to introduce or to extend the system of absorption costing. By contrast, in the same time period 23% changed their methods in order to render the charges made more controllable by the division and to avoid arbitrariness and disputes. Although the fairness of any allocation method depends on the subjective judgement of a divisional manager, there is widespread academic agreement that the practice is useless for planning and evaluation purposes, and is wholly arbitrary and needless (see Thomas, 1980b, for a review of this literature). The BIM (1974, p. 40) survey concludes that:

Profit centre accounting in some form is accepted by a large number of companies. However, the results suggest it is not always used to full advantage in controlling management service costs (both at the centre and within units); nor does it always incorporate the principles of 'responsibility accounting' to the full since many profit centres have to accept the charges without involvement in their calculation or right of appeal.

The findings of Tomkins' survey also substantiate these claims, and further cause for concern is provided by Vancil's (1979, p. 105) conclusion that:

Corporate managers do use the calculation of profit to influence the behaviour of each profit center manager, and the message they are sending to him in deciding to assign the costs of shared resources is that the scope of his initiative should not be restricted solely to the resources for which he has functional authority.

In addition, top management seemed to assess the viability of the profit centre on a total cost basis that included allocated costs. As a result, it appears that financial responsibility always exceeds the delegated authority of the divisional manager, although this is a matter of degree, and can be mitigated in several ways.

Firstly, managers in multidivisional companies tend to have physical custody over a wide range of facilities, and this reduces the amount of central service charges that need to be allocated. Secondly, the decision to allocate central expenses varies with the type of service provided. In some companies, none of the central research and development costs are assigned to profit centres. Vancil found that 87% of companies allocated electronic data processing costs, whereas 60% charge profit centres for public relations, operations research and top management services. Lastly, the basis of allocating different costs varies. Actual usage, negotiation and apportionment on sales revenues or assets appeared to be the three most common methods.

The diversity of practices is bewildering, but despite the virtually unanimous academic agreement that joint- or common-cost allocations should not be used in internal decision making, there is disquieting evidence to suggest that they are. Any performance measure that incorporates non-controllable cost allocations is imperfect when used to evaluate the performance of a divisional manager. The problem may be overcome, as Horngren (1982) shows, by excluding such allocations from the manager's performance measure although allowing them to remain in the divisional measure.

Profit performance, evaluation and rewards

Ezzamel and Hilton's study revealed that over half their respondents used the profit performance measure as one of the major factors in deciding whether to promote a divisional manager. Virtually all the companies surveyed used the performance measures in evaluating the future viability of the divisions. The earlier US studies offer no insights except that 'many companies tie their executive compensation programs to the size and trend of divisions' ROI ratios' (Mauriel and Anthony, 1966, p. 103).

The most extensive evidence relating rewards to financial performance measures is provided by Vancil's study. Annual bonuses were received by 90% of the managers in this survey, and current financial performance played an important role in determining the annual bonus. For two-thirds of the managers, the size of the bonus was calculated by means of a defined formula rather than the subjective judgement of the superior manager. From a total of 282 profit centre managers, 30% believed the bonus was determined solely by financial performance and a further 35% believed it to be partly determined in this way. Even when there was no defined formula, 18% still perceived financial performance to be very important, 13% that it was somewhat important with only 4% believing that it was not important in determining rewards. The annual bonus also seemed to comprise a significant part of the manager's income and the median bonus amounted to 25% of annual salary in these companies. Vancil argues that psychic rewards, such as self-esteem and recognition by one's peers and superior, are reinforced by the annual bonus. Although limited, the available empirical evidence thus suggests that financial performance measures are an important element in determining the tangible and intangible rewards of divisional managers in the USA. The incidence of reward and incentive schemes associated with accounting performance measures in the UK is less well documented. However, it would appear that even if managers merely perceive the performance measures as part of an evaluation procedure not linked in any strict way to rewards, the measures still carry the potential to be used to attach blame or inflict penalties.

Controllable performance measures

Our earlier review of the empirical evidence revealed that rate of return on investment (ROI) and residual income (RI) appear to be the most popular measures used in practice. The question now to be answered is whether companies formally distinguish in their evaluation and measurement systems between the performance of the manager and the performance of the economic unit? This is not a trivial question because, as Solomons (1965) notes, the brightest managers are sometimes promoted to turn around the lamest divisions. If a budget-constrained style of evaluation is used and no distinction is made between the manager and the division in measuring performance, then bias and manipulation of accounting reports seem rational responses.

Again, the empirical evidence is limited. Reece and Cool (1978, p. 46) comment that: 'many investment managers ... feel that their superiors at corporate headquarters do not adequately make this economic – managerial performance distinction when they evaluate these investment centre managers' performance', and Vancil's evidence corroborates this finding. In the British context, Tomkins provides evidence that the same measures are used to evaluate the divisions and the divisional management. The most common measures used are return on capital, net residual income before taxes and controllable operating profit. Tomkins found that over 90% of the companies used more than one measure to evaluate managerial and divisional performance and that over 50% used three or more measures. Further, his respondents indicated that monthly financial reporting to the central office is common. The actual and budgeted details of production, sales and other individual elements of the profit calculation are included in the evaluation process, which suggests that managers may have the opportunity to substantiate the reasons for their decisions. However, 'no company referred to the need for a different evaluation for the divisional manager' (Tomkins, 1973, p. 168), and the same measures seem to be used to evaluate both managerial and economic performance. These findings are in direct contradiction to the exhortations of academic writers such as Solomons (1965) and Shillinglaw (1977), who argue that separate performance measures are an essential prerequisite to effective responsibility accounting.

Further, the calculation of profit by multidivisional companies appears to be subject to significant differences of interpretation and various measures of profit can be defined, as shown in Table 9.3. Net income determined by GAAP includes tax, interest and the allocation of central expenses in its calculations. Mauriel and Anthony (1966, p. 105) offer no details but state 'that generally accepted principles for calculating corporate profit and investment are also applied to investment centre accounting'. In the UK reliance on GAAP appears to be less with different profit measures being used more frequently.

Table 9.3 Definitions of divisional profit in practice

Alternative definitions of divisional profit	Reece & Cool (1978)	Tomkins (1973)
Net income under GAAP	40%	10%
Controllable profit	2	19
Controllable RI before tax	2	5
Net RI	2	21
Net profit before tax	10	14
Net profit before tax, interest and central allocations	25	5
Net profit before tax, interest and after central allocations	18	24
No answer	1	2

The most concrete conclusion is that multidivisional companies are either still experimenting with alternative profit performance measures or that they adopt different measures depending on their perception of which is most appropriate.

Overall, the combined results of these surveys give cause for concern. At the risk of oversimplifying, the typical multidivisional company uses some form of profit measure to evaluate divisional and managerial performance. No distinction is made between measuring divisional and managerial performance, and it is likely that allocated costs will be included in both the accounting measures. Divisional management are rewarded on the basis of their actual profit performance compared with budget or by interdivisional comparisons of similar performance measures. It therefore appears that the use of the AIS to contribute to management control, in practice, closely follows the conventional view of Gordon and Thomas, outlined earlier.

POTENTIAL DEFECTS OF ACCOUNTING PERFORMANCE MEASURES

For the conventional AIS to fulfil its potential contribution to management control effectively, it is necessary for complete, accurate and neutral accounting performance measures to be developed. Some of the problems likely to be encountered when applying the conventional AIS to non-programmed decision making are as follows:

1. *Completeness:*
   (a) corporate and divisional goals can only be selected in those areas where quantitative, financial performance information is available (Mintzberg, 1975);
   (b) the control mechanism stresses short-term performance measurement which may not reflect the long-term trend (Hopwood, 1974);
   (c) the performance measure is a surrogate and disguises the variability and interdependence of the component parts (Ijiri *et al.*, 1966).
2. *Accuracy:*
   (a) the targeted performance measure is set in an unfair manner and does not reflect a reasonably attainable standard (Hofstede, 1968);
   (b) the comparison of targeted and actual performance provides variances that can be interpreted ambiguously (Hopwood, 1974);
   (c) the valuation rules based on GAAP are inappropriate for internal control purposes (Solomons, 1965).

3. *Neutrality:*
   (a) the performance measure does not reflect managerial effort, only results (Drucker, 1964a);
   (b) the performance measure is effected by interdependencies and decisions taken elsewhere in the company (Shillinglaw, 1977);
   (c) the rigid style of evaluation, concentrating on the accounting performance measure, causes opportunistic behaviour (Hopwood, 1974).

In the dynamic environment in which non-programmed decisions are taken, several of these potential defects may combine to make the overall effectiveness of accounting performance measures highly questionable. Several of the defects can be traced to one major attribute of the non-programmed decision, namely the inability to predict outcomes accurately.

The impact of inaccurate prediction

In an uncertain environment, top management cannot precisely define the actions it wishes divisional managers to take, and hence it cannot specify their precise area of autonomy. When circumstances are very changeable, it may be necessary to allow divisional managers to set their own targets. In more stable circumstances, top management may use past performance records or the performance of independent, external companies as reference points to influence divisional targets. No clear guideline on what constitutes an appropriate level of expected performance can be given, save that divisional managers should perceive it as fair, and can thus commit themselves to it. Allowing divisional management to participate in planning and target-setting is more likely to achieve this commitment than merely handing down targets from top management to the divisions. Even the appropriateness of an undefined target, as for example an instruction to improve on the last period's performance, should be open to questioning by divisional management in order to discover the basis on which top management believes this to be feasible.

The divisional manager's perception of the completeness of the performance measure in reflecting the agreed target should be considered. Accounting measures of performance may be subject to more inaccuracy than measures expressed in other terms. The profit performance measure may be regarded as inadequate by the manager of a division developing a new product line, introducing new technology or new work methods. He may perceive productivity data as more important initially and marketing effectiveness as more important at a later stage. When the division reaches a more mature position, profit measures may still be less than complete indicators of the effectiveness of his personnel and labour relations policies, the internal communication system and the social roles in the local community that he has developed. He may argue that the results of these efforts will only become apparent in the long term and that his performance and the division's are not synonomous. For a contrasting view of the validity of distinguishing managerial and divisional performance measures, see Demski (1976). The manager's perception of the completeness of the performance measure also depends on how it is influenced by allocations of joint costs and transfer pricing practices, and how significant an impact these inter-dependencies have.

Additionally, the manager's perception of the evaluation process and the provision of rewards is conditioned by its predictability. The traditional feedback control mechanism compares budgeted or targeted performance with actual performance to evaluate managerial effort. The resultant variances may be due to a combination of conceptual errors in the predictive model, unforeseen environmental changes, intentionally biased forecasts and managerial inefficiencies (Horngren, 1982). The 'management by exception' evaluation that budgeting allows seems inappropriate when the inter-relationship between the division and its environment is uncertain. Without an accurate prediction of outcomes, performance evaluation by comparing budgeted and actual accounting measures appears of dubious merit. As Hopwood (1974, p. 107) suggests, 'the problem is insoluble . . . but if such a (predictive) model existed might not the manager be redundant'.

Management perceptions

The evidence gathered by cross-sectional analysis and postal questionnaires is especially weak in eliciting details of personal feelings and beliefs. Nevertheless, it offers some insights into divisional managers' perceptions of accounting performance measures and their association with reward schemes.

In Vancil's (1979) survey, over a third of the profit centre managers recognized profit performance measures as incomplete, and certainly not all-inclusive reflections of long-term potential. Another frequent response concerned the measures' inability to handle changing environmental conditions. Managers wanted to know how well they had done, but many felt that a comparison with the budget was misleading. Over a quarter of the respondents gave comments similar to the following (Vancil, 1979, p. 91):

My profit performance last year may not have looked good compared to my budget or even to prior years, but in the light of chaotic conditions that existed in our industry, I think my performance was outstanding.

In addition, the failure of the performance measures adequately to handle structural interdependencies contributed to the managers' perception of the unfairness of the measurement system. As a result, Vancil found that only 42% of the managers regarded the profit they earned as a fair reflection of their performance.

When a link between incomplete performance measures and rewards is perceived to apply, non-neutral behaviour may be induced. The use of a budget-constrained style of evaluation based on the manager's ability continually to meet the budget on a short-term basis appears inconsistent with the reasons for divisionalization. It represents an attempt to superimpose a rigid control mechanism on a non-programmed decision. Given that rewards are perceived to be conditional upon meeting budgeted levels of performance, divisional managers may be motivated to indulge in opportunistic behaviour owing to the unfairness they perceive in the control mechanism. Behavioural theorists claim that rewards used to motivate managers may result in managers charging items to incorrect accounts or time periods, adjusting the timing of reports and generally submerging detailed information that may prove harmful to the claiming of the reward (see Chapter 3). It can be argued that they are responding in a rational manner to the imperfect performance measures and the rigid evaluation use. Hence one of the aims of the behaviour congruent AIS may not be met, namely that performance measures will not encourage divisional managers to operate in the best interests of the organization.

Drucker (1961) pin-points a major defect in this use of performance measures. Although a resurrected Isaac Newton could still watch apples falling off a tree and observe the effect of gravity, when we try to measure human performance, the mere act of observation may change the behaviour observed. It is unrealistic to believe that people will supply information that may adversely affect their own well-being. That is, information is always oriented towards the production of outcomes that are desired by the sender, and in situations that are complex and/or uncertain, there is no guaranteed method of overcoming this.

Imagine yourself in the position of a divisional manager whose position depends, at least in part, on attaining a targeted profit performance. If the target is not achieved, you believe that your promotion or bonus will be adversely affected, and your status as a competent manager may be lost if top management assigns a headquarters team to help you operate your division. You are aware that the performance measure is an imperfect reflection of the effort you make and yet, the company evaluates your short-term performance in this way.

Outlining the imperfections of the present system to the top management may prove effective. It may also isolate you if no other divisional manager has complained. Top management will be in a very difficult position if an alternative means of evaluating your performance *vis-à-vis* other divisional heads is agreed. 'Besides, this has always been the way in the past, and you've lived with it up until now' seems a likely reply to maintain the existing system.

The least troublesome action is to manipulate actual performance, or reports of actual performance, so that it accords with the target. Such practices as charging costs to incorrect accounts and delaying repairs are not uncommon under the budget-constrained style of evaluation (Hopwood, 1974). Stockpiling excess production to supplement a future period's low productivity, trimming quality control and other discretionary costs or shifting those resources to other uses are some of the other options available to the divisional manager. Alternatively, the manager may avoid taking decisions that reduce his short-term performance, by ignoring opportunity costs and including allocated costs, even though acceptance of the decisions would be in the company's best interests (Thomas, 1980b).

The manipulation of actual results is only one side of the coin. On the obverse is the possibility of biasing the target itself, and non-programmed decisions offer plenty of scope for this (see Chapter 7). Essentially, it is the non-programmed nature of the tasks involved that renders the attachment of rewards or blame to variances meaningless. An accurate model of the division's relationship with its environment is needed if variances due to the manager's efforts as opposed to uncontrollable environmental factors are to be distinguished. Using participation as a means of obtaining reasonably accurate information for divisional target setting is completely futile if a budget-constrained style of evaluation is subsequently employed. Divisional managers will be acting rationally by manipulating actual results and biasing the targets. As Dearden (1962a, p. 87) has stated:

There is thus a conflict between the planning and control uses of the budget. To motivate the best possible level of actual performance the budget must be set at a level above that which will, on average, be attained. Adverse budget variances will thus be generated, but these are a sign that the budget system is working as intended. A budget that is always achieved with no adverse variances indicates that the standards are too loose to motivate the best possible results. To obtain the desired motivational effects from an appropriately set budget target thus requires that adverse budget variances are treated appropriately; small adverse variances are a healthy sign and should not be treated as something to be avoided.

An important implication of these findings is that the budget level which motivates the best performance is one that is somewhat more demanding than the level of performance that will actually be achieved. However, a budget that is likely to be achieved will motivate only a lower level of performance, as shown in Fig. 9.1. The budget level that most usually motivates the optimum results (a challenging target accepted by the manager) is in excess of the average performance actually attained by that manager. But if it is reduced to a less demanding level, actual performance also decreases.

Under a profit centre system, the divisional manager is expected to improve the profits of his division. It should not be any surprise if he takes the most direct route toward this accomplishment.

In summary, the application of the conventional AIS to the multi-divisional company will result in behaviour congruence only by coincidence if the profit measure is incomplete, inaccurate or non-neutral. This is because:

1. the manager's responsibility under the AIS always appears to be greater than the autonomy and discretion he has; and
2. the emphasis on short-term performance and the provision of rewards may encourage self-interest and the manipulation of performance standards and/or measures.

Before considering alternative forms of AIS which may promote behaviour congruence and effective management control, it will prove useful to examine the role of the divisional accountant.

The divisional accountant

It may be argued that for rigid evaluation procedures to be useful they must be accompanied by strict central monitoring to detect biased estimates and manipulated reports. The burden of such monitoring is likely to fall on the accounting staff. In the non-programmed situation, the accountant may not only be required to fulfil the role of a watchdog, but also to act as a bloodhound to discover the basis on which the divisional manager has constructed his budget. As Golembiewski (1964) and others have noted, this emphasis on score-card keeping and stewardship is likely to occur at the cost of providing information for managerial decision making and attention directing.

Sathe (1978b) provides evidence that accountants who report directly to the head office chief accountant are more likely to give priority to information that stresses central regulations than are those who report to a divisional or subsidiary manager. In the latter instance, the information needs of the division tend to be given precedence. By decentralizing the accounting function, the accountant becomes part of the management team at the division and provides a broader range of management services designed to improve self-control (Hofstede, 1968). However, such close personal contact may encourage the accountant to collude in the manipulation of control data flowing upwards (Schiff and Lewin, 1970). Empirical research conducted by Hopper (1980) has revealed that when the accounting function is decentralized, lower-level and divisional managers interact more with accountants, assess the accountant's performance more favourably and tend to use the accounting information more. Interestingly, Hopper found line managers who freely admitted to the manipulation of accounting information only in organizations having a centralized accounting function. The negative and defensive attitudes engendered by the emphasis on score-card keeping and evaluation led one department to operate its own accounting system as a source of information for decision making and to challenge the results of the official system! (Hopper, 1980). Limited though the evidence is, it does suggest that centralization of the accounting function narrows its role to one of primarily score-card keeping, and results in managerial distrust of accountants and the information they provide. To expect accountants to act as bloodhounds and to check the details of divisional performance records is likely to cause open conflict and to place the accountant in an invidious position.

TOWARDS A CONTINGENCY FRAMEWORK: PERFORMANCE EVALUATION

Recognition that accounting performance measures are incomplete, inaccurate and non-neutral for non-programmed decision making does not necessarily mean that the AIS should be abandoned in multi-divisional companies. Modifications in the way profit is measured, expressed and used may improve the effectiveness of the AIS. Expanding the evaluation process to include both quantitative but non-financial measures, and qualitative information, may usefully augment the accounting information. Further, some of the monitoring devices developed in personnel management may be used. Any or all of these alternatives may have a part to play in improving the fit of the AIS with the multidivisional structure and non-programmed decision taking. In addition, modifications to profit measurement calculations, reward schemes and evaluation styles may improve the effectiveness of the AIS in restraining managerial self-interest.

The use of performance measures

One avenue to explore is to change the style by which performance is evaluated. Hopwood's profit-conscious style (see Chapter 7) advocates using budgetary information in a careful and flexible manner, with the manager's ability to improve the effectiveness of the division being assessed by the trend of performance over time. This may avoid some of the worst effects of short-term performance evaluation, and indeed, Hopwood found that this style resulted in less manipulation of accounting reports. However, accounting information still remained the prime means of evaluation, and to avoid the neutrality problem it may be appropriate for separate measures of managerial and divisional performance to be developed.

The concept underlying responsibility accounting is disarmingly simple: 'that costs should be borne by, and revenues should be credited to, the segments of the business responsible for them' (Solomons, 1965, p. 55). Where the responsibility for the incurrence of a cost is shared by two divisions, it should be charged to the division that will accept the invoice or pay the labour, but an offsetting charge to the benefiting division should also be made. As Solomons (1965, p. 54) states:

This accounting activity is concerned not only with the evaluation of past performance but also, importantly, with the motivation of managers to conduct their operations in a manner calculated to serve the best interests of the company as a whole.

So responsibility accounting is designed to promote behaviour congruence by distinguishing financial results that are controllable by the divisional manager from those that are non-controllable, although this is difficult to apply in practice.

Normally, accounting texts stress the analysis of budget variances as a means of control. Even in the programmed situation, where budgets can be determined accurately, problems can arise. For example, does the materials price variance reflect the performance of the purchasing manager, and the materials efficiency variance the performance of the production manager? By purchasing at lower than the standard price, the purchasing manager can ensure a favourable variance. If this results is sub-standard materials being used in production, the actual quantity used may increase, thereby increasing the favourable price variance reported still further. Conversely, a favourable materials efficiency variance may be due to the production manager's insistence on higher quality material than is required. In judging who is responsible for a cost, it may be necessary to distinguish between responsibility for the standard cost and responsibility for the ensuing variance. These difficulties are compounded when standard costs include indirect costs.

Divisional overheads will normally include items of indirect supplies, indirect labour and services, such as those offered by the central computer department, power plant, etc., whose usage may be controlled by the divisional manager. The rate at which these services are charged may be pre-determined, and probably is set by top management or the service department. The user division only controls the use made of the service, and a variance expressed in physical, not financial, terms may be more reflective of the divisional manager's responsibility. However, even this variance may be inconsistent with divisional responsibility for the amount of service used depends on its quality and its availability, both of which are factors that the divisional manager does not control.

In addition, the division may be allocated central overheads. These include items such as corporation tax, head office and administration expenses, and finance costs that are incurred for the common benefit of all divisions and are then allocated to the divisions on some 'incorrigible' basis. The term 'incorrigible' is used by Thomas (1974, 1978) to emphasize that all methods of allocation are essentially unverifiable and irrefutable. The most recent analysis from this author concludes that 'no individual allocation method even approaches being reliably behaviour-congruent with respect to all decisions and circumstances' (Thomas, 1980b, p. 111). Nine allocation methods are subjected to a rigorous analysis to determine their ability to guide managers to corporately optimal decisions, and also their propensity to guide managers to accept decisions that are not corporate optimal. At this stage, we highlight just one conclusion (Thomas, 1980b, p. 9) of the study, namely that:

most joint-cost allocation methods tend to confuse the central office's evaluation of divisions, products and division managers by violating a key tenet of responsibility accounting: that the figures used in such evaluations should reflect only the division's, product's or manager's efforts and accomplishments (as distinct from those of others).

Only the 'democratic method' that divides all joint costs equally among divisions is consistently behaviour congruent for evaluation purposes. Actions taken by other divisions will not adversely or beneficially affect a division's evaluation, nor will actions taken by the individual division to improve efficiency rebound upon it in the form of an increased cost allocation. Hence, the concept of responsibility accounting requires interdependent decisions to be recognized and may give rise to more complete performance measures being calculated if allocated costs are specified as controllable or non-controllable. However, it should be noted that there is an alternative view that allocations provide useful information to divisional managers of the total costs that their operations are required to cover (Zimmerman, 1979).

Zimmerman offers an explanation for the widespread practice of allocating costs by means of two arguments. The first identifies cost allocations as useful ways to constrain managers' consumption of perquisites. Based on Williamson's (1964) concept of managerial utility and placed in an agency framework, it is argued that allocations represent a lump-sum tax which reduces the divisional manager's discretion to increase staff, re-furnish offices, etc. This occurs because financial performance measures are lowered and the potential to share in any incentive scheme is reduced. The second argument identifies allocations as approximations of 'difficult-to-observe' costs. When, for example, a long distance telephone line is shared and no allocation is made, incorrect over-use of this facility will result in additional costs to the firm. These costs arise because the service is degraded, managers find the line occupied and have to wait. To avoid this, managers may turn to telex, fax or other costly means of communicating. Allocating the costs of the long distance telephone line may proxy these 'difficult-to-observe' opportunity costs and constrain excessive mis-use.

Under either argument, it is not intended to demonstrate an optimal cost allocation, but rather to explain why allocations persist in practice. Allocation of costs will be rational as long as the costs of administering allocations are less than the costs of perquisite consumption and the costs incurred due to degraded service. Viewed from this perspective, it may be argued that allocations of cost are consistent with the notion of behaviour congruence. That is, managers' actions are positively affected by the allocation to take decisions consistent with the company's overall interests. At a different plane of debate, however, the actual allocation of costs may cause managers to make dysfunctional decisions, as Thomas (1980b) illustrates.

Additionally, the choice of the profit measure used can promote behaviour congruence by being a relatively complete measure for evaluative purposes. The choice of profit measure to be adopted by multidivisional companies has been the subject of intermittent debate since 1965, when Solomons published the General Electric

Company's method of residual income (RI). We will deal with the relatively short-term aspects of this debate here, and analyse the claim that RI has the 'maximization of the discounted present value of the enterprise' as its long-run counterpart in Chapter 12.

The RI versus ROI debate

Residual income is the excess of net earnings over the cost of capital employed. It is therefore an absolute profit performance measure rather than a rate, and it is also the only profit performance measure that explicitly provides a separate measure for divisional and managerial performances. Controllable RI before taxes is suggested as the measure of managerial performance and net RI before or after taxes as the measure used to evaluate the division. It therefore appears to be consistent with the aims of responsibility accounting.

There is broad agreement that controllable profit or controllable contribution is an appropriate measure of performance for profit center managers. The differences of opinion arise when considering investment centre managers. Traceable profit (the lower left-hand column of Table 9.4) rests upon the conventional cost accounting concept that all costs and revenues that can be unambiguously identified with the division should be included in the performance measure (Amey and Egginton, 1973). The alternative performance measure, Controllable RI, rests upon the concept of controllability and emphasizes responsibility accounting (the lower right-hand column of Table 9.4), a distinction clearly argued by Samuels (1970). On the one hand, there is Amey's view (1969, p. 145) that 'in the interests of achieving the firm's overall objective, divisions should not ... have the power to determine their own capital investment', whereas, on the other hand, Solomons (1965, p. 77) believes that 'divisions have a much greater degree of control over important segments of their total investment than, for instance, a plant manager in a centralized company'. The implications of these conflicting views for the combined effects on short-term evaluation of performance and capital investment decisions will be studied in Chapter 12. For the moment, we concentrate on the short-term comparison of RI and ROI.

The measures as targets

RI is argued to provide a better guide for divisional management decision making than ROI. In terms of developing a target, the level of the standard set is equally problematic, regardless of whether ROI

Table 9.4 Alternative forms of divisional profit measures (adapted from Solomons, 1965, and Amey and Egginton, 1973)

Sales to outside customers		XXX
Internal sales		XXX
		XXX
Less Variable costs of goods sold externally and internally		XXX
Variable divisional expenses		XXX
CONTROLLABLE CONTRIBUTION		XXX
Less Controllable divisional overhead		XXX
CONTROLLABLE PROFIT		XXX

Less Depreciation and expenses on divisional fixed assets	XXX		Less Depreciation on controllable fixed assets		XXX
Non-controllable divisional overheads	XXX		Expenses (e.g., leases) relating to controllable fixed assets		XXX
			Interest on controllable investments		XXX
TRACEABLE PROFIT	XXX		CONTROLLABLE RESIDUAL INCOME BEFORE TAXES		XXX
Less Allocated central expense	XXX		Less Depreciation on non-controllable fixed assets		XXX
			Allocated central expenses		XXX
			Interest on non-controllable investments		XXX
NET PROFIT	XXX		NET RESIDUAL INCOME BEFORE TAXES		XXX
Less Taxation on divisional income	XXX		Less Taxation on divisional income		XXX
NET PROFIT AFTER TAX	XXX		NET RESIDUAL INCOME AFTER TAXES		XXX

or RI is used. However, it is possible that a target expressed in RI terms will guide divisional managers more clearly towards a level of operations consistent with a particular investment base than will ROI. This suggests that the RI performance measure is neutral, and will avoid directing divisional managers to take decisions not in the company's best interests. This planning advantage stems largely

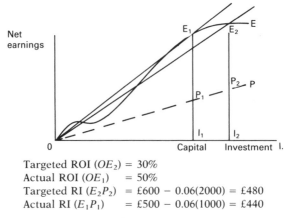

Targeted ROI (OE_2) = 30%
Actual ROI (OE_1) = 50%
Targeted RI (E_2P_2) = £600 − 0.06(2000) = £480
Actual RI (E_1P_1) = £500 − 0.06(1000) = £440

Fig. 9.1 RI and ROI targets.

from the fact that the RI target states an absolute profit figure, whereas ROI sets a rate. This may be shown by considering Fig. 9.1.

Let the set target be expressed by the point E_2, with the ROI required being the slope of the line OE_2. The broken line, OP, is the cost of capital and we assume that OI, the capital investment base, is subject to significant influence by the divisional manager. In its simplest form, the argument runs that the divisional manager given the ROI target can improve upon it by cutting his level of investment from I_2 to I_1 and achieve a return indicated by the slope of the line OE_1. The slope of OE_1 is greater than OE_2 and hence indicates a better ROI. However, any movement away from I_2 may cause the RI, represented by E_2P_2, to fall.

To demonstrate this numerically, let us assume that:

$$I_1 = £1000 \qquad I_2 = £2000$$
$$E_1 = £500 \qquad E_2 = £600$$
$$P \text{ is a constant } 6\%.$$

At the extreme, the divisional manager given a target in ROI terms could operate at the initial kink of the earnings curve and still obtain or improve upon the target set. The RI associated with this level of investment will clearly indicate that this was not the level of operation intended by the target set. The ROI target gives only ambiguous guidance to the manager who is able to control his investment base, for there are several levels at which the target can be attained or bettered. The RI target, on the other hand, narrows this range of possibilities. Hence, use of RI may confine the scope for opportunistic behaviour. The importance of this potential advantage depends on two real-world conditions being met. Firstly, can divisional managers adjust their investment bases to the target set in the short-term? Secondly, how realistic is the net earnings curve used in this example?

If the items in the investment base are truly controllable by the divisional manager, then the opportunistic behaviour associated with the ROI target seems likely. For example, the manager of a hypermarket may control stocks, debtors and expenditure on fixtures and fittings. The decision to build his store is unlikely to have been influenced by him, and therefore its value does not form part of his controllable investment base. But in this instance, the possibility of operating at different levels of working capital investment in the short run is extremely likely. When the investment base included in the target closely reflects the manager's degree of control, then the benefit of using controllable RI as opposed to ROI should be considered.

Amey's (1969) argument against the inclusion of an interest charge in computing traceable profit is that divisional managers are or should be given a set of assets to operate. Then a target ROI is equivalent to the divisional manager attempting to maximize profit. But this is true if, and only if, the divisional manager's control over his investment base is minimal. The variety of assets and current liabilities that multidivisional companies include in the investment bases of their divisions implies that some effort is made to match these with the control managers actually exercise. Tomkins (1973) confirms this implication in the UK setting, especially in terms of working capital management.

This is an area where the distinction between the profit centre and investment centre may be rightly questioned. Operating decisions, such as the level of output to be produced, will directly result in working capital changes that may be permanent in nature. Is a profit centre manager to be held responsible for these changes in investment? When, as a direct consequence of an operating decision to increase output, additional distribution vehicles are bought or the construction of extra warehousing facilities is necessitated, is it not more realistic to treat the manager as responsible for investment and not merely for profit? Perhaps the type of capital expenditure that can be typically authorized at the divisional level is characterized by relatively small amounts, non-specific in use or directly contingent on operating decisions (Emmanuel and Otley, 1976). Nevertheless, the use of targets expressed in ROI terms contains the potential to misdirect managers over the level of controllable investment to be used.

The importance of the potential defects of using ROI depends on the shape of the net earnings curve. If it is horizontal, both ROI and RI will guide divisional managers to disinvest in order to obtain improved accounting measures. Actual performance as measured by ROI and RI will increase, but neither measure will indicate that the divisional manager is not operating at the investment level expected. This reaction may be due to the evaluation – reward scheme, or it may alternatively be viewed as an action taken in the company's best interests to obtain the same level of earnings with less assets.

The shape of the earnings curve in Fig. 9.1 indicates at first an increasing rate of return secured by economies of scale as the division's activities grow. Then earnings continue to rise with increasing investment, but at a lesser rate with a more or less constant gradient until a plateau is finally reached. It can be argued that this is broadly consistent with product life cycle trends put forward by marketing experts (Wright, 1974). The actual shape of the net earnings curve remains a matter for investigation at the individual division level. To be consistent with controllable residual income, earnings should be measured by controllable profit less the depreciation and expenses associated with controllable assets, regardless of whether these are classified as fixed or current. This gives a target expressed in controllable RI terms that can guide a divisional manager in a relatively unambiguous way and that is consistent with the degree of short-term control he exercises. The motivation to achieve the target controllable RI should be positive if the categorization of investment into controllable and non-controllable is accepted by both divisional and top management. However, there are technical defects in any accounting measure, and to the extent that these are incorporated in controllable RI, the manager's commitment to it will be diminished.

The measures as means of performance evaluation

There are several technical accounting problems that apply with equal force to the use of both ROI and controllable RI. The technical choice between the measures is little affected by:

1. calculating profit pre- or post-tax
2. calculating profit pre- or post-depreciation
3. measuring asset values pre- or post-depreciation
4. basing asset values on historic or current costs

For a survey of the potential shortcomings of using either net or gross book values, see Dearden (1960, 1961) and Vatter (1959). The empirical studies suggest that net book values are most commonly used and thus both ROI and RI measures will increase with the passage of time, given a constant contribution margin or controllable profit, whereas gross book values will present stable ROI and RI measures over time. The impact of these different treatments depends on the age structure of the assets held at the division and the capital replacement policy. The significance of the impact is greater in respect of ROI because of its use in comparing divisional performance. RI, whether controllable or net, has a built-in bias that favours larger divisions and is, therefore, not recommended for inter-divisional comparisons (Anthony and Dearden, 1980, chapter 8).

The substitution of replacement costs or current costs for historic costs may yet gain momentum, given the past adoption and introduction of SSAP 16 (ASC, 1980) in the UK and FAS 33 (1979) in the USA. Under the now defunct British standard, the current cost of replacement was the more likely valuation base to be used. The guidance notes that accompanied the Standard offered practical help to determine current costs, but these were not mandatory. As Sizer (1979) states: 'While indices may be adequate for external reporting, managers may argue that they are not sufficient when assessing their own performance and will pressurize accountants to employ the concept of the modern equivalent asset' or some equally subjective valuation method. Again, the impact of such changes should affect the ROI and RI calculation equally.

The technical problems that distinguish the ROI and RI calculations are:

1. Controllable and non-controllable investments must be determined to calculate controllable and net RI accurately.
2. The interest rate or cost of capital to be applied to the controllable and non-controllable investments under RI must be determined.
3. The need to use annuity depreciation in order that the short-term RI measure is consistent with the discounted cash flow techniques used to evaluate capital projects.

Discussion of this last problem explores the relationship between short-term performance measurement and investment decisions and is examined in detail in Chapter 12. Of the remaining two problems, any ROI measure that provides separate calculations for divisional and management performance will encounter the same problems of distinguishing controllable and non-controllable investments as RI. Thus, the determination of the cost of capital provides the only significant distinction in the calculation of RI as opposed to ROI.

In order to compute the interest charge on investment, a cost of capital must be applied to the investment base. This interest charge is an imputed cost and, in the sense of Solomons' (1965) proposal, it is an acknowledgement that equity capital, retained earnings and debt finance are not cost-free. The use of this imputed cost is designed to promote divisional managers' awareness of the cost of using capital assets and to avoid the potentially harmful substitution of capital assets for labour. Also the imputed interest charge is an opportunity cost, in that it measures the sacrifice of investing scarce resources in a division's assets. Amey's (1979, p. 144) counter-argument is:

... that once investment has taken place opportunity cost is only relevant when the firm has to take further decisions concerning the use to which the asset is put, not in evaluating performance.

However, it can be equally argued that this is the responsibility of the manager of an investment centre ... to decide whether to continue using the asset, to replace or abandon it (Emmanuel and Otley, 1976). We believe that it is necessary to impute a capital charge when evaluating managerial and divisional performance, to avoid managers being motivated to take decisions that harm the overall company.

Solomons' preferred method of establishing what the charge for capital should be is to compute the weighted average cost of capital from the projected capital structure that the company has set itself. An alternative to calculating a weighted average is to allocate debt finance costs to the divisions and impute an interest charge based on the pure equity cost of capital. Again, the 'optimal', future capital structure needs to be estimated. Neither is satisfactory because it is assumed that any investment project must have the same risk class as the average risk of the firm. This is highly unlikely in multi-divisional, diversified companies. The question then becomes whether a single cost of capital should be applied uniformly to the divisions or whether separate rates should be developed that reflect their relative risk, growth and profitability profiles. Solomons (1965) and Flower (1971) argue for the former view; Gordon and Halpern (1974), Ma (1969), Jarrett (1978) and Ezzamel (1979) support the latter.

In point of fact, developments in finance theory which rely on the efficient market hypothesis and the capital asset pricing model (CAPM) allow divisional cost of capital rates to be calculated fairly simply. The return required for an individual investment j is given by the expression:

$$R_j = R_f + B_j(R_m - R_f)$$

where

R_m = the return on the market portfolio of all risky assets;
R_f = the riskless rate of interest;
B_j = beta, a measure of how the returns on the investment vary with the returns on the market.

Determination of individual division's costs of capital requires identifying a twin security listed in the stock market which matches the risk class of the division (Keane, 1983). For example, Corinthian plc has three operating divisions:

	% of Firm Value
Distribution division	50%
Sports goods division	30%
Property division	20%

Corinthian has identified the following three principal competitors:

Company	Estimated Equity Beta	Proportion of Debt in Capital Structure
TSP Transport plc	0.8	0.3
Cheetah plc	1.6	0.2
Southern Homes plc	1.2	0.4

The riskless rate of interest (R_f) is 7% while the expected return on the market portfolio of all risky assets (R_m) is 15%. Corinthian plc presently has a capital structure comprising 60% equity and 40% debt, and for the moment, it is assumed that debt for Corinthian and the competitor companies is risk-free.

Divisional Cost of Capital

	Distribution division	Sports goods division	Property division
Asset beta	$0.7(0.8) = 0.56$	$0.8(1.6) = 1.28$	$0.6(1.2) = 0.72$
Required return	$7 + 0.56(15 - 7)$ $= 11.5\%$	$7 + 1.28(15 - 7)$ $= 17.2\%$	$7 + 0.72(15 - 7)$ $= 12.8\%$

Corinthian Cost of Equity Capital

$$0.5(0.56) \quad + \quad 0.3(1.28) \quad + \quad 0.2(0.72) = 0.808$$

Required return $= 7 + 0.808(15 - 7) = 13.464\%$

If the assumption about risk free debt is removed, and a beta of 0.2 is regarded appropriate for each company's debt, then divisional and corporate costs of capital or required returns become:

Divisional Cost of Capital

	Distribution division	Sports goods division	Property division
Asset beta	$0.7(0.8) + 0.3(0.2)$ $= 0.62$	$0.8(1.6) + 0.2(0.2)$ $= 1.32$	$0.6(1.2) + 0.4(0.2)$ $= 0.8$
Required return	$7 + 0.62(15 - 7)$ $= 11.96\%$	$7 + 1.32(15 - 7)$ $= 17.6\%$	$7 + 0.8(15 - 7)$ $= 13.4\%$

Corinthian Cost of Equity Capital

$$0.5(0.62) \quad + \quad 0.3(1.32) \quad + \quad 0.2(0.8) = 0.866$$

Required return $= 7 + 0.866(15 - 7) = 13.928\%$

This example illustrates that the uniform application of the company's cost of capital may result in two divisions – distribution and property – being asked to submit individual investment proposals which are inconsistent with the required market return (more on this shortly).

Whilst the above calculations may appear straightforward, there are several difficulties. CAPM is essentially a single-period model, and this limits its applicability to multi-period investments. Also there is the problem of identifying the market portfolio precisely and hence determining R_m. In the context of the investment centre manager in a multidivisional company, there is the question of whose risk is incorporated in the required return or cost of capital. As we shall explain in Chapter 12, the risk profile of individual managers may have a more significant influence over which capital projects are formally submitted than divisional costs of capital or hurdle rates. The determination of divisional costs of capital is hampered by the inability to find independent companies of approximately the same scale of operation as individual divisions, the allocation problem and the practical constraints of applying the capital asset pricing model. Of the 25 companies participating in Solomons' (1965) study, only a few charged their divisions for the use of capital, and all of these used the same rate for all divisions.

However, the case for developing separate divisional cost of capital rates seems strong. The use of a single cost of capital rate uniformly applied to all divisions' capital projects would result in favouring high-risk, high-return divisions. The total diversified company's risk profile may therefore change adversely over an extended period of time. Given the absence of a reliable method to develop divisional cost of capital rates, one suggestion by Shwayder (1970) seems worth pursuing.

It is proposed to use the default-free rate as the implicit interest rate for all divisions' investments, and then for the user (top and divisional managements) to attach their own risk penalty to performance results. This suggestion rests on the assumption that risk is only partly a function of time (Robichek and Myers, 1965), so that the time preference component of the investors' required rate of return can be usefully approximated by the return of default-free bonds. This default-free rate is used to compute controllable RI, and then net RI may be adjusted in line with the uncertainty top management perceives as appropriate to particular divisions. Note that the suggestion is that the division's performance measure is adjusted for risk, whereas the divisional managers are charged the default-free rate in the calculation of controllable RI. This may help to defuse the personal commitment of divisional managers to capital projects they have proposed, in that top management may argue that the manager is making an adequate contribution, but that the project's riskiness cannot be offset by other compensating activities or projects at this time. Top management should be concerned with the overall company's risk profile, and perhaps the application of Shwayder's modification to the RI calculation is one way to achieve this without demotivating the divisional managers or reducing their commitment to the controllable RI performance measure. Almost incidentally, the use of a default-free interest rate simplifies the problem of determining a corporate cost of capital appropriate for use at the divisional level.

A more recent development (Gregory, 1987) using the default-free rate treats divisional managers as lessees of headquarters assets. The behaviour congruent properties of this alternative performance indicator, especially with regard to long-term decisions, are examined further in Chapter 12.

The profit conscious, controllable RI combination

The development of *ex post* measures of performance that are consistent with responsibility accounting and that may potentially lead to behaviour congruence is a difficult task in practice. We may argue that in the multidivisional company:

1. A flexible, profit-conscious style of evaluation should be used to reduce the tendency of divisional managers to regard the short-term financial performance measure as an end in itself. This may improve the completeness property of the measure.
2. Separate performance measures should be created for the evaluation of the manager and the division. This improves the completeness and accuracy of the performance measures used.
3. Wherever possible, the manager's performance measure should not include allocated costs. This improves the neutrality of the performance measure.
4. Controllable residual income may be superior in providing a less ambiguous target for divisional managers than ROI, although this depends on:
   (a) controllable investment being correctly defined, and
   (b) the shape of the net earnings curve relative to the investment level.
5. A default-free interest rate should be used when computing controllable residual income.

The combination of a profit-conscious style of evaluation and a profit performance measure which emphasizes controllability represents a potential improvement. We acknowledge that there is no guarantee that these changes in the AIS will result in a change of emphasis from control of divisional managers to control by those managers. But the close association between the manager's performance measure and the control he exercises, coupled with the evaluation on a longer-term trend, may lead the manager to use the accounting information for self-control. With top management support, the divisional manager may be more inclined to set higher targets, examine the accounting variances more closely to discover the effects of his past decision making, and to view his task more as adapting to an uncertain environment than merely meeting a rigid performance measure. The decentralization of the accounting function and the establishment of divisional accountants is one positive way by which top management may show its commitment to self-control.

Unfortunately, this combination does not offer a totally satisfactory solution. Controllable RI still resembles an all-inclusive measure of performance; the non-neutral aspect depends on how long the trend will be before evaluation takes place; the biasing of targets and manipulation of information is not prevented by using controllable RI. All that can be claimed for this package of suggestions is that it begins to recognize the need of the divisional manager to obtain feedback consistent with the control he exercises. Wherever possible, the accounting information should not disguise the effect of the decisions he has taken by including non-controllable charges and allocations.

The non-accounting, multiple performance measure combination

It can be argued that any divisional profit measure has too narrow a perspective to indicate adequately the progress made towards maintaining the division as a useful part of the overall enterprise. In his prize-winning article, Parker (1979, p. 317) advocates that:

... if accountants wish to claim that they serve the creators of company goals, they should turn their attention to providing performance measures for divisional self-assessment, since much of the corporate 'goal set' appears to be generated from the actions of divisional personnel as well as higher management.

He suggests that additional quantitative measures of performance are needed to reflect productivity, marketing effectiveness, social responsibility and human resource management. The relative importance of profit, ROI or controllable RI in the top management's evaluation of the manager's performance will decline as a result. When the budgeting information plays this minor role, Hopwood (1972) calls it a non-accounting style of evaluation (see Chapter 7).

In Hopwood's study, the non-accounting style of evaluation resulted in little manipulation of accounting information and low involvement in costs. The preoccupation with financial and quantitative outcomes is not necessarily consistent with the circumstances in which non-programmed decisions take place. Profit may be an indicator of effective management, but its relationship with efficient work methods, good employee relations and an astute promotion policy within the division is debatable. The actions of past divisional managers may well have contributed to this period's profit. The inherent uncertainty surrounding the divisional manager's task may indeed merit a multidimensional evaluation.

Monitoring devices

One possible compromise to promote both control by divisional managers and control of divisional managers is to build non-quantitative monitoring devices into the AIS. For example, the process of top management authorizing capital projects and conducting post-completion audits alerts divisional management to additional monitoring devices. As Scapens and Sale (1981, p. 22) state:

These monitoring processes are independent of the evaluation of operating activities and if they are effective, the operating activities can be evaluated without reference to the capital base of the division.

Similarly, the planning assumptions and key variables that divisional managers disclose may act as a monitoring device when the actual events become known.

The provision of direct contact by means of face-to-face meetings between top and divisional managements may promote a 'joint problem-sharing' atmosphere. In much the same way as planning assumptions may be mutually disclosed, top management may be able to monitor the heuristic decision rules and uses of accounting information made by the divisional managers. The aim is not that these rules and uses (or non-uses) should be scrutinized or critically analysed, rather it is to gain some impression of how complex or simplistic, how broad or narrow, is the information base of the predictive model being used. For example, the experienced research supervisor does not attempt to over-structure his student's work, but rather monitors the information sources used, and the logical build-up of the assumptions made. With the provision of a supportive climate, top management may monitor information sources and uses without attempting to control the divisional manager. The existence of direct contact or temporary committees may serve a monitoring role independent of the periodic reports of operating performance. The monitoring process cannot contribute to enforcement to meet a specific target because top management is unclear as to what that target should be, but the feasibility of different courses of action may be agreed. By acknowledging this, the possibility of creating a supportive, 'joint problem-sharing' atmosphere is enhanced. However, it should be recognized that the number and frequency of monitoring devices may reduce rather than improve divisional managers' performance if they feel over-monitored (Marris and Mueller, 1980).

Personnel devices

The personnel management literature offers several additional means of evaluating managerial performance via quantitative but non-financial measures. With a recognition of the high degree of skill, knowledge and decision making discretion in the actual work being done by divisional managers, it is argued that top management's 'primary task is to stimulate rather than drive, and develop rather than reward in a purely material sense' (Thomason, 1978, p. 69). The selection procedures for divisional managers therefore comprise part of the management control process. Before employment, the candidate may be subjected to rigorous training and socialization processes, and during employment, promotion is subject to the building of a performance history over several years.

Some managerial evaluation schemes have focused on the information processing dimensions of the manager's work (Cummings and Schwab, 1973). In the Nestlé Company head office, for example, a manager's evaluation is dependent upon his ability to recognize and decode a barrage of information, collect information, plan a decision and its execution and to adjust and re-adjust during the process of implementation in order to achieve the expected outcomes. Although the means for measuring each aspect of this information processing capability may be regarded as imperfect, the overall measure can indicate the complexity, amount of information and the changeable conditions under which managerial decision making takes place. The use of these personnel measures as complements to the accounting performance measures may therefore be appropriate. Personnel measures that focus on the information processing part of the divisional manager's work may cause top management to interpret the financial results more sensitively. As with budgeting, the process of identifying information needs should aid the divisional manager to comprehend the complexities of his task and to effect his own improvements. Top management, through the use of such measures, should also be made increasingly aware of the non-programmed decisions the manager has to take, and this may result in more joint problem sharing than when evaluation is based purely on financial performance measures.

We have already referred to the confusion that multiple performance measures can cause (see Chapter 7). The possibilities of misdirecting the divisional manager and causing opportunistic behaviour appear endless. However, these shortcomings may be largely due to their inappropriate use as short-term evaluation tools with little or no effort being made to develop agreed courses of action. For multiple performance measures to work effectively not only is a non-accounting, long-term style of evaluation required, but also a continual dialogue between top and divisional management to build consensus. Under this combination, rewarding and penalizing divisional managers appears extremely difficult to accomplish on other than an arbitrary basis, and it is of prime concern that the 'right' personnel are selected to become divisional managers. Monitoring devices developed in the personnel management literature to gauge individual characteristics, as well as information processing and communication skills, appear to have an active role to play in selecting managers for promotion and monitoring their performance subsequently. In the multidivisional organization where non-programmed decisions are most frequent, top management's faith in the individual divisional manager to take decisions in the company's best interest may be a necessary condition for effective management control.

The combination of a non-accounting style of evaluation and multiple performance measures attempts to:

1. Extend the evaluation of performance both in terms of the dimensions measured and the time periods covered. A more complete evaluation of performance may result.
2. Reflect the multidimensional nature of the divisional manager's work by indicating variances on several aspects. A more accurate assessment of performance may result.
3. Indicate that managerial effectiveness is not a short-term or financially apparent phenomenon. Effectiveness is maintaining the division within the feasible region and taking actions in the company's best interests. The multidimensional trend evaluation may stimulate neutral or non-opportunistic behaviour.

Contingent performance measurement

All AISs rely on the assumption that actual performance can be measured accurately. Evaluation by means of a profit performance measure in multidivisional companies leads to a short-term emphasis in management control. Rewards linked to the attainment of a financial target or budget are used as enforcement devices to gain lower-level managers compliance. Unfortunately, in the non-programmed situation, managerial judgement is required to set targets and, if a profit measure is used, this will not encapsulate all aspects of the manager's efforts. The link with rewards also suggests that managers will not be indifferent in reporting actual performance. Budget-constrained evaluation is likely to encourage the divisional manager to perceive the short-term accounting performance measure as the overriding aim of his decision making. By manipulating accounting reports and biasing targets, the divisional manager is reacting rationally to the use of a formal control system being inappropriately applied to non-programmed decisions. In the short-term, the company appears to be making progress, as reflected by the accounting

Table 9.5 Contingent performance measurement to lead to management control

Characteristics of:	Unitary	Multidivisional
Performance		
Decentralization	Limited	Full
Performance measures: manager	Budgeted cost, revenue, profit	Budgeted controllable RI
Performance measures: division	Budgeted cost, revenue, profit	Budgeted net RI/ROI
Other measures	–	Productivity Marketing
Monitoring devices	–	Direct contact Joint problem sharing Heuristics and sources
Personnel measures	–	Individual character development
Valuation bases	GAAP	Responsibility accounting
Evaluation		
Time span	Short-term	Long-term
Purpose	1. Division viability 2. Corporate plans 3. Management	1. Managerial self-control 2. Division viability
Style	Budget constrained	Profit conscious/ non-accounting
Rewards formally linked to financial performance	Absolute	Partial/none

performance measures but, in fact, it may be causing managers to take decisions that are incompatible with actions that maintain the division in the firm's feasible region. In short, the system may not be promoting behaviour congruence.

The appropriateness of the traditional AIS for management control is likely to vary with the degree of decentralization allowed by different companies. As the degree of delegated decision making increases in response to the incidence of non-programmed decisions, so must the emphasis of accounting control, use of performance measures and the style of evaluation change (see Table 9.5).

Categorization of these changes solely by reference to organization structure is an oversimplification. Within unitary structured companies, the separate managers responsible for advertising and research and development may use as much discretion and jusgment in setting their targets or budgets as managers of product line divisions in the multidivisional firm. Therefore, a profit-conscious or even non-accounting style of evaluation may be appropriate in these instances. When accounting measures are used, the distinction between managerial and departmental effectiveness should be followed as far as possible. But these areas of discretion in the unitary organization are regarded as isolated instances for, if non-programmed decisions are widespread, a change to the multidivisional structure is to be expected. Similarly, the suggested modifications in the AIS may prove more appropriate to the divisional manager in the multi-divisional organization than to his subordinate, functional managers.

Opinions are rightly divergent on this point (McNally, 1980). The hypermarket manager's problem in deciding which items and lines to purchase involves consultation with his purchasing and sales or layout managers. Once a decision is reached, the purchasing and layout decisions are capable of being programmed, and the more traditional uses of the accounting measures may be appropriate for these lower-level managers. By contrast, when the functional managers in the division face non-programmed tasks, the problem becomes more than one of coordination. The purchasing manager's judgement about if or when a substitute material will become available and at what cost; the production managers' judgement about how efficiently the workforce will learn to use the substitute material, whether its introduction will involve changes in work flows, different combinations of people and machines, whether new skills or technologies need to be learnt; the sales manager's expectations of increasing market share with and without the new material given various degrees of competition, fluctuating customer loyalties in response to price, credit and discount terms that can themselves be varied, suggest a need for joint responsibility. It is necessary for the divisional manager to involve the functional managers in the planning and target setting process, to incorporate their individual predictive models and assumptions and modify them relative to the plans of the other functional heads. The presence of budget-constrained evaluation and an emphasis on accounting performance measures may cause these managers to be less than honest in stating their plans and actual results in much the same way as we argued the divisional manager may behave. A reduction in emphasis on financial measures of performance and a long-term evaluation based on trends may appear more appropriate in these circumstances.

We are therefore recognizing that effective management control and performance evaluation follow a continuum contingent upon the incidence and frequency of non-programmed decisions. At the extremes, this implies that different performance measures and styles of evaluation may be used, but within the continuum the differences will be changes of degree or in the combination of controls used.

EXERCISES

1. What are the limitations of all financial performance measures? Compare and contrast the relative advantages and disadvantages of RI and ROI. When would you consider the use of RI to be more appropriate and when, if at all, would you be indifferent?

2. In many universities and polytechnics, student performance in a particular course is evaluated by means of regularly submitted course-work and a final examination. Assume that you participate and contribute in classes and conscientiously undertake and submit course-work, but that the scores you obtain are always below those you expected. What do you do?

   Compare and contrast your reactions with those of a divisional manager whose annual bonus is solely determined on the basis of budgeted versus actual financial performance.

   What changes or modifications would you recommend in both cases?

3. A university teacher, active in teaching, administration and research, wishes to obtain further finance from a government research agency. The new research project will build on the findings of his existing and continuing projects. Some of these findings have already been incorporated in the courses he teaches and he hopes to employ a student who has taken these courses as a post-graduate research assistant on the new project.

   Submissions for research funds are handled by the university's central administration. The professor provides an estimate of his time needed to complete the project. The administration then prepares the following statement:

Research Project XYZ Cost Statement

Professor X's salary (based on the proportion of research hours to total hours of teaching, administration and research)	XXX
Central overhead charge (central administration, electricity, other utilities and rates allocated on the basis of the professor's estimate of hours to be spent on this project)	XXX
Department overhead charge (shared equipment costs, departmental administration costs, research assistant salaries allocated by means of negotiation between research directors and the head of department)	XX
Total research grant requested	XXX

The research agency is concerned that this system does not result in the best allocation of resources and that it is not getting 'value for money'.
Comment on the strengths and weakness of the system from:
(a) The individual professor's perspective.
(b) The central administration's perspective.
(c) The research agency's perspective.
Under this system, will a comparison of budgeted (i.e., total research monies requested) and actual costs be useful?

4. Jayhawker Enterprises has four divisions that produce toasters, washing machines, electric carving knives and tumble driers respectively. They share the same brand name, and the company's reputation has been built on the quality of its products. For this reason, quality control is centralized and maintains exacting standards for all the product divisions. In any one month during the forthcoming year, the following data is likely:

Product Division	*Separable cost per batch (£'000)*	*Sales price per batch (£'000)*
Toaster	24	19
Washing-machines	54	55
Electric carvers	3	82
Tumble driers	41	195

Quality control Department cost: £100 000 per month in total.
Assume that one batch of each product is produced each month.
Required:
(a) Discover the book profit of each product using the:
   (i) NRV.
   (ii) Democratic (i.e., dividing the common costs equally be-
        tween the number of users) allocation methods.
(b) Repeat the exercise in (a), above, on the basis that the toaster
    divisional manager has improved efficiency and succeeded in
    reducing his separable costs to £16 000 per batch without
    adversely affecting quality.
(c) Repeat the exercise in (a), above, using the original data
    except that now the toaster divisional manager has increased
    the selling price to £27 000 per batch without adversely
    affecting demand.
(d) What are the implications on your analysis in (a)–(c), above,
    for rewarding the individual managers on the basis of the book
    profits recorded?
5. Mr T.G.R. Davies of the Grand Slam division has just submitted a
   budgeted ROI for the next year of 60%. Mr G. Wheel of the Triple
   Crown division has submitted a 15% budgeted ROI. The company,
   Cambrian plc, has a cost of capital of 30%, and accepts both the
   target ROIs. Actual performance during the year results in Grand
   Slam achieving 64.3% and Triple Crown 15% ROIs.
   Both divisional managers have substantial influence over their
   respective divisions' investment bases and the following information was used when they set the targets:

Grand Slam		Triple Crown	
Controllable profit (£m)	Investment (£m)	Controllable profit (£m)	Investment (£m)
1	3	0.18	3
2	4	0.48	4
3	5	0.75	5
3.75	6	1.08	6
4.5	7	1.75	7
5	8	1.6	8
5.5	9	1.35	9
5.8	10	1.2	10
6.0	11	1.1	11
6.2	12	0.96	12

Required:

(a) To present a reasoned argument and analysis to help explain why each manager chose the ROI target he did.

(b) To determine whether targets expressed in RI terms would have altered the divisional managers' actions in any way. (Hint: a comparison of budgeted and actual performance may prove useful.)

(c) To explain the effect on each manager's target-setting if Cambrian imputed a cost of capital charge of 60% to Grand Slam and 15% to Triple Crown.

6. The Blackstone Engineering Company Ltd is a multiproduct firm organized on a product-division basis. The 1986/87 summary of management accounts is as follows:

	Div. A £000	Div. B £000	Div. C £000
Net sales	9000	6450	5250
Direct production costs	4500	3000	2400
Direct expenses	1350	750	600
Overheads			
Depreciation	600	450	300
R & D	300	300	150
Administration	450	375	225
Selling expenses	900	600	300
Financial expenses	450	300	300
Corporation tax	300	300	375
Net profit after tax	£ 150	£ 375	£ 600
Capital employed	£7500	£3750	£3000

Required:

(a) Restructure the above data into a residual income statement, which clearly distinguishes managerial and divisional performance; calculate divisional and corporate ROI; and evaluate the performance of the company and its divisions insofar as the available information permits. The following further data are relevant to your solution:

(i) Sales are made by divisions direct to external customers in all cases, using exclusively their own sales staffs and facilities.

(ii) Depreciation includes an allocation of HQ and central R & D facilities' depreciation, the allocation being equal to 1% of net sales per division.

(iii) R & D is conducted centrally and costs have been

allocated to divisions on the basis of notional benefits estimated by the Research Director. Inquiry ascertains that 40% of all R & D expenditure is on basic research, while the remainder is development work contracted for by the 3 divisions in the cost proportions of A (25%), B (50%) and C (25%).

(iv)   Administration expense includes an allocation of HQ expense, equal to 2% of net sales per division.

(vi)   Financial expenses, including interest, insurance and rates, etc., include an allocation of non-traceable central financial expenditure equal to 4% of total capital employed per division.

(vi)   Corporation tax appears to have been fairly allocated.

(vii) Divisional capital includes an allocation of centrally controlled capital totalling £3 000 000, which for historical reasons has been allocated to A (60%), B (20%) and C (20%).

(viii) Corporation cost of capital is assessed at 10%, post-tax.

(b) Outline the arguments for and against the allocation of common costs and give your opinion on whether such allocations are useful.

(c) What theoretical and practical advantages does residual income offer as opposed to rate of return on investment?

7. Cubic plc is a multidivisional company which has principal activities organized into consumer durable, industrial plant hire and leisure divisions. These 3 divisions comprise 60%, 20% and 20% of the total firms value respectively.

Cubic is attempting to identify separate costs of capital for each division and has discovered the following three competitors:

Company	Estimated equity beta	Proportion of debt in capital structure
Icelandic plc	0.9	0.2
B & H Plant Hire plc	1.3	0.4
Ladswell Leisure plc	1.9	0.3

The riskless rate of interest is 7%, while the expected return on the market portfolio of all risky assets is 15%. Cubic plc presently has a capital structure comprising 60% equity and 40% debt.

Required:

(a) Outline the potential advantage of discovering the cost of capital for individual divisions.

(b) Determine the corporate and divisional costs of capital when:

  (i) debt for Cubic and the competitor companies is regarded as risk-free.

  (ii) debt for each company has a beta of 0.3.

  Explain the assumptions underlying your calculations. How reliable are they likely to be over time?

(c) What are the implications of the divisional costs of capital for short-term performance measures?

8. Cathcart Industries plc began trading in 1926 when Theophilus P. Cathcart started the mechanical engineering business. Success in manufacturing machine tools for the automobile industry allowed Cathcart to expand into engine production, and with the declaration of war, involvement in automobile, aeroplane and marine engine production. These were and are sold world-wide.

The Cathcart family connection with the firm ended in 1955 and since then there have been five different chief executive officers (CEO). Each can be said to have brought a distinct leadership style to the firm and to have definite ideas on how activities should be organized. For example, John Drake, the penultimate CEO, organized the company by geographical divisions recognizing the distinctions between trading in North America as opposed to the Pacific Rim countries, in Europe as opposed to Africa. His successor, Emile Fox, restructured Cathcart Industries along functional lines, emphasizing the fact that there was a common technology at the core of all the product ranges. Most recently, James Christopher who was appointed 4 months ago, has explored the possibility of restructuring the firm again, this time on multi-divisional product market lines. This appears to mean that where growth and profitability seem merited, a separate marine engine division serving Pacific Rim countries should be recognized or a separate automobile engine division serving Europe, and so on. Cathcart's consolidated turnover for 1988 was in excess of £2206 million with profits of £398 million.

Required:

(a) With reference to Cathcart Industries plc, analyse the potential advantages and disadvantages of

  (i) maintaining the functional or unitary organization structure.

  (ii) restructuring along a multidivisional product market basis.

(b) James Christopher views the restructuring as beneficial, at least from the point of view of developing costs of capital for each specific division. Explain the problems of using a single cost of capital to appraise all investment projects and the possible benefits of the approach he favours.

(c) James Christopher is especially interested in the marine engine operations. This activity he estimates to comprise 40% of total value of Cathcart Industries plc. Cathcart's present capital structure comprises 80% equity and 20% debt.

He has identified an independent competitor, Avon Engines plc, which has 30% debt as a proportion of its capital structure and an estimated equity beta of 1.5.

Christopher estimates the riskless rate of interest to be 9%, while the expected return on the market portfolio of all risky assets is 18%.

Determine the marine engine activity's cost of capital when:

(i) debt for Cathcart and the competitor company is regarded as risk-free.

(ii) debt for each company has a beta of 0.3.

Explain the assumptions underlying your calculations. How reliable are they likely to be over time?

10

Rewarding managerial performance

SUMMARY

The final link in the management control cycle is to connect the achievement of desired results with incentives for managers, so that they are motivated to achieve the performance targets that are set. The linking of rewards with performance helps ensure that effort is devoted in desirable directions.

However, there are a variety of possible rewards, both financial and non-financial and the link can be made with both short-term performance measures, such as annual profit figures, and longer-term evaluations of overall managerial performance. Despite a considerable amount of experience with systems of performance-related pay, especially in the USA, there is remarkably little hard evidence as to their relative effectiveness, and thus little guidance as to how they should be designed.

INTRODUCTION

With rare exceptions, organizations control managers' behaviour by promising them rewards for generating the desired results. This motivational form of control is indirect because it focuses on results rather than the actions that will generate those results. Such indirect control is necessary because it is not usually possible to specify completely what actions managers should be taking, and it can also be costly to monitor their actions closely, even if it is possible to know what these should be.

The sets of promises of rewards for the generation of desired results and threat of penalties for the absence of those results are usefully labelled as 'contracts' between the corporation and the employee (Jensen and Meckling, 1976). Some of these contracts meet the legal definition of the word 'contract' because their terms can be enforced through the courts. Other contracts are not legally enforceable, but their terms and effects are virtually indistinguishable from those of legal contracts. The terms are enforced by corporate administrative processes or labour-market forces. If corporations renege on their promises and the relevant labour markets are at least partly competitive, employees will leave, and firms will find it difficult to hire talented replacements because their reputation for trustworthiness will be damaged.

This chapter provides a discussion of the many rewards (and punishments) that can be and are promised to managers as part of these motivational contracts. Since penalties are just negative rewards – or the absence of positive rewards – the term 'rewards' will be used here to refer to allocations of things that managers both value and those they would like to avoid. The chapter distinguishes the rewards in terms of their form (e.g., cash, share options and improved promotion possibilities), the bases organizations use for assigning the rewards, the shape and the explicitness of the function linking rewards with performance measures, and the size of the results-dependent monetary rewards.

FORMS OF REWARD

The rewards included in motivational contracts can be in the form of any item that managers value. The valued items can be understood in terms of any of the many motivational theories, such as Maslow's hierarchy of needs, as was discussed in Chapter 3. 'Wants' is probably a better term for the items Maslow describes than 'needs' because few, if any, of the items in the hierarchy are essential, and individuals can and do make trade-offs among items at different levels in the hierarchy. It should be recognized, however, that the mix of desires managers have is likely to be, on average, different from those of production-line workers; for example, their physiological and safety requirements are largely assured.

Vancil (1979, pp. 93–4) distinguished three categories of rewards managers receive. Firstly, they derive pleasure from managing an entity of their own. Secondly, they enjoy the power and status that accompanies their position. Thirdly, they earn monetary rewards. These rewards can come in multiple forms, including salary, bonuses, share options, and promotions that will cause them to earn higher rewards in the future. Organizations can derive some motivational value from their contracts if they link promises of any of these valued rewards to measures of performance that the managers can influence. For example, corporate managers can and do threaten to reduce the pleasure middle managers derive from managing their entity by refusing to fund ideas for expenditures in entities where performance is not good. They grant managers additional power and increase their status within the firm by publicizing their good results. And they grant additional pecuniary rewards in the form of cash, delayed payments of cash and shares.

It is obvious that organizations should attempt to promise those rewards that provide the most cost effective motivational effect, but this is not easy to do because the effects of each of the various reward forms vary depending on manager's personal tastes and circumstances. Some managers are greatly interested in immediate cash awards, whereas others are more interested in increasing their retirement benefits, in increasing their autonomy, or in improving their promotion possibilities. However, some systematic taste patterns are apparent. For example, as compared with top executives, lower-level managers are probably more interested in protecting their autonomy and in improving their prospects for promotion. Eaton and Rosen (1983) provide evidence that they are also less interested in the stability of their short-term income (after their base salaries are assured). It is also apparent that reward tastes also vary systematically across cultures, at least partially because of local income tax rates. If organizations can tailor their reward packages to their manager's individual preferences, they can provide meaningful rewards at the lowest possible costs.

Unfortunately, this tailoring is not easy to accomplish, and only scattered evidence exists as to the motivational effects of the various forms of rewards. For example, a recent review article by Ehrenberg and Milkovich (1987, p. 87) concluded that:

While a variety of theories exists about the effects of various [management] compensation policies, surprisingly little evidence exists on the extent to which compensation policies vary across firms and more importantly on the effects of pursuing alternative compensation strategies.

Thus, it is not surprising that most compensation textbooks (e.g., Henderson, 1985) devote most of their discussion to compensation of lower-level employees, not managers. The most comprehensive handbook of reward management in the UK (Armstrong and Murlis, 1988) devotes just one chapter to performance management, although it explicitly excludes shop-floor incentive schemes to concentrate on managerial compensation.

Agreement does not even exist about the basic question as to whether it is desirable to provide results-dependent monetary rewards. Some authors (e.g., Jensen and Murphy, 1988; Foulkes, 1985; Opsahl and Dunnette, 1979; Wilson, 1973) maintain that pay is obviously a powerful motivator, and Bellah *et al.* (1985) add that many managers use the size of the monetary awards they receive as a standard by which to judge their own self-esteem. Other (e.g., 'Management Bonuses: Do You Need Them?', 1979) suggest that performance-dependent bonuses may just waste money because they do not cause managers to work any harder. Still others (e.g., Kohn, 1988; Pearce, 1987; Hamner, 1975) believe that bonus plans often actually diminish motivation because they are easy to misdesign and mismanage. It seems clear if communications to the managers about what it is important are not correct, that error is compounded if the communications are reinforced with promises of large incentive awards. However, there has been an increasing trend in the UK during the late 1980s to include a performance-related element into the remuneration package of middle managers (Murlis, 1988).

Observing organizations' reward practices does not easily provide definitive clues as to which rewards the organizations have found to be more effective in a motivational sense. This is because some choices of reward forms are affected by other than motivational considerations. Some choices are affected by tax considerations, such as whether the income is taxable to the employee and at what tax rate, and whether the corporation can deduct the expense. It is probably that the observed trend in the UK has been considerably affected by the reduction in higher rates of taxation and by reducing the range of perquisites that are not subject to tax when received by an employee. The company car is perhaps the last major non-monetary reward commonly used and that is not usually subject to variation because of performance. Some choices are also made to improve employee retention. Some reward forms are promised because the organization wishes to offer total compensation packages comparable to those offered by their competitors. And long-term incentive awards reduce turnover through the provision of a form of 'silver handcuffs'; the managers forfeit the awards unless they stay with the firm for a period of years. Finally, some choices are made to get company shares in managers' (and other employees') hands as part of a defence against hostile takeover.

THE LINK BETWEEN REWARDS AND RESULTS

Any of the reward forms listed above can be linked with any performance measure or combination of measures that can be used to distinguish good from mediocre or poor performance. The evaluation of most managers in profit-making organizations generally involve measures that include combinations of the financial performance measures, described in Chapters 8 and 9, such as profit after tax or ROI measured over annual and sometimes multi-year performance periods. Even in profit-making organizations, however, the financial measures are usually supplemented by some non-accounting measures, such as market share, growth, customer satisfaction or achievement of specific product development milestones. Merchant (1989) concluded that the primary function of these other measures is to provide leading indicators of forthcoming financial performance. Their use helps offset the short-term bias inherent in accounting income measures of performance; for example, earnings can be increased in the short-run by reducing expenditures on investments that will pay off in future periods (e.g., for research and development).

In most organizations, the link between rewards and financial results measures, however defined, is linear. The linear function is the simplest to communicate and administer. Rewards are typically promised only over a restricted performance range, however. The typical results – reward function is shown in Fig. 10.1 (Merchant, 1989). The function has lower and upper reward cut-offs, and it is linear in shape between the cut-off extremes. Merchant found that 9 of the 12 firms he studied set a lower cut-off in their short-term incentive compensation contract. Below some significant fraction, approximately 80% of targeted annual performance (which is typically the budget), these corporations promised profit centre managers no incentive compensation for financial performance.

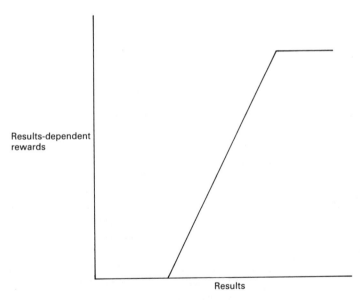

Results-dependent rewards

Results

Fig. 10.1 Shape of typical results – reward function.

These corporations set this lower cut-off because they do not want to pay any bonuses for performance they considered 'mediocre'. The fraction of the target set as the lower limit varies with predictability of the target; it is a lower fraction where the predictability is lower.

Nine of the 12 firms (not the same 9) defined an upper cut-off on incentive payments for profit-centre managers, although the pay out functions for higher-level managers were less likely to have an upper cut-off level. No extra rewards are provided for results above this upper cut-off. The cut-offs are set at a broad range of results, but they are also typically set at a percentage of the annual performance target (the range observed was 105–150%).

Upper cut-offs appear to be set for a number of reasons, including:

1. a fear that the high bonuses that would be paid might not be deserved because of:
   (a) a windfall gain;
   (b) behaviour that increased current period reported profit at the expense of the long term;
   (c) a faulty plan design (the fear is greatest when the plan is new);
2. a desire not to encourage unsustainably high growth and profitability;
3. a desire not to pay lower-level managers more than upper-level managers earn (vertical compensation equity);
4. a desire to keep total compensation consistent over time, so that managers are able to sustain their lifestyle;
5. a desire to adhere to standard corporate and industry practices.

EXPLICITNESS OF THE REWARD PROMISES

Another potentially important feature of motivational contracts is the explicitness of the reward promise. Sometimes the forms of the rewards promised and the bases on which the awards will be given are communicated to the managers explicitly. Some of them are described in writing in great detail. Other, often quite important, contracts are left mostly implicit. The implicit, unwritten 'understandings' between managers are implemented on a case-by-case basis and used to fill the gaps left either intentionally or unintentionally in the written contracts. For example, the bases on which the rewards are assigned may be left vague because the evaluations are done subjectively. Or managers may be told that the corporation will try to protect them against the harmful effects of certain economic factors that they cannot control if it turns out to be a 'bad' year. The important promotion-prospects contract is almost invariably implicit.

Managers infer the factors that are used to determine promotions by observing, over time, the skills, personal qualities and accomplishments of those who are promoted. Indeed, this appears to offer the most potent form of control as the criteria can be varied over time. However, because managers are not certain as to what the criteria are, they have to try to perform adequately on all the dimensions of performance they believe are important. Thus, the vague promotion-prospects contract can be used to counteract the short-term opportunism that more explicit contracts may engender.

Superiors sometimes leave contract terms purposely implicit for any of several reasons. They may not know how to describe the bases for the rewards or the weightings of importance of each of the individual items in the set of evaluation criteria prior to the performance period. They may want to keep the contract flexible to avoid motivating managers in directions that turn out to be no longer appropriate as environmental or competitive conditions change. They may want to encourage managers to 'do their best' and not to give up when they perceive a performance target as impossible or coast after achieving a target. Or they may want to reduce manager's propensities to engage in short-term manipulations of the performance measures.

However, the fact that a contract (or contract element) is unwritten does not necessarily mean that it is implicit. Some contract terms are communicated in ways that are so clear that the employees immediately understand their terms, such as in direct face-to-face meetings. For example, a simple verbal order that the manager will be fired if the budget targets are not achieved this year is quite explicit. Explicitness depends on the clarity of the communication between the managers and their evaluators. Clear communication is desirable, unless a chance exists that the contract terms will quickly become obsolete.

SIZE OF RESULTS-DEPENDENT MONETARY REWARDS

Monetary rewards play an important role in the managers' motivational contracts in the USA and increasingly in those of other countries. It seems natural to conclude that the motivational impact that monetary rewards provide is directly related to the size of those rewards, except perhaps for a wealth effect that causes somewhat diminishing motivational returns as total compensation becomes larger. Surprisingly, however, and despite the plethora of compensation surveys that have been undertaken, little evidence exists to support that conclusion. Little information exists even about the size of the controllable, at-risk (performance-dependent) rewards that managers are promised. Reward analyses are also complicated because it is difficult to quantify the expected values of many forms of rewards, even some that are monetary.

Data certainly do exist about size of annual bonuses and salary increases. For example, data collected from 4000 US executives in 350 organizations by the Hay Group (1987) show that average annual bonuses for chief executive officers (CEOs) of corporations of over $1 billion in annual revenues was 47% of salary in 1984 and 59% in 1987; they are smaller for lower-level employees and for CEOs of smaller companies. Annual base salary increases for CEOs in large companies were in the range of 6.5% in 1987, and slightly higher than that in the immediately preceding years. Vancil (1979) and Merchant (1989) presented data about the annual bonuses promised profit centre managers. Vancil (1979) found that 90% of his sample of 317 profit-centre managers receive annual bonuses, and the median bonus was 25% of the salary. Merchant (1989) found that all 12 firms that he studied promised profit centre managers annual bonuses. The size of a typical bonus varied considerably (from 10% to 100% of salary), but he also found that a bonus of 25% of salary was typical.

In the UK, the Incomes Data Service reported that in June 1988, 50% of maufacturing organizations and 40% of service organizations had some form of performance-related pay scheme. However, many such schemes applied at the most senior levels only, and others only to shop floor employees, so the proportion of middle managers paid in this way is probably still quite small; but the trend is towards more middle management schemes of this sort. In particular, the financial services sector has been at the forefront of introducing performance-related pay schemes, as a response to an increasingly competitive environment. It is also of increasing importance in the public sector, including the civil service and local government, as evidenced by the UK employment minister, Kenneth Clark: 'It is only right to pay more to those who bring to their job enthusiasm, enterprise and initiative than those who are prepared merely to idle along.'

However, the real motivational effects of these performance-dependent rewards are much smaller than these data would make them appear, for any one of three reasons. One reason is that not all of this performance-dependent pay is at risk. Most firms use achievement of budget targets as the primary standard for assigning annual bonuses. Merchant and Manzoni (1989) found, however, that these budget targets were likely to be exceeded by the vast majority (80–90%) of profit centre managers and, as described above, firms pay bonuses after only a fraction (e.g., 80%) of the target is exceeded. Thus, it is not logical to consider all of the annual bonus at risk; if, for example, 60% of a bonus is virtually guaranteed because the performance targets are guaranteed to be achieved, then only 40% of the bonus can be considered to be at risk.

Secondly, some firms' performance evaluation processes do not do a good job of discriminating between above- (and below-) average performers, and superiors are reluctant to make sharply differentiated monetary rewards that they find uncomfortable to explain. Medoff and Abraham (1980) and Lawler (1971, p. 158) cite evidence showing a weak relationship between pay and performance. For example, in their study of the pay practices in two large manufacturing corporations, Medoff and Abraham found that the firms were unable to discriminate much among the performances of their managerial and professional employees; the performances of the vast majority of them (95%) were rated good or better. Furthermore, the employees rated highest were paid only 6–8% more than those rated lowest (unacceptable).

The third factor limiting the motivational impact of some performance-dependent rewards is the controllability of the measures of performance on which the rewards are assigned. For example, Merchant (1979) found the typical annual bonus award was 25% of salary, as described above. But he also found that in 9 of the 12 firms he studied, the award was either partially based on or potentially limited by the performance of the corporation (or another higher-level entity such as group). This assignment is made despite the fact that the profit centre managers had virtually no control over the performance of the corporation taken as a whole. Thus, the bonus award based on results that are controllable is less than the average 25% figure would suggest.

The expected values of the monetary, but non-cash, rewards are even more difficult to determine than those of the annual bonuses. The value of a share option, for example, varies with market values. Thus, it is not surprising that the Hay Group (1987) found the median value of stock options granted CEOs in large companies was 80% of salary in 1984, 97% in 1985 and 160% in 1986. After the October 1987 market crash, the values undoubtedly declined sharply. It is even more difficult to put a monetary (or utility) value on other forms of rewards such as additional autonomy or an improvement in promotion prospects. Merchant (1989), however, concluded that these other forms of rewards are sometimes much more important than the monetary rewards. He found that when profit centre managers are struggling to meet budget targets, the avoidance of missing the targets becomes their dominant concern. They are not as concerned about their bonuses as they are with the penalties that may be awarded if they miss targets, including loss of autonomy, loss of ability to get their own ideas funded, loss of promotion possibilities and, possibly, even loss of their job.

Also the values to the managers of all these forms of rewards are significantly affected by the timing of reward provision. Costello and Zalkind (1963) cited evidence showing that rewards provided soon after actions are taken have a far stronger motivational effect than those that are delayed; prompt rewards increase the speed and permanence of any learning that takes place. Merchant (1989) also concluded that managers appear to discount delayed rewards at a rate much greater than the time value of money. This discount factor sharply limits the motivational effect of long-term incentive plans because the rewards for taking an action are not received until some years into the future.

CONCLUSIONS

Rewards are an important part of the contracts used to control managers' behaviours. Rewards that can be linked to measures of performance or subjective performance evaluations come in many forms, but evidence about the effects of the various forms of rewards is not solid. It is widely, but not universally, believed that monetary rewards are important for motivation, but certainly other forms of rewards, such as praise, recognition and promotions, can also be powerful motivators.

However, motivational contract design presents problems far larger than just the choice of rewards. For instance, it seems to be cost effective to tailor rewards to managers' individual reward preferences. But contract costs can be borne in many forms, and the tailoring of reward promises to individual managers' taste is not necessarily an optimal control design choice because it increases the potential for managers' perceptions of contract inequities and the costs of contract administration.

Similarly, it is well recognized that organizations' total compensation package must be competitive to attract and retain qualified employees. If a portion of the compensation package, such as base salaries, is not competitive, perhaps because a salary cut or freeze was applied during a difficult operating period, then the results-dependent reward function may have to be adapted to compensate.

The most solid advice that can be provided is that performance-dependent rewards should be sufficiently meaningful to offset other incentives employees have to act in ways that are contrary to their organization's best interests, but the rewards should not be greater than those necessary to provide the needed motivation. However, solid evidence as to the positive and negative effects of most of the specific reward choices is only just emerging.

EXERCISES

1. In many corporations, managers are asked not to pursue blindly their quantitative goals, but to 'do what's best for the company' in taking their decision. Is this a motivational contract? If not, why not? If so, how is this contract enforced?

2. In corporation A, a large, divisionalized firm, managers are motivated by different factors. A number of managers, particularly the younger ones, are most interested in improving their promotion prospects. Some others want to build capital, so they are interested in high cash incentives and, particularly, stock ownership. A few managers nearing retirement are interested primarily in job security because they know it would be difficult for them to obtain another good position at an advanced age. How should corporation A design its reward structures so as to motivate all of these managers without wasting money on rewards that are not valued by some managers?

3. Many firms have found stock awards (e.g., stock options, restricted stock) to be effective in motivating managers. Such awards have the advantage of providing managerial rewards that are proportional to those earned by shareholders. Additionally, if the stock appreciates in value, the awards can be quite lucrative without creating a cash drain on the corporation. But what if the stock fails to continue appreciating in value? Do stock awards (e.g., options) still have a motivational effect? If not, is motivating managers a tougher task in firms that are not profitable and not growing?

4. Assume as a division manager in a large corporation that you have been promised the choice of two incentive plans. The first plan will pay you an annual bonus of 30% of your salary if you achieve your budget targets. The second plan will pay you a bonus of 30% of the salary you earn over a 5-year period, at the end of that period, if you achieve the cumulative targets in your 5-year strategic plan. (Assume the annual and 5-year targets are equally difficult to achieve.) Which plan would you prefer, and why? How large would the 5-year plan's promised bonus have to be to equal the motivational impact of the annual bonus plan?

5. Why do firms set lower performance cut-offs in their incentive compensation contracts? What is the danger in so doing?

6. Why do firms set upper performance cut-offs in their incentive compensation contracts? In what types of firm are these cut-offs

most valuable? What is the danger in setting upper cut-offs?
7. What are the advantages and disadvantages of providing bonuses 'by formula', as opposed to assigning them subjectively?
8. If you were a division manager in a large firm, which of the following compensation packages would you prefer:
   (a) salary of £50 000, with no bonus;
   (b) salary of £30 000, plus an annual bonus of 10% of the excess of your division's profit over budget. (You are not sure exactly what to expect because the environment is uncertain, but your best guess is that your division will exceed its profit budget by £200 000.)

   Does your choice identify you as risk averse or risk loving? If all managers in the firm were like yourself, what implications would that have for the design of incentive compensation schemes?

11

Interdependence and transfer pricing

SUMMARY

In comparison with many other accounting issues, transfer pricing may be regarded as a relatively small nut, but it is one which has proved difficult to crack. This may be due to the pervasive nature of transfer pricing. At one level, the issue has the attributes of a zero sum game, one divisional manager benefiting at the expense of another. At a totally different level, transfer pricing may be viewed as part of corporate strategy influencing the desired degree of integration and differentiation.

This chapter examines the literature, both empirical and theoretical, in an attempt to explain transfer pricing systems. We undertake the analysis within the multidivisional company and attempt to identify that set of circumstances in which the transfer pricing and allocation problems can be distinguished. When information economies, decentralization of the make or buy decision and a differentiation strategy are present, it is argued that the transfer price will not only affect individual division's profit performance, but also that of the company.

Also recent organizational studies have indicated the importance of divisional management autonomy and the need for mediation and arbitration procedures. Undoubtedly, there is an encouraging trend to view the transfer pricing system as an integral part of the management control process. Inappropriate systems may lead to a lack of behaviour congruence and encourage divisional managers to become over-competitive, myopic and parochial. One possible system to diminish these defects is offered by the introduction of the fair and neutral transfer pricing procedure.

INTRODUCTION

The degree of interdependence that exists between the divisions of a company is determined by the way in which its economic activities are organized. When each division operates in a separate product market then the degree of interdependence between the divisions is likely to be slight. However, even here the operating divisions may share common resources, such as a central computer or repair shop. Also, although the matching of strategy and organization structure may be sound at the outset, applications of new technology or the appearance of new product markets may break down the logic of maintaining the original separate divisional identities. But in other circumstances, particularly those that encourage vertical integration, there may be very considerable interdependence between divisions. The way in which the AIS accommodates the varying degrees of divisional interdependence is an important consideration in assisting the company to adapt to its changing business environments. The AIS should assist the company and its divisions to recognize new areas of activity and promote the establishment of new inter-divisional relationships.

The effective integration of divisional activities is one role that the transfer pricing system, as part of the AIS, can play. At the extremes, transfer prices may promote the integration of the activities of distinct divisions, or they may serve to differentiate the divisions still further by actively discouraging cooperation. Ideally the AIS should provide a transfer pricing system that encourages the matching of organization structure with the evolving business strategy. It is also important that the transfer pricing system chosen is compatible with the performance evaluation role played by the overall AIS.

There are many methods of setting transfer prices, but virtually all of those found in practice have one common attribute. That is, the transfer price represents a revenue for one division and a cost, of an equal amount, to another division. An increased transfer price improves the revenue of the supplying division and simultaneously increases the costs of the purchasing division. This zero sum game aspect of the transfer pricing system affects the reported performance of the division, both absolutely and relatively to other divisions. The potential for divisional managers to indulge in opportunistic behaviour to improve their individual performance at the expense of overall company performance is difficult to ignore.

This chapter begins by investigating the role of transfer pricing in the multidivisional company. The different forms of interdependence and the various types of transfer prices found in practice are presented and the roles they play are examined. In particular, we concentrate on balancing the need to maintain the freedom of action of divisional management and the need for overall integration. Next, alternative transfer pricing systems designed to promote behaviour congruence are examined. Finally, their consistency with an AIS which uses a profit-conscious style of evaluation and controllable RI as opposed to a non-accounting style with multiple performance measures is gauged.

INTERDEPENDENCE

Organizational structure

Developing an AIS that is capable of handling interdependence in a multidivisional company is something of an acid test. By matching the organization's structure with the product market environments in which it wishes to operate, interdependence between divisions may be reduced so as to be minimal. However, as business environments change and company strategy evolves, its organizational structure may remain static. This is because major reorganizations are costly and thus tend to occur infrequently. The burden of making the new strategies effective within the confines of the existing multidivisional structure may fall on the AIS.

The AIS may be required to provide information either to promote the links between separately identified divisions or to enhance the differentiation of the activities of the divisions and the markets served. For example, consider a company that manufactures electric motors, and bearings and other components, and sells these to other independent companies that assemble washing machines. The creation of separate divisions for motors and for bearings and components may be compatible with a strategy of differentiation. Each division has separate markets, and may develop customer loyalty for its particular products. However, if the number of washing machine assembly companies diminishes, there may be increasing pressure to maintain customer loyalty for the total package of the company's products. The need for the two divisions to interact on matters such as design specifications, quality and even pricing policies becomes greater. However, if the motor manufacturing division develops a new market for its products, for example, by selling motors to water pump assembly companies, the need for interaction is reduced. The structure of the firm may not change, but the AIS may be expected to assist the firm to adapt to greater or lesser interdependence between the divisions.

It may be argued that a multidivisional company should be more than just the sum of its parts by profiting from cross-fertilization of ideas and products between the divisions. The development of a new marketing strategy in one division may be capable of successful application in another; a new product of one division may complement an existing product in another division; a component part may have wider application than just within the division that first re-

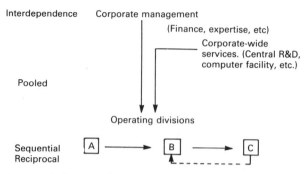

Fig. 11.1 Potential forms of interdependence (adapted from the MBS Survey Report, 1974).

quired it, and so on. From this perspective, the successful AIS in a multidivisional company is a mechanism that permits and promotes the blend of differentiation and integration necessary for successful adjustment to changing environments. The system should instil a need for flexibility between divisions in their dealings with each other. Thus, interdependence places a further requirement on the company's AIS if divisional managers are to interact effectively. The concept of behaviour congruence with its emphasis upon the development of consensus regarding actions in the feasible region seems appropriate. The notion that accounting information should not misdirect decision makers by encouraging opportunistic behaviour appears particularly relevant when dealing with interdependence in the multidivisional company.

Interdependence can take several forms. A decision to invest in a specific machine constrains expenditure on other assets and confines expenditure in the future to assets compatible with the original machine. There is interdependence between the short term and long term, such as the effects of investment on production, of advertising upon sales, or of the failure of one event occurring increasing the probability of failure of another event. Our concern relates to the interdependence of work flows, products and services. Hence, Thompson's (1967) categorization of technological interdependence appears useful (see Fig. 11.1).

Pooled interdependence is characterized by divisions that do not interact directly but who share a common source for a scarce resource. Sequential interdependence occurs when the output of one division becomes the input of another, and reciprocal interdependence occurs when the outputs of divisions become the inputs for each other. As we move from pooled to reciprocal interdependence, the complexity and the degree of interdependence increases substantially. Thompson argues that under conditions of extensive inter-dependence, in all but the most stable environments, a highly adaptive process of coordination is desirable, that is, coordination by mutual agreement, or feedback. However, as Baumler (1971, p. 342) states the conventional AIS which employs profit performance targets 'is clearly not a highly adaptive process based on mutual agreement; rather it contributes to the illusion of separation between sub-units'. The results of Baumler's laboratory experiment testify to the in-appropriateness of using a specific target when interdependence is extensive. Performance improved when specific targets were used only when interdependence was minimal. The conclusion of his research is clear: the effectiveness of the specific performance measure approach depends upon the degree of interdependence. It may be possible that the adoption of the profit-conscious or non-accounting styles of evaluation may partially overcome this difficulty, but we also need to examine whether the accounting treatments of interdependence are capable of generating a flexible attitude to inter-dependence amongst divisional managers.

The accountant's interpretation

Interdependence between operating units can be handled either by cost allocation or by transfer pricing. Wells (1978) suggests that the main historical reason for cost allocation is that it was used to develop full costs for pricing purposes. Stone (1973) found that even in 18th century England, cotton mill owners wished to know which were the profitable parts of their businesses and used transfer prices to help identify these.

We have already seen how pervasive the practice of allocation is on both sides of the Atlantic. However, it is worth noting that:

1. not all companies allocate all central costs;
2. when they do, they use different methods, such as apportionment, negotiation and actual use, which, it can be argued, reflect different degrees of interdependence.

Non-allocation of central joint costs indicates to divisional managers that these are outside their control. For example, top management may believe that basic research should be conducted although it may not give rise to commercial applications in the foreseeable future, and thus choose to bear the cost centrally rather than allocating it to divisions. The apportionment of central costs on a basis such as the number of employees, sales revenue, or square footage of floor space occupied, suggests to operating managers that they have some re-sponsibility for these costs and encourages them to question the size of the allocated amounts. Negotiation of a charge for shared resources induces this questioning to be more active and formal, whereas an allocation based on actual usage allows the divisional manager greater independence, as he may determine the use that he makes of the central service himself. At both extremes, namely non-allocation and a charge based on actual usage, interdependence is actually or at least apparently, minimal. This argument, which is based on Vancil's (1979) observations, can be applied to the three forms of interdependence defined by Thompson. Not to allocate costs relating to sequential and reciprocal interdependence leads to 'free' goods and services being provided by divisions for each other and results in financial performance reports being meaningless. We will therefore discuss this alternative no further.

A transfer price is a monetary value that is attached to a movement of goods from, or the rendering of services by, one organizational unit for another in the same company (Wells, 1968). In theory and practice, transfer prices can be attached to the movement of goods or services under all three forms of interdependence, and the cost allocation methods of apportionment, negotiation and actual usage have counterparts in transfer pricing. If allocation and transfer pricing are similar responses to the same phenomenon, namely interdependence, are not transfer prices also arbitrary and incorrigible?

Allocation and transfer pricing: the incorrigible twins

First of all let us examine the similarity of the two accounting treatments. We will assume that Division 1 produces a component part that costs £5000 per batch. Division 2 packages the components at a cost of £1000 per batch and then sells them to the retail trade for £12 000. The total profit earned by the divisions and the company is £6000. A transfer price of £11 000 per batch gives Division 1 the entire profits; a transfer price of £5000 completely reverses this result, and a mid-way transfer price of £8000 allows the divisions to share the profits equally. In the absence of an external market for the component part, any transfer price is irrefutable and unverifiable. All the allocations of profits to the divisions by means of these transfer prices are incorrigible (Thomas, 1980b), i.e., incapable of being verified by empirical evidence. Without a means of verifying the transfer price, a divisional manager's profit performance may increase due to his bargaining or political ability rather than any improvement in the efficiency or effectiveness of his division. This is analogous to the case where costs allocated to one division are increased because of actions taken by other divisions. If a divisional manager is aware that his performance measure includes incorrigible amounts over which he has no control, he will logically prefer a lower allocated cost or lower transfer price, even under a profit-conscious style of evaluation.

Hence transfer pricing and allocation seem to exhibit the same incorrigible characteristics. Both accounting treatments affect performance measurement and because a manager's financial responsibility exceeds his actual authority, the opportunistic actions associated with non-neutrality are likely to occur. The accounting treatment of interdependence can thus work against behaviour congruence for these reasons (Thomas, 1980b).

THE SPECTRUM OF ACCOUNTING TREATMENTS

Cost allocation by apportionment is but one way of promoting the degree of integration that top management believes to be appropriate. It suggests that there is a stable, if not fixed, inter-relationship between the provision and use of central and divisional goods and services. Cost allocation on the basis of actual usage, on the other hand, suggests that divisional users are able to vary their demands. The underlying assumptions here are that the user divisional manager can either do without the product or service without adversely affecting his division's effectiveness or, if the product or service is a necessary input to his business, he can obtain it more efficiently elsewhere. It implies that divisional managers are free to use alternative sources and that, as a result, the use made of internally provided goods and services will fluctuate. The manager of the electric motor division operating under a strategy of differentiation does not have the sale of his output underwritten or guaranteed by the component parts division, whereas this division may form a captive market for the motor division under a strategy of integration. An AIS that employs the actual usage or apportionment treatments reinforces these perceptions of freedom or captivity.

Basing cost allocation on actual usage is consistent with divisionalization, in that no division or central service department is protected from market forces. No service or intermediate product supplier can guarantee its existence by having a captive, internal group of user divisions. Hence, the initial view that profit, or any specific divisional performance measure is incomplete when the degree of interdependence is extensive may be tempered. When a manager has freedom to choose the amount of internal product or service his division uses, the resulting performance measure is substantially under his control. Giving divisional managers the freedom to take such actions means that the performance measures used should reflect the costs and benefits of these actions.

One of the external conditions necessary for the actual usage basis of cost allocation to be successful in promoting behaviour congruence is that alternative sources of supply exist. Some of the problems here are that the internal service or product is either unique or is not available in the quantities required (Anthony and Dearden, 1980). The uniqueness may derive from product quality, its secret composition, or advanced technological applications that are governed by patents. Independent external suppliers may be unwilling to earmark large proportions of their available capacity for a division if they know that another division in the same company is capable of producing the identical product, and the divisional manager's freedom to take alternative action is thus constrained. In the short term at least, the unavailability of alternative sources of supply increases the dependence of the user division upon other divisions unless it has alternative uses available for its resources or can do without the product. If the product is essential, the alternative uses of divisional resources are limited or external sourcing is infeasible, then there is a prima facie case for questioning the maintenance of a separate division.

So far, we have merely isolated the conditions under which a divisional manager may be prepared to accept accounting information involving cost allocations as part of his measure of performance. Of equal importance in maintaining the manager's commitment is the role the accounting information plays in influencing decision making. To promote behaviour congruence, the accounting information should guide the manager to take decisions that are in the best interests of the firm. The decisions that divisional management are most involved in will include whether to sell externally or internally, whether to buy externally or internally, and in what quantities. Making these decisions with relevant, neutral information should, over an extended period of time, indicate whether a more formal relationship between the divisions is required or whether the existing, flexible interaction should continue. The provision of accounting information that does not guide the manager to promote his self-interest is therefore important. This is evident when it is recognized that the same accounting information used in decision making will invariably contribute to the performance measures used to evaluate the division, the manager and the products concerned. Through performance evaluation, the information used to decide where to buy and where to sell provides an input to other decisions, such as the continuing or discontinuing of a product or service, the expansion or contraction of the division, the promotion or sacking of the manager, all of which have some effect on resource allocation within the firm. Hence, the monetary value placed on the internal good or service may have far-reaching consequences.

Relevant costs

In the transfer pricing literature, transfer prices ranging from the marginal cost of manufacture, to full-cost plus a profit element, to adjusted market prices, have all been advocated and, as we shall see, this diversity is also to be found in practice. Appendix 1 at the end of this chapter shows a simple example where market values may be thought relevant for purposes of performance evaluation; avoidable or incremental costs appropriate for the decisions to make internally or buy externally, and marginal costs are employed to determine the optimal output levels for the trading divisions. A rigorous analysis is not attempted here, because Thomas (1980b) has already accomplished this task. Instead, we highlight his conclusions, which are that:

1. No transfer price can promote behaviour congruence with regard to all the decisions and circumstances in which it will be used.
2. No transfer pricing approach can simultaneously guide divisional managers to take corporately optimal decisions and provide relevant information for separate profit performance evaluation. [The only exception to this conclusion occurs when there is a perfectly competitive external market for the internally traded good or service (Hirshleifer, 1956; Tomkins, 1973). The market price is equal to the marginal cost of the supplying division, and the company and the divisions are indifferent whether the trade takes place externally or internally.]

These conclusions hold when divisional managers are motivated and evaluated by profit measures. With a reduction in emphasis on short-term profit performance and the association with rewards, the divisional manager may subordinate his self-interest in order that the actions taken benefit the firm as a whole. However, for the individual divisional manager to know which course of action is in the company's best interest, more and more information needs to be transmitted. The market price is relevant only if the purchasing division is made aware of the alternative actions the supplying division can take to avoid a situation of excess capacity, and a breakdown of this division's avoidable and non-avoidable costs is thus needed. Further, to determine the quantities to be traded internally, the cost behaviour patterns of the divisions need to be compared in order to reach a decision in the company's best interests.

Chapter 6 illustrated how one technique, linear programming, can be used to handle large amounts of detailed data to obtain a corporately optimal solution. But this approach inevitably led to thinly disguised centralized decision making. The LP analysis assumed, just as the example in Appendix 1, that the relationship between costs and volume is precisely known. Additionally, the decisions presented in Appendix 1 assume that revenues obtainable in an external market can be determined with certainty. Once we recognize that the external markets for intermediate products are dynamic and subject to imperfections, then the entire linear programming and relevant cost analyses are in danger of collapsing.

For arguments sake, let us assume that the divisional managers are willing to subordinate their self-interest in order to obtain a corporately optimal solution. The presence of market uncertainty makes the forecasts of respective divisional managers concerning the prices they would have to pay externally subject to unintentional bias and inaccuracy. Subsequently, the over-optimistic or over-pessimistic forecasts of one manager may be interpreted by the other as intentional. Opportunistic behaviour may be set in motion if the affronted manager perceives that the other divisional manager is rewarded for an increased profit performance.

So, in terms of using the relevant cost information to determine the appropriate levels of interdependence in the multidivisional company the following observations are pertinent. Firstly, different transfer prices are needed for the inter-related decisions taken by divisions. Secondly, market prices, avoidable costs and marginal costs are all relevant, but their application will result in a plethora of different profit measures. Thirdly, even if short-term profit performance and incentive schemes are de-emphasized, the inherent uncertainty associated with external intermediate product markets allows the possibility of unintentional inaccuracy in the estimates to occur. The mere perception that one manager is taking advantage of this may lead another to provide intentially biased estimates of costs or revenues in future. In short, the assumptions of the relevant cost analysis may be regarded as inconsistent with the existence of uncertain, dynamic markets, which is the basic reason why the multidivisional structure was adopted. The relevant cost analyses only work because a non-programmed decision is treated as programmed.

Negotiation

Negotiation of the cost of central services to be borne by divisional managers may occur in conjunction with freedom to decide whether or not to seek alternative sources of supply. Negotiation of the cost of central services may centre around the estimated use to be made of the resource by the divisions or an attempt to spread the cost 'fairly' between the divisions. There is a parallel proposal in the transfer pricing literature (Cook, 1955, p. 93) that a:

... free negotiation system could satisfy the basic criteria ... that a transfer price that will not lead to transfers which will reduce the company's profit but which will permit and encourage any transfer which increases the company's profit ...

will be achieved by this means. Dean (1955) elaborates on the basic approach by recommending that the role of a price mediator is created to constrain the negotiations.

Support for the negotiation approach is also given by Shillinglaw (1977) and Fremgen (1970), but virtually all of these writers agree that the divisional managers should be free to take alternative actions. 'Free access to markets and sources of supply' is recognized as a necessary condition by Dean; 'the ability to test and verify the price by means of market transactions' is required by Shillinglaw. If there are no true alternatives, then negotiation merely creates pseudo-profit centres.

Watson and Baumler's (1975) support of negotiation is based on the notion of conflict resolution. They argue that although divisions are differentiated, their managers are still members of a single organization, and that a skilled price mediator and the provision of various accounting data (e.g., cost schedules, mathematical programming solutions, etc.) will provide guides to decision making. Divisional managers may indeed belong to a single organization but, as we have seen, little effort at present seems to be made to develop shared values or assumptions between top and divisional managements. Instead, commitment to imperfect financial targets is required and rewarded, and in these circumstances it seems likely that negotiation will be primarily motivated by self-interest. The use of a non-accounting style of evaluation, linked only weakly to rewards may allow the conflict resolution powers of negotiation to emerge. Certainly Arvidsson's (1973) laboratory experiments substantiate the use of face-to-face, direct contact negotiation as a positive means to create a joint problem-solving atmosphere. Nevertheless, its effect must be related to the importance of profit in evaluating divisional managers' performances and the ability of the AIS to overcome the non-neutrality aspect of accounting information in non-programmed decisions.

Divisional management autonomy

Taking the perspective that the accounting treatment should be consistent with achieving behaviour congruence and enabling the company's strategy to evolve within a multidivisional structure, instances where problems arise can be identified as follows:

1. When divisional managers do not have the freedom to choose alternatives for the goods or services offered internally, either:
   (a) because the company's policy does not allow this degree of delegated authority; or
   (b) because the unique quality or volumes required of the internal goods or services are unavailable outside the company.
2. When the divisional manager is required to take decisions affecting other divisions using the relevant accounting information because:
   (a) divisional autonomy is sacrificed by the necessary transmission and centralization of information; and
   (b) the inherent uncertainty of market prices makes the whole idea of optimality questionable and may instigate opportunistic behaviour such as the manipulation of cost and revenue forecasts.

This analysis suggests that specific performance measures for segments of a multidivisional company can be calculated even when the manager's freedom to take alternative actions is constrained by the requirement that relevant cost information is used. However, the communication of this information to other divisional managers and the top management suggests that ultimately the decisions about whether to trade internally or externally are taken centrally. The divisional management's commitment as an independent manager is thus reduced. Alternatively, if the managers are allowed to take alternative actions such as purchasing or selling externally, there is the possibility that they will manipulate the cost or revenue information in order to improve their division's reported profit. In the former instance, divisional management may argue that the use of relevant cost concepts is contrary to decentralization, whereas in the second case, the company should be aware that the divisional manager's decisions may not be in the company's best interests.

Whilst the trade-off concerning transfer prices which ensure optimal solutions but require centralized decision-making and those which maintain decentralization but can result in sub-optimal solutions has long been recognized (Grabski, 1985), the debate has been somewhat lopsided. Optimality or sub-optimality can be calculated whereas the costs and benefits of decentralization are largely unquantifiable and intangible. However, the application of organization theory offers some insight into the potential relationship between divisional management autonomy and appropriate transfer prices.

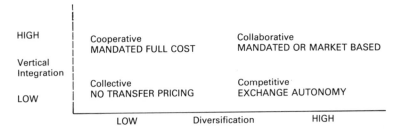

Fig. 11.2   The manager's analytical plane.

Swieringa and Waterhouse (1982) applied four models to the well known Birch Paper Company case. The Behavioural (Cyert and March, 1963), the Garbage Can (Cohen, March and Olson, 1972), the Organizing (Weick, 1979) and the Markets and Hierarchies (Williamson, 1975, 1979) models each gave a different perspective on the same problem. Firmly placing transfer pricing in an organization context led these writers to conclude that the process of devising transfer pricing rules, procedures and prices may be as important in achieving organizational control as the rules, procedures and prices themselves.

However, the practical problem of which form of transfer price to apply was largely ignored and prompted Eccles (1983, 1985) to develop a deductive theory based on in-depth interviews conducted with 150 executives in thirteen US companies. Identifying the transfer pricing system as dependent on the strategy companies adopt, Eccles developed 'The Manager's Analytical Plane' or MAP.

The collective organization resembles most closely the small business where divisionalization is absent and close central control is found. The competitive organization is akin to a conglomerate, divisional managers enjoying significant discretion over decision-making and being evaluated on profit performance. In this case market based transfer prices are recommended because divisional autonomy extends to control over the make or buy decision.

A mandated cost transfer price is suggested for cooperative organizations where the divisions are not primarily profit centres, performance being evaluated on a comparison of budgeted and actual results. The strategy requires that internal demand is satisfied before contact is allowed with external parties and the use of a mandated or formula based transfer price allows simplicity in operation and ease of understanding.

The most difficult organizational context is the collaborative where Eccles recommended a mandated or market based transfer price. Mandated prices are required to ensure that the benefits of vertical integration are attained but high diversification with an emphasis on separate divisional profit performance required market based transfer prices. Eccles felt that constraining the sourcing decisions of divisional managers and employing dual prices, that is, the revenue to the supplier division is not the same as the cost to the buying division, may be appropriate in this instance. The autonomy afforded divisional managers under different strategic and structural conditions is therefore important and Eccles emphasized the need for transfer pricing policies to be responsive to continuous changes in organizational circumstances. Although the theory can be criticized for being based on limited empirical evidence from a few industries and for not providing a categoric recommendation for the collaborative organization, it nevertheless provides a rich understanding of transfer pricing in practice.

If the existence of uncertainty makes the multidivisional structure appropriate, then the designer of the AIS should be aware that information for optimal decision making is unlikely to be available. The non-programmed nature of the decisions means that even well-intentioned managers cannot supply unbiased and accurate cost and revenue forecasts. With an evaluation scheme that is based on short-term divisional profit, managers have an incentive to manipulate their forecasts. Solomons (1965) recognized the incompatibility of using 'ideal' transfer prices together with divisional profit as a measure of managerial responsibility, and Naert (1973, p. 100) also expresses this clearly:

If profit of one division depends on the performance of the other division, the first purpose of decentralization is not served, since decentralization does not result then in a better means of controlling managerial performance. Neither will the second purpose of decentralization, namely to improve motivation, be realized for the same reason. Divisional performance should then be measured on a cost performance rather than on a profit performance basis.

Therefore, it seems that accountants and designers of systems should be as concerned with the divisional manager's perception of his freedom to take alternative actions as with the financial numbers placed on the internal movements of goods and services. In the multidivisional company, the aim should be to provide accounting information for feasible rather than optimal solutions.

ACCOUNTING TREATMENTS IN PRACTICE

We will concentrate on empirical studies dealing with transfer pricing practices in this section, partly because the evidence concerning cost allocation has been given in Chapter 9 and also because

Table 11.1 Transfer prices in practice

	BIM (1971)	MBS (1974)	Tomkins (1973)	Emmanuel (1976)	Vancil (1979)
No. of companies participating	293	44	51	92	291
% age using transfer prices on the following basis:	70%	100%	89%	100%	85%
Variable/direct costs		5.8	4.5	2.9	4.6
at standard				2.9	2.9
at actual				–	1.7
Full cost (incl. overhead)	39*	44.5	13.4	17.7	25.5
at standard		26.4		13.2	12.5
at actual		18.1		4.5	13.0
Full cost-plus specific		12.1	12.0	16.2	16.7
return on sales					2.9
return on investment					2.9
mark-up					10.9
Market price	38	37.6	46.2	44.1	31.0
competitor's price		26	32.8	10.3	11.7
list price		–	–	16.2	17.2
most recent bid		–	–	–	2.1
adjusted by discount		11.6	13.4	17.6	–
Negotiated	23	–	21	19.1	22.2
Other	–	–	2.9	–	–

* This report indicates that 39% of the respondents use a cost basis for transfer pricing.

the evidence is more explanatory in nature. The reader should be warned that these explanations are subject to considerable subjective interpretation and that the data were again collected by means of postal questionnaires.

The percentage of participating companies using transfer prices in two of the studies (MBS, 1972; Emmanuel, 1976) is high because the stated focus of this research was confined to transfer pricing alone. Nevertheless, the studies concerned with financial planning (Tomkins, 1973) and decentralization (Vancil, 1979) also suggest that transfer pricing is found in most large companies. The types of transfer prices used are interestingly uniform, as shown in Table 11.1.

If the MBS survey replies for full cost-plus, and the adjusted market price are aggregated (23.7%) to indicate bases where negotiation is plausible, common features are apparent. Over a third of

Table 11.2 Freedom to take alternative action

	BIM (1971)	MBS (1974)	Tomkins (1973)	Emmanuel (1976)	Vancil (1979)
The decision to trade externally					
Has to be approved	73%	80%	69%	69%	61%
Never has to be approved	27%	20%	31%	31%	39%

Table 11.3 Freedom to set/change price

	BIM (1971)	MBS (1974)	Tomkins (1973)	Emmanuel (1976)	Vancil (1979)
Corporate management alone	61	35	5	32	7
Corporate management and the divisional management	21	43	38	39	39
Divisional management alone	13	22	57	29	54
Other	4	–	–	–	6
No answer	1	–	–	–	–

companies used some form of market price; a fifth used negotiated transfer prices and between a third and a half based their transfer prices on costs. These surveys indicate that market-oriented transfer prices are important in industrial practice. Earlier studies in the USA, conducted by the NICB (1967) and Mautz (1968), substantiate this contention. The discretion of divisional managers to decide where to sell and where to buy their respective outputs and inputs is shown in Table 11.2.

The approval required may be that of top management or of other divisional managers. The BIM data, when related to the respondent's perception of the degree to which their company was decentralized, indicate that the freedom to determine the source of supplies is positively correlated with decentralization. Vancil provides evidence that the freedom is positively related with the manager's functional authority over manufacturing. Again, the uniformity of practice, particularly in the UK, appears noteworthy.

Table 11.3 indicates who is responsible for setting or changing prices. The Tomkins and Vancil responses refer to divisional price setting, in general, whereas the other three survey responses relate to the setting of transfer prices. The BIM and Emmanuel studies find no significant difference between the management groups responsible for setting and changing the transfer price. Divisional management involvement in transfer price determination increases for those companies which regard themselves as fully decentralized (BIM, 1971). No real pattern of divisional management involvement emerges, and one reason for this may be the diverse ways in which the questions were asked. It is feasible that the use of the market list price, for example, may be categorized as top management alone setting the transfer price. Vancil observes that the divisional manager's influence over prices varies with his functional authority over sales personnel and the importance of divisional sales relative to total corporate sales.

Data on the degree of divisional inter-dependence is difficult to present in a single table because different researchers have chosen different percentages of internal sales to total divisional sales to indicate low, medium or extensive interaction. Some research studies focus on inter-dependence company-wide (BIM, 1971; Tomkins, 1973; Vancil, 1979), whereas others collect data about the 'typical' or main operating units degree of inter-dependence (MBS, 1974; Emmanuel, 1976). No generalization of the survey data is appropriate. In fact, it may be argued that discovering the amount of inter-dependence is irrelevant. The stability or flexibility of the interdependence may give a more meaningful reflection of the requirements placed on the AIS.

EXPLANATIONS OF PRACTICE

Tomkins did not find any relationship between the volume of internal transfers and the transfer pricing basis used. He concluded that the basic conflict in fixing transfer prices was to decide the degree to which divisional autonomy was desirable. Vancil observed that diversification was negatively related to inter-dependence. Not surprisingly, companies having related businesses are more involved in internal transfers of goods and services. The results of this survey show that the degree of inter-dependence was positively related to divisional profit performance. One possible explanation is that transfer pricing poses fewer problems when divisions are delegated the necessary authority to take alternative actions, and engage in internal trade on the same basis as external sales or purchases. The inference that companies which try to maintain the independence of profit centres by using market-oriented prices tend to be more successful is the only significant explanation offered. This is perhaps

Table 11.4 The relationship between transfer pricing objectives and combinations of organizational variables

Combinations of organizational variables*

Benefits of integration	EXIST								NON-EXIST							
Cost of using external market	EXIST				NON-EXIST				EXIST				NON-EXIST			
Degree of interdependence	EXTENSIVE		SLIGHT		EXTENSIVE		SLIGHT		EXTENSIVE		SLIGHT		EXTENSIVE		SLIGHT	
Units identified by:	FUNC-TION	PROD-UCT	FUNC-TION	PROD-UCT	FUNC-TION	PROD-UCT	FUNC-TION	PROD-UCT	FUNC-TION	PROD-UCT	FUNC-TION	PROD-UCT	FUNC-TION	PROD-UCT	FUNC-TION	PROD-UCT
Transfer pricing objectives																
differentiation	0	3	0	1	1	4	3	3	0	0	1	2	1	1	6	6
integration	7	3	3	1	3	10	3	4	2	1	1	0	1	0	0	0

* The incurrence of incremental costs of using the external market are entirely conditional upon the existence of an external market, hence, this latter variable is excluded from this part of the analysis for ease of presentation.

not surprising, given the potentially large number of intervening variables that may influence the transfer pricing base in a particular company.

Table 11.4 shows the objectives that companies adopt for transfer pricing relative to various combinations of organizational characteristics (Emmanuel, 1976). A continuum is evident, with some clustering at the extremes, which suggests that the organizational characteristics may distinguish transfer pricing objectives in those extreme cases. However, there is no clear explanation of the role chosen for transfer pricing when, let us say, benefits of integration exist and the costs associated with differentiation are low.

Our inability to explain the reasons for various transfer pricing practices may eventually be overcome by adopting more clinical and longitudinal research techniques. In recent years, the approach of building a normative theory based on practice has gained support (Kaplan, 1986), and Hopwood (1983) has argued that organizational research to date has been limited in scope, fragmented and scarce. From a completely different perspective to Eccles and the other empirical researchers, Spicer (1988) has attempted a rectification of these deficiencies.

Spicer relies on inductive reasoning to develop an organizational theory of transfer pricing. Taking Watson and Baumler's (1975) behavioural approach as a starting point, the growing literature on the economics of internal organizations (Williamson, 1975, 1979) are integrated to formulate six testable hypotheses. Again, the role of divisional management autonomy is highlighted and, in addition, the role which top management may play in conflict resolution and the arbitration of disputes arising from inter-divisional trade. Spicer concentrates on three aspects of transaction costs, namely:

1. the investment characteristics of the transaction (the degree of specific investment required in the intermediate good);
2. the frequency or volume of internal transfers;
3. the degree of uncertainty and/or complexity associated with internal transfer.

Firms are assumed to face two fundamental decisions. Firstly, they must decide the design feature of products; and secondly, whether to make or buy the product. The make or buy decision is assumed to be made in order to limit the transaction costs involved. Spicer proceeds to develop hypotheses related to the design characteristics of products. One of these hypotheses is shown in Fig. 11.3.

Although there have been over 50 empirical studies of transfer pricing undertaken since 1960 world-wide, evidence to substantiate

Fig. 11.3   Transfer prices and product design characteristics.

or reject this and Spicer's other hypotheses is limited. However, on the relationships suggested in Fig. 11.3, a survey undertaken by one of the authors (Emmanuel, 1976) provides confounding data. For standardized products, for example, half the sample companies used full cost prices, with the remainder equally divided between the use of negotiated and market-based transfer prices. A more recent survey (Price Waterhouse, 1984) provides some support for Spicer's hypothesis, in that 90% of the 74 US companies participating in the study used market prices for standardized products. For customized products, the Emmanuel survey found two forms of transfer price were equally popular, namely adjusted market price and cost-plus. From the same survey, 50% of the UK companies participating employed a cost-based transfer price, but a third used market-based and the remainder a negotiated transfer price. The Price Waterhouse survey reports similar results, whereas the Manchester Business School study (1972) offers support of Spicer's hypothesis. This survey reveals that when specially made production equipment is transferred, actual full cost is by far the most popular pricing base. Additionally, the majority of companies limit divisional managers' freedom to trade externally in this situation.

The evidence is incomplete and limited but Spicer's hypotheses may form the foundation on which future empirical research may usefully be undertaken. More gloomily, it may be that we shall never be able to determine why a particular transfer price is chosen except in specific cases, and we thus may have reached an intellectual impasse. On the one hand, there is the school of thought begun by Coase (1937), and reinterpreted by Henderson and Dearden (1966, p. 145) and others, that states:

integrated performance should exceed the performance achieved when the two operations [divisions] are kept separate. If it does not, why integrate?

On the other hand, there is general agreement that intermediate product markets are imperfect and may involve considerable costs to the company when used by divisions. The trade-off between the internal benefits of integration and the external opportunities of differentiation is not likely to be stable. Yet the AIS can impose a degree of rigidity on divisional managers that confirms the continued use of strategies of integration or differentiation regardless of such changes.

At the risk of repeating ourselves, it seems timely to review the foregoing arguments and research. First, the current empirical evidence does not explain transfer pricing in practice. Secondly, advances in developing an organization theory of transfer pricing are in their infancy. Thirdly, and more positively, recent empirical and theoretical contributions have recognized that the system is as important as the actual transfer price employed or recommended. Definition of the system may be confined to arbitration and adjustment procedures, or more broadly, performance evaluation of divisions and their managers and corporate structure and strategy. The inter-meshing of these and other variables provides a rich and fertile area of research if clinical, in-depth case studies are undertaken. At this point, what is clear is that decentralization, especially in terms of the make or buy decision, occupies a central position in the analysis of attempting to explain why certain transfer pricing systems are employed.

TOWARDS A BEHAVIOUR CONGRUENT TRANSFER PRICING SYSTEM

At risk of adding yet another proposal to the transfer pricing litera-ture, we shall present a transfer pricing system that provides a learning effect that may lead to behaviour congruence in the multi-divisional company. It is not contended that this proposal offers a complete solution, but rather that by working through it the reader will be able to appreciate the issues that exist in this area. The astute reader will be aware too that we have not addressed inter dependence in the multinational company. International transfer pricing gives rise to additional problems over and above those already outlined, and a review of the empirical and structural evidence is given in Appendix 2. Although the international case is more complex, the interrelationship of business strategy, organization structure and the accounting treatment of the inter dependence may be no less im-portant than in the domestic transfer of goods and services.

The response to the absence of perfectly competitive external markets for intermediate goods and services may be to limit decentralization, in practice, or to impose accounting treatments that are only successful in circumstances in which decentralization is necessarily limited. Under the former policy, negotiated transfer prices provide results that satisfy neither division. 'Everyone feels cheated, and everyone has an alibi for his profit ... results' (Dean, 1955, p. 72). This reaction is also likely where a formula, full cost-plus transfer price is imposed or negotiated (Lambert, 1979). A transfer price designed to give corporately optimal decisions renders the subsequent performance measures unreliable as indicators of managerial effectiveness and may also prompt manipulation of information. The accountant's role is to develop a system that maintains divisional authority but also limits the incentives for opportunistic decision making, especially in terms of the decision to make internally or buy externally. From this perspective, just one transfer pricing problem is isolated. All other problems are similar to problems of allocation.

This transfer pricing problem occurs when:

1. A strategy of differentiation is followed and a multidivisional structure is adopted.
2. There are alternatives to the internal trade available that the divisional manager is free to use.
3. The amount of information transmitted between divisions and top management, to ensure an 'optimal' solution, should be kept strictly limited.

When a perfectly competitive external market for the internally traded product or service exists, the transfer price is given by the market price. Perfect competition assumes many suppliers and users, a homogeneous product, insignificant transportation costs and perfect knowledge between all the parties involved. As Hirshleifer (1956) shows, this is the one situation where multidivisional performance measures and corporate optimality can be attained without concern for the opportunistic behaviour of managers. The question therefore arises as to the extent to which such markets exist in real life.

Imperfectly competitive markets

Solomons (1965) outlined some common features of imperfection in intermediate markets. The transferred good may be differentiated; discounts may be given for particular types of trade or for different conditions of sale; the spot and long-term prices may be significantly different. The net result is that the price obtainable by the seller may be very different from the price payable by a buyer as when, for example, there are selling costs, debt collection costs and other costs of finding a customer in the external market.

Studies of intermediate product markets by Stigler and Kindahl (1970), and Atkin and Skinner (1975), suggest that sellers' discount terms and amounts are not uniform. Further, the range of prices facing the selling division overlap only in part with that facing the buying division. The conventionally made assumption that a consensus of divisional and top management beliefs with respect to market prices is possible becomes dubious in these circumstances. Market prices may be uncertain because the market is dynamic, subject to product innovation and new competitor entry. Any agreement on a market based transfer price may, through the passage of time, require time-consuming renegotiation of that budgeted price.

In these circumstances, the use of a market-oriented transfer price may well lead to the unintended decision making indicated in the first part of Appendix 1. The properties of transfer pricing that are most important when the external market is imperfectly competitive are:

1. That the transfer price can be verified by the divisional managers as fair and accurate.
2. That the transfer price minimizes the inducements for self-interest or improving one division's profit at the expense of another; that is, it is neutral.

Solomon's suggestion of a two-part tariff transfer price seems to satisfy the second of these conditions, but not the first. His proposal involves charging the user division the variable costs of the transferred product, plus a lump-sum period cost. The period cost is based on the proportion of the supplier division's capacity that is budgeted to serve the user division. Hence, if 10% of the annual capacity is required by the user division, the supplier will charge 10% of its budgeted fixed costs as a period cost. The proposal therefore avoids the inclusion of fixed costs in the price of every unit of the intermediate product traded internally. Variable costs are not distorted and provide proxies of marginal, avoidable costs relevant for decision making. The supplier division's performance is not compromised to the extent that a realistic proportion of fixed costs are recouped via the period cost charge. Thus, the neutrality of the transfer pricing system to provide relevant cost information that may guide divisional managers to take where to buy, where to sell decisions in the company's best interests, is served. However, the profit performance status of the supplier division may be adversely affected.

The product and period charges contribute to the recovery of costs, but fail to provide a profit for the supplier division in terms of the internal trade. The accuracy of the two-part tariff in reflecting the supplier division's contribution to corporate profit may be questioned. The manager of that division may perceive the profit performance measure as consistently understated. This conviction may strengthen when external sales, at a price greater than the two-part tariff, have to be relinquished because of internal trade. Uncertainty over the prices at which the supplier may be able to charge external customers and the prices the user may have to pay external suppliers may cause the conviction to be persistent. The supplier division may be unwilling to earmark capacity at the two-part tariff price if it is thought that external sales may be made at a higher price during the period covered by the budget. Similarly, the user division may be unwilling to accept the internal trade at the two-part tariff price if it is believed that the price of external purchasing will be lower in the period covered by the budget.

A proposal by Emmanuel and Gee (1982) addresses this problem and outlines a procedure to obtain fair and neutral properties for market-oriented transfer prices. In shortened form, the procedure charges a transfer price in two instalments. The first instalment is a product cost equivalent to the standard direct or variable costs of manufacture, and the second instalment represents a period cost. The period cost is calculated at the end of the reporting period by determining the contribution that the supplier division earned during the period through the external sale of the equivalent product to that traded internally. This procedure is made known in advance to divisional managers and appears to be consistent with maintaining decentralization and the freedom of action of divisional managers. It is also made known in advance that a lost contribution charge will be made against any division that fails to reach the level of budgeted capacity utilization agreed between the individual divisional manager and top management. This charge is unrelated to the ex-post period cost of the transfer price, but it is an integral part of the system. The aim of the lost contribution charge is to reverse any inducement the supplier division may have to sell limited quantities externally in order to inflate the market price.

A simple example may illustrate the procedure. Note that the large gap between the divisions' expectations of market prices is primarily for clarity of illustration, but such differences may be found in practice (Atkin and Skinner, 1975). Division A, the supplier, has capacity available to make 100 000 general purpose motors in the forthcoming half-year. No other use for the resources combining to make the motors is available in this time period. The standard variable costs of manufacture are £5 per motor and the divisional manager believes that 70% of total capacity can be sold externally at a price of £10 per motor.

Division B, the user, requires 50 000 of these motors in the next six-month period, but the divisional manager reckons that, on average, the purchase cost will amount to £7.50 per motor. At an initial meeting to decide whether to trade internally or not, this mixture of opinions about future market conditions and costs should be readily available. The difference in expected market prices may be due to the managers' expectations of excess demand or excess supply and the different marketing policies appropriate to meet these circumstances, the discounts the user division has obtained previously, the extra costs the supplying division incurs in trading externally, as well as concern for quality, delivery date and other dimensions of non-price competition.

If the external market is imperfectly competitive, and if the managers' expectations are realized, the optimal solution for the company is to transfer 30 000 motors from Division A to B. The problem is twofold; firstly, how can the managers be convinced that internal trade is appropriate; and secondly, that it can be conducted at a price that will subsequently be viewed as fair to both parties in terms of the effect on the profit performance measures.

The cost of manufacture which may be taken to approximate incremental cost (£5) is lower than the cost of external purchase, £7.50. Internal trade is therefore feasible. It is not appropriate to trade internally before satisfying external demand because the contribution from this trade is double that of the internal transfer. In these circumstances, general policies for divisional managers to satisfy internal customer demands first will be inefficient, and what constitutes a fair transfer price still requires resolution. With complete confidence in his expectations, the supplier can determine the maximum range of the discount he is willing to offer to secure the internal trade without adversely affecting his division's profit performance by using the following formula:

$$(1 - dt_{j\,max})M_s = 2S_t - M_b$$

Where M_s is the market price of motor expected by the supplier; S_t the standard variable cost of manufacture; M_b the price the user is expected to pay for the motor; and $dt_{j\,max}$ is the maximum discount the supplier should be willing to offer. Thus:

$$(1 - dt_{j\,max})10 = 2(5) - 7.5$$

and:

$$dt_{j\,max} \qquad = 75\%$$

This algorithm incorporates the saving on trading internally and adjusts the selling price accordingly. The transfer price is therefore a product cost (S_t) plus a contribution equivalent to that expected on external sales during the same period. This latter period cost cannot be determined until the end of the reporting period. To verify the effect on divisional profit performance, the following computations are given. Note that the lost contribution charge is independent of the period cost of the transfer price. The lost contribution charge provides an incentive for the supplier to consider seriously the internal trade when expecting excess capacity:

Division A: No internal trade	£
Revenue (70 000 × 10)	700 000
Standard variable cost (70 000 × 5)	350 000
Contribution	350 000
Less lost contribution charge	
$(M_b - S_t)(Q_s - Q_a)$	
(7.5 − 5)(100 000 − 70 000)	(75 000)
	£275 000

Division B:	
Purchase costs (50 000 × 7.5)	£375 000

The computation that follows shows the lowest price Division A can charge as a transfer price (i.e., £2.50) and still maintain divisional profit at £275 000:

Division A: With internal trade	£
Revenue (70 000 × 10)	
(30 000 × 2.5)	775 000
Standard variable cost	
(100 000 × 5)	500 000
Divisional contribution	£275 000

Division B:	
Purchase costs	
(20 000 × 7.5)	
30 000 × 2.5)	£225 000

However, the supplier need not give a 75% discount. Based on the supplying manager's expectations and assuming perfect prediction, this is only the upper limit of the discount he could give and still attain the same level of financial performance with the internal trade as without it. Let us assume that a 25% discount is offered and accepted by the managers. If the expectations of the divisional manager of A are confirmed, then at the end of the 6-month period, the transfer price is:

		£5
Product cost (S_t)		
Period cost $M_s(1 - dt_j)$	7.5	
less S_t	5	2.5
		£7.5 per motor

The manager's expectation of the £10 selling price is upheld, and the division's performance contributes £425 000 (i.e., (70 000 × 10) + (30 000 × 7.5) − 500 000). The user division pays an equal per unit cost for motors whether these are sourced internally or externally in this instance. Alternatively, let us assume that the expected selling price of £10 did not materialize and, on average, the motors sold for £8:

Division A: Actual performance	£
Revenue (70 000 × 8)	
(30 000 × 6)	740 000
Actual variable cost	
(100 000 × 5)	500 000
Divisional contribution	£240 000

The transfer price becomes:

		£5
Product costs	6	
Period cost $M_s(1 - dt)$	5	1
less S_t		
		£6 per motor

We have assumed actual variable costs to equal standard, and the £185 000 contribution variance is made up of adverse price variances on external sales (70 000 × £2) and internal sales (30 000 × £1.5). The buying division benefits from this outcome because his expectation of the market price proved to be more accurate:

Division B:

		Budget		Actual
Transfer price	30 000 at £7.5	225 000	at £6	180 000
External purchase	20 000 at £7.5	150 000	at £7.5	150 000
		£375 000		£330 000

Fairness and neutrality

At first glance, it may appear that the manager of Division A bears all the risks associated with this transfer pricing procedure. When the supplier expects to sell the entire capacity externally, there is no incentive to provide a discount because no lost contribution charge is expected to be levied. A premium may be set on the internal trade when excess demand is forecast. Also, in the circumstances given above, the supplier cannot claim that it was manipulation of the transfer price that caused the poor performance. His market predictions proved inaccurate, and his financial performance suffered because of this. The effect of the lower market price did not disproportionally affect the transfer price, because it was based on the actual market prices obtained less the agreed discount. If the manager had not agreed to the internal sale, divisional performance would have been even lower. A similar argument applies when the supplier exceeds the selling price expected and the transfer price is increased. In both instances, neither manager is to be blamed: the decision not to operate with excess capacity is correct, only the prediction of the ultimate transfer price is inaccurate, and that is to be expected under conditions of uncertainty. The calculation of the ultimate transfer price is not subject to bargaining, because it is market determined and thus provides allocation-free information for performance appraisal.

The divisional managers' freedom to use external markets is not constrained. Also they are aware that the only means at their disposal to influence the transfer price is through the accurate predictions of market behaviour. The focus of attention should therefore become how the market will operate in some future period, and not on how to set a transfer price beneficial to the individual division. This recognizes that divisional managers may still make decisions not in the company's best interests because of forecast inaccuracies. In non-programmed decision making, we have argued that the feasibility, not optimality, of the agreed action is the important criterion. It is this emphasis that the proposal follows.

CONCLUSIONS

We must remind ourselves that the above transfer pricing proposals apply only to a specific set of conditions concerning inter-dependence in the multidivisional company. These are that each division faces an uncertain product market environment; that all divisional managers are free to trade internally or externally; and that divisional and managerial performance is evaluated or perceived to be evaluated by some form of profit performance measure. Under these circumstances, the transfer price needs to provide information that will have a neutral effect on divisional managers' behaviour and will contribute to the completeness and accuracy of the separate performance measures. A market-based transfer price may prove defective when the external market is so dynamic or imperfect that divisional managers cannot agree on what the likely price will be. Opportunistic behaviour, such as gaming, introducing phantom quotes or spurious expectations of demand may be introduced to increase one division's share of the profit on the internal trade at the expense of the other. There is also the possibility that such behaviour may cause the internal trade not to take place, to the detriment of the company overall.

Faced with these possibilities, multidivisional companies may reduce the incentives for opportunistic behaviour by using their AIS in a way that de-emphasizes the importance of profit performance measures. For example, a non-accounting style of evaluation and multiple performance measures may be used. The absence of rewards associated with performance measures may encourage divisional managers to reach consensus on the merits of internal trade relative to the uncertain, external environment without recourse to evaluating the decision in terms of their self-interest. The manipulation of cost and revenue information may be substantially reduced because there is much less concern about profit. In order for the divisions to agree actions about the levels of inter-dependence, time-consuming, wide-ranging discussions about the assumptions affecting the merits of the internal trade will need to take place for a consensus to emerge.

Alternatively, the relative importance of the profit performance measure may be maintained, but with evaluation occurring over a sustained period of time. The AIS may be used in a profit-conscious manner and may focus on controllable RI. Evaluation by means of the trend in controllable RI may mitigate some of the worse aspects of opportunistic behaviour. Divisional managers may perceive the setting of the transfer price as a swings-and-roundabouts exercise, the price favouring one manager on one occasion and the other on another occasion. However, this may be too hopeful a view, because the inclusion of cost or revenue information in a performance measure that is supposed to reflect managerial control may cause opportunistic behaviour. The case for a fair and neutral transfer price seems to be strongest under this use of an AIS. In order to secure behaviour congruence, the AIS needs to show that the transfer prices used are not being manipulated by a divisional manager or top management. Negotiated, full cost-plus, marginal costs and LP dual prices all suffer from this potential defect when decisions are recognized as being non-programmed. The assumptions that allow these forms of transfer pricing to be optimal from the company's perspective are that there is perfect knowledge about future costs and market prices and that divisional managers will freely and unbiasedly provide this information.

The AIS that attempts to use LP dual prices, for example, to provide an optimal solution results in re-centralization and diminishes the control that divisional management has over profit performance measures. The circumstances in which these techniques are appropriate, namely where no external market for the output of the supplier division exists or the external market is sufficiently stable to provide a market price, appear inconsistent with the reasons for the adoption of the multidivisional company. We may therefore conclude that accounting treatments of inter-dependence in multidivisional firms must be as concerned with the behavioural effects of transfer prices as with their ability to secure feasible solutions. The procedures for setting, mediating and negotiating transfer prices should be of concern to the designers of the AIS in attempting an appropriate match with the strategic aims of the decentralized organization.

APPENDIX 1   RELEVANT COST CONCEPTS FOR DECISION MAKING

Division A can supply Division B with a component at a price of £500 per batch. Division A incurs costs of £400 per batch in producing the component, half of which are variable costs. Division B, after further processing costs of £250 per batch, converts the component into a final product that it can sell for £800 per batch. An external supplier has approached Division B with an offer to supply an identical component for £450 per batch.

Performance evaluation of the internal/external purchase

	Internal		External		
	A	B	A1	A2	B
Revenue	500	800	500	–	800
Associated costs	400	750	400	200	700
Profit/(loss)	£100	£50	£100	£(200)	£100

The cost concept is market prices.

Note that the decision to buy externally by Division B may either increase or decrease corporate profits. This depends on Division A's ability to generate alternative uses and buyers for its outputs. The

£100 profit (A1) assumes that it can do this; the £200 loss (A2) shows the effect when it cannot. To improve profit performance, Division B is likely to buy externally if allowed to do so.

The make or buy decision

Division B buys externally

Incremental analysis

	A has excess capacity	A sells excess capacity
Costs avoided by external purchase	£200	£200
Cost incurred by external purchase	450	450
	250	250
Contribution due to external sale	–	300
Net incremental gain/(loss)	£(250)	£50

The cost concept is avoidable costs and incremental/differential analysis.

These figures reconcile with the comparison of the combinations of profit in the first example, that is total company profit when A has excess capacity (£100) and when it sells the excess, £200. To conduct the above analysis, the divisional manager of B needs a detailed breakdown of the avoidable and non-avoidable costs of A. By accommodating this, B may argue that A can meet the external supplier's price and still make £50 per batch profit. Without the provision of the avoidable cost information, B cannot gauge the effect of his decision to buy externally.

The output-level decision

The data has been modified to allow the marginal analysis to be illustrated. We will assume that the internal purchase takes place at a price of £500 per batch:

	Division A	Division B	Selling price
Average cost per batch	$200 + 0.05Q$	$250 + 0.00835Q$	800
Total cost	$200Q + 0.05Q^2$	$250Q + 0.00835Q^2$	$800Q$
Marginal cost	$200 + 0.1Q$	$250 + 0.0167Q$	800

Optimal output: $800 = 200 + 0.1Q + 250 + 0.0167Q$

$Q = 3000$

Optimal transfer price: $200 + 0.1(3000) = 500$

or: $800 - 250 + 0.0167(3000) = 500$

Profits of £450 000 and £74 850 result for Divisions A and B respectively.

The cost concept is marginal analysis.

For this decision, both or one of the managers or the top management must have access to the detailed information shown above. Note that if 3000 batches are traded internally, the profit performance under our original analysis indicates £300 000 and £150 000 will be earned by the respective divisions. Under marginal analysis, the results indicate that Division A is three times more profitable than B. This is due to the treatment of Division A's transfer price as an average cost including non-marginal costs, in our first example, and as an increasing marginal cost now, namely $200 + 0.1Q$ (Thomas, 1980b).

The sequence of decisions indicates that divisional managers may evaluate a make internally or buy externally decision by gauging the effect on their individual performance measures. To determine the appropriateness of their decision, the alternative actions available to sister divisions need to be known. Even then, the relevant information needed must include a breakdown of the other divisions' avoidable and non-avoidable costs. Having decided to trade internally, the quantity to be transferred or used requires additional knowledge about the sister divisions' cost behaviour patterns over relevant output ranges.

APPENDIX 2   INTERNATIONAL TRANSFER PRICING

Multiple objectives

Although we have argued that transfer pricing in the domestic situation is contingent upon the company's choice of business strategy and is part of the autonomy – control debate, international transfer pricing is more complex. Here the movements of goods and services are between related segments of the same company, but the divisions are located in different countries. The impact of the interdependence carries more implications than merely accommodating divisionalization.

Shulman (1967), Thomas (1971), Stewart (1977) and Verlage (1975) are some of the writers who have identified the broader group of objectives that international transfer prices can pursue. Perhaps uppermost in this group is the use of transfer prices to minimize tax liabilities for the company internationally. Stated very simply, a high transfer price to a division operating in a country where its profits are subject to higher rates of tax is beneficial. The tax incurrence is minimized when small or no profits are recorded in high tax rate countries and large profits are reported in relatively low tax rate countries. This is subject to freedom to transfer profits within exchange regulations. International transfer pricing may facilitate this beneficial shifting of profits between divisions.

Import duties and ad valorem taxes can be minimized by transferring products at low prices to a division located in a country with high import duties. Transfer pricing may also play a role in avoiding currency fluctuations. A high transfer price may recoup more purchasing power of a falling currency, earlier. In addition, a high transfer price may circumvent restrictions placed on multinational companies by host countries. When countries restrict the repatriation of dividends or profits, a higher transfer price for imports may lessen their impact. Alternatively, a low transfer price may be a relatively cheap way of financing an overseas division and may give it a competitive edge in the host country's markets.

This is merely a selection of alternative objectives that international transfer pricing may follow. They add financial inter-dependence to the technological inter-dependence that is usually considered in the domestic movements of goods and services. Just as domestic transfer pricing has to trade-off the benefits of differentiation and integration, determining an international transfer price's role also involves trade-offs. For example, minimizing corporate tax liability and import duties are incompatible roles when transfers are made to a country with high import duties and high income tax rates. (Plasschaert, 1979, provides numerical examples of this problem.) The use of transfer prices to counter currency exchange fluctuations may render financial evaluation of the overseas division's performance extremely difficult. Owing to the pervasive effect of the pricing policy, the fiscal agencies of several countries have powers to investigate the values placed on the international movements of resources between segments of the same multinational company.

Fiscal and other constraints

Section 485 of the Corporate and Income Tax Act 1970 allows the UK Inland Revenue to investigate international transfer prices and to substitute alternative 'arm's-length' prices when assessing companies and individuals for taxes. Little is known about this branch of the Inland Revenue's work, but *The Economist* (11 October 1980) reported that out of 18 cases that were heard in court, only 4 have been won by corporate or individual taxpayers.

In the USA, Section 482 of the Internal Revenue Code provides specific rules to control international transfer prices. Three methods of pricing are allowed, and in descending order of acceptance these are the comparable uncontrolled price, the resale price and the cost-plus price. A fourth method includes a plethora of pricing bases that are firm-specific, but that in special circumstances, the fiscal authorities may accept as approximations of arm's-length values (Benke and Edwards, 1980). The effectiveness of these powers is largely unknown because, as in the UK, most of these cases are settled by negotiation between revenue agents and corporate management before coming to court. Recently, the Internal Revenue Service has adopted functional analysis as a means of evaluating alternative transfer pricing policies. This is an essentially subjective exercise where economic risk borne by the parties is compared with economic value or return. The burden of proof remains firmly with the multinational company.

Increasingly, minority shareholders in subsidiaries of multinational companies, host governments and organized labour in the host countries are becoming aware of the potential impact international transfer prices may have. The trend towards greater segmental disclosure in the annual reports of multinational companies may be seen as a reflection of this concern. Currently it is a problem of special interest in the context of the development of Codes of Conduct for Multinationals at the level of the United Nations and OECD. Yet our knowledge about the pricing policies adopted is meagre and inconclusive.

The empirical evidence

The incidence of international transfer pricing is reported by Arpan (1972), Franko (1974) and Milburn (1976). In 1971, for example, almost 30% of total Canadian imports and exports were accounted for by transactions between Canadian companies and their foreign parent companies. In the USA, the fiscal authority estimated that intra-group transactions have grown from $662 million in 1973 to $4.4 billion by 1982. A United Nations report (1978) stated that 30% of UK exports were of an intra-group nature and there is every likelihood that this has increased over time.

More recent empirical surveys by Tang (1979), Wu and Sharp (1979), Tang and Chan (1979) and Hoshower and Mandel (1986) attempt to use statistical analysis to explain the reasons for transfer pricing practices. Wu and Sharp examined whether the objective, pricing method and arbitration system differed between 61 companies representing 11 industries. They also tested the hypothesis that different objectives, methods and systems would be used when international as opposed to domestic transfers are made. Postal questionnaires were used to collect the data, and the Kendal coefficient of correlation and chi-square tests of significance are applied to the ordinally ranked data.

Very briefly, these researchers found that there is a contrast between the roles domestic transfer prices and international transfer prices play. Maximization of overall company profits, performance evaluation of the segments and compliance with US government restrictions are the top three objectives for domestic price setting, whereas compliance with foreign tax and tariff regulations, profit maximization and compliance with US tax regulations and IRS rulings appear as the three top ranked roles of international transfer pricing. Very little difference is noted, however, in terms of the transfer prices used. For both domestic and international movements, market price is ranked first; for domestic pricing, the negotiated and full cost-plus methods are next in popularity, and this order is reversed for international transfers. It was also found that companies employ consistent arbitration methods for settling both international and domestic transfer price disputes. The most popular method is to use two levels of arbitration: an initial reconciliation at the local, divisional level, and if this fails, the corporate management settles the matter.

The Tang and Chan (1979) survey obtained responses from 75 US and 50 Japanese companies concerning environmental variables that may influence international transfer pricing. Again, the respondents ranked the objectives of their pricing policies. Companies in both countries ranked the role of obtaining overall profit as most important, and there was broad agreement on the importance of securing the competitive position of subsidiaries in foreign countries and the repatriation of profits or dividends.

The admittedly meagre empirical evidence suggests that transfer prices do follow different objectives in the international and domestic situations. Opinions that suggest a transfer pricing problem does not exist (Stobaugh, 1970), or that it can be solved by concerted government action (Plasschaert, 1981), seem to ignore the interaction between financial and technological inter-dependence. International transfer prices may be developed to reduce tax liabilities and import duties, but will these satisfy the behaviour congruence objective and allow overseas divisional managers to feel responsible for their financial performance? International transfer pricing is a most complex and multidimensional subject. Any attempt at developing a contingency approach must await the accumulation of empirical evidence not only from multinational companies, but also from fiscal agencies.

EXERCISES

1. The accountant's response to inter-dependence between parts of an organization is to allocate costs or charge transfer prices. What

properties do these treatments have in common, and when can they be distinguished?

2. International and domestic transfer prices should always be calculated in the same way in order to avoid governmental and fiscal interference. Do you agree?

3. The Plantaganet Company is a large conglomerate that has 40 divisions. Division X wants to buy a component for its final product and receives bids from separate external suppliers of £500 and £550. The supplier who bid £550 will buy raw materials for £100 from Division Z, which has excess capacity. The variable costs associated with the raw materials is £40. The supplier who bid £500 will not buy any raw materials from Plantaganet. Division Y is working at full capacity, but can provide the component part to X at a price of £550. Division Y purchases its raw-material requirements externally from an unrelated party at £50 and incurs additional variable costs of £300.

Required:

(a) to identify the potential work flows and forms of inter-dependence;

(b) to discover which offer Division X should choose in the company's best interests;

(c) to outline the arguments likely to be heard in seeking to apply the corporate optimal decision;

(d) to decide at what price the transactions should take place.

4. Peat, Ernst and Touche (PET) is a very large accounting firm. Its main activity and revenue earner is undertaking audits of publicly owned companies' accounts. Increasingly, the audit teams have made use of PET's central computer facility and staff, whose prime role had been to serve senior partners in the administration of the firm. The senior partners are in favour of the increased use of the central computer and staff, and their services have not previously been charged to audit team users.

However, the supervisor of the central computer has recently submitted a budget that requires 5 extra staff and capital expenditure of £200 000 in meeting the expected demand for computer services.

Required:

(a) to isolate clearly the factors that the senior partner should consider in deciding whether to charge the audit teams for the computer services or not;

(b) to evaluate the merits and limits of using a marginal cost transfer price for the services in the short and long term;

(c) to outline the financial performance measure for the audit team consistent with a marginal cost transfer price.

5. The Baron Company consists of 2 divisions that trade extensively

with each other. The relevant revenue and cost functions for the final product are given below:

$$R = 205 - 0.5Q \qquad (1)$$
$$C_m = 19 + Q \qquad (2)$$
$$C_d = 10 + 0.7Q \qquad (3)$$

where R is the unit revenue of the final product, C_m is the unit cost incurred by the supplier division in making the product and C_d is the unit cost function associated with the distribution and sale of the final product by the user division. Q is the quantity of product transferred.

Required:

(a) to determine the optimal output level to maximize Baron's profit, and the transfer price consistent with this level;

(b) to show the profits of each division at the optimal solution;

(c) to show the profits for each division and the transfer prices associated with:
   (i) the supplier acting as an internal monopolist;
   (ii) the user acting as an internal monopsonist;

(d) to show the effect on divisional profits when the supplier's unit cost (C_m) is:
   (i) 99
   (ii) $107 - 0.1Q$
       instead of $19 + Q$

(e) Given the results of (d) above, what might the supplier contemplate doing to improve his profit performance?

(f) From the perspective of business strategy, what action would you suggest that Baron take?

6. 'If I were to price these boxes any lower than $480 a thousand', said James Brunner, manager of Birch Paper Company's Thompson division, 'I'd be countermanding my order of last month for our salesmen to stop shaving their bids and to bid full-cost quotations. I've been trying for weeks to improve the quality of our business, and if I turn around now and accept this job at $430 or $450 or something less than $480, I'll be tearing down this programme I've been working so hard to build up. The division can't very well show a profit by putting in bids that don't even cover a fair share of overhead costs, let alone give us a profit.'

Birch Paper Company was a medium-size, partly integrated paper company, producing white and kraft papers and paperboard. A portion of its paperboard output was converted into corrugated boxes by the Thompson division, which also printed and coloured the outside surface of the boxes. Including Thompson, the company had 4 producing divisions and a timberland division, which supplied part of the company's pulp requirements.

For several years, each division had been judged independently on the basis of its profit and return on investment. Top management had been working to gain effective results from a policy of decentralizing responsibility and authority for all decisions except those relating to overall company policy. The company's top officials believed that in the past few years the concept of decentralization had been successfully applied and that the company's profits and competitive position had definitely improved.

Early in 1957, the Northern division designed a special display box for one of its papers in conjunction with the Thompson division, which was equipped to make the box. Thompson's staff for package design and development spent several months perfecting the design, production methods and materials to be used. Because of the unusual colour and shape, these were far from standard. According to an agreement between the two divisions, the Thompson division was reimbursed by the Northern division for the cost of its design and development work.

When all the specifications were prepared, the Northern division asked for bids on the box from the Thompson division and from two outside companies. Each divisional manager was normally free to buy from whatever supplier he wished; and even on sales within the company, divisions were expected to meet the going market price if they wanted the business.

In 1957, the profit margins of converters such as the Thompson division were being squeezed. Thompson – as did many other similar converters – bought its paperboard, and its function was to print, cut and shape it into boxes. Though it bought most of its materials from other Birch divisions, most of Thompson's sales were made to outside customers. If Thompson got the order from Northern, it probably would buy its linerboard and corrugating medium from the Southern division of Birch. The walls of a corrugated box consist of outside and inside sheets of linerboard sandwiching the fluted corrugating medium. About 70% of Thompson's out-of-pocket cost of $400 for the order represented the cost of linerboard and corrugating medium. Though Southern had been running below capacity and had excess inventory, it quoted the market price, which had not noticeably weakened as a result of the over-supply. Its out-of-pocket costs on both liner and corrugating medium were about 60% of the selling price.

The Northern division received bids on the boxes of $480 a thousand from the Thompson division, $430 a thousand from West Paper Company and $432 a thousand from Eire Papers Ltd. Eire Papers offered to buy from Birch the outside linerboard with the special printing already on it, but would supply its own inside liner and corrugating medium. The outside liner would be supplied by the Southern division at a price equivalent of $90 a thousand boxes, and it would be printed for $30 a thousand by the Thompson division. Of the $30, about $25 would be out-of-pocket costs.

Since this situation appeared to be a little unusual, William Kenton, manager of the Northern division, discussed the wide discrepancy of bids with Birch's commercial vice-president. He told the vice-president: 'We sell in a very competitive market, where higher costs cannot be passed on. How can we be expected to show a decent profit and return on investment if we have to buy our supplies at more than 10% over the going market?'

Knowing that Mr Brunner had on occasion in the past few months been unable to operate the Thompson division at capacity, it seemed odd to the vice-president that Mr Brunner would add the full 20% overhead and profit charge to his out-of-pocket costs. When asked about this, Mr Brunner's answer was the statement that appears at the beginning of this case. He went on to say that having done the developmental work on the box, and having received no profit on that, he felt entitled to a good mark-up on the production of the box itself.

The vice-president explored further the cost structures of the various divisions. He remembered a comment that the controller had made at a meeting the week before to the effect that costs which were variable for one division could be largely fixed for the company as a whole. He knew that in the absence of specific orders from top management, Mr Kenton would accept the lowest bid, which was that of the West Paper Company for $430. However, it would be possible for top management to order the acceptance of another bid if the situation warranted such action. And though the volume represented by the transactions in question was less than 5% of the volume of any of the divisions involved, other transactions could conceivably raise similar problems later.

(a) In the controversy described, how – if at all – is the transfer price system dysfunctional?

(b) Describe other types of decisions in the Birch Paper Company in which the transfer price system would be dysfunctional.

7. Helman plc is a diversified company having, among others, major interests in the mechanical, civil and structural engineering industries and in motor pump manufacturing.

The motor pump division is a separate profit centre, although a significant proportion, sometimes as much as 60%, of its output is sold to other divisions. Up until now the inter-divisional transactions have not attracted top management's attention. However, a situation has arisen where the engineering division has appealed to top management to intervene.

The motor pump division has quoted a price of £180 per batch of 100 pumps. The engineering division has obtained quotations from external suppliers of as low as £135, although £160 per batch of 100 pumps seems to be the norm. Neither division is willing to negotiate further, and top management has requested and obtained the following data from the respective divisions:

Motor Pump Division
  Average cost of manufacture of one batch of
  100 pumps $10 + 1.5Q$
Engineering Division
  Average Distribution cost of one batch of
  100 pumps $25 + 8.8Q$
  Average Revenue of one batch of 100 pumps $305 - 0.6Q$

Q is the quantity of pumps in batches of 100 which can be transferred.

Required:

(a) Determine the optimal solution to maximize Helman's profit, and calculate the optimal transfer price, assuming there is no alternative external supplier of motor pumps. Show each division's profit.

(b) Clearly identify the main issues and recommend a course of action for Helman's top management when the alternative external suppliers are recognized to exist.

(c) Outline the operational difficulties of applying the optimal economic solution in practice.

(d) Identify the circumstances when the transfer pricing problem can be distinguished from the allocation problem.

8. The Earlswood Company is a multidivisional company which holds divisional managers responsible for their individual profits. The Squire Division produces, among other items, an electric motor which the Knight Division uses.

The following information relates to the average unit costs and revenues associated with the electric motor:

Squire Division   *Knight Division*
  Manufacturing cost $28 + 2Q$ Distribution cost $14 + 0.7Q$
                                     Revenue $350 - 0.8Q$

Q is the quantity of product which can be transferred.

Required:

(a) Determine the optimal output level to maximize Earlswood's profit and calculate the optimal transfer price consistent with this level. Assume that there is no external market for the intermediate product.

(b) Show the profits of each division under the optimal solution.

(c) Outline the operational difficulties of applying the optimal solution in practice.

(d) Provide a reasoned argument to identify the circumstances in which the 'true' transfer pricing problem exists and suggest a transfer pricing procedure which may be appropriately used in these circumstances.

12

The capital investment decision in the multidivisional company

SUMMARY

The need for the accounting information system to promote behaviour congruence is possibly most pronounced for investment centre managers. The importance of capital projects to the long-term effectiveness of the company means that the interactions between results, action and personal controls cannot be overlooked.

In-depth studies of the capital budgeting process indicate the significant influence which divisional managers may exercise over project generation and the estimation of associated cash flows. Discounted cash flow techniques are recommended to evaluate such projects but the divisional manager's financial results may be evaluated on an accruals income basis. A fundamental concern is that managers will propose projects which improve short-term accounting profit for the division but which are second-best ones for the company. Alternatively, projects acceptable to the company will not be formally submitted if divisional profit – however measured – falls.

A detailed examination of the equivalence of residual income (or rate of return on investment) and net present value (or internal rate of return) when annuity depreciation is used, indicates a technical solution. However, the cumbersome nature of this solution is revealed when cash flow operating budgets are employed. This analysis prompts the question, 'Why measure divisional performance by means of income?'. For investment centre managers in multinational companies, the inclusion of budgeted versus actual cash flow as a complementary performance measure compatible with achieving behaviour congruence appears worthy of consideration.

INTRODUCTION

The capital investment decision is possibly the most important decision taken by any economic enterprise. Generally such decisions commit a substantial proportion of the firm's resources to actions that are largely irreversible. Further, by means of capital investment decisions, the firm's strategy evolves and is implemented. Most capital investment decisions are non-programmed by their very nature and hence, in a multidivisional company, are subject to influence by divisional management. The effectiveness of the divisional management's involvement in the capital budgeting process is partly conditioned by the nature of the AIS. The ability of the AIS to encourage managers to generate investment opportunities that further the company's best interests is of crucial importance. If the AIS provides inducements for the divisional managers to promote their own self-interests at the expense of overall welfare, then behaviour congruence is unlikely to occur. Our focus of attention will therefore be on the development of the AIS to accommodate changes in strategy via capital investment decisions taken in multidivisional structures.

This chapter outlines the main stages of the capital budgeting process in the multidivisional company. Empirical evidence that relates to divisional management's influence on each stage is introduced, and the potential adverse effects are outlined. Of particular concern is the compatibility of the profit performance measure included in the AIS as a means of evaluating the performance of divisional managers and the discounted cash flow techniques typically used to evaluate capital projects. A lengthy illustration is given to examine the inducements ROI or RI measures may provide relative to the discounted cash flow techniques. The potential of cash flow evaluations of managerial performance to moderate incentives for opportunistic behaviour is examined, and we conclude with a reappraisal of the type of AIS which uses the profit-conscious style of evaluation and controllable RI as its overall performance measure.

THE CAPITAL BUDGETING PROCESS

The long-term success of any economic enterprise rests on its ability to take effective capital investment decisions. One potential advantage of the multidivisional firm over the unitary firm is the improved quality of capital investment decisions it is able to make. The increased visibility of the separate divisional activities and performances allows top management to allocate resources between the divisions more efficiently. In addition, top management is able to call for and obtain whatever information is regarded as pertinent to the investment decision. Top management may be able to re-allocate resources, should an initial project not meet expectations. Hence, the multidivisional company may be viewed as a mini-capital market

(Williamson, 1970), in which top management acts as an allocator of resources, better informed than external investors and even large institutional investors. Further, the actions that top management can take, such as the discontinuation of a project or the removal of a divisional manager, may not adversely affect the company's share price. By contrast, the removal of a managing director by the shareholders in a general meeting may have serious repercussions on the market value of a firm. It may be argued that the top management of the multidivisional firm is better positioned to identify investment opportunities and to ensure their effective implementation than either the top management of unitary firms or external investors.

For such arguments to be upheld, the capital investment decision must be assumed to take place in a stable, if not completely certain environment, where information symmetry is absent. Top management is assumed to know what investment opportunities are available, which implies that it is as aware as divisional management of the various activities taking place throughout the firm. If it is true that top management possesses such knowledge, then a main reason for adopting the multidivisional structure is removed. Alternatively, the argument seems to presume that top management has sufficient confidence in the monitoring devices, including the accounting performance measures in the AIS, to pinpoint areas where investment is worthwhile. As we have suggested in Chapter 9, the accuracy, completeness and neutrality of any profit performance measure is open to question and needs to be interpreted carefully. Top management's reliance on formal accounting measures of performance may well be misguided. Just as an AIS that emphasizes the attainment of short-term profit performance may cause opportunistic behaviour in respect to rewards or transfer price manipulations, so its influence may extend to investment decisions if the divisional manager perceives that this is a means of increasing his share of available resources.

When the uncertainty associated with diverse environments is acknowledged as a reason for adopting the multidivisional structure, then the possibility of information asymmetry must also be recognized. There is a likelihood that divisional and top management levels will possess different pieces of information relevant to the investment decision requiring the participation of divisional management in planning. The need for the assumptions of divisional and top management to be communicated to each other so that a consensus on feasible actions may emerge (Chapter 8) is especially important when taking capital investment decisions. One useful role the AIS may play is to encourage divisional management to contribute effectively to the selection and detailed planning of capital project proposals. It is from this perspective that we now review the empirical evidence relating to the involvement of divisional management in the capital budgeting process.

The empirical evidence

The capital budgeting process may be broadly viewed as comprising of six stages (King, 1975):

1. project generation or origination;
2. estimation of cash flows;
3. progress through the organization;
4. analysis and selection of projects;
5. authorization of expenditure;
6. post-audit investigations.

Several authors (Marsh, 1976; Pinches, 1982) have argued that the analysis and selection stage of the process has pre-occupied academic researchers to the exclusion of all other stages, although this misplaced emphasis is gradually being rectified in the literature. We shall therefore examine each stage in turn.

Project generation
There are many different forms of capital investment projects. For example, modern business enterprises are required to invest in filtration plant and equipment to meet pollution control legislation. Improvement to existing canteen or cafeteria facilities for employees, or the establishment of an educational endowment are further examples of investments where profit or rate of return criteria are inappropriate. Projects such as these can involve significant sums of money, but they are subject to wider criteria of evaluation than merely profit, rate of return or net present value. The type of capital projects over which the AIS has significant influence are those that are expected to earn a tangible return.

The influence divisional managers exert over the capital investment decision begins with their power to reject, or their failure to generate project proposals. If capital investment proposals start within the divisions, then the divisional management's power to reject emanates from not submitting proposals, or more realistically, only generating those projects that are prefered. The total number of proposals that have been considered by the division is unlikely to be known by top management and alternative or competing projects not favoured by divisional management can be ascertained only with difficulty and with increased monitoring costs. Top management may remain blissfully unaware of projects generated but rejected by the divisions.

Rockley (1973) found that approximately 60% of all investment proposals originated from line managers in the 69 UK companies he surveyed. Istvan (1961) also found, based on data collected from 48 US companies, that most investment proposals originated with line management but were usually of an obligatory, or replacement, nature. Projects of a more strategic nature originated from top management. In a more recent survey of 211 companies, Scapens *et al.* (1982) concluded that the choices made by divisional management were constrained by the strategic plan developed by top management. Such a plan generally outlines the areas of the business where capital investment is to be directed and expresses, in broad terms, the maximum amounts of expenditure to be allocated to each area. However, the preparation of capital budgets relating to specific projects is normally the responsibility of divisional management (Marsh *et al.*, 1988). It therefore seems that divisional managers are constrained in their choice of projects both by the strategy adopted by top management and by the level of expenditure allocated. However, the specific projects to be undertaken within these constraints are heavily influenced by them.

In large British firms the existence of self-imposed limitations rather than market-imposed limitations on capital expenditure is more common and important (Pike, 1983). Within these self-imposed constraints, the opportunity to choose both obligatory and expansion-oriented projects preferred by the divisional managers appears to be relatively unfettered. In addition, some firms provide only a general outline of the areas where proposals are likely to be approved; in others the divisional management help develop the strategic plan through membership of the relevant planning committee. The scope for divisional management to dismiss or to exclude projects from the capital budgeting process is substantiated by the findings of several clinical studies where researchers have spent considerable periods of time investigating individual companies' practices.

Berg's (1965) study of a US engineering conglomerate that comprised 6 groups and 40 divisions, provides one insight. At top-management level, consideration of individual projects proved impossible because of the large number involved (i.e., 5000 per year), the variety of technologies and markets and the absence of complete information. Instead an allocation of funds was made to the 6 groups, with an emphasis being placed on the group's achievement of short-term profit targets in order to reduce the number of project proposals. At group level, the number of businesses and projects (almost 1000 per year) was still too large to allow individual consideration.

The group tended to allocate funds to specific divisional projects based on the group's estimates of divisional growth and return. Only at the divisional level was it possible to consider all projects individually. Again, it proved difficult for the divisional staff to disagree with the estimates made by the originators of the project, and the allocation of funds tended to be influenced by opinions of the sub-unit's or plant's business potential, and the previous performance of the project proposer. Plant managers originated projects with a view to the impact on their own operations. Risky projects were frequently not proposed, even though the risk could be diversified and substantially reduced when placed in the context of the company as a whole.

Sihler (1964) also discovered that plant level managers had a significant influence on the capital budget. In the large US-based metals and chemicals company he studied, operating managers submitted to their superiors only a relatively small proportion of the opportunities that were available at plant level. Again, the projects that were submitted were chosen on the basis of their impact on operating plant problems. Considerations of corporate objectives, strategy and the net present value of the investment carried little or no weight with plant management.

Aharoni (1966) argued that project generation was influenced by the personal risk to which the originator was exposed. He found that there was a risk threshold beyond which project consideration was abandoned. Carter (1971) confirms this finding in his study of a small computer firm. King's (1975) study involved two large UK companies, and he also recognized that investment project proposals involved a large amount of work for the originator, accompanied by a high level of personal risk with little tangible reward. Hence, King prefers the term 'triggering' to 'generation' because he found that many investment opportunities were ignored until the need for them became pressing. Again, the element of choice seems to rest with lower-level managers.

A clinical study by Ackerman (1970) compared project origination in two integrated and two diversified US firms. He found that top management generated capital investment projects more frequently in the integrated firms than in the diversified firms. Project generation in the diversified firms was an outgrowth of product market strategy, where top management's information was incomplete and a greater reliance had to be placed on divisional management as project originators.

From the available empirical evidence it seems that individual management can exercise choice by influencing projects that are submitted into the capital budgeting process. The constraints imposed by the top management via the strategic plan and the level of allocated expenditure may limit divisional management's discretion, but these are unlikely to curtail entirely the freedom to generate proposals. A sub-set of projects may be recognized as unlikely to gain top management approval, but the choice of projects to submit, within the limits of the strategic plan and the allowed expenditure, seems to remain firmly with divisional management.

Estimation of cash flows

The important question to pose now is: 'On what criteria will divisional managers submit capital investment projects?' In general terms, only those projects that are thought to have a good chance of acceptance are likely to be submitted. Also the impact of the project in terms of the divisional manager's exposure to risk appears to be a significant influence. Several of the clinical studies found evidence that project originators biased information to make their proposals more attractive (Aharoni, 1966; Carter, 1971; King, 1975). Berg (1965) observed that the capital budgeting process in the company he investigated was really a 'game' with the rules being defined by the measurement, control and reward schemes, the pressure for current profits and the administered profit goals. In a similar vein, Scapens *et al.* (1982) acknowledged that acceptance of a particular project depends upon it meeting certain financial criteria. Divisional managers will probably not include proposals that seem unlikely to meet these criteria. The divisional managers will therefore generate their own financial information and forecasts prior to the formal submission.

It can be argued that the project originator is best placed to provide this information given his intimate knowledge of the product, market and technology involved. However, Berg argues that a management incentive scheme based on current profits encouraged managers to have very short time horizons and to favour using short pay-back periods and high discount rates. Similarly, Bower (1970) viewed the central problem in the large, highly diversified US company operating in chemicals, electronics and engineering that he studied, as disentangling the forecasts of financial information from the commitment of divisional managers to the project. Tying rewards to the differences between results and forecasts may produce downward biased estimates. Not tying rewards to results may induce optimistic bias and reduced motivation. It seems illogical to believe that divisional managers who have to make estimates in an uncertain environment will not favour information that shows the project in the best possible light and is least harmful to their well-being in the firm. This suggests that there is a second layer of choice exercised by the divisional manager and governed by his commitment to the project. Having generated a set of projects, cash flow estimates reduce the number to which the divisional manager remains favourably disposed. The likelihood of a project's inclusion in the division's capital budget then depends on how the manager's performance is evaluated and rewarded. The consistency between the methods of project appraisal and the means used to evaluate managerial performance is therefore of crucial importance. We will consider this further at the evaluation and analysis stage, but let us first examine the relationship between commitment and the development of divisional capital budgets.

Progress through the organization
The divisional capital budget represents the formal request for funds and is used in most UK and US companies, although below a certain limit of expenditure (below £104 000 and $136 000, on average) top-management approval is not required (Scapens *et al.*, 1982). Divisional managers include those projects in their capital budgets that are likely to be found acceptable by top management. So far, what is acceptable has been found to mean (a) lying within the strategic plan, and (b) not harmful to the divisional manager's well-being. This implies that the proposed project, if accepted, will improve the manager's performance measure and enhance the possibility of him being rewarded.

Further, the studies conducted by researchers who spent considerable periods of time in particular firms indicate that, as a project progresses through an organization, the changing commitment of different groups to the project has an influence on its eventual acceptance. Berg notes that alliances changed as proposals progressed upwards in the organization, and once the group level had screened their divisions' proposals, divisions and group became allies in competing against other groups. Aharoni (1966) argues that there is no one investment decision made at a single point in time, but instead a long process involving many people at different organizational levels. The collection of information necessitates contact with other parts of the firm, the revision of subjective estimates and the exchange of tacit promises of support. The accumulation of commitments limits the fredom of action in subsequent stages until the almost inevitable decision is reached. Strong commitment, especially from the project's originator, is required in order to devote the time necessary to extract promises of support.

The exact timing of this gathering of support may occur before or after the inclusion of the proposal in the divisional capital budget. King (1975), for example, found that the need to justify the project took place at the evaluation stage. Increased commitment here inevitably led to bias in the information used for evaluation. He identified a project's upward progress through the organization as a political process in which the originator continually seeks higher-level sponsors. The findings of these, admittedly isolated, examples suggest that there is a social or group aspect to the acceptance of a project. It also appears that the greater the commitment of the divisional manager who originates the project, the greater is its likelihood of being accepted.

Analysis and selection of projects

Academic textbooks argue for the evaluation of capital investment projects using discounted cash flow techniques. The effective management of cash, and more important, the timing of cash flows are the means of ensuring corporate survival and the increase of shareholder wealth. Divisional managers' performance is most often measured in terms of a rate of return on investment or profit before interest and tax (Scapens *et al.*, 1982). Typically, incentive schemes are linked to these accrual based income measures, which means that the manager who submits a project and ignores the effects on the profit measures may be disadvantaged. The most common techniques used to evaluate capital projects are indeed net present value (NPV) or internal rate of return (Scapens *et al.*, 1982). The divisional manager may therefore find a conflict between his self-interest, as measured by some form of profit, and the corporate interest as measured by the discounted cash flow (DCF) techniques (Barwise *et al.*, 1987).

When this inconsistency between measurement techniques occurs, there is the potential for the divisional manager to reject projects on a further criterion. Inclusion in the capital budget is reserved for those projects that are both likely to be accepted using corporately determined hurdle rates, and those that will improve or maintain the profit performance measure on which the manager's rewards are based. Table 12.1 indicates the potential conflicts and outcomes.

A real danger exists that divisional managers will reject, and hence fail to submit, capital projects that meet the firm's criterion of acceptance, but that lower current performance as measured by some form of accrual income. This relates to project proposals falling in the top right-hand quadrant. There is also the potential danger that divisional managers will bias the estimates of cash flows for projects that would otherwise be rejected when evaluated using the discounted cash flow hurdle rate. The improvement that acceptance of these capital projects can make to the short-term managerial performance measure is the incentive here. Hence proposals falling in the bottom left-hand quadrant may be submitted by the divisional manager if he believes that his over-optimistic cash flows will be

Table 12.1 Potential conflicts between short-term and long-term evaluation techniques

	MEASURES OF SHORT-TERM PERFORMANCE, ROI, RI, etc.	
	Improves current performance	Lowers current performance
Long-term performance measures, NPV, IRR, etc.		
Acceptable project	SUBMIT	?
Unacceptable project	?	NON-SUBMISSION

accepted. For the projects in the top-right quadrant, top management will be unaware that such proposals were originated; and for the projects in the bottom-left quadrant top management may have great difficulty in detecting the bias. The development of increasingly sophisticated DCF techniques offers no solution to these problems. We shall examine later in this chapter whether or not the extent of these problems is reduced by developing evaluation techniques consistent with project selection methods, but first the remaining stages of the capital budgeting process are discussed.

Authorization of expenditure
Top management takes the final decision to accept a project included in the divisional capital budget. The overwhelming impression given by the empirical evidence, such as that of Bower (1972), Morgan and Luck (1973) and Scapens *et al.* (1982), is that this may amount purely to 'rubber-stamping'. Capital investment proposals that reach the stage of formal application for authorization by top management are very rarely turned down. This is because the selection of capital projects is made informally, lower down the organization. By the time authorization is requested, the acceptability of the project to the originator plus a large section of the organization has already been determined.

The authorization stage may be regarded as a monitoring device to ensure that the project has undergone the normal planning procedures, but the effectiveness of such a device to prevent projects preferred only by divisional managers from being authorized must be questionable. It is therefore open to serious doubt whether top management's authorization of capital expenditure can mitigate or prevent the opportunistic behaviour of divisional managers at the earlier stages of origination, estimation of cash flows and even selection.

Post-audit investigations

After the authorized project has been implemented and operated for a period, often one year, an audit of the actual results may be taken. Post-auditing of capital projects is less common in the UK than in the USA, and the popularity of the practice, at least in Britain, does not seem to have grown. Rockley (1973) found that 56% of UK companies carried out post-audits, whereas Scapens *et al.* (1982) reported that only 36% of the UK companies surveyed used the practice.

The purpose of the audit is to compare all or some of the project outcomes with the original estimates. Rockley found that the comparisons were not used to criticize the manager or group which made the forecasts, but were used instead as an educational device to improve future forecasts. This enlightened view is necessitated by the changes in inflation, market conditions, etc., that are normally outside the divisional manager's control, but that nevertheless occur between the time of making the forecasts and operating the project for at least one year. Scapens *et al.* (1982) also report that post-completion audits are used for learning rather than control purposes. One participant in that study stated that the benefits of post-completion audits are 60% psychological and 40% technical. The normal practice for British companies surveyed by Scapens *et al.* (1982) is for divisions to audit their own projects, but they are required to send the detailed comparisons of actual and estimate to head office.

An evaluation of the capital budgeting process

It is difficult to deny that divisional management can, and does, exercise significant influence over certain stages of the capital budgeting process. The generation of projects, the estimation of cash flows and their progress through the organization all appear to be subject to a high degree of divisional control and influence. The formal evaluation and authorization stages seem to have relatively little direct impact on the ultimate set of projects that the firm undertakes because of the decisions taken at prior stages. A specific problem for accountants in this context is to ensure that the AIS does not misdirect divisional management to select projects that are not in the organization's best interests. This can occur when the divisional manager's reward is linked to a short-term, accrual income measure of performance which is inconsistent with the discounted cash flow techniques used to evaluate the capital project. It is therefore time to re-open the ROI versus RI debate, and to investigate Solomons' (1965) claim that RI is the short-run counterpart of net present value.

ROI, RI AND PROJECT EVALUATION

Two grave consequences of a defective AIS used for performance evaluation are:

1. that divisional management will fail to submit projects that the company would find acceptable;
2. that divisional management will submit projects which give expectations of higher personal rewards in the short term at the expense of projects giving higher net present values.

In order to illustrate these defects and to suggest potential improvements, we will now embark on a lengthy example. Several simplifying assumptions are made, but our central focus is upon the compatibility of different forms of short-term profit measures and accepted DCF techniques, such as NPV, to guide divisional managers to propose those capital projects that are in the best interests of the company.

One of the most important assumptions made is that relating to the cash flow estimates of the capital projects to be reviewed. We assume that these are known with certainty. This is contrary to the empirical findings of Sihler (1964), Berg (1965), Aharoni (1965) and King (1975), who found that capital project proposals were influenced by the personal risk to which the originator was exposed. Divisional managers may be risk averse, in the sense that they may regard the loss of a current bonus as more unpleasant than the gain of a future bonus of an equal amount. Hence managers may be reluctant to generate investment proposals where the predictions of likely outcomes are highly uncertain. They may prefer to do nothing, or to select projects with lower returns but whose outcomes can be predicted within a more well-defined boundary. In the illustration that follows, we assume that the managers are risk neutral and that the cash flow estimates are not biased. We also assume that the annual profits of the projects are equal to the net cash inflows less depreciation, we ignore the effect of taxation, and we accept the company's cost of capital or hurdle rate as given. It should, however, be noted that most firms correctly take account of taxation in their DCF evaluations, but use profit before tax in their measures of divisional performance, thus introducing a further possible inconsistency. The aim of the following analysis is to gauge the compatibility of ROI, RI and discounted cash flow techniques to guide divisional managers to propose investment projects that are in the firm's best interests. The influence of the AIS and the short-term profit performance measures may misdirect the divisional manager to suggest actions that will not be totally consistent with the company's feasible region or strategic plan.

The Kinetic Compounds Company

The Kinetic Compounds Company is a large conglomerate company operating in the electronic, engineering and chemical industries. There are over 20 divisional managers responsible for activities identified by separate product markets. Each divisional manager receives a cash bonus and a promotion evaluation based on his division's annual rate of ROI. The investment base is calculated using net book values.

The new chief accountant has recently convinced top management that RI is a more appropriate measure of both the division's and divisional management's performance than the ROI measure previously used. At a specially convened meeting with divisional management, the chief accountant finds that some divisional managers regard RI as misleading and refer to it as 'accounting gobbledygook'. In making these arguments, the managers produce the following case.

There is a division in the company that is considering a project that will produce net cash inflows of £350 000 per annum for the next 5 years. The initial investment of £1.2 million will then be obsolete and worthless. Using the usual straight line depreciation, the project gives a stable profit over its useful life but its RI will vary in each of the 5 years (Table 12.2). At present, this division is earning a 14% ROI. It is agreed that the company's cost of capital is 10%.

The managers' case seems clear. The imputed charge for interest on capital in the RI calculation causes RI to vary significantly from year

Table 12.2 The division's case against RI

	Year 1	Year 2	Year 3	Year 4	Year 5
Asset balance at year beginning	£1.2m	£960K	£720K	£480K	£240K
Net cash inflow	350K	350K	350K	350K	350K
Depreciation	240K	240K	240K	240K	240K
'Profit'	110K	110K	110K	110K	110K
Interest on capital	120K	96K	72K	48K	24K
Residual income	(10K)	14K	38K	62K	86K
ROI on net book value	9.2%	11.5%	15.3%	22.9%	45.8%

Table 12.3 The company's view using NPV

$$
\begin{aligned}
I_0 \quad &= \text{£}1.2\text{m; life 5 years;} \\
&\quad \text{annual cash inflow} = \text{£}350\text{K}; i = 10\% \\
\text{NPV} &= -1.2 + 0.350 a_{5 \rceil .1} \\
&= -1.2 + 0.350\,(3.7908) \\
&= -1.2 + 1.32678 \\
&= \text{£}126\,780 \text{ positive}
\end{aligned}
$$

to year. The chief accountant now offers his interpretation of the case and begins by calculating the net present value of the project to discover whether it is worthwhile accepting from the company's point of view (Table 12.3). He then shows the RI calculations using annuity depreciation (Table 12.4). The NPV is positive and therefore, from a financial perspective alone, the project is worthy of consideration for acceptance.

The accountant's case rests on the assumption that the usual divisional management performance measure will be based on annuity depreciation instead of straight line depreciation. Further, the annuity depreciation calculated using the same rate, 10%, as that used for the NPV project. With a constant stream of net cash inflows, the divisional evaluation needs only to check whether the first year of the project gives a positive RI in order to accept the project. Using the information in Table 12.4 to calculate a rate of ROI, it is doubtful whether a divisional manager currently earning a ROI of 14% would accept the project because of its low returns in the first two years. By contrast, the results shown by the RI measure of performance are consistent with the decision that the company would take using NPV. This consistency is always maintained because discounting the RI for each year at the hurdle rate gives the net present value of the project.

The chief accountant is also able to show the effect of the firm changing its policy on the hurdle rate. Instead of using the 10% hurdle rate let us evaluate the project using an internal rate of return (IRR) criterion of, say, 14% and discover how this effects the RI figures (see Table 12.5).

On this occasion, the annuity depreciation is determined by the 14% IRR requirement. A small positive RI results for each of the 5 years, indicating that this project gives a return just in excess of the 14% required. Again, there is consistency between the DCF and the managerial performance results, and in addition the ROI figures in Table 12.5 reflect this. Mepham (1978), in particular, has promoted this method of capital investment evaluation.

The accountant has therefore been able to show that either RI and NPV or ROI and the IRR, can be employed together to obtain

Table 12.4 ROI, RI with annuity depreciation at 10%, the company's hurdle rate

Depreciation charge + interest = $£1200K \div a_{\overline{5}|.1} = £316.6K$

	Year 1	Year 2	Year 3	Year 4	Year 5
Asset balance at year beginning	£1200K	£1003K	£786.7K	£548.8K	£287.1K
Net cash inflow	350K	350K	350K	350K	350K
Interest on capital	120	100.3	78.7	54.9	28.7
Depreciation	196.6	216.3	237.9	261.7	287.9
	316.6	316.6	316.6	316.6	316.6
RI	33.4	33.4	33.4	33.4	33.4
ROI	153.4K ÷ 1200K = 12.8%	133.7K ÷ 1003K = 13.3%	112.1K ÷ 786.7K = 14.2%	88.3K ÷ 548.8K = 16.1%	62.1K ÷ 287.1K = 21.6%

NPV $= 33.4a_{\overline{5}|.1}$ = £126 000

Table 12.5 ROI, RI with annuity depreciation at 14%, the company's required internal rate of return

	Year 1	Year 2	Year 3	Year 4	Year 5
Asset balance at year beginning	£1200K	£1018.5K	£811.6K	£575.7K	£306.8K
Net cash inflow	350K	350K	350K	350K	350K
Interest on capital	168	142.6	113.6	80.6	43
Depreciation	181.5	206.9	235.9	286.9	306.5
	349.5K	349.5K	349.5	349.5	349.5
RI	0.5K	0.5K	0.5K	0.5K	0.5K
ROI	168.5K ÷ 1200K = 14%	143.1K ÷ 1018.5K = 14.1%	114.1K ÷ 811.6K = 14.1%	81.1K ÷ 575.7K = 14.1%	43.5K ÷ 306.8K = 14.2%

consistency between the method of project appraisal used and the managerial performance measures used. Both combinations may help to avoid the problem of managers not submitting projects that adversely affect their current performance as measured by the AIS. Hence behaviour congruence may be improved as long as annuity depreciation is used in constructing the short term management profit-performance measure.

A divisional manager from the electronics group now raises another problem. He states that in his line of business, there is never just one way to improve a process or product. There is always a choice, which means that, inevitably, there are competing projects. How can RI help divisional managers to choose the right project?

Let us consider a competing project to the original proposal we have just evaluated. Again, to simplify matters, we assume that this project has the same economic life of 5 years, the cash flow estimates can be regarded as certain and the relevant cost of capital is known. Table 12.6 shows the company's evaluation of the competing project with its associated NPV. Table 12.7 evaluates the project in terms of the management performance measures, ROI and RI including straight line depreciation.

In comparison with the original project, this proposal offers a lower NPV, £121 000 as opposed to £126 780, but a higher ROI in each of the first 2 years, 15% and 15%, as opposed to 9.2% and 11.5% respectively. If the divisional manager wishes to show an improvement on the current ROI, which we assume is 14%, he may be tempted to accept the competing project instead of the original project. On strictly financial grounds, this is not in the firm's best interests.

The chief accountant suggests the application of annuity depreciation to determine whether ROI or RI will be capable of choosing

Table 12.6 The company's view of the competing project using NPV

	$I_1 = £1m$ Life 5 yr $i = 10\%$		
	Net cash inflow	V^n	PV
Year 1	350	0.9091	318.2
Year 2	320	0.8264	264.5
Year 3	290	0.7513	217.9
Year 4	260	0.6830	177.6
Year 5	230	0.6209	142.8
			1121
		NPV = £121 000 positive	

Table 12.7 The division's view of the competing project using ROI, RI

	Year 1	Year 2	Year 3	Year 4	Year 5
Asset balance at year beginning	£1000K	£800K	£600K	£400K	£200K
Net cash inflow	350K	320K	290K	260K	230K
Depreciation	200K	200K	200K	200K	200K
Profit	150K	120K	90K	60K	30K
Interest on capital	100K	80K	60K	40K	20K
RI	50K	40K	30K	20K	10K
ROI on net book value	15%	15%	15%	15%	15%

between the projects in a manner consistent with the DCF techniques. Tabler 12.8 illustrates the application of annuity depreciation at the company's assumed hurdle rate of 10%, and Table 12.9 follows the change of policy to a 14% internal rate of return criterion. Table 12.10 brings together the results as measured by the different criteria for both the original and the competitor projects.

Table 12.10 reveals that a divisional manager who is intent on improving his short-term performance measure, whether it is calculated by means of ROI or RI, will favour the competing project when straight line depreciation is used, despite the NPV of the projects indicating that the original project should be preferred. When annuity depreciation is substituted for straight line depreciation, the same incentive to improve short-term performance may result in a preference for the competing project. At both the 10% and 14% hurdle rates, the competing project has a ROI and RI that is greater than those expected of the original project for each of the first 2 years of operation. Only by evaluating the results over the full 5 years will the divisional manager appreciate that his interests are best served by proposing the original project. However, the divisional manager may expect to have moved jobs within the firm or to have left the firm within that period. In any event, the competing project is only seriously detrimental to his performance measure in years 4 and 5, and by then the environment may have changed sufficiently for the expected advantages of the original project to be lost. So, it may be argued, that neither RI nor ROI (even with annuity depreciation) give divisional managers clear guidance about which project to propose when the expected cash flows are different from year to year.

At this stage, the chief accountant may point out that there is a way to overcome this problem of comparability by using an adjusted RI

Table 12.8 ROI, RI with annuity depreciation at 10%, the company's hurdle rate

Annuity depreciation ÷ interest = $1000K \div a_{\overline{5}|.1} = £263.8K$

	Year 1	Year 2	Year 3	Year 4	Year 5
Asset balance at year beginning	£1000K	£836.2K	£656K	£457.8K	£239.8K
Net cash inflow	350	320	290	260	230
Interest on capital	100	83.6	65.6	45.8	24
Depreciation	163.8	180.2	198.2	218	239.8
	263.8	263.8	263.8	263.8	263.8
RI	86.2	56.2	26.2	(3.8)	(33.8)
ROI	186.2K ÷ 1000K = 18.6%	139.8K ÷ 836.2K = 16.7%	91.8K ÷ 656K = 14%	42.0K ÷ 457.8K = 9.2%	(9.8K) ÷ 239.8K = (4.1%)

Table 12.9 ROI, RI with annuity depreciation at 14%, the company's internal rate of return

Annuity depreciation ÷ interest = 1000K ÷ $a_{\overline{5}|.14}$ = £291.3K

	Year 1	Year 2	Year 3	Year 4	Year 5
Asset balance at year beginning	£1000K	£848.7K	£676.2K	£479.6K	£255.4K
Net cash inflow	350	320	290	260	230
Interest on capital	140	118.8	94.7	67.1	35.8
Depreciation	151.3	172.5	196.6	224.2	255.5
	291.3	291.3	291.3	291.3	291.3
RI	58.7	28.7	(1.3)	(31.3)	(61.3)
ROI	198.7K ÷ 1000K = 19.9%	147.5K ÷ 848.7K = 17.4%	93.4K ÷ 676.2K = 13.8%	35.8K ÷ 479.6K = 7.5%	(25.5K) ÷ 255.4K = (10%)

Table 12.10   A comparison of the projects using various evaluation measures

Evaluation Measures	Year	Original project	Competing project
ROI using straight- line depreciation	1	9.2%	15%
	2	11.5	15
	3	15.3	15
	4	22.9	15
	5	45.8	15
RI using straight- line depreciation	1	£(10K)	£50K
	2	14	40
	3	38	30
	4	62	20
	5	86	10
NPV		£126 780	£121 000
ROI using annuity depreciation @ 10%	1	12.8%	18.6%
	2	13.3	16.7
	3	14.2	14
	4	16.1	9.2
	5	21.6	(4.1)
RI using annuity depreciation @ 10%	1	£33.4K	£86.2K
	2	33.4	56.2
	3	33.4	26.2
	4	33.4	(3.8)
	5	33.4	(33.8)
ROI using annuity depreciation @ 14%	1	14%	19.9%
	2	14.1	17.4
	3	14.1	13.8
	4	14.1	7.5
	5	14.2	(10)
RI using annuity depreciation @ 14%	1	£0.5K	£58.7K
	2	0.5	28.7
	3	0.5	(1.3)
	4	0.5	(31.3)
	5	0.5	(61.3)

approach, where depreciation is calculated by deducting interest on the capital sum outstanding from the expected cash receipt for the year, the ability to compare projects with uneven cash flows may be enhanced (Tomkins, 1973). Tables 12.11 and 12.12 show the results using this method for the original and competing projects respectively.

This procedure does seem to overcome the problem of comparability, but at the cost of having a depreciation charge that can increase and decrease over the project's life dependent on the changes in cash flows. In addition, the adjusted RI may stimulate divisional managers to prefer short-lived projects at the expense of longer-lived projects that have higher NPVs. The adjusted RI procedure is therefore unlikely to be acceptable to divisional managers or most accountants who are used to applying a specific depreciation method.

In this last respect, it is also debatable whether ROI or RI with annuity depreciation will be found acceptable in practice. In contrast to all other depreciation methods, the annuity method provides increasing charges over the life of an asset, whereas conventional methods either provide stable or reducing charges. The compatibility between RI with annuity depreciation and NPV is only apparent to the divisional manager if the results over the project's entire life are investigated. With an AIS used in a way that emphasizes short-term performance, the managers may be disinclined to do this. The chief accountant may be theoretically correct, and in fact the illustration demonstrates that RI using annuity depreciation is equivalent to NPV, but as a guide to encourage behaviour congruence, its use is limited by the short-term emphasis in using the accounting information.

Thus, the following conclusions seem to apply. The use of RI with annuity depreciation gives guidance compatible with the firm's evaluation criterion, NPV, as long as the results are viewed over the project's entire life. A clear policy statement that divisional management performance is to be determined by a profit-conscious style may ensure that managers look at the RI results for all years of the project's life. Secondly, even using RI with annuity depreciation does not seem to give clear guidance to divisional managers choosing between competing projects. Only the DCF techniques appear capable of doing this, and divisional management is not regularly evaluated on this basis. The conventional AIS normally uses some form of accrual income to measure managerial performance. The unacceptability of annuity depreciation highlights the accountant's difficulty to measure the investment base in a manner which is both consistent with the long-term decision model and the generally accepted practices of accrual accounting. A novel suggestion by Gregory (1987) seeks to overcome this problem by treating the division as lessees of capital assets owned by top management.

This alternative results in an absolute profit measure where lease payments are related to the net cash flows of each year of the asset's use. The relationship is determined by the proportion of the initial

Table 12.11 The original project using adjusted RI

		Year 1	Year 2	Year 3	Year 4	Year 5
Asset value at year beginning		£1200K	£970K	£717K	£438.7K	£132.6K
Net cash inflow		350	350	350	350	350
Interest on capital	120	97	71.7	43.9	13.3	
Depreciation	230	253	278.3	306.1	132.6	
		350	350	350	350	145.9
RI		—	—	—	—	204.1

$$\text{NPV} = 204.1\ (V_{.1}^{5}) = £126\,726 \text{ positive}$$

Table 12.12 The competitive project using adjusted RI

		Year 1	Year 2	Year 3	Year 4	Year 5
Asset balance at year beginning		£1000K	£750K	£505K	£265.5K	£32.1K
Net cash inflows		350	320	290	260	230
Interest on capital	100	75	50.5	26.6	3.2	
Depreciation	250	245	239.5	233.4	32.1	
		350	320	290	260	35.3
RI		—	—	—	—	194.7

$$\text{NPV} = 194.7\ (V_{.1}^{5}) = £120\,714 \text{ positive}$$

investment to the present value of the project. Using the original project data of the Kinetic Compounds Company, the following divisional performance measure may be developed:

Lease payment as a proportion of annual cash inflow:

$$\frac{I}{P.V.} = \frac{£1.2m.}{£1.32678} = 0.90445$$

NPV = £126 780

Lease payment £350 000(0.90445) = £316 558

Divisional performance measure:

	Net cash inflow
Less	Lease payment
	Divisional income

In this case, divisional income becomes £33 442 per annum because the net cash inflows are constant over the project's life. Discounting the income stream gives an NPV £126 772 [33 442 $a_{5\rceil,1}$] which is equivalent to the original calculation.

The simplicity of this approach is a major advantage but it is not without its difficulties. Divisional managers may still be tempted to misjudge future cash flows in later years especially if, in the short term, improvements in the divisional performance measure can be obtained. As Gregory (1987) recognizes, this temptation is enhanced when divisional managers consider a termination or abandonment decision. By convincing top management that cash flow prospects are expected to be lower, a decrease in lease payment can be accomplished and income apparently increases. There is an additional problem, in that the lease payment charged under this method may bear little or no resemblance to market leasing arrangements. For the investment centre manager, his decision to lease internally or externally may rest, in part, on the extent to which financial accounting statements about 'off-balance sheet financing', for example, are adopted for internal reporting purposes. Somewhat gloomily, we may conclude that no practically acceptable profit performance measure exists that will guarantee consistency with the results given by the DCF techniques. However, there is a further possible (if somewhat radical) alternative.

CASH FLOW AS A MEASURE OF MANAGERIAL PERFORMANCE

When it is recognized that divisional managers may significantly influence the early stages of the capital budgeting process, it seems essential that the profit performance measures incorporated in the AIS do not mislead managers to submit projects that are not in the firm's best interests. It seems relevant therefore to consider budgeted and actual cash flow comparisons as measures of managerial performance.

There have been many proponents of cash flow accounting, of whom the most notable are Lee (1972), Lawson (1978) and Thomas (1980a). Especially in times of inflation, accrual profit before depreciation tends to run ahead of operating cash flow, increasing working capital requirements lead to an enhanced risk of overtrading. With the reliance large companies place on funding capital projects from internally generated cash flow, it is not surprising to learn that 79% of British companies require divisions to return surplus cash to the central common pool (Scapens *et al.*, 1982). In the USA, the practice is even more established, with cash typically being returned on a daily basis.

In theory, either profit before interest and tax or cash flow provide a satisfactory measure of divisional performance when divisions are unable to influence their capital asset base (Emmanuel and Otley, 1976). When the divisional managers can influence the asset base, these measures may be less appropriate because of the omission of any information about capital investment. In the context of the true investment centre, it is worth considering how a cash flow accounting system may encompass capital investment information and still avoid giving the managers an incentive to choose projects not in the firm's best interests. To conclude the Kinetic Compounds case, Table 12.13 illustrates the consistency of comparing the incremental cash flows and NPV of the projects. However, to contemplate seriously using an AIS based on cash flows, we need to discover how it can be extended to include all aspects of a divisional manager's decision making.

Table 12.13   The incremental cash flow and NPV comparison of the projects

		Year 1	*Year 2*	*Year 3*	*Year 4*	*Year 5*
Original project	£1200K	350K	350K	350K	350K	350K
Competitor project	£1000K	350K	320K	290K	260K	230K
	200K	–	30K	60K	90K	120K
Discount at 10%			24.8K	45.1K	61.5K	74.5K

$$\text{NPV} = -200K + 205.9K$$
$$= \text{£}5900 \text{ increase over the competing project}$$

Henderson and Dearden (1966) provide, possibly, the best suggestion for integrating divisional capital and operating decisions within an AIS. (For a more specific illustration of using cash flow to measure divisional performance with a special emphasis on the post-audit of capital projects, see Gee, 1980). The Henderson and Dearden proposal for cash flow accounting focuses on the integration of three budgets. The first is a contribution budget consisting of the expected revenues less the costs of doing business, that is variable costs. They suggest that this budget is prepared annually and that the comparison with actual costs is made monthly. The other two budgets, called the fixed/managed cost budget and the capital budget feed information into the contribution budget. The fixed/managed cost budget is made up of those costs that would still be incurred under short-term shut-down conditions (from 2–4 weeks) and may include fixed manufacturing costs, marketing costs incurred before the point of sale, research and development costs and the administrative costs of the division. Only cash costs are included, and depreciation and other costs representing allocations of previous investments are excluded. The fixed/managed cost budget is prepared annually. When costs incurred by increasing (or savings from decreasing) the present level of operations are approved, the promised future increases in contribution are included in the appropriate year's contribution budget. Similarly, the cash flows on which a capital investment proposal is justified are included in the appropriate year's contribution budget. Thus, the same data used to take a long-term decision are included in the short-term performance measure. A simplified illustration of the system is shown in Table 12.14.

The original budget for the year is based upon the contribution expected from day-to-day operations. The additional information under the fixed/managed budget heading has resulted from the expectations of changes in fixed costs for the year. These changes are illustrated in Table 12.15.

Table 12.14 The integrated contribution budget (after Henderson and Dearden, 1966)

	Original budget (£'000s)	Fixed/ managed (£'000s)	Capital (£'000s)	Adjusted budget (£'000s)
Revenue	1000	+75	0	1075
Variable costs	500	0	−400	100
Contribution	500	+75	+400	975

Table 12.15   The fixed/managed cost budget (after Henderson and Dearden, 1966)

	Plus approved expansion (£'000s)	Less approved contraction (£'000s)	Budget (£'000s)
Revenue	+150	−75	+75
Variable costs	+ 80	−80	0
Contribution	+ 70	+ 5	+75

Note that these entries refer to the expected cash cost and revenue changes. The explanation of the approved expansion is that an improved marketing programme costing £80 000 is expected to increase sales by £150 000, and a contraction in inventory sizes stocked is expected to reduce revenue by £75 000 but will cut costs by £80 000. The capital budget entry in Table 12.14 indicates that expenditure is not expected to affect revenue this year, but manufacturing and direct labour costs are expected to diminish by £400 000 in this year of the project's life.

As with all proposals for the improvements of AISs, this suggestion has its drawbacks. Firstly, the manager responsible for the contribution budget may have little incentive to divest himself of unused assets. The investment base of the division affects the contribution budget only indirectly by determining the capacity available to generate revenues. Secondly, when transfer prices are involved, the manager working to a contribution budget may try to inflate the expected revenue or may not attempt to improve efficiency if a standard cost base is used. An opportunity cost approach is required, so that at full capacity a transfer price equivalent to some market price is charged, whereas at below full capacity the marginal cost approximated by standard variable cost is applied to the internally traded goods or services. Estimating which of these situations is likely to occur over a future period of time is problematic, but not insurmountable (Chapter 11).

There is, of course, the more fundamental question of whether transfer prices should be included under a divisional cash flow accounting scheme. In practice, when inter-divisional trading occurs, records of the transfers and their prices are made, but no cash passes between the divisions in respect of the trade. The argument may then be advanced that the revenue and cost of the contribution budget should exclude non-cash transactions. However, this would not reflect the level of operation of individual divisions and may disguise the importance of a division servicing several others with, for example, specially designed component parts. It may also disadvantage capital expenditure projects in one division that result in the lowering of costs of transferred goods to other divisions. This aspect of the transfer pricing problem specifically relating to capital expenditure proposals has received little attention. Ackerman (1970) states that even in integrated companies, investment analyses were confined to one division and excluded the impact of the proposed project on the profitability or need for additional capacity in other divisions linked to it by product transfer. From the authors' casual observations, this attitude appears common in diversified British companies also, and may provide a logical explanation why divisional managers tend not to generate capital projects that involve the uncertainties associated with inter-divisional trade.

There is also the possible difficulty that an AIS based on cash flow is more easily manipulated by divisional managers (Rutherford, 1982). Careful timing of invoice payments and receipts can distort the comparison between budgeted and actual results. Inevitably, capital budget estimates of cash flow will require adjustment over time and may provide divisional management with another opportunity to exercise bias. However, any revision should be accompanied by a review of the key assumptions on which the original cash flows were based and the possibility of learning may be a beneficial result. Again, the style of evaluation may be decisive in determining whether this occurs.

In favour of an AIS based on an integrated cash flow budget, it may be stated that top and divisional management use the same measure to evaluate capital projects and that the on-going performance report, the contribution budget, is expressed in the same terms, that is cash flow. The assumptions upon which the project cash flows are based may help the divisional manager to re-appraise the assumptions underlying the on-going operations of the division. Also the integrated cash flow AIS has the advantage of flexibility of application to a profit centre or an investment centre. For the former, a contribution budget that includes the original plus fixed/managed cost changes is appropriate; whereas for an investment centre, the capital budget is included as well. The cash flow AIS may therefore offer adaptability in line with the divisional manager's influence over types of capital expenditures. Finally, the resultant measure of performance may be regarded as more consistent with economic profit than either accounting profit, ROI or RI.

This final point requires elaboration. Scapens (1978) argues that economic value is normally defined in terms of the NPV of future net receipts, and economic income is defined as the amount that can be consumed in a period without impairing this economic value. Multi-divisional companies appear to have tentatively embraced the DCF techniques, but their measurement of accounting profit is not equivalent to economic income. Economic income or economic profit may be defined as the excess of benefits over costs of productive activities in each period when all relevant costs are measured in terms of their opportunity costs. The merit of the cash flow AIS budget is that, wherever possible, allocations of historic cost are excluded. However, the contribution budget may not exactly reflect economic profit, because cash flows are only approximations of opportunity cost values. Nevertheless, by excluding the confounding effect of historical cost allocations, it may give divisional managers better signals as to what level of operations to aim for, which products to produce, etc., that will result in activities closer to maximizing economic value than may be obtained when using an AIS based on accrual income.

CONCLUSIONS

The available empirical evidence suggests that divisional managers may influence strategically important stages of the capital budgeting process in multidivisional companies. The size and diversity of these companies means that top management's knowledge of specific aspects of the divisions' operations is inevitably deficient. The inherent uncertainty surrounding the particular product markets increases the likelihood of information asymmetry.

The important question arises of what influences divisional managers in their choice of capital projects to generate formally. Self-interest and self-preservation may motivate the managers to propose capital projects that will improve or, at least, not harm the measures by which their performance is evaluated. The prevalance of ROI, comparisons between actual and budgeted profits, and to a lesser extent RI, suggests that the impact of the proposals on these measures will be assessed by the managers before formal submission. Even when a reward is not linked with these short-term performance measures, the manager's perception that these are controls of top management may influence the choice of projects generated. Hence it is important that the short-term performance measures incorporated in the AIS guide divisional managers to propose capital projects consistent with the best interests of the company.

Although Solomons' (1965) contention that RI is the short-run counterpart of net present value is found to be theoretically correct, it has two practical defects. RI requires some form of annuity depreciation to be used, and current practice in both the UK and the

USA suggests that this is not acceptable to managers or accountants. Secondly, even the RI measure with annuity depreciation gives the manager a clear signal to accept or reject the capital project if, and only if, the annual cash flows are constant. If they are not, then the annual RI figures must be discounted over the life of the project. The possibility of managers favouring projects with higher RIs in the early years but yielding lower NPVs than competing projects cannot be ignored. However, the combination of controllable RI with a profit-conscious style of evaluation may encourage the manager to examine the trend of RI results over the entire life of the project.

Nevertheless, the conventional AIS appears defective in providing a measure for short-term performance evaluation and incentive purposes that is compatible with the measure that should be used to evaluate long-term capital projects. One potential reason for this incompatibility is that the short-term performance measures use accrual accounting concepts, whereas the long-term planning models use cash flows. Certainly, there may be advantages in maintaining consistency between the income measures reported in financial accounts and management accounts, but there is the competing advantage of gaining consistency between management accounts and the evaluation of capital projects. The importance of cash management for the firm as a whole is supported by the empirical evidence, which indicates that divisions are required to remit cash surpluses on a frequent and regular basis to the centre. Given this attention to cash flow management, it seems worthwhile to examine short-term performance measures for divisional managers based on the cash flow concept. The integrated cash flow AIS using a contribution budget satisfies the requirement that manager's short-term and long-term decisions are not evaluated by different accounting concepts. With the adoption of a profit-conscious or more flexible trend-oriented style of evaluation, the incentive for managers to concentrate on the short term at the expense of the long term may be significantly reduced. Additionally, the contribution budget offers greater compatibility as an approximation for economic profit than does either ROI or RI. In turn, economic profit may be regarded as a more accurate proxy for economic value than any existing accrual based measure of income. The possibility of incorporating the assumptions of capital projects with the proposals in the formal capital budgeting process may improve the likelihood of consensus management. Simultaneously, the relationship between these assumptions and those under which the day-to-day operations are conducted may help divisional managers to react to the uncertain environments they face. By acknowledging the importance of matching top and divisional managements' assumptions, we are perhaps moving towards a less accounting oriented and towards a more multidimensional AIS.

EXERCISES

1. Identify the stages of the capital budgeting process. Suggest ways in which top management could improve the accuracy and completeness of the information associated with capital project proposals.

2. Assume that you are part of the top-management team of a large, diversified company. You are aware of the incentives that divisional and lower-level managers have to pre-select projects and provide biased estimates, but the company policy is still to evaluate these managers on a short-term accruals income basis. Give reasoned arguments for and against each of the following separate suggestions:
   (a) To create the additional head office position of a capital budget 'supremo' whose remit is to monitor and check each project before ultimate authorization.
   (b) To issue a policy that all capital project proposals that are generated should be evaluated by the divisional accountants and the results sent to the chief accountant at head office.
   (c) To create a head office based team who are automatically called in by divisional managers to give advice at the cash flow estimation stage.
   (d) To issue a policy statement that all capital projects will be considered on their merits regardless of their evaluation under the company's DCF criterion.

3. Compare the relative advantages and disadvantages of RI, ROI and the integrated contribution budget as measures of managerial performance. Comment on each measure's compatibility with the DCF techniques.

4. An integrated cash flow AIS does not encourage opportunistic behaviour such as the manipulation of actual results and the provision of biased estimates by divisional managers. Discuss.

5. Hal Edstrom is the divisional general manager of the Electrical Goods Division of Associated Engineering. The company has used a divisionalized control system for several years. The performance measure of prime concern to divisional general managers was ROI using net book values. This determined each managers' bonus, and affected the assessment of his potential for promotion at the end of each year.
   A new chief accountant, Jeremy Grissle, has convinced corporate management that RI is a better measure of division and

divisional manager's performance. Jeremy is now trying to convince the divisional managers of the superiority of RI at a special meeting.

Hal Edstrom argues that RI is misleading and gives the following example to illustrate his objections: 'I have a project that will produce net cash flows of £400 000 per annum for the next 5 years. It will then be obsolete and worthless. The initial investment is £1 500 000 and Associated Engineering uses straight line depreciation. Under RI, my performance varies for each of the 5 years, which is quite ridiculous, as my true performance as shown by profit (i.e., net cash flow less depreciation) remains stable. RI is obviously accounting rubbish!'

Required:

(a) Demonstrate, using the example provided, how Hal Edstrom has reached his conclusion. The company's cost of capital is 10% per annum.

(b) How would you counter his argument that RI is nonsense?

(c) What are the technical and theoretical advantages of using RI as opposed to ROI?

6. The performance of the Triple Crown Chemical Division of Industrial Chemicals Ltd is appraised by the residual income method, and the divisional manager, Dr Williams, has the power to dispose of redundant assets.

The division has an asset with a written-down value of £50 000. For the purpose of calculating residual income, the asset is depreciated at £5000 per annum (10-year life, nil scrap value). Residual income is charged with interest at 10% per annum on written-down value at the beginning of the year.

Dr Williams considers that the asset's cash flows, net of out-of-pocket costs, will be £7000 per annum for 5 years and £3000 per annum for a further 5 years, giving an expected present value of £33 657. An opportunity to sell the asset for £30 000 has arisen. After the current year, the disposal value of the asset will be negligible. Residual income will be charged with any book loss on the disposal of the asset.

Required:

(a) If Dr Williams decided to sell the asset, would his decision be in the best interests of Industrial Chemicals Ltd?

(b) Should Dr Williams, who is ambitious and believes that his promotion prospects depend on high profit performance in the current period, retain or sell the asset?

(c) If Dr Williams had only recently been appointed as divisional manager, would he retain or sell the asset?

(d) What difference, if any, would it make to your decisions in parts (a) and (b) if the asset could be sold for £35 000 instead of £30 000? What conclusions might you make about the usefulness of RI in this instance?

7. The Angler-Cost Company recently established two new plants for the manufacture of toy go-carts (plant X) and skate-boards (plant Y). The investment decisions were made on the following basis:

	Plant X	Plant Y
Initial investment	£300 000	£400 000
Present value of future cash flows discounted at cost of capital 8% p.a.	£340 000	£480 000
Economic life	5 yr	5 yr
Scrap value	Nil	Nil

Expected cash flows were £50 000 in year 1 and £100 000 in year 2; both plants achieved expectations in year 1.

In year 2, plant X earned a cash flow of £80 000. A competitor's innovation of replacing the conventional wheels of toy go-carts with low friction skate-board wheels resulted in a fall in demand. The plant manager estimated that £25 000 cash flow had been lost as a result.

In year 2, plant Y earned a cash flow of £105 000. Of this £10 000 related to the sale of skate-board wheels to an external third party, the innovative competitor of X, which had not been included in the original investment decision.

Assuming that cash flows approximate to controllable profit, calculate the residual income in year 2 for each plant (adopting straight line depreciation).

Discuss the appraisal of performance and the assumptions of the original expectations.

Briefly outline what action, if any, should be taken in respect of the individual plant manager's performance.

8. A divisional manager is considering the following two machines, each of which has an initial cost of £800 000 and an optimal useful life of four years, with an estimated scrap value of zero. The machines produce constant outputs from year to year:

		£
Machine I	Annual operating costs in each of years 1 to 4	247 600
Machine II	Operating costs: Year 1	100 000
	2	200 000
	3	340 000
	4	400 000

You may assume that the company owning the machines has a required rate of return of 10% per annum, and that sales revenues and operating costs are settled in cash at the end of the year to which they relate.
Required:
(a) Determine the minimum annual sales revenue required to justify the purchase of each of these machines.
(b) Using the calculation in (a), above, determine the ROI and RI for each machine each year of its life. Straight-line depreciation is the company's preferred policy.
(c) Follow the instructions in (b), above, except that now annuity depreciation is to be applied.
(d) Give reasoned arguments to help the manager decide which machine to submit in his formal capital budget.
Show all calculations. State your answers to the nearest £1000. Ignore taxation and inflation.

9. Cathode plc has 2 divisions. The managing director has told the divisional managers that a bonus will be paid to the more profitable division. However, absolute profit as conventionally computed will not be used. Instead the ranking will be affected by the relative investments in the 2 divisions. Both of the managers have now written to claim the bonus. The following data are available:

Division	Assets at original cost	Assets at net book value	Net income after depreciation
	£	£	£
Electrolysis	380 000	190 000	46 000
Ergometer	250 000	125 000	32 000

The company's cost of capital is 10% per annum.
Required:
(a) Which method for computing profitability do you think each manager chose to show that his results were the best?
Briefly state to which manager you would award the bonus and give your reasons.
(b) Each divisional manager is actively contemplating a project with the following cash flows:
Investment of £30 000 now, giving expected net cash inflows beginning in one year's time of £4000 per annum for 10 years. There will be no scrap value at the end of the project's life.
(i) What will be the likely investment decision each manager will make when appraising this separate project? Will each manager's decision be consistent with the

company's best interest? (You are to assume that from the first year of operation the project's net cash inflow is equivalent to net income after depreciation.)

(ii) Under which set of conditions may residual income measures lead to corporately acceptable investment decisions?

(c) Why is it important that in the multidivisional company the short-term performance measure coincides with the long-term planning model to evaluate capital projects?

10. Oklahoma Chemicals Inc is contemplating changing the method of measuring divisional performance. At present, rate of return on investment (ROI) is used. Each division's return is calculated by dividing net income by the net investment base at the beginning of the year. Straight line depreciation is included in the net income computation. The alternative is to measure performance by means of residual income (RI).

Dr Larry Nathy, the manager of the Ozark Division, is considering an investment now and asks you to evaluate the following data, particularly in respect of the effect on his division's ROI and RI measures:

	£
Initial investment (t_0)	100 000
Expected net cash flows ($t_1 - t_6$) per annum	23 000
Expected scrap value (t_6)	4 000
Oklahoma Chemicals Inc cost of capital	10%
Ozark Division current ROI	15%
Economic life of asset	6 years

The proposed RI measure will also use straight-line depreciation and the net book value of the asset at the beginning of the year. Assume that the net cash flow is equal to net income before depreciation.

Required:

(a) Provide the information requested by Dr Nathy and also advise him as to what to do in the company's best interests. Why may he not accept your advice?

(b) Show him how the RI computation can be adapted to give a decision consistent with the company's view, and list the conditions under which it will hold.

(c) Demonstrate how Gregory's leased payment scheme would achieve equivalence with NPV.

(d) The discretion which investment centre managers have over the capital budgeting process makes the choice of short-term performance measures by which they are evaluated of paramount importance. Discuss.

(e) Evaluate the suggestion of Henderson and Dearden (1966) that an integrated cash flow budget would overcome many of the defects of accrual income performance measures.

11. (a) Why do companies divisionalize?

(b) What advantages, if any, does the multidivisional structure possess as opposed to the unitary or functional structure?

(c) Peter James is an investment centre manager in the divisionalized company named the T. Tilling Co. Peter has an opportunity to invest £60 000 now in machinery that will generate the following data over the next 3 years:

	£
Variable costs per item produced	5.00
Revenue per item	7.00
Annual maintenance costs associated with the new machinery	620.00

The number of items expected to be sold are 15 500, 18 600 and 19 600 in years 1, 2 and 3 respectively.

The company's policy is to depreciate equipment and machinery on the straight line basis and a minimum rate of return of 20% is required on new investments. Peter's current rate of return is 30% as measured by net income after depreciation expressed over the net book value of assets at the beginning of the year.

Assume that *net cash flows* are equal to net income/contribution before depreciation. At the end of the third year, the machinery has no scrap or salvage value.

Required:

(a) Show whether the present short-term performance measure (ROI) will lead Peter to take an investment decision that is consistent with the company's best long-term interests.

(b) Provide an alternative analysis that will bring the long-term planning and short-term control models into coincidence. Make clear the assumptions under which this solution applies.

Part Four

A Framework for Analysis

In earlier parts of this book, we have outlined the significant influences on the design of the management control system. Concentrating on the programmed, non-programmed dimension explicitly recognizes that different managers will encounter different degrees of unpredictability when making decisions. Organization structures like the multidivisional can be argued to reflect the unpredictability of a number of diverse environments. Given the assumptions on which the traditional AIS is based, the question must be asked 'Can effective management control be achieved with an AIS of the same design?'

Contingency theory suggests that universal application is inappropriate and a framework for analysis is developed in this chapter to suggest alternative performance measures, incentives and evaluation uses in the multidivisional organization. No general prescriptions can be offered because the design of the successful management control system will depend on what the individual company is seeking to achieve. Just how the management control system maintains its effectiveness in the face of changing corporate aims and actions is a second significant, and as yet, unanswered question.

One conclusion alone appears self-evident. Future generations of management accountants may be as concerned with events occuring outside as within the large business enterprise. The need for their AIS to be flexible in order to continue to contribute to the management control process may become of fundamental importance.

13

Accounting for management control

SUMMARY

While the limitations of the contingency approach are recognized, it seems heroic to assume that a single accounting information system will work equally well in all types of companies. We have identified one contingent variable – the incidence of non-programmed decision making – as a potentially significant influence in the design of accounting information systems. Within an organizational theory perspective, the multidivisional company was chosen to exemplify the difficulties of applying conventional accounting systems because of the high incidence of non-programmed decision making. Whether or not the conventional system can be modified or requires replacement is our concern in this chapter.

Results, action and personnel controls are shown to be in conflict when the conventional accounting information system is applied to the multidivisional company. Furthermore, the encouragement given to divisional managers to mis-record, manipulate and bias does nothing to promote behaviour congruence. Hence there seems to be a *prima facie* case for change.

De-emphasis of profit performance measures, adoption of non-financial measures and the use of profit conscious or non-accounting styles may be appropriate. But additionally, the significance of corporate culture and personnel development seem necessary for success. It must also be recognized that the design of management control systems must interact with corporate strategy. Our knowledge about how these systems are used over time is only beginning to emerge. Perhaps the single most important change for the management accountant is to develop feedforward controls to, at least, the same level of sophistication as feedback controls. To do this effectively, and to become a useful adviser, the accountant will need to monitor external as well as internal variables which critically effect divisional plans. Translation of changes in key variables to show the effect on financial plans may re-orient the accountant to make a more balanced commitment to providing information relevant for decision making, attention-directing and score-keeping.

INTRODUCTION

An organizational view of accounting provides the possibility of moving beyond the constraining technical orientation to the subject that has dominated so much of professional and scholarly dialogue to a view of accounting that emphasizes the organizational and social roles that the technology serves and the human processes through which it becomes effective.

(Hopwood, 1984)

The emphasis on the multidivisional form of organization has been taken to highlight the problems of applying conventional accounting information systems for management control. Recognition of the importance of companies adopting this organizational form is given by Hill (1985). In a survey conducted in 1982, just over 60% of 144 large UK companies exhibited a multidivisional structure. Adoption of the structure in the USA can be traced to the 1950s and 1960s (Rumelt, 1974), where it is estimated that almost 80% of the largest 200 companies have multidivisional structures. The introduction to France, Italy, West Germany and Japan is more recent but the trend of adoption by large companies appears to be gaining acceptance (Cable, 1988). Given the economic significance of these enterprises, the emphasis on the multidivisional form seems quite appropriate.

Companies adopting this structure exercise management control in a different manner. Perhaps due to the size of their operations, their geography and line of business diversity, and the many potential relationships between divisions of the company, managing becomes increasingly complex. Hence multidivisional companies tend to have two broad layers of managers, corporate or headquarters staff and line or divisional general managers. The role of corporate or top management is to perform strategic planning, monitor the efficiency and performance of divisions within the firm, award incentives and allocate resources, (Williamson, 1985). The crucial implication is that divisional managers are afforded greater control over operating decisions. This quasi-autonomous status allows divisional managers to take decisions more quickly and for the entire company to become more responsive to market changes.

Decentralization is therefore a distinguishing feature of multi-divisional companies but it does present a major difficulty for the AIS. How can top management be certain that divisional managers will make decisions in the company's best interests? Will the regular financial reports accurately reflect and justify the decisions taken, or will they merely give the appearance that all is well when in fact it is not? At the very least, corporate management should have sufficient faith in the design of the AIS that it will not provide incentives for divisional managers to mis-record or manipulate financial information. Hence our emphasis on the concept of behaviour congruence as an attempt to recognize the need to redirect managers' attention away from the means (financial performance measures) towards the ends (agreement on an appropriate set of actions). The implications for the AIS to achieve management control successfully in the multi-divisional company is our concern in this chapter. However, there remains one other important factor to consider in our analysis.

The conscious delegation of decision-making authority to divisional managers suggests that these managers will take different types of decisions to their counterparts in other forms of organizations. We have concentrated on the programmed, non-programmed dimension. This continuum suggests that at one pole decision making is repetitive, in accordance with a well-known plan where the relationship between actions and results can be clearly specified and measured. Virtually the opposite conditions exist at the non-programmed pole where intuition and judgement are required, there is no explicit plan and the relationship between actions and results is at best hazy. Unique decisions frequently occur because the internal and external environments are constantly changing. Unpredictability in some shape or form, we have argued, will characterize the average divisional managers' decision making. This seems consistent with the top management's perception of the need to decentralize. The position on the continuum cannot be exactly specified, but the usefulness of the programmed, non-programmed dimension allows the introduction of environmental uncertainty. Whether the uncertainty takes the form of dynamism, heterogeneity and hostility in product markets (Gordon and Miller, 1976) or static-dynamic, simple-complex forms, (Waterhouse and Tiessen, 1978) is not our concern. It is important to recognize the uncertainty and the effect on the predictability of decisions because effective controls (whether financial or others) will be contingent upon environmental circumstances. The design of the AIS needs to take this into account with the aim of promoting behaviour congruence.

THE CONTINGENCY APPROACH RESTATED

The contingency theory approach firmly places the design of the AIS in the context of organizational responses to a wider environment, such as firms' business strategies and organizational structures. The effectiveness of the design of the AIS depends on its ability to be adaptive to changes in external circumstances and other internal responses. When business strategies are developed in response to environments that are characterized by dynamic and unpredictable changes, the requirements placed on the organizational structure and AIS may be quite different to those necessary in an environment characterized by stability. The best way to structure and manage a firm depends on the uncertainty associated with the activities it undertakes or proposes to undertake in the future. The uncertainty of operating in diverse technological and market environments will affect the design of the organization and its accounting system. Hence the underlying premise of the contingency approach is that there is no universally appropriate AIS that applies equally to all organizations in all circumstances. We have shared this view and have outlined some of the problems that can occur when conventional AISs are applied in uncertain situations.

However, we have taken great care not to imply that specific contingent variables will effect the AIS in a particular way. As one of the authors has concluded elsewhere, the contingency theory of management accounting is based on an insufficiently articulated model, it gives scant attention to developing a working definition of organizational effectiveness and empirical support for it is limited and weak (Otley, 1980). Therefore to link specific contingent variables with specific features of AIS design is currently unsubstantiated and may ultimately be fallacious. Instead we have used the contingency approach to broaden the framework within which the design of the AIS can be evaluated. As a general framework, the contingency approach has two advantages. Firstly, it explicitly recognizes that environmental uncertainty and organizational complexity are important factors influencing both organizational design and AIS design. Secondly, it draws our attention to the support that the AIS can give to help managers take decisions where outcomes cannot be accurately predicted because of environmental uncertainty. Hence we have simplified and condensed the complex interrelationships that undoubtedly exist between the many potentially influential variables by concentrating on that combination of conditions that gives rise to non-programmed decisions. In essence, we have argued that the conditions that make decentralization of decision making and a multidivisional organizational structure appropriate increase the incidence of non-programmed decision taking (Chapter 8). The implications of this type of decision making for the effectiveness of the AIS have been examined in the remainder of Part Three with regard to performance measurement, transfer pricing and capital budgeting.

The assumptions made in Part Three are in marked contrast to those found in Part Two. In Chapter 6, for example, it was argued that the successful application of linear programming and using relevant costs for decision making depends on complete and certain information being available. A predictive model that is capable of accurately forecasting outputs given a knowledge of inputs is required. Such a model may exist for a clearly defined production process, but the advent of new mass-production techniques of considerable complexity makes it increasingly less feasible (Kaplan, 1984). Inevitably, conventional accounting techniques need to assume that the external environment is relatively stable and predictable. When this is so, centralized decision making becomes efficient and the behaviour of individuals within the firm also becomes more predictable. Yet as Chapter 2 pointed out, individuals have varying and possibly conflicting, motives for working. Their involvement and commitment to work in organizations cannot be evaluated by ignoring the social and cultural context in which the work is done. In essence, a conventional AIS makes assumptions similar to those made by the cybernetic control model, introduced in Chapter 1. When clear objectives, a well-understood predictive model, accurate measurements of actual outcomes and clearly definable alternative actions exist, programmed decision making is the norm and conventional accounting techniques are appropriate. Scapens (1980) reaches a similar conclusion when evaluating the role of quantitative models in programmed and non-programmed decisions. In these circumstances, conventional accounting techniques may be seen as promoting managerial efficiency. However, the important question to pose is whether an over-emphasis on efficiency by vigorous appli- • cation of the conventional AIS will hinder managerial attention to effectiveness.

Non-programmed decision making

Non-programmed decisions are those whose outcomes cannot be accurately predicted. They require a high degree of judgement, they are often unique, their effect on other parts of the business can only be guessed at, and their outcomes are largely non-quantifiable. A homely example is the decision of whether to get married; a business example is the decision of how much money to allocate to research and development activities. Both decisions are capable of either producing great benefits or, alternatively, resulting in great harm!

The reasons associated with non-programmed decision making also instigate the organizational response of decentralization and the adoption of the multidivisional structure and are a source for concern in continuing with a conventional AIS. Once a significant amount of non-programmed decision making occurs at lower levels of management, the problem of information asymmetry within the firm cannot be ignored. Divisional and lower-level managers may possess more detailed, up-to-date and valid models of the specific activities for which they are responsible than the top management. The possibility that the different management levels will not share exactly the same aims, preferences or beliefs about actions to be taken places a great, if not overwhelming, burden on the AIS as an aid to effective management control. The traditional reliance on accounting measures of divisional performance will be inappropriate because they are incomplete, inaccurate and non-neutral. Unless changes are made to the design of the AIS, it will provide powerful incentives for managers to indulge in opportunistic behaviour. The linking of reward schemes (Chapter 10) to accounting measures of performance may result in the manipulation of actual results and the introduction of bias in forecasts (Chapter 7). The idea of superimposing the same AIS on the divisional management of a decentralized firm as was appropriate for the top management of a centralized firm represents a failure of the accountant or designer of the AIS to recognize the need for a system to be compatible with its organizational context. We will therefore examine what the likely repercussions will be of applying a conventional AIS to a multidivisional structure. It should constantly be remembered that this structure has a higher incidence of non-programmed decisions, taken at a lower level, than the unitary organization because product markets are more differentiated and dynamic and a greater degree of decentralization has been adopted.

It should also be noted that attempts to prescribe the design features of a general AIS contradict the contingency approach to some extent. What follows is a general form of analysis which would require further refinement before application in a specific multidivisional company.

The multidivisional AIS mismatch

A mismatch between a multidivisional structure and its accounting information system can occur at one of three levels, as illustrated in Figs 13.1–13.3. At the first level, a lack of participation in standard setting will result in standards and targets being seen as inappropriate by the managers responsible for attaining them. At the second level, even if participation in standard setting occurs, the linking of rewards directly to the achievement of financial measures of performance will result in bias and manipulation of accounting reports. Even if no direct link between rewards and financial measures of per-

Implications: Standards or targets of performance
irrelevant, or perceived as irrelevant;
resource allocation inappropriate or
perceived as such by the divisional
manager

Fig. 13.1 Sequentially applying the traditional AIS to the multidivisional company.

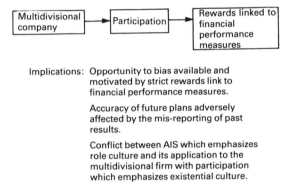

Implications: Opportunity to bias available and
motivated by strict rewards link to
financial performance measures.

Accuracy of future plans adversely
affected by the mis-reporting of past
results.

Conflict between AIS which emphasizes
role culture and its application to the
multidivisional firm with participation
which emphasizes existential culture.

Fig. 13.2 Sequentially applying the traditional AIS to the multidivisional company.

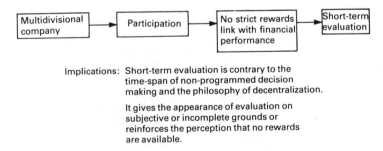

Implications: Short-term evaluation is contrary to the
time-span of non-programmed decision
making and the philosophy of decentralization.

It gives the appearance of evaluation on
subjective or incomplete grounds or
reinforces the perception that no rewards
are available.

Fig. 13.3 Sequentially applying the traditional AIS to the multidivisional company.

formance is made, a short-term approach to performance evaluation may result in a third level of mismatch and cause similar effects.

The non-programmed decision is essentially one where the alternative actions are novel, unique and heavily dependent on the judgement of the divisional manager as to their likely outcomes. A high incidence of non-programmed decisions results in plans being manager-specific and heavily influenced by his experience, attitude and judgement. The AIS should promote an attitude where positive actions in the firm's best interests are taken unaffected by short-term evaluations, mechanical reward schemes and dictats from top management. Hence a closer fit of the AIS to these circumstances is desirable.

Matching the AIS to the multidivisional structure
A closer match of the AIS to the multidivisional structure is obtained by having managerial participation in standard-setting, no strict link between rewards and financial performance measures, and performance evaluation being conducted in a more flexible manner with a longer time horizon, as outlined in Fig. 13.4.

Some suport for these recommendations is given by the research which has investigated environmental uncertainty and the design of AIS. Amigoni (1978), for example, found that increasing structural complexity led to additional accounting tools being employed whereas environmental uncertainty caused the replacement of obsolete tools with new ones. Govindarajan (1984) found no direct connection between evaluative styles, reward systems and effectiveness until uncertainty was considered. Then, under conditions of high uncer-

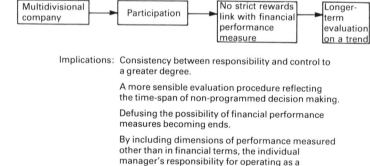

Implications: Consistency between responsibility and control to a greater degree.

A more sensible evaluation procedure reflecting the time-span of non-programmed decision making.

Defusing the possibility of financial performance measures becoming ends.

By including dimensions of performance measured other than in financial terms, the individual manager's responsibility for operating as a quasi-autonomous member of the firm is recognized.

Fig. 13.4 Sequentially applying the traditional AIS to the multidivisional company.

tainty, a correlation between more subjective methods of evaluating performance and effectiveness emerged.

THE ROLE OF FINANCIAL MEASURES OF PERFORMANCE

Given that we have advocated the use of profit-conscious or non-accounting styles of evaluation, we now require to assess how much emphasis should be placed on financial performance measures. The questionable accuracy of accounting measures of ROI, RI or profit over a period of time suggests that any over-emphasis on a particular accounting measure may cause opportunistic behaviour at the divisional management level to re-emerge. Top management may mistakenly accept these accounting measures as accurate indicators of efficiency and attempt to instruct lower-level managers to seek optimal solutions. In the face of environmental uncertainty, information asymmetry and a lack of clear objectives, optimality is an ephemeral concept. Agreement on actions that maintain the divisions within the feasible region determined by the dynamic interactions of the groups comprising the firm and its environment is a more attainable aim. The notion of behaviour congruence stresses the feasibility rather than the optimality of solutions.

The task of forecasting the future and predicting the likely outcomes of actions taken in an uncertain environment is a sufficiently difficult task without the AIS providing incentives for managers to intentionally bias the information they provide or to misuse their opportunities for participation. The AIS needs to provide feed-forward and feedback information that will aid divisional managers in their future decision making. The dynamic nature of each divisional manager's environment requires the operational plan to be set by him within relatively wide guidelines set by top management. The need to integrate both the activities occurring within his division and the inter-relationships that exist with other divisions results in the divisional manager having a major influence on management control. Anthony's view of the role of accounting information being categorized into the distinct compartments of strategic planning, management control and operational control (Chapter 4) seems inappropriate and inoperable.

The permeating influence of the divisional manager over all aspects of planning in the multidivisional firm requires that feedback is not confined to financial measures of performance alone. Objective measures of results in terms of staff turnover, productivity, customer returns and complaints and other non-financial statistics should be reported. These should be complemented by subjective qualitative data such as the manager's ability to create a sound management team within the division, his ability to forecast market changes, to redistribute resources within the division and his ability to maintain a positive leadership style including cooperation with other divisions. In short, the more feedback the AIS can provide for self-learning by the manager the better, although the precise information that each manager will regard as relevant will depend on the detailed manner in which the plans are developed. Hence the relevance of feedback controls depends on divisional management's involvement in feed-forward controls and planning.

The qualities required of the divisional manager to plan for non-programmed decisions will vary both within and between firms but, as a generalization, the following seem relevant:

1. The divisional manager should actively evaluate the assumptions on which his plans are based in order to detect changing key variables.
2. The divisional manager should continually scan the environment, both externally and internally, to update his predictive model and to adjust for changed relationships as he perceives them.
3. The divisional manager should be willing to plan actions consistent with challenging the environment and his predictive model in order to maintain or expand the feasible region of activities of the division.

We shall consider one specific decision as an example to illustrate these attributes. A divisional manager plans to increase production by 5% over the next month in order to meet a special order from a customer. In order to do this, it will be necessary for the existing workforce to work overtime. To assess whether such overtime working is feasible, he must have some conception of the way his labour force is motivated and the rewards it will react favourably to. He also needs to predict how trade union officials will react and, if their reaction should be unfavourable, what the likelihood of organized industrial action will be. He may also have to assume that central maintenance and repair services will be available when required to ensure that breakdowns do not prevent the increased production. In a similar vein, the amount of raw materials needed for the extra production may not be strictly proportional to normal production requirements. Whether the labour force is required to work just a few nights overtime in the month or whether it is spread evenly over each evening, or whether it is offered to only specific individuals rather than the entire workforce, may affect material usage, productivity, and union and individual reaction. In addition, there are predictions that need to be made about the special order itself. Will the order require different material inputs, work flows or different skills to complete on time? Are the quality specifications different from normal production and will this involve any retraining? Will the special requirements placed on the labour force for handling the extra order affect normal production? The practising manager would no doubt add many other considerations, but these are perhaps sufficient to illustrate the choices that have to be made, the key variables that need to be detected and the need to update the predictive model. Most if not all of these predictions require both qualitative and non-financial information, as well as financial and other quantitative information to be used. Ultimately, the manager will have to use his judgement about the acceptability of the proposed production plan to accommodate the interests of the trade unions, labour, customers and the company's overall strategy. His willingness to accept another special order in the future is likely to be conditioned by the feedback he receives from attempting to implement this production plan.

When the AIS provides a monthly comparison of budgeted and actual results in financial terms, many of the impediments to the effective use of information mentioned by Mintzberg (Chapter 4) may emerge. Customer satisfaction and labour productivity relating to the special order will not be shown in the accounts; even the costs and revenues associated with the specific order will probably be embedded in aggregate data relating to both special and normal production. The timing of the report at the month end may make even tentative judgements about the relationship between the special order and the financial results difficult to interpret because the events to which it refers are over and done with. A misguided emphasis on the financial results to appraise managerial performance may adversely affect the manager's future willingness to develop effective plans. Instead of discovering assumptions, key variables and changed relationships, the manager may be inclined to use his detailed knowledge of what might go wrong to set easily attainable targets or to provide alibis for not attaining the targets. The formal accounting system comparing budgeted and actual results whether in controllable RI, ROI or cash flow terms is unlikely to surmount these problems.

The emphasis on financial results therefore appears to be misplaced in the extreme case of highly non-programmed decision making. A move away from the role culture to one that recognizes the need for democratic interaction between the management levels seems appropriate. This may be enhanced by adopting a non-accounting style of evaluation in which feedback is provided by various performance measures on several dimensions. An outline of these arguments is

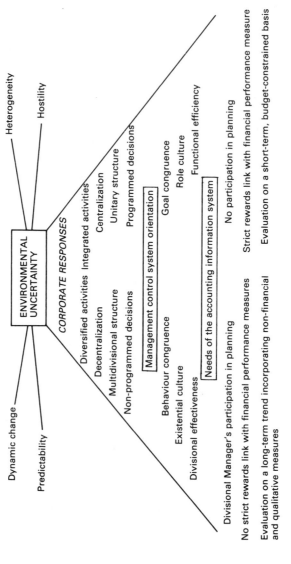

Fig. 13.5 The design and contingent characteristics of the AIS.

shown in Fig. 13.5, together with an indication of the design of the appropriate AIS at the two extremes.

SPECIFIC IMPLICATIONS FOR THE AIS

The loaded question now needs a response: 'Can the conventional AIS be modified to cope with the demands of a multidivisional structure and a higher incidence of non-programmed decision making?' Throughout this book, we have tried to emphasize that although distinctions can be made between unitary and multidivisional structures, between centralization and decentralization and even between integrated and diversified operations, these are really differences of degree. We have contrasted the extremes whereas, in reality, there is a whole spectrum of possibilities lying in between. In fact, the distinction between programmed and non-programmed decisions is itself a continuum, with changed conditions resulting in decisions previously considered programmed becoming less programmed. Conversely, the discovery of previously unknown relationships between factors will have the opposite effect of making non-programmed decisions more programmed.

The crucial factor is the provision of feasible feed-forward controls or planning methods. Without these, the provision of feedback controls, performance measures and budget variances is unlikely to lead to effective management control. Motivation and measurement are inextricably linked under the conditions of uncertainty. The knowledge that performance will be measured along certain dimensions provides the motivation for managers to make their performance look good in the interests of self-preservation. Participation in planning allows the manager the means of securing relatively easy standards of performance. These standards are difficult for top management to question, unless significant monitoring costs are incurred to discover as much about the divisional activities and environments as the lower-level managers already know. Hence there is the need for an AIS which will encourage managers to provide honest, intentionally unbiased plans of action.

One way ahead may be to redirect the budget setting process. Instead of the main focus being on financial items, an alternative concentration on assumptions should be made. Feed-forward control is concerned with predictions about what outputs are expected to be at some future time. If those expectations differ from what is desired at that time, control actions can be taken to minimize such differences. The predictive models used are specific to each manager and the AIS should ensure that each manager produces as unbiased and as challenging a set of predictions as is possible. When a planning gap between the expected and desired outputs is recognized, divisional and top management should explore the alternative assumptions on which their views are formed, and attempt to discover the alternative control actions that are available. This iterative development of operating plans allows top management to reveal assumptions about how the division's activities fit the desired overall strategic plan. The process also gives divisional management the opportunity to question these assumptions and to re-assess its own assumptions. The role of the AIS need not be passive. The collection of financial and non-financial data to verify assumptions, especially by monitoring external sources, trade journals, economic forecasts, etc., may prove to be the most useful role the AIS can serve.

Such an iterative development of a plan allows managers to concentrate on the differences of opinion that exist between divisional and top management concerning the validity of the assumptions each has made. Clarifying and communicating these assumptions should improve the understanding of both levels of management and allow agreement to be reached on what is feasible. Acceptable actions become more clearly associated with key assumptions and help direct the AIS in its role of gathering relevant feedback information. Additionally, as planning extends to strategic decisions, the consistency between the assumptions made about the key variables in operational planning may be assessed. It is a valid use of the AIS to perform the role of recording assumptions and ensuring that updated versions of agreed assumptions are carried forward. Top management's views of economy-wide or world-wide prospects can complement the divisional managers' views concerning particular markets and products. The integration of planned actions over time may be more efficiently taken when agreement on key variables and their likely changes are discussed openly. The monitoring role of the AIS in respect to these key variables should allow the service it provides to divisional managers to be improved. Hence feedback provided by the AIS is not necessarily restricted to monthly or annual reports. It will be as frequent as necessary to monitor changes in important key variables in order to provide the divisional managers with timely warnings that alternative actions are called for.

Of equal importance is the service the AIS can provide in assessing how actual events matched the assumptions that were made when the plan was developed. Divisional and top management may thus become more aware of defects in their identification of key variables or their ability to predict how these variables interact in the uncertain environment. The evaluation process is much richer when the actual events and assumptions are compared. This is because the assumptions are not limited to events that can be measured in financial terms, but also include opinions gathered from external market intelligence, informed communications within and outside the company and management hunches.

The aim of this design of AIS is quite simply to improve learning. At both top and lower management levels, awareness of the many sources of uncertainty that effect decision making is improved. The AIS has the role of scanning the environment to determine whether key assumptions remain valid. Predicting the likely impact of such changes on expected financial performance is a function that accountants are well qualified to undertake. But the service function of the accountant should be emphasized, and this may well be enhanced, even with the reduced emphasis on financial performance.

The democratic atmosphere by which planned actions are agreed requires a more democratic evaluation process to be created. Blame should not be attached to individuals, but may be traced to an intransigent, uncertain environment that will very rarely behave as was expected. The aim is therefore to play the game of beating the environment rather than 'beating' the divisional manager unfortunate enough to have mis-estimated the value of a key variable. Such an existential culture is reinforced by not linking incentives too closely to financial performance measures, and by appraising the performance of the divisional manager over a substantial period of time. The ability of the manager to develop predictions, assumptions and actions that are compatible with maintaining the division's effectiveness within an uncertain environment should form an important part of this evaluation. Top management's role in the iterative development of plans allows both a qualitative and quantitative judgement of the divisional manager's ability to be made.

THE DESIGN OF MANAGEMENT CONTROL SYSTEMS

We have said relatively little about the dynamics of management control systems design, that is the processes by which the need for improved management control systems become apparent and how such improvements become incorporated into existing systems. The reason for this lack of attention is not that the topic is unimportant, indeed it is of crucial importance to effective organizational functioning, but rather that there has been little empirical work that has addressed itself to these issues. Most empirical studies have considered only the interaction of influencing variables within an organization, or across a sample of organizations at a single point in time. That is, they have been cross-sectional studies rather than the longitudinal studies necessary to understand the patterns of evolution and adaptation of control systems. Obviously, part of the reason for the dearth of such studies is that they take a great degree of effort over a considerable period of time to undertake.

However, from the observations gathered in an informal manner during the conduct of management control system research, it may be possible to piece together some general patterns of issues that tend to recur as organizations attempt to adapt their control systems to meet new circumstances. For example, it appears to be common that control systems design is rarely static; most control systems, in practice, seem to be an untidy amalgam of components put together at different times for different purposes. In addition, parts of the systems are likely to be undergoing adaptation to meet new challenges that have emerged in the recent past. Although many management accountants may have a yearning for a single, tidy, integrated system of control, the reality appears to be that this is highly unusual, such systems existing only in relatively static environments where it might be argued that sophisticated control systems are not necessary. More commonly, the control system is untidy and satisfies the requirements laid upon it only imperfectly. In these circumstances, attention is paid to the more major imperfections with additional or adapted systems being implemented where necessary.

However, within this somewhat chaotic environment, it appears that three main areas of concern are typically being addressed, all of which can significantly influence the control system's behaviour congruent properties. These can be represented by three questions, to which new and more refined answers are continually being developed. In one sense, the evolution of management control systems design can be seen as the continual development of new answers to the same fundamental problems. The three questions are:

1. What are the dimensions of good performance that the organization is seeking to promote?
2. What are the appropriate standards of performance in each of these areas, both for the organization as a whole and for the segments which make it up?
3. What rewards (penalties) are to be associated with the achievement (non-achievement) of these performance targets?

We shall consider each of these questions, in turn, to examine some of the mechanisms that are used to develop new and more relevant solutions to what are evidently fundamental issues that all organizations have to continually resolve.

Dimensions of good performance

The first question is the most fundamental as it concerns the underlying *raison d'être* of an organization, that is, what is it trying to achieve? At one level this is a question of corporate strategy, with long-term objectives and plans that are capable of attaining them being developed and refined. In terms of Anthony's (1965, 1988) categorization, the processes that resolve such issues are the subject matter of corporate strategy and thus outside the scope of this text. However, the question needs to be resolved not only in terms of long-term corporate plans for the organization as a whole, but also in terms of more detailed plans for parts of the organization and for shorter-term horizons. It is here that overall corporate strategy merges into issues of management control.

At the level of the overall organization there is not usually a single overall criterion that defines what good performance should be. Even if profitability is taken as a major objective, there are still questions as to the relative importance of long-term and short-term profitability, how profitability should be measured (profit, return on capital employed, residual income etc.), and its relationship to growth, liquidity and share price considerations. More crucially, how to obtain good profitability in a complex and uncertain environment is not a well-understood process. Thus subsidiary dimensions of good performance do not necessarily follow from an overall goal, even where one exists.

Next, such overall goals as are developed have to be decomposed into subsidiary goals relating to such matters as product range, product quality, customer service, market segmentation and so on. Further, goals need to be developed for each part of the organization and for each of the business functions which comprise it. Thus the dimensions of performance that are defined for a segment of the organization are likely to be multiple and probably partially conflicting (e.g. product price versus product quality; quantity sold versus price obtained).

Finally, although some aspects of performance can be quantified, many other aspects are less quantifiable (e.g. product image, employee morale) although no less important. And whether quantified or not, the means by which a goal can be achieved may not be well understood. Thus any programme of action designed to achieve these goals is likely to be debated both in terms of its likely effectiveness and in terms of its general desirability.

The processes of developing corporate strategy thus begin to merge into issues of more detailed management planning and control as they work their way through the organization and down the managerial hierarchy. Ambiguities in overall goals and the problems of designing appropriate plans to achieve them in a complex and uncertain environment make this process one which requires considerable managerial judgment. It is a process which is continually being adapted in all organizations because of the need to respond or pre-empt to a continually changing environment. To the extent that changes are made to the dimensions of performance that are being pursued, the rest of the management control system will have to follow in order to ensure that such new goals result in appropriate actions designed to attain them.

Setting standards for performance

The second question is closely related to the first. Even when an adequate set of dimensions of required performance have been developed, standards of achievement on each of these dimensions need to be set. Here there is an immediate conflict between what is desirable and what is attainable, with both being subject to considerable ambiguity. Top management will reflect the pressures that they feel from the various interest groups associated with the organization, most obviously customers and shareholders. But they may have relatively little direct knowledge about how feasible it is to achieve such standards of performance, and of the detailed actions necessary to implement them. This problem is confounded by the fact that the people in the best position to make judgements about the feasibility of proposed targets are also the managers who will ultimately be held accountable for meeting the standards that are set. In such circumstances, there is an obvious motivation for managers to be less than totally candid in the information they give.

This conflict between what is desirable and what is attainable reverberates up and down the organization, with senior managers tending to emphasize overall desirability and lower-level managers being more concerned with feasibility. It affects matters such as planning procedures (top-down versus bottom-up), participation in budget setting (participation or consultation or imposition) and organizational design (span of control versus number of organizational levels; centralization versus decentralization), as well as the design of information and control systems. The basic issue is one of information asymmetry, with senior managers being better informed as to what is necessary for overall organizational survival and success, and lower-level managers being better informed as to what can actually be achieved by their division. The process by which standards of performance are set and codified into formal procedures such as budgetary control are a fundamental part of the management control process. This can never be a totally mechanistic process, but it is one which is subject to alteration as a better understanding of how the organization actually operates is achieved. However, as some areas become better understood and more suited to the application of formal controls, so other areas emerge where past experience is inadequate to allow standards to be developed in other than a tentative and subjective manner.

Linking performance to rewards

The final question is concerned with the association between reward structures and performance target attainment. It is all very well to set quantitative performance targets for managers, but they will be effective only to the extent that managers perceive desirable rewards flowing from their achievement (or penalties flowing from their lack of achievement). This requires the establishment of mechanisms linking target achievement to valued, although not necessarily financial, rewards. These mechanisms can take a variety of forms, ranging from the encouragement of cohesive peer groups (characteristics of Japanese styles of management) to the explicit linking of substantial monetary rewards to target attainment (most prevalent in the USA, but also inherent in all types of incentive payment schemes). Interestingly, the use of systems of performance-related pay seems to be most easily accomplished at the top and bottom organizational levels, through share-option plans or profit-sharing schemes at the top and incentive or piecework payment schemes at the bottom. It proves to be more problematic at middle management levels, mainly because of the difficulties, referred to earlier, of establishing suitable targets in an objective and reliable manner.

There is no doubt that incentives can be devised that will encourage managers to achieve, or at least report, a high level of target attainment, but the means by which targets are attained may not be those which were intended or desired. In particular, such schemes tend to emphasize the independence of one organizational unit or division from another, and encourage a high level of competition between managers. Such behaviour may be harmful where cooperation between managers is necessary for successful organizational performance. In addition, such schemes may encourage the bias and manipulation of management information, so that senior managers become increasingly misinformed about what is actually happening, while believing all is well.

This linking of rewards with results is essentially part of an organization's accountability process, which is central to effective management control. It includes not only the use of short-term rewards, but also overall judgements concerning managerial performance that may heavily influence long-term promotion prospects. It needs to be borne in mind that the bulk of a manager's financial remuneration is likely to come from base salary, supplemented by annual increments and promotions, rather than from any short-term payment by results schemes. Nevertheless, this seems to be an area in which there is a tendency constantly to tinker with the precise links between performance and pay. Evidently, it links with the setting of performance standards, but the point at which bonuses begin to be paid and the gradient at which they rise with increasing performance are also likely to affect motivation. The development of new targets, new standards and new links with pay seem to be an increasingly important part of the design of a management control system.

The dynamics of systems control

The emergence of new answers to all three of the questions posed above does not necessarily conflict with the contingency theory of accounting information systems. The latter may suggest a steady state towards which organizations may try to evolve. The former is more concerned with the processes and mechanisms that are used to move towards new steady states. However, it does beg the question of the rate of change and evolution. It may be that environmental and organizational changes are now occurring so rapidly that the idea of a steady state is outmoded and that we need to be concerned only with processes of change. There is some indication that this may be increasingly true and that the poor results associated with some contingency-based studies may be due to their attempt to take a snapshot of a rapidly changing set of circumstances. On the other hand, there is some evidence that organizational accountability and control procedures are relatively permanent in most organizations, and that the changes described are primarily superficial.

Recognition of the management control process as comprising results, action and personnel controls seems, at least, a step in the right direction. Our understanding of how these controls are used is only beginning to emerge. The traditional view of management control systems as passive and relatively unchanging reflections of corporate strategy is open to doubt. Management control systems may also be used interactively by top management to focus organization members' attention on the threats and opportunities presented by a changing, uncertain environment.

Simons (1989) demonstrates through his research in the health-care industry in the USA just how varied and rich can be the choice of management control system. Abstracting from the cases where the traditional approach is taken and where the controls are diagnostic, that is a primarily management by exception role, he concentrates on the interactive use of management control systems. Controls become interactive if top management personally and regularly involve themselves in the decisions of subordinates. The emphasis in some organizations may be on budget planning controls or revenue budgets, programme or project management systems, intelligence or human development systems, or on all five simultaneously. The choice of which system or controls to emphasize conveys to members of the organization the current strategic uncertainties top management wishes to stress. The system or controls chosen provides the focus for agenda setting, discussion at meetings and the means of re-directing attention to strategic uncertainties. Different strategic uncertainties seem to merit the interactive use of different controls.

This approach does not contradict the underlying premise of contingency theory. However, Simons' analysis offers a more dynamic explanation of why different control systems are used and changed in practice. Inductive reasoning along these lines offers a worthwhile avenue to research the process of management control in the future. The use of control systems is an area of fundamental importance to organizational functioning and requires urgent attention.

THE WAY AHEAD

There is a growing awareness of the contribution the AIS can make to organizational effectiveness, but this is conditioned by the circumstances in which the firm has grown and operates. The attempt to match the AIS with the circumstances faced by the firm is not made any easier by the fact that our knowledge of how firms operate is in its infancy. Neo-classical economic analysis offers predictions about how groups of firms will operate in product markets, but it offers very little insight into the internal operations of the individual firm. It may be argued that traditional economic theory assumes information asymmetry, in that superior managers are expected to know the optimal decisions subordinate managers should take! Behavioural and managerial theories of the firm address this weakness, but as yet, provide only generalizations that are not empirically substantiated. The emergence of principal – agent theory concentrates on individual employment contracts and provides only very limited explanations of managerial behaviour. Thus, there is a vast and fertile area for research that is of interest to accountants as designers of systems to improve or maintain organizational effectiveness.

The contingency theory of management accounting provides a more complete theoretical framework within which to develop guidelines for AIS design. But although interesting theoretical explanations and predictions have been developed, to date little empirical justification for these has been amassed. In part, this has been due to an over-reliance on arm's length, questionnaire-based methods to disentangle the complex, and often subtle, processes of management control. However, it is clear that the package of controls used by an organization interact in a very complex manner, and that there is a great deal of managerial choice and judgement involved in developing an effective control package. Future research in this field will probably be most successful if it begins by attempting to understand the processes of control that are observed to operate in a single organization, before attempting to generalize its findings by generating a more complete theory.

The perspective taken here includes micro, macro, context and process elements. We have been concerned with the decision making behaviour of individual managers and with their mutual interdependence; we have tried to predict behavioural traits within different firms in terms of the structures or degrees of diversification which they reflect; and we have examined the interrelationship between aspects of the AIS, and incentive schemes, participation and evaluative style. A pluralistic approach has been taken where the insights offered by managerial and behavioural theories have been used to identify potentially important parameters in which the AIS must operate. Whether or not the most important insights have been identified, and whether or not the most appropriate implications for the AIS have been drawn, only time will tell. The main purpose has been to improve the understanding of a future generation of AIS designers to take into account the need for adaptability and flexibility in the face of an ever-changing corporate environment. Only you, the reader, can determine the utility of this framework by its value in the future decisions you make.

EXERCISES

1. Identify the AIS design problems in the following abbreviated cases, and suggest ways for improvements:
   (a) You have discovered by on-site inspection that a manager is consistently mis-recording the amounts of materials used on individual jobs. In total, the amounts recorded equal the budgeted total.
   (b) The head of an airframe design section continually uses component parts that result in the aircraft working perfectly but being overweight. On inquiring, the head of design argues that if his design fails, the blame can be traced back to him. For any one section, the part is only a few kilograms overweight, but the company has 100 other design sections all having the same attitude and all contributing designs that, in total, result in the aircraft being several hundred kilograms overweight.
   (c) The manager of the quality control section associated with the new microcomputer project approaches you informally with a problem. The project chief is not allowing him to spend the

funds allocated for quality and reliability testing. Instead some of these funds are being siphoned off to ensure that production remains on schedule and that output is at the expected level.

2. In broad outline, suggest the main features of an AIS designed to be appropriate for:
   (a) a production process whose output is standard steel rods made for stock;
   (b) a division producing microchips;
   (c) a company making chocolate confectionery in which it is the brand leader;
   (d) a division producing gas which is used mainly by other divisions in the firm.

3. Brian Catchpole is the manager of the rubber hose department of the BBR Company. His department manufactures hose of a single quality, although the lengths and specific nozzle attachments comply with individual customers' instructions. The department's workforce consists of 25 people, of whom 5 are supervisors reporting directly to Brian.

   Just over a year ago, Brian returned from a course on managerial decision making convinced that he should involve his supervisors more in departmental decisions. He was certain that the standards needed revising and gave the supervisors as a group the chance to discuss and decide what the new performance standards should be. To his surprise, the group argued that the standards were too tight. After extensive discussion with the head office staff, Brian gained approval for a 10% reduction in the standards which the supervisors accepted.

   The financial results using the new standards have just become available for the year ended 31 October 1985:

	Budget	Actual
Production (linear feet of hose)	8.0m.	8.8m.
Direct labour hours worked	20 000 hrs	18 000 hrs
Materials used	100 000 lb	104 000 lb
Costs	£	£
Direct labour	20 000	21 600
Direct material	50 000	62 400
Overhead costs – fixed	40 000	49 000
– variable	60 000	64 000
Total costs incurred	170 000	197 000
Revenue from sales	240 000	264 000
Net profit	70 000	67 000

Overheads include all factory, selling and administration costs, and are applied on the basis of standard direct labour hours.

All the hose produced during the year is sold, and no inventory exists as at 31 October 1985. During the year, the sales have been greater than anticipated in the budget, but this is regarded as a temporary fluctuation.

Required:

(a) Prepare a statement analysing the differences between actual and budgeted costs and explain the most important of them.

(b) Would you recommend that Brian continues to allow the supervisors to set standards in this situation?

(c) Outline the motives individuals may generally have to bias budgets and steps that may be taken to counter bias.

(d) What changes in the overall design of the AIS might you recommend?

4. The Bailriggers Division specializes in manufacturing rigging for sailing dinghies and small yachts – a growth industry. But the firm also has a sideline in wire products for garden use, including Twisteze, a high-quality, plastic coated wire supplied in small drums for various uses in domestic gardens. Twisteze is sold through garden shops at £4.50 recommended retail price, the normal trade discount being 32%.

The company is currently producing and selling 252 000 drums per year of Twisteze, which represents 70% of annual capacity. Factory accounts show the following monthly costs for average output:

	Total cost £	Unit cost £
Materials	13 650	0.65
Wages and salaries	16 800	0.80
Depreciation	5 250	0.25
Rent	6 300	0.30
Sundry plant expense	6 720	0.32
Delivery costs	1 470	0.07
Sales commissions	9 450	0.45
	£59 640	£2.84

A chain store offers to buy on contract a quantity of Twisteze that may average 4000 drums per month at £1.75 per drum. The chain store would re-sell the drums under their own brand name: costs of colouring and substitute labelling of the drums are insignificant and may be ignored. Sales to the chain store would give rise to no sales commission or delivery costs (the customer would collect in his own transport).

Inquiry elicits that wages are directly variable with output up to 22 000 units per month, but rise to £1.00 per unit thereafter. Capacity per month is limited to one-twelfth annual capacity – there is no slack labour or machinery transferable in the short run from other products. 60% of the material costs concern wire transferred in from another division of the firm at a price yielding 40% contribution to that division. Sundry plant expense is 25% fixed.

Required:

(a) present a report calculating the probable advantage or otherwise of accepting the chain store order. Clearly explain the assumptions on which your calculation is based.

(b) re-appraise your decision above in the light of new information concerning the 40% of materials not transferred in from the other division. The historical/book cost of this material to satisfy one month's production of the order is £1040. It can be sold now for £1500, less 10% selling costs. Alternatively, it can be converted at a cost of £1000 into material used for sailing dinghies whose present replacement cost is £3100.

(c) Using your analysis in (a) and (b), above, how will the accounting information for decision making differ from that used for control purposes?

(d) What are the implications of your analysis for achieving behaviour congruence?

5. The Carberg Corporation manufactures and sells a single product. The cost system used by the company is a standard cost system. The standard cost per unit of product is shown below:

Material – one pound plastic @ £2.00	£2.00
Direct labour 1.6 hours @ £4.00	6.40
Variable overhead cost	3.00
Fixed overhead cost	1.45
	£12.85

The overhead cost per unit was calculated from the following annual overhead-cost budget for a 60 000 unit volume.

Variable overhead cost:	
Indirect labour 30 000 hours @ £4.00	£120 000
Supplies – oil 60 000 gallons @ £.50	30 000
Allocated variable service – departmental costs	30 000
Total variable overhead cost	£180 000

Fixed overhead cost:

Supervision	£27 000
Depreciation	45 000
Other fixed costs	15 000
Total fixed overhead cost	£87 000
Total budgeted annual overhead cost at 60 000 units	£267 000

The charges to the manufacturing department for November, when 5000 units were produced, are given below:

Material: 5300 pounds @ £2.00	£10 600
Direct labour: 8200 hours @ £4.10	33 620
Indirect labour: 2400 hours @ £4.10	9 840
Supplies – oil: 6000 gallons @ £.55	3 300
Other variable overhead costs	3 200
Supervision	2 475
Depreciation	3 750
Other	1 250
Total	£68 035

The purchasing department normally buys about the same quantity as is used in production during a month. In November, 5200 pounds were purchased at a price of £2.10 per pound.

Required:

(a) Calculate the following variances from standard costs for the data given:
   (i)   materials purchase price
   (ii) materials efficiency
   (iii) direct labour wage price
   (iv) direct labour efficiency
   (v)   overhead budget.
(b) The company has divided its responsibility such that the purchasing department is responsible for the price at which materials and supplies are purchased. The manufacturing department is responsible for the quantities of materials used. Does this division of responsibilities solve the conflict between price and efficiency variances? Explain your answer.
(c) Prepare a report that details the overhead budget variance. The report, which will be given to the manufacturing department manager, should display only the part of the variance

that is the responsibility of the manager and should highlight the information in ways that would be useful to that manager, in evaluating departmental performance and when considering corrective action.

(d) Assume that the department manager performs the time-keeping function for this manufacturing department. From time to time, analysis of overhead and direct labour variances have shown that the department manager has deliberately mis-classified labour hours (e.g., listed direct labour hours as indirect labour hours and vice versa), so that only one of the two labour variances is unfavourable. It is not feasible economically to hire a separate time-keeper. What should the company do, if anything, to resolve this problem?

(From: Horngren, 1982.)

6. Examine the following annual operating budget report for a divisional manager responsible for the manufacturing and marketing of a wide range of garden tools and utensils.

   Required:
   (a) highlight any unusual features it contains.
   (b) explain why these features are included.
   (c) explain in which set of circumstances such a report may be viewed as appropriate.
   (d) Outline the ways to improve the report.

Garden Tools and Utensils Division
Annual operating budget report for year ending 31.12.85

Assumptions: at 1.1.1985

Product sales growth expected to be 5% subject to
1. GNP remaining stable
2. competitor's new brands unavailable this period
3. impact of change in credit terms to customers assumed to be zero

Product cost savings expected to be reduced by 2% subject to
1. labour turnover confined to 5% in respect to skilled craftsmen
2. union agreement on washing-up time allowance and productivity payments
3. replacement of machine M2

Product profit expected to be £1 450 000 an increase of £250 000 over last year.

Financial highlights

	Budget	Actual	Flexible budget
Expected output (units)			
Sales	£		
Controllable costs			
labour	£		
materials	£		
administration costs	£		
Service costs			
maintenance	hrs		
lighting	hrs		
central computer	hrs		
Non-controllable costs			
central allocation administration			
corporation tax			

Events: at 31.12.85

Product sales
1. GNP stable
2. competitor's brand test marketed on East coast
3. credit terms reduction caused 1% of customers not to purchase
Product costs
1. labour turnover rose to 10%, among skilled craftsmen
2. union did not agree to washing-up allowance and productivity proposals
3. machine M2 and M3 replaced
Product profit £1 185 000

Part Five

Case Studies

The case studies in Chapter 14 have one element in common: they allow some aspect(s) of the management control system to be explored in a specific organizational setting. As with all worthwhile case studies, there is no single solution or set of recommendations which can be seen to be totally superior to all the others. The process of building to a set of recommendations is the key feature. This requires critical analysis of the case facts, a clear presentation of logical arguments and, in many instances, a recognition of essential, additional information.

All of the seven cases in this chapter have undergone the acid test of student examination, either at final year undergraduate or postgraduate level. The concern of each is to look at management control issues within the specific organization. The Permaclean Products case focuses on pricing, and the Nutone Housing Group of Scovill Inc. examines labour standards and responsibility accounting, while BBR and Beech Paper concentrate on transfer pricing; cash flow management provides the main issue in Altex Aviation and HCC concentrates on the practical benefits and detriments of designing an incentive scheme; and ES Inc. examines the issues of developing performance measures with a corporate objective of creating value for shareholders.

The chronology of the cases has no special significance, though the issues they address broadly follow the format of Part Two through to Part Four of this book. In including these cases, we hope that some of the ideas contained in the book may prove useful in analysing real-life situations. The reader may even find that concepts have some merit when dealing with ill-defined practical problems!

14

Management control
case studies

PERMACLEAN PRODUCTS PLC

Permaclean Products is an old-established firm, located in Dunstable, which manufactures a comprehensive range of domestic cleaning materials. It has a sound reputation and a well-known brand name which has made it a market leader in a wide range of products designed for home use. Although Permaclean has several competitors, the total sales of each are small in comparison with those of Permaclean, mainly because none offers such a complete product range.

In 1986 the price of one of Permaclean's major products, Permashine, was raised from 75p per bottle to 99p when the product was re-packaged in a newly designed bottle; however, the contents were identical to the previous pack, both in formulation and quantity. During the following two years sales fell by 27 per cent. At 75p per bottle Permashine had been competitively priced but when its price was increased manufacturers of similar products had not followed. In the period from 1984 to 1987 the price of competing products had been raised by only 5p.

Prices were fixed once a year, to come into force on 1 February, before the annual peak demand which occurred in the spring. In January 1988, John Williams, the marketing manager, met with Andrew Dutton, the chief accountant, to review the company's pricing policy for the coming year.

Permashine

Permashine is a proprietary cleaning product for bathrooms and in 1985 had accounted for over 10 per cent of the company's sales.

Although there are a variety of competing products on the market, Permashine has special properties which make it especially suitable for cleaning baths made of acrylic materials. Such baths are becoming increasingly common, but great care has to be taken to avoid scratching them when they are being cleaned. Permashine contains no abrasive materials yet is able to clean acrylic surfaces with great efficiency, giving a surface shine that is very durable. No competing product appears to have this combination of advantages.

The process used in the manufacture of Permashine involves a hazardous chemical reaction that has to be precisely controlled. Production therefore takes place in a separate building on the same site as the main factory where the other products are made but some distance from it. This production unit, which was constructed in 1980 for safety reasons, is not capable of being adapted for the manufacture of other Permaclean products without substantial expenditure. Although the manufacture of Permashine is potentially hazardous, no serious accidents have occurred during the 15 years in which it has been produced and the final product is itself completely harmless.

In early 1986, Andrew Dutton had installed an improved cost-accounting system which allowed product costs to be determined and product profitability to be reviewed. With regard to Permashine, this took into account the new packaging costs, as well as the over-head costs that were separately attributable to the production unit. His analysis, shown in Table 14.1, indicated that the total cost of Permashine was greater than the current selling price of 75p. As a

Table 14.1 Estimated costs of Permashine at various production volumes

Cost (p/bottle)	Annual production ('000s of bottles)						
	250	300	400	500	600	700	800
Direct labour	17.5	17.5	17.0	17.0	17.0	17.5	18.0
Materials	8.0	8.0	8.0	8.0	8.0	8.0	8.0
Department overhead							
Variable	9.0	9.0	9.0	9.0	9.0	9.0	9.0
Fixed	14.4	12.0	8.0	7.2	6.0	5.1	4.5
Factory overhead							
(20% of direct labour)	3.5	3.5	3.4	3.4	3.4	3.5	3.6
Factory cost	52.4	50.0	45.4	44.6	43.4	43.1	43.1
Selling and administration cost							
at 80% of factory cost	41.9	40.0	36.3	35.7	34.7	34.5	34.5
Total cost	94.3	90.0	81.7	80.3	78.1	77.6	77.6

result, at the annual pricing review in 1986 the selling price was increased to 99p.

Although total industry sales continued to rise during 1986 and 1987, Permashine suffered a reduction in both its market share and its total sales, as shown in Table 14.2.

Table 14.2 Permashine: sales and prices

	1981	1982	1983	1984	1985	1986	1987
Permashine sales ('000s of bottles)	400	429	486	525	536	462	391
Total industry sales ('000s of bottles)	2000	2050	2250	2200	2300	2650	2900
Permashine % of market	20	21	22	24	23	17.5	13.5
Permashine price (p)	60	70	70	75	75	99	99
Competitors' price range (p)	56–62	65–70	65–70	69–75	69–75	70–9	75–80

The 1988 pricing review

Both Mr Williams and Mr Dutton were concerned to improve the profitability of Permashine, as it was one of the company's major products. Mr Williams had joined the company in 1980 and had introduced a number of changes in the firm's marketing methods. One of his major successes had been his decision to replace wholesalers with a team of salaried sales representatives who sold the company's full product range direct to retailers. Mr Dutton had been appointed in 1984, following the retirement of the previous chief accountant, and has been responsible for installing a modern computer-based accounting system.

Mr Williams pressed for a return to the previous price of 75p for Permashine; at this price he was confident that the market share of the product could be increased to 20% in 1988. He thought that total industry sales would continue to increase to at least 3 million bottles in 1988, and that Permashine was capable of regaining its previous position, provided that it was competitively priced. Because Permaclean had a modern production facility and a manufacturing output greater than any competitor, he was confident that factory production costs were the lowest in the industry. He therefore supported a policy of reducing the price, so that other firms would find it uneconomic to continue to compete.

Mr Williams was convinced that sales would continue to fall if the price were to be maintained at 99p, although he believed that there would always be a premium market for Permashine because of its unique qualities. He thought that annual sales were unlikely to fall below 250 000 bottles, even at the current price.

Mr Dutton replied that he was well aware of the problems being experienced in selling the higher-priced product. Nevertheless, his analysis showed that the 99p price covered the costs of the product, even at the lowest volume envisaged. If the price were reduced to 75p costs would fail to be covered, even if sales volume rose to the 800 000 bottles which represented the maximum practical capacity of the plant. He referred to his detailed costings (Table 14.1) to support his argument. These figures, he stated, were based on actual data from past years; where data were not available, he had made what he regarded as realistic assumptions.

Question

What price would you recommend for Permashine? Support your recommendation with detailed calculations, making the underlying assumptions on which your analysis is based as clear as possible.

SCOVILL INC.: NUTONE HOUSING GROUP

In January 1982, in his first month with the company, Bob Hager, Scovill's new treasurer/controller, faced a difficult issue. He discovered that one of the major operating groups of the company, the NuTone Housing Group, was using direct labour-time standards that were purposely overstated. The overstated standards caused large, favourable labour-efficiency variances, overstated product costs and, until year end, a substantial understatement of inventory values. Accounting adjustments had to be made at year-end to total cost of sales and inventories. For the year 1981, this adjustment totalled $2.8 million.

After studying the situation, Mr Hager decided to approach Jim Rankin, executive vice-president in charge of the Housing and Security Products groups, with a request to make the labour standards more realistic. Mr Rankin was against making the change:

'This issue has come up before, and I feel strongly that making the change would not be in NuTone's best interest. We make a lot of special quotes, and sometimes the pressures to squeeze margins on these quotes are too strong. That's where our inflated standards play an important role; they give us a cushion to protect our margins when we are making price decisions. This business has been very successful over the years, and I would go as far as to say that the way we've used the standards to protect our margins has been the single most important management practice that has contributed to our success.

The overstated costs also make our monthly financial reports conservative because we do not capture the favourable efficiency variances until year-end, and I like that. I love to take inventory at year-end and find that we've got some extra in there. It's like Santa Claus has arrived. The extra profit takes care of a lot of little costs that occur at year-end.'

Mr Hager, however, still thought it was important that NuTone's labour standards be made realistic:

'I realize that NuTone has been operating the way they have for many years; this problem has been mentioned in the auditors' management letter for each of the last six years, and I'm sure it goes back before that. But the distortions are getting larger and larger. The 1981 end-of-year adjustment was

This case was prepared by Research Assistant Lourdes Ferreira and Associate Professor Kenneth A. Merchant as the basis for class discussion rather than to illustrate either effective or ineffective handling of an administrative situation.

more than a month's income for NuTone. It's not just that this is bad account-ing; I'm really concerned that we may not know our real product costs, and as a consequence we may be making some bad decisions. I'm also disturbed that Mr Rankin has no interest in fixing an obvious problem.'

Scovill's operating groups had considerable autonomy, so Mr Hager's primary option, if he wanted to pursue this issue, was whether to raise it with the audit committee of the board of directors. He did not take this step lightly. He had had to make such an appeal only three times in his career, for issues of major importance, and he did not wish to force a confrontation with a line manager, particularly since he had just joined the company. The questions he had to ask himself were: how important is it to have realistic cost standards? How much merit do Mr Rankin's arguments have?

Scovill Inc.

Background

Scovill Inc. was a leading producer of quality consumer and industrial products. The company had started operations in 1802 in Waterbury, Connecticut, USA, as a brass works and over the years had grown both internally and through acquisition. By 1981, Scovill had become a diversified international company with total annual revenues in excess of $800 million. (Exhibit 1 shows a financial summary for the years 1978–81.) Scovill had been paying dividends for 126 con-secutive years, longer than any other industrial company on the New York Stock Exchange.

The corporation was organized into 6 product groups (see organ-ization chart in Exhibit 2). Exhibit 3 describes the groups' major prod-uct lines and shows their 1981 sales and operating income numbers. All of the groups benefited from well-known product trademarks, and most of their products were leaders in their market segments.

Scovill was operated in a highly decentralized fashion. The product groups were allowed considerable discretion in establishing and implementing the strategies appropriate to their areas of business. The primary control mechanisms employed by headquarters were annual reviews of the budgets submitted from each of the groups and quarterly reviews of actual results compared with the budgets.

Scovill did not have a single unified accounting system that was used in all of its operating units. This was due to the fact that Scovill had acquired many companies over the years, and the acquired companies were allowed to continue with most of the elements of their accounting systems, even after they became a part of Scovill. The accounting policies set at corporate tended to describe minimum reporting requirements and very general accounting policies rather than detailed instructions that had to be followed. For example, the accounting policy manual specified that the operating units were to follow the full absorption method of accounting, 'whereby most fixed and variable costs are recognized in inventory and cost of sales accounting', but it did not provide further description as to how the full absorption method was to be accomplished.

Bob Hager, Scovill's treasurer and controller, joined Scovill in January 1982. Bob had a solid accounting background and substantial experience. He had earned an MBA with a concentration in production and was a certified management accountant. While employed at the General Electric Company early in his career, he completed that company's well-regarded financial training programme. Later he served as a divisional controller at Pennwalt Chemical and Bristol-Myers and as corporate controller of Marine Midland Bank and Loctite Corporation.

NuTone Housing Group

Background
NuTone was founded in 1936 in Cincinnati, Ohio, USA, as a manufacturer of door chimes. After the Second World War, the company extended its product lines to include auxiliary heaters, kitchen and bathroom fans, intercoms and range hoods. NuTone merged with and became an operating group of Scovill Inc. on 15 September 1967.

The acquisition proved to be a great success. NuTone had consistently been the company's most profitable group, and it was often referred to as the 'jewel' of Scovill. In 1981, NuTone had total annual sales of just over $200 million, and the group's gross margin percentage was still hovering near its historical average of about 40%. Exhibit 4 shows summary group financial data.

Products and production
NuTone competed in two broad markets: the new housing and remodelling market and the consumer durables market. It manufactured and sold approx. 5000 products in 11 product lines, including exhaust fans, heaters, range hoods, door chimes, bath cabinets, radio-intercoms, paddle fans, lighting fixtures and security systems. Exhibit 5 presents data on the size and profitability of NuTone's major product lines.

NuTone had been very successful in maintaining a market leadership position in most of the market segments in which it competed. It had good products with well-known trademarks, an experienced sales force, long-standing relationships with distributors, and an extensive service and technical support network. It also made the highest expenditures in the industry for promotional items such as catalogues, displays and cooperative advertising. NuTone products were generally sold at premium prices because they offered superior designs, more features and higher quality.

NuTone manufactured for stock according to demand forecasts by product line. The sales of many of the product lines were cyclical and/ or seasonal, but the variations in demand were smoothed out to some extent by NuTone's broad product line. The broad product line also had an advantage in attracting large distributors who preferred to deal with manufacturers who could supply products in multiple product categories.

Each product had to go through a number of different manu- facturing operations such as punch pressing, welding, painting and assembly. Because of the cyclical demand and capacity constraints, NuTone kept multiple buffers of work-in-process inventory. If neces- sary, most products could be expedited through the factory from raw materials to finished goods in two days.

Organization

NuTone was organized functionally, as shown in Exhibit 6. Most of the NuTone employees had been with the company for over 10 years. All of NuTone's top management group had been with NuTone before the merger with Scovill, with the exception of Pat Dionne, director of finance, who had just recently joined the company.

The group's main manufacturing facilities were in Cincinnati, adjacent to the group headquarters. The experienced labour force, which was not unionized, was paid higher wages than the industry average.

Jim Rankin, executive vice-president, had been with NuTone for 27 years. He had worked his way up through marketing, having served as a product manager, vice-president of sales and marketing, and general manager of NuTone. Mr Rankin was an outgoing, people- oriented manager who was well-liked by employees at all levels at NuTone. Mr Rankin was appointed to his present position as executive vice-president of the Housing and Security groups of Scovill in 1980. Even after assuming the executive vice-president position, Mr Rankin maintained hands-on responsibility in the areas of marketing and strategic planning at NuTone. NuTone's president, Mr J. William Cahill, was primarily involved in operations.

Pricing

Prices for NuTone products were set in three different ways: catalogue pricing, quantity-quote pricing and special-quote pricing. The prices in the catalogues were set at NuTone headquarters to yield gross margins of 50–60%. NuTone's direct sales force of over 200 (the largest in the industry) could sell at the catalogue prices without consultation with management. Management was constantly alert for conditions that might warrant price changes, particularly material cost increases. The catalogue prices were updated as necessary, usually from one to three times per year. Changes usually took about two months to take effect.

If a customer wanted a discounted price, the salesperson would have to consult with a regional sales manager, who could offer quantity discounts off a quantity-quote pricing (QQP) list. This list, also prepared at NuTone headquarters, offered discounts of up to 20% depending on the types of products the customers wanted and the quantities to which they were willing to commit. Historically, the discounts offered on the QQP lists had not been changed frequently.

Special-quote prices were offered for very large sales, generally to large builders and distributors. Requests for special quotes went to sales administrators at group headquarters who prepared the quotations in close consultation with Jim Rankin (executive vice-president). The first step in developing a special quote price was to apply the standard gross margin rule. Then the price was shaved depending on a number of factors, including what levels of stock were on hand, whether sales and profits were needed to meet the group's monthly budget, and whether strategic considerations were involved, such as penetrating a new market, using a new distributor or meeting the competition.

These special quotes were an important part of NuTone's business, at times comprising up to 50% of total sales. On average, 15–20 requests for quotes were received each day and, as Jim Rankin observed: 'The tighter the business, the more quotes there are out there.' Mr Rankin took care to review each of the special quotes personally. He even called in each day when he was out of town to review them.

Product line decisions

NuTone management was constantly refining the product-line offerings. In recent years, on average, approximately 60 new products were offered each year, and 100 products were discontinued. The product lines were reviewed formally twice a year – in April and November – to identify products that should be discontinued. The reasons that could cause a product to be discontinued included low sales volume, low profitability, problems in producing the necessary volumes, or problems in sourcing the necessary production materials.

NuTone management continued to produce some products that could not be sold profitably, however, because they considered it desirable to offer a full product line. Unprofitable items that the company continued to produce tended to be relatively simple, commodity-type products which could be produced more cheaply by smaller competitors with lower labour costs, but which complemented other products in the NuTone product line.

Market trends

In the early 1980s, NuTone's traditional market leadership position was being threatened by three major changes in the housing market. First, demand for new houses was dropping because of high interest rates, and price pressures were pushing builders to use fewer and cheaper add-on products. Secondly, the market was shifting towards the south and west regions of the USA, where 75% of the building in the USA was taking place, instead of the north-east where NuTone had traditionally dominated. NuTone executives were wont to observe, wryly, that: 'The market has gone south on us.' Thirdly, competition was increasing. Some smaller competitors had entered some of NuTone's markets, and as John Cruikshank, NuTone's manager of sales and marketing observed:

'We're the high-cost producer in many of our markets. Some of our competitors have labour rates of $4.50, compared to our $10.50 plus liberal fringe benefits, and they're willing to operate with profit margins of only 6 percent of sales. Scovill wants 14–16%.'

To reduce manufacturing costs, NuTone shifted some of its production, starting in 1979, from in-house to offshore purchasing. But this shift caused a much longer production cycle and larger inventories, as the shipment time from the Far East to Cincinnati was approx. 4 months.

Incentive compensation

Personnel at most levels of NuTone were given incentive compensation. The top-level managers were provided annual bonuses based on the performance of the entire corporation. If Scovill met its annual earnings per share (EPS) goal, bonuses of 50% of salary were provided. No extra awards were provided if actual EPS exceeded the target. If actual EPS was 10% or more under the target, no bonuses were provided. The bonuses were scaled linearly with actual EPS within these two extremes.

Middle-level NuTone managers were primarily rewarded based on achievement of goals specific to their own functional areas, but they were also rewarded depending on the group's profit performance compared with plan on a basis very similar to that done at the corporate level. For example, regional sales managers could earn an annual bonus of up to 50% of salary; 80% of this bonus could be earned by meeting a total regional sales quota and certain sales targets set for some of the major product categories. The other 20% of the bonus was provided if NuTone met its profit targets.

Personnel in the direct sales force were paid a straight commission on sales volume, with no reimbursement of expenses. The commission rate was scaled down depending on the amount of discount off catalogue prices the customer received. For example, the commission rate was 50% higher if the sale was made at catalogue prices instead of at QQP pricing.

Cost accounting

Cost accounting at NuTone dated back to 1954, when time studies were done to establish labour standards for incentive purposes. At that time, the standards were set very leniently, at approximately one-third of the level an experienced worker could achieve, so that bonuses were virtually assured. For those production employees whose output was determined by their work pace, not the speed of a machine (approximately 50% of the total workforce), the bonus was computed as the basis of $1 per hour times the difference between actual efficiency and the lenient standard, with no maximum imposed on the total bonus paid. For example, workers who performed at 300% efficiency (the average level) would be paid as follows:

Base pay (per hr)	$2.00
Bonus for achieving 300% of standard	2.00 (= $1 × [300% − 100%])
Total expected hourly wage	$4.00

Over the years the cost system evolved, and by the late 1970s NuTone's system was fairly typical for a manufacturing company. *Direct materials* were costed at standard costs, plus an allowance for material overheads which were estimated for 22 categories of materials (e.g., raw materials, purchased products, motors, mirrors) to cover freight-in, scrap and materials variances. The materials overhead rates ranged from 3% to 7%.

Direct labour costs were calculated by extending the time standard for an operation by the departmental labour rate. Time standards were established by the manufacturing department on each of the approx. 50 000 operations being performed in the plants; an operation was defined as somebody doing something to a particular product. Departmental labour rates, including fringe benefits, were calculated for each of 26 departments in the group.

Overhead costs, such as personnel, maintenance, utilities and taxes, were allocated to departments based on 'the most rational means' available. For example, payroll insurance and taxes were allocated on the basis of the number of employees per department; routine maintenance expenses were allocated on the basis of square footage used; inventory, insurance and taxes were allocated on the basis of material costs. Overhead costs were then charged to inventory as a percentage of direct labour dollars, with the overall average departmental overhead rate slightly less than 150%. By product line, the average overhead rates varied from 100% to 300%, depending on the mix of departments the products went through.

Special tooling was charged directly to the particular model or models being produced. Depreciation was taken over a four-year period from the date of installation.

Variances were recognized as follows: material price variances were recorded when the materials were entered into inventory. Material efficiency and labour and overhead variances were recognized in the month incurred, with the exception of the 'conversion cost adjustments', as described below.

Routine reviews of the standards were conducted annually. The material standards were updated based on the price paid on the latest purchase order. The labour rate standards were updated, based on the new departmental labour rates. The labour efficiency standards, being tied to compensation, were changed relatively infrequently. They were revised only if a change had been made to the production process, if an employee requested a review of a labour standard, or if they looked grossly out-of-line. The overhead standards were re-calculated, based on the forthcoming year's budget.

The conversion cost adjustment
The one major feature of the NuTone cost-accounting system that was unusual was that the labour standards were still set such that the workers would achieve average efficiency rates of around 300%, not 100%, when they were working at a normal pace. Most of the actual efficiency rates for performing the various operations in the plan varied from 240% to 360% of standard. The $1.00 bonuses for achieving each additional 100% efficiency over standard were still being provided, although the incentives were now a much lower percentage of total compensation because the base pay had risen from the old average of about $2.00 per hour to a higher average of about $8.50 per hour.

Monthly, actual labour costs (regular payroll, including bonuses and fringe benefits) and the overhead applied on them were debited to inventory, with the corresponding credit to cash or a liability account. As units were sold, inventory was credited and cost of goods sold debited by an amount calculated according to standard. The variances between actual and standard caused inventory to be understated, and cost of goods sold to be overstated, during the year. At year-end, these favourable variances were used to cover unfavourable variances that could be determined only after the physical inventory had been taken at year-end. The unfavourable variances included losses due to scrap (which was not tracked well during the year), shrinkage, mis-reporting (such as over-reporting of labour hours or re-work reported as direct labour), employee thefts, direct labour overtime, differences in daywork rates, components purchased abroad (that required just assembling) and differences across plants. Historically, these unfavourable variances totalled approx. 30% of the total favourable variances. The unused portion of the favourable variances was then credited to cost of goods sold as a 'conversion cost adjustment' (CCA) and debited to labour inventory, to correct for labour and overhead costs that had been overstated during the year. The CCA variance had existed since the institution of inflated labour standards at NuTone in 1954, but the size of the variance had been growing much larger in recent years, as shown in Table 14.3.

The CCA increases were caused by NuTone's sales growth, which caused a concomitant growth in inventories, and increases in labour rates which had been running at an annual rate of over 10% per year in the recent inflationary period. Because of the size of the end-of-year accounting adjustments being made in NuTone's books, it was noted by some people at Scovill headquarters that 'at NuTone, the 13th close is the most important'. Headquarters personnel could easily see the favourable variances that were building up but they could not estimate accurately how much would be left after the unfavourable variances were subtracted at year-end.

Even harder to estimate was the impact of inflated labour costs on

Table 14.3 The size of variance trend

Year	Conversion cost adjustment ('000s)
1977	$ 772
1978	1108
1979	1499
1980	1912
1981	2778

the profitability of each individual product line. Average product costs were approx. 55% material, 20% direct labour and 25% overhead, but the cost proportions varied considerably across product lines. Exhibit 7 presents some examples of the distortions caused by the inflated labour standards. The last two columns on the right reflect actual labour and actual overhead (allocated on the basis of actual labour) costs by product line. The actual data could be estimated from information maintained by the cost accounting staff at NuTone.

The conflict

Bob Hager knew that to be able to implement more realistic labour standards, he needed the cooperation of NuTone management. The NuTone accounting personnel all reported to group management, not to Scovill headquarters and, in any case, the NuTone manufacturing department, not accounting, was responsible for setting and maintaining the labour standards.

Most people at headquarters who had thought about the issue were convinced that the standards should be made more realistic, but NuTone personnel, even those in the accounting department, were not convinced. Here are some representative views:

Bob Hager:
'I know that NuTone has been a very profitable group for many years, and that's why it has been allowed to run so independently. The NuTone group uses the distorted labour standards to manage earnings over the year; they have ways of capturing some of that favourable variance if they need it to achieve monthly earnings targets. My predecessor, who was nearing retirement, allowed the situation to exist; he endorsed the philosophy of understating income in the first three quarters and then pulling it out at year-end.

'This is not a technical or systems problem; it is a philosophical problem. I worry about whether we really know what is happening to margins on specific line items of business because the labour and overhead content varies significantly in products of different types. I also worry that we don't have good monthly and quarterly profit numbers that should be providing us early warning indicators.'

Paul Bauer (director of corporate planning at Scovill headquarters):
'The NuTone labour standards just provide a way of salting profit away until the end of the year. Scovill's primary objective is to meet or exceed the chairman's stated annual EPS target, and the NuTone managers have been the heroes because they have been producing it at year-end. I don't think that's sound business because we've distorted all the product costs. Without special analyses of both labour and overhead allocations, they can't tell which products are dogs and which are earning us money. On a macro basis, their game is to generate an extra profit at the end of the year.'

Jim Rankin:
'I have run six different companies, and to be honest with you, I haven't had a

lot of good experiences with standard cost systems. Manufacturing in this business consists of a lot of short runs with change overs requiring set-ups. A standard cost system works best with long runs. A smart manufacturing manager can appear to make a lot of money just by making long runs.'

. . .

'If this group was run by an engineer or a manufacturing person, I'm sure we would have a typical standard cost system. But this group has been run by marketing people for many years, and this system has worked for us. If corporate forces us to go to a typical standard cost system, I am sure it will cost us margin.'

. . .

'You might say, "Why not put in the system and price at, say, 70% margin rather than 50%?" That sounds logical but I don't think it would work. The higher cost numbers are a crutch. Even though I know the costs are overstated, when I do my pricing calculations, I unconsciously believe those figures are the real costs. It's just like the crutch some people use of setting their clocks 10 minutes fast to ensure that they won't be late for their appointments. Overstating the costs causes us to keep our actual margins up. I like the fact that we have a little extra in there.'

. . .

'Would the rankings of products by margins change if the labour standards were accurate? Sure they would. But I know this business inside and out – I've been running it since 1967 – and I know what our products cost. If corporate makes us go to accurate labour standards, we'd have to run with two sets of books because I don't want to change what we've been doing. It has worked well for many years. We have pride in being the high-earning group at Scovill.'

. . .

'I like to have the monthly financials be conservative. There are a lot of things that can go wrong at year-end, particularly in the inventory areas, and I don't want any of those unpleasant surprises that can occur at year-end. In fact, I've told my financial people, "If there's ever an inventory loss at year-end, don't even bother to stop in the office on your way out."'

Bill Hanks (manager of cost accounting and payroll at NuTone):
'I'm not sure that the people at corporate realize what a monumental job it would be to change these standards. We have 26 manufacturing departments and 50 000 operations. Our cost accounting group consists of only 6 people, and manufacturing has only two industrial engineers. Doing the whole job could take years to complete.'

Exhibit 1

SCOVILL INC.: NUTONE HOUSING GROUP Scovill Inc. Financial and Statistical Highlights (1978–81)

Selected Scovill data	1978	1979	1980	1981
Net sales from continuing operations	633.4	788.1	793.0	817.9
Earnings from continuing operations	29.9	35.3	27.4	30.0
Earnings (loss) from discontinued operations	0.8	(3.3)	(3.4)	(34.5)
Net earnings (loss)	30.7	32.0	24.0	(4.5)
Per share of common stock:				
Net earnings (loss)	3.35	3.46	2.56	(0.50)
Cash dividends	1.40	1.43	1.52	1.52
Price range	$24\frac{7}{8}-17\frac{1}{4}$	$21\frac{1}{2}-17$	$19\frac{7}{8}-13\frac{7}{8}$	$21\frac{5}{8}-15\frac{1}{8}$
Number of employees	15 918	20 396	18 416	17 526

Source: Scovill Annual Reports.

Exhibit 2
SCOVILL INC.: NUTONE HOUSING GROUP Scovill Inc. Organizational Chart

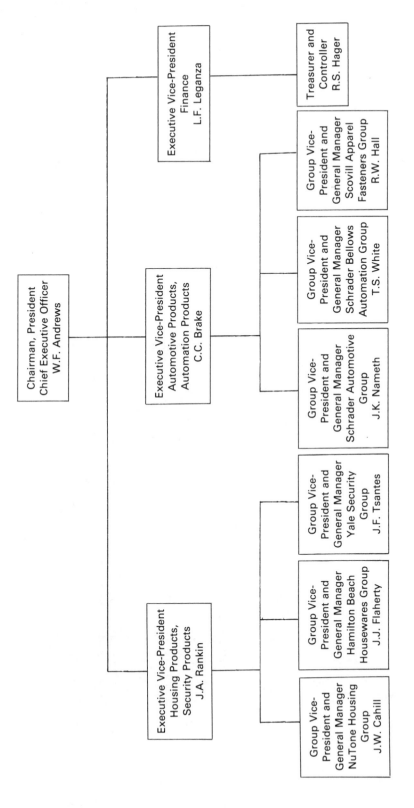

Exhibit 3

SCOVILL INC.: NUTONE HOUSING GROUP Group Product Lines, Sales, Operating Income ($m)

Group	Major Product Lines	1981 Sales	1981 Operating Income
NuTone Housing	Exhaust fans, intercoms, chimes, paddle fans	$200.5	$31.8
Yale Security	Locksets, padlocks, door closures, electronic locking systems	112.6	12.3
Hamilton Beach Housewares	Blenders, food processors, irons, coffee makers, electric knives	149.3	4.4*
Scovill Apparel Fasteners	Snap fasteners, rivets, burrs, brass zippers	149.1	21.7
Schrader Automotive	Tyre valves	83.2	4.3
Schrader Bellows Automation	Pneumatic valves, cylinders, regulators	123.2	12.0

* Includes a $2.4 million intangible asset write off and a $2.5 million provision for plant shut down and product discontinuance.

Exhibit 4
Selected Financial Data for NuTone (1978–81) ($m)

	1978	*1979*	*1980*	*1981*
Sales	207.3	197.1	183.9	200.5
Total Standard Variable Costs	118.2	117.9	120.5	121.7
Gross Margin	89.1	79.2	63.4	78.8
Gross Margin (%)	43.0	40.2	34.5	39.3
Operating Income	27.0	28.5	21.1	31.8
Total Assets	57.6	56.3	59.1	77.9
Inventories	26.3	27.2	30.1	36.7

Source: Scovill Annual Reports (non-publicly available numbers disguised).

Exhibit 5
SCOVILL INC.: NUTONE HOUSING GROUP
NuTone Product Lines: Financial and Marketing Highlights[a]

Product Line	*% of NuTone 1981 Sales*	*% of NuTone 1981 Contribution*	*Market Share (%)*	*Relative Position in the Market*
Exhaust Fans/Heaters	25.3	29.0	34	1st
Intercoms	12.2	18.1	65	1st
Chimes	9.3	12.7	55	1st
Central Vacuums	6.0	8.6	40	1st
Bath Accessories	6.8	5.9	20	1st
Range Hoods	6.5	5.1	10	2nd
Bath Cabinets	6.3	4.8	18	2nd
Food Centers	2.5	3.1	95	1st
Paddle Fans	13.8	8.5	5	4th
Lighting	4.5	3.2	N/A[b]	N/A[b]
Security Systems	1.2	0.9	20	N/A[b]
Others	5.6	0.1	–	–
TOTAL	100.0	100.0	–	–

[a]Based on the most recent estimates.
[b]Not available.

Exhibit 6
SCOVILL INC.: NUTONE HOUSING GROUP NuTone's Organization Chart

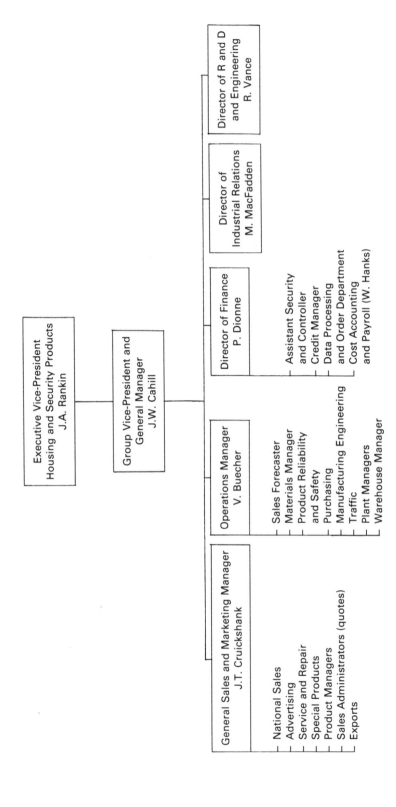

Exhibit 7

SCOVILL INC.: NUTONE HOUSING GROUP Examples of Product Costs and Profitability Levels

Products	Selling Price	Standard Costs Per Unit				Actual Costs Per Unit	
		Material	Labour	Overhead	Total	Labour	Overhead
Bathroom Exhaust Fan (Model 40)	$ 26.69	$ 8.40	$ 4.20	$ 5.35	$17.95	$ 2.47	$ 3.71
Door Chime (Model 15)	3.40	1.25	1.21	1.27	3.73	0.67	0.82
Kitchen Range Hood (Regular)	64.45	21.84	8.75	11.88	42.47	5.95	8.88
Kitchen Range Hood (Deluxe)	108.69	35.98	10.08	14.80	60.86	7.32	11.86

BBR PLC

'BBR prides itself on being a growing, prosperous company, its success being partly due to a good management team which fully participates in its development via a decentralized control system.' This statement was questioned at the meeting which took place between John North, group finance director of BBR and Paul Giddings, divisional general manager of the Shrewsbury plant. The surprise came when Paul revealed that he did not believe he was responsible for his division's profitability. This, he claimed, was due to the company's transfer pricing policy.

Historically, Paul's division bought over 50% of its total input of rubber hose from a sister division located in Preston. This trade annually accounted for about 25–35% of the Preston division's total output. Paul felt that the transfer price was unfair, and hence his division's reported profit was not a true reflection of his operational effectiveness. In the ensuing conversation both men agreed, in principle, that divisional general managers are delegated discretionary control over short-term strategy development, day-to-day operating decisions and capital expenditure decisions up to a prescribed limit. However, Paul claimed that, in practice, other factors intervened to reduce the divisional manager's degree of control and took, as an example, the inter-divisional trade in rubber hose.

The Rubber Hose Trade

Fundamentally, the Preston division produces rubber hose which is then sold to, among others, Paul's Shrewsbury division where it is 'tailored' for hydraulic uses in pit props, aircraft undercarriages and heavy plant and equipment.

Before the annual budgets are compiled, the divisional general managers enter into negotiations about fixing the transfer price. Three months' notice is required before any mutually agreed price can be revised. The managers themselves spend one or two days negotiating the transfer price for the forthcoming months. At this meeting, information provided by their respective management accountants and annual cost variances provided by the central purchasing officer of BBR are available. The Preston division provides cost data relating to standard variable and fixed costs traceable to the division, plus an apportionment for selling, administrative and distribution costs. Normally, these data provide a platform price for the negotiations. The forecasts given by the central purchasing

Professor C.R. Emmanuel prepared this case as the basis for discussion rather than to illustrate either effective or ineffective handling of an administrative situation.
© 1989 Clive R. Emmanuel

officer are included in these cost estimates. The Preston subsidiary is unaware of the assumptions on which the purchasing forecasts are based, but nevertheless accepts them as relevant to the fixing of the transfer price.

The Shrewsbury division also compiles standard cost data and, in addition, presents price list information with the likely allowable discounts it can hope to receive from alternative suppliers. On some occasions, these latter estimates form the ceiling price for the negotiations on the transfer price. One of the difficulties that has been experienced is that the range between the cost estimates at Preston and the competitor list prices at Shrewsbury can be vast. So much so that the platform price exceeds the ceiling price. This may occur when excess supply is expected to characterize the external market. Hard-nosed negotiations can result in the ultimate transfer price being less than satisfactory to both parties, and there is always the possibility for unrelated disputes to interfere with the unstructured negotiations on the transfer price.

When a transfer price has been negotiated, this is incorporated in the annual budgets of the divisions resulting in separate profit targets. The Preston division requires large volume production in order to obtain economies of scale and to maintain its competitive position in the external market. Manufacturing 'set-up' costs are high, and hence there are real cost savings in having long production runs. The Shrewsbury division, on the other hand, is committed to increasing its share of the final product market which is price-sensitive. The end-product users are mainly multinational companies and have access to world-wide suppliers. The differing orientations are perhaps best illustrated by the responses to a question put to the respective divisional managers about the degree of autonomy which they exercise:

Does the authority to use external markets freely, to develop and innovate products, and to plan the division's future:

	Preston Division	Shrewsbury Division
(a) reduce the inter-dependence between the companies of the group?	Agree	Disagree
(b) make compliance with corporate plans more difficult?	Agree	Disagree
(c) allow your division's performance to be a more realistic reflection of your worth or effort?	Agree	Agree
(d) motivate you to use more your ingenuity, imagination and creativity?	Agree	Agree

(e)	cause corporate/group objectives to give ground to division's goals?	Agree	Disagree
(f)	enhance the competitive effectiveness of the group as a whole?	Disagree	Agree

Paul Giddings feels that at the transfer price negotiating stage, he is always in a weak position. There are only two other domestic suppliers and three overseas who could supply the rubber hose in the volume he requires. Even then it is unlikely that any one of these five external suppliers would be willing to handle more than 20% of his division's total needs. His input to the negotiations is based on volume discounts likely to be available from the external suppliers and he argues that the Preston division should give a substantially better discount when he is buying internally because Preston avoids the problems of the settlement and payments, advertising and some transportation costs. In fact, he argues that the economies of scale Preston enjoys from the internal trade are being passed on in disproportionately lower prices to potential competitors of the Shrewsbury division! The Preston division counters that the savings obtained by the large volume of internal sales enables it to be cost-efficient and innovative in developing new production techniques.

Exhibit 1 provides cost data which the managers are using in their current negotiations. The transfer price proposed by the Preston division is £12.50 per metre of rubber hose.

Overlaying all of this is the difficulty both parties have in trying to forecast whether the future market will exhibit excess demand or excess supply. It is this problem which had led to the regular revision of the transfer price during the budget year in which it has been set.

Questions

1. Using the data provided, explain Paul Giddings' misgivings about a transfer price of £12.50. Indicate the actions he may take to source his rubber hose requirements and identify those which are in BBR's best interests.
2. Analyse the transfer pricing procedure of BBR within the management control system. Outline clearly all the hidden costs associated with the existing procedure.
3. Suggest and examine alternative transfer pricing procedures and transfer prices which may lead to an improvement.

Exhibit 1 Cost Data Available for the Transfer Pricing Negotiations
Preston Division

Output (thousand metres of rubber hose)	Average material cost (£ per metre)	Average direct labour cost (£ per metre)
100	8.00	5.00
200	7.70	4.80
300	7.50	4.70
400	7.20	4.50
500	7.00	4.10
600	6.50	4.00
700	6.00	3.80
800	5.50	3.60
900	5.00	3.40
1000	4.50	3.20
Annual Budgeted Divisional Fixed Costs	£160 000	
Annual Budgeted Allocation of Selling, Administration and Transportation Costs	£ 40 000	
Proposed Transfer Price	£12.50 per metre	

Shrewsbury Division

Buy-in order size (thousand metres of rubber hose)	Average external Suppliers list price (£ per metre)	Average discount (% per metre)
100	14	nil
200	14	3.57
300	14	7.15
400	14	11.6
500	14	15.0

BEECH PAPER COMPANY

Background

The Beech Paper Company is a medium-sized, partly integrated, company producing a variety of specialist papers and paperboard. It is wholly owned by a large conglomerate, but it maintains its own Head Office in Warrington, Lancashire, and is subject only to overall financial control by its parent company. It has 5 operating divisions: the Waste Paper Division, which supplies most of the company's pulp requirements; the Northern, Western and Southern Divisions which produce paperboard and a variety of other paper products for both outside customers and for internal use by other divisions; and the Carton Division which converts some of the paperboard output of the Southern Division into corrugated boxes with colour printed outside surfaces. The output of the Carton Division is sold both to external customers and to the Western and Northern Divisions.

Control system

Each of the five divisions is headed by a general manager. Following a re-organization of the company three years ago, divisional general managers were given considerable autonomy and told that they were expected to act as if they were the managing directors of independent companies. Each division is regarded by Head Office as a profit centre, and the performance of each divisional general manager is evaluated on the basis of his profit performance.

In specific terms, each division is expected to achieve a net return on sales of at least 6%. Operations are planned on an annual basis, linked to a financial year end of 30 June. Prior to the beginning of each financial year, divisional general managers are required to submit budgets showing the net profit, in excess of the 6% of sales revenue required, that they expect to earn. At this stage, adjustments are often made to the budgets, as a result of consultation and negotiation between divisional managers and Head Office. Once agreed, this budget forms the basis for evaluating performance in the ensuing year.

Each Divisional General Manager is primarily responsible to the Operations Director at Head Office. The Operations Director reviews divisional budgets and closely monitors actual performance, in comparison with budget, on a monthly basis. He is also required to resolve problems within a particular division, or between divisions, from time to time. However, he prefers not to interfere in what he considers to be normal operating matters, and has previously refused to intervene in inter-divisional squabbles. This is in keeping with the company philosophy of decentralization which he was instrumental in establishing two years ago. Under this philosophy, the Head Office is responsible primarily for strategic planning, capital investment decisions and the overall control of divisions, including the appointment of divisional general managers.

Inter-divisional transfers

A substantial volume of production is transferred between the divisions within Beech Paper, as it operates as an integrated paper company, with each division having specialist skills. The Waste Paper Division provides most of the pulp used by the three paper-making divisions, as well as supplying external customers. The output of the three paper-making divisions goes to one another, as well as to outside customers. The Carton Division does a significant amount of paperboard conversion and printing for Western and Northern Divisions, and usually purchases linerboard from the Southern Division.

These inter-divisional transfers present a special problem of management accounting, as the operating divisions are viewed by Head Office as independent profit centres. The problem is resolved by using transfer prices to account for the internal transactions. Thus, a product which is transferred internally generates a credit for the supplying division, and an equal and opposite debit for the user division.

There are several methods by which transfer prices can be determined. In Beech Paper, consistent with its philosophy of decentralization, transfer prices are set on a bid-and-negotiate basis. Upon request, the selling division submits a quotation to the buying division; at the same time, the buying division also solicits quotations from outside suppliers. Beech operates on the general principle that the buying division should attempt to place orders internally, where possible. So where the selling division's bid is too high, the selling and buying divisions should attempt to reach a mutually acceptable price by negotiation. The problem may also be referred to the Operations Director, although he may refuse to interfere in what he regards as a normal operating matter. At this point, if agreement is not achieved internally, the buying division is free to accept an outside bid.

Setting

The date is 10 June 1990. Preliminary budgets for the year ending 30 June 1991 have been submitted by the Divisions to Mr Hodge, the

Operations Director. The budgets have been based on the assumption that all purchases have been made internally, where possible, but they are still subject to discussion and final agreement.

Role for Mr John Clark

You are the Divisional General Manager of Beech Paper Company's Carton Division. Some months ago, you became concerned over a widespread tendency among your salesmen to discount their prices on boxes. After carefully investigating the issue, you wrote a strong memo directing the salesmen not to sell boxes below cost plus the normal 20% mark-up. This directive is consistent with your long-standing policy and is designed to ensure that a fair share of overhead costs, and a reasonable profit margin is obtained from each sale. This is important since you and your division are evaluated on your return on sales revenue.

You have analysed your markets carefully and are convinced that your best strategy is to maintain your normal prices, even if you fail to operate at capacity. The level of competition is increasing, but you have a reputation as a reliable supplier of a quality product that you believe will allow you to command premium prices. However, you also believe that it is important that you are seen to apply the same pricing policy to all your customers in order to maintain this position.

Recently, Mr David Norton, Divisional General Manager of the Northern Division, put out an order to tender. This was for the supply of 1500K boxes over the coming year that he would use to package his other products. He received bids from the Scott Packaging Company for £410 per thousand, from the Irish Paper Company for £432 per thousand and from your own division for £480 per thousand. Since he was aware of the fact that you were currently operating at less than 90% of your capacity, he contacted Mr Hodge, the Operations Director, to receive guidance on where the contract should be placed. Mr Hodge suggested that Mr Norton should discuss the matter with you. Mr Norton is now on his way to see you.

MEMO

FROM: John Clark, General Manager, Carton Division
TO: All Sales Representatives, Carton Division
DATE: 20 March 1990

Pricing policy

1. The prices currently being obtained for our products are not adequate. Our budgeted profit target cannot be achieved unless our normal pricing policy can be re-established. This memorandum is to re-affirm that policy, and to make it clearly understood that I intend to hold all sales representatives accountable for achieving the 20% mark-up included in it.

2. Our pricing structure is intended to provide for three elements:
   (a) The variable costs of production and marketing of an order.
   (b) A contribution towards the recovery of divisional fixed costs and Head Office costs.
   (c) A profit margin.

   The current policy is to price at 120% of the identifiable variable costs of production and marketing. The 20% 'add-on' cost represents a contribution towards fixed overheads and profit, and is crucial to the continued success of our business. In future, no order will be accepted at a lower price unless specifically authorized by the Marketing Manager.

3. The reasons I have heard from salesmen for not adhering to this policy are two-fold. First, it has been argued that we need to price lower to meet competition. Secondly, it is stated that we do not adhere to this policy on internal sales.

   I have no sympathy with these arguments. If a competitor wishes to fill his plant with low priced business, then let him. We wish to obtain good quality business, even if that means we sometimes operate at less than maximum production; I would rather turn away such low margin business in the expectation that we will obtain sufficient full price business. Given our reputation for quality and service, we should be able to compete effectively with this pricing policy.

   Regarding internal sales, I agree that it is potentially harmful if we do not adhere to the same policy for these sales. Let me assure you that inter-divisional sales will be subject to exactly the same pricing policy as external sales.

   ALL sales quotations *must* therefore include the full 20% mark-up.

SUMMARY BUDGET
CARTON DIVISION – BEECH PAPER COMPANY
Year ending 30 June 1991

	£'000	£'000
Sales Revenue		
From external customers outside of Beech	3300	
Northern Division	720	
Western Division	1080	
		5100
Costs		
Manufacturing		
Materials	2972	
Labour	574	
Variable overhead	286	
Fixed overhead	210	
		4042
Marketing		
Commissions	99	
Order-filling	111	
Advertizing	33	
Other	105	
		348
Administration		260
Share of Head Office costs		100
Total costs		4750
Budgeted gross profit margin		350
Required profit (6% of sales revenue)		306
Budgeted excess/(deficiency)		44

Notes:

1. All marketing costs are variable, except for £35 000 order-filling and £70 000 other costs. Administrative costs are also variable except for £85 000 fixed costs.
2. The budget is based on the assumption that the order from Northern Division for 1500K boxes will be obtained at a price of £480 per thousand.

BUDGET SUPPORTING SCHEDULES
CARTON DIVISION – BEECH PAPER COMPANY
Year ending 30 June 1991

(1) Pricing assumptions: unit costs and prices

	Northern Division	Western Division	External customers
Variable costs:			
Manufacturing			
Materials			
Linerboard, etc. (note 1)	280	305	310
Printing materials	20	24	29
Labour	56	66	65
Variable overhead	29	33	32
Marketing			
Commissions (note 2)			18
Order-filling	5	8	16
Administration (variable)	10	14	24
Promotion costs (note 2)			6
TOTAL VARIABLE COSTS	400	450	500
20% addition for fixed cost recovery and divisional profit margin	80	90	100
PRICE (per '000 boxes)	£480	£540	£600

Notes:
1. Linerboard is usually purchased from the Southern Division. The variable costs of production amount to about 60% of the transfer price.
2. Sales commissions, advertising and promotion costs are not incurred on sales within Beech. The £6000 per thousand box cost for advertising represents the £33 000 total advertising cost allocated on a per thousand basis.

(2) Estimated demand

	£'000
External customers:	
5500K boxes @ average price of £600/K	3300
Internal sales:	
Northern Division	
1500K boxes @ average price of £480/K	720
Western Division	
2000K boxes @ average price of £540/K	1080
Total demand (9000K boxes)	£5100

Notes:
1. Maximum practical capacity is approx. 10 250K boxes.
2. The above-average prices differ because of differences in specification of boxes supplied to different customers.

Role for Mr David Norton

You are the Divisional General Manager of the Northern Division of the Beech Paper Company. Recently, while examining bids from different companies for a major order of 1500K boxes that your division was planning to buy over the coming year, you discovered the following. One company, Scott Packaging, had submitted a bid for £410 per thousand boxes. A second company, Irish Paper, had bid £432 per thousand boxes. The Carton Division of your own company had also been asked to bid, as was normal practice, but had submitted a bid of £480 per thousand boxes.

Since you know that the Carton Division has been operating at only about 90% of its capacity for some time now, you were surprised at this difference in price. You telephoned Mr Hodge, the Operations Director of your company at Head Office, to ask his advice on how you should proceed, since it seemed undesirable to let the business go outside of the company. He suggested that, consistent with the decentralized philosophy of this company, you should discuss the matter with Mr Clark, the General Manager of the Carton Division.

You are now on your way to see Mr Clark. Your objective is to resolve this issue in a way which is best for the company, but you are also very conscious of the fact that you and your division are evaluated according to your return on sales revenue, and that you must remain competitive.

NORTHERN DIVISION
BEECH PAPER COMPANY
SUMMARY OF BIDS FOR SPECIAL DISPLAY BOXES

Scott Packaging Company	£410 per '000
Irish Paper Company	£432 per '000
Carton Division	£480 per '000

Note:

The Irish Paper Company would buy the ready printed outside linerboard from the Carton Division of Beech Paper, but supply its own internal liner and corrugating material. The outside liner would be supplied by Southern Division at a price equivalent to £90 per thousand and would be printed by the Carton Division for £30 per thousand. Southern and Carton Divisions' variable costs are about 60% and 5/6 of these prices respectively.

SUMMARY BUDGET
NORTHERN DIVISION – BEECH PAPER COMPANY
Year ending 30 June 1991

	£'000	£'000
Sales Revenue		
From external customers outside Beech	6000	
Western Division	500	
		6500
Costs		
Manufacturing		
Materials		
Purchased from outside	1320	
Purchased from Carton Division	720	
Purchased from Waste Paper Division	1340	
Labour	625	
Variable overhead	330	
Fixed overhead	470	
		4805
Marketing		
Commissions	290	
Order-filling	150	
Advertising	110	
Other	125	
		675
Administration		590
Share of Head Office costs		100
Total costs		6170
Budgeted gross profit margin		330
Required profit (6% of sales revenue)		390
Budgeted excess/(deficiency)		(60)

Role for Mr Andrew Sutherland

You are the Divisional General Manager of the Southern Division of the Beech Paper Company. During the past year your division has been operating at less than its full capacity, due to a lack of orders. However, in the past few weeks you have received a considerable number of inquiries from potential customers and you are now confident that the internal and external business you can expect will enable you to operate at full capacity.

Your normal pricing policy has been to mark-up your variable costs of both manufacturing and marketing an order by two-thirds to cover both your heavy fixed costs of plant and machinery, and also to provide you with a profit margin. During the past year, you have not always been able to implement this policy and have taken some orders at a lower price so as to ensure that you obtained the business. However, because of the improved order position, you now believe that all orders should be priced according to your normal policy, and you have prepared your budget submission on that basis.

You are a strong believer in the policy of decentralization that has been introduced by your Operations Director, Mr Hodge, and have been pleased to accept the responsibility of running your division as if it were an independent company, despite your poor performance in the current year which has been mainly due to lack of market demand for your products. But you are not convinced that all your colleagues share these views. You have been approached in the past by the managers of other divisions seeking preferential terms because you are all part of the same company. In your view, this is inappropriate, except insofar as internal prices are lower than external prices because you do not include sales commission, advertising and promotion costs in internal transfer price quotations.

SUMMARY BUDGET
SOUTHERN DIVISION – BEECH PAPER COMPANY
Year ending 30 June 1991

	£'000	£'000
Sales Revenue		
From external customers outside Beech	6865	
Carton Division	2735	
		9600
Costs		
Manufacturing		
Materials		
Purchased from outside	400	
Purchased from Western Division	600	
Purchased from Waste Paper Division	2600	
Labour	900	
Variable overhead	450	
Fixed overhead	2250	
		7200
Marketing		
Commissions	360	
Order-filling	150	
Advertising	130	
Other	170	
		810
Administration		690
Share of Head Office costs		100
Total costs		8800
Budgeted gross profit margin		800
Required profit (6% of sales revenue)		576
Budgeted excess/(deficiency)		224

Notes:
1. This budget assumes that Southern Division will be able to work at production capacity for the whole year.
2. Marketing costs are all variable, except for £50 000 of order-filling costs and £120 000 of other costs. Administrative costs include £520 000 fixed costs.

Role for Mr Jim Hodge

You are the Operations Director of the Beech Paper Company at the Head Office in Warrington, Lancashire. Recently, Mr David Norton of your Northern Division telephoned you and confronted you with the following facts. In receiving bids for a large order of 1500K boxes which his division needed to buy, he received the following quotations:

Scott Packaging Company	£410 per thousand
Irish Paper Company	£432 per thousand
Carton Division, Beech Paper	£480 per thousand

Since he was aware of the fact that the Carton Division was currently operating at under 90% of its capacity, he felt that this business could best be undertaken internally, and asked for your advice on what should be done.

You recently set up the Beech Paper Company's system of decentralized management, in which each division is evaluated on its return on sales revenue, and believe that it provides the best structure for flexible and competitive operation. While you could intervene and make special arrangements to adjust the reported profit figures of each division, you are very reluctant to do so. However, it does seem that there is something wrong if the Carton Division cannot compete on the open market, and it concerns you that such a large order might be lost to the company.

You have asked your Chief Accountant to analyse the situation, and he has produced a schedule of the costs to the company of accepting each alternative. Nevertheless, consistent with your style and philosophy of management, you suggest to Mr Norton that he visits Mr Clark, the Carton Division Manager, to discuss the matter, and that they handle the matter themselves. It is possible, however, that they will come back to you later for help.

Note: Mr Hodge should receive copies of the summary budgets for each division.

MEMO

FROM: Mr A. Smith, Chief Accountant
TO: Mr J. Hodge, Operations Director
DATE: 9 June 1990

Comparison of bids

I append my notes on how the 3 bids received by the Northern Division for the supply of boxes appear to affect the profitability of the Beech Company overall. It is clearly in the company's interest that this transaction should be undertaken internally.

	Carton Division	Scott Pckg	Irish Paper
		Supplier	
Quoted price (per '000)	£480	£410	£432
Variable cost to Southern Division	168		54
Variable cost to Carton Division	120		25
Payments to suppliers		410	432
Payment from Irish Paper			(120)
Total cost to Beech	$288	$410	$391

Note: This analysis assumes that no external order would be refused if this order were supplied internally.

ALTEX AVIATION

Assuming control at Altex Aviation

'We closed on Altex Aviation in the late evening of 29 December 1971. Frank flew back to Los Angeles that night and I went up to Dallas immediately thereafter to pick up some papers and to resign from McKenzie & Booze. I took a check for $100 000, which represented all the cash we had, gave it to Bill Dickerson, who no longer owned the company, and said, "Would you give this to Sarah and have her deposit it?" He said, "Fine"; and he gave it to Sarah and she deposited it the next day. I went down to McKenzie & Booze, resigned, and then about lunch time, after saying goodbye to folks, I picked up the phone and called Sarah. With the $100 000 we gave her, Altex had $102 000 in the bank. I said, "Hello, Sarah, this is Ted Edwards", "Oh, Mr. Edwards", she said, "I am so glad you called. When will you be in?" I said, "I will be in shortly". She said, "Oh good, I have a few cheques for you to sign." I said, "That's wonderful. What are the cheques for?" She said, "I have written checks *only* for our most pressing bills. I tried very hard to make sure that only those that are most important be paid." I said, "That's fine. What's the total of the checks you have written?" She said, "$92 000". I said, "We'll discuss it".

I drove very calmly down to Altex Aviation to have my first confrontation with Sarah Arthur. Now I had envisioned, as every business school graduate does, that when I bought my company, I would walk in the front door the next morning; everyone would bow down; and there would be a brass band. Instead, I'm walking in through the back door (a) realizing that I have a crisis on my hands, (b) hoping no one is going to see me so I can deal with this crisis and (c), of course, I don't really know how I am going to deal with it. What I did was, I said to Sarah, "We are *not* going to pay these bills". And she said, "Oh, but you *must*". And I said, "No, I will decide what bills we are going to pay". She said, "OK". And then sat back to watch this idiot make a fool of himself – that was my first day.'

Thus did Ted Edwards describe the beginning of Frank Richards' and his ownership of Altex Aviation.

The purchase
Theodore Edwards and Frank Richards met in 1968 as graduate students at the Harvard Business School. Although planning on working initially for large companies, they decided that they eventually wanted to own their own business. Upon graduation in 1970, Frank took a job in the corporate finance department with an elec-

This case was prepared by Professor Neil C. Churchill of SMU, Edmund M. Goodhue of MIT and Kenneth A. Merchant of HBS as a basis for class discussion rather than to illustrate either effective or ineffective handling of an administrative situation.
© 1982 President and Fellows of Harvard College, Harvard Business School and Neil C. Churchill. Case 9-183-058.

tronics firm in Los Angeles, and Ted went with a New York consulting firm's Dallas office doing market planning.

After six months, Frank transferred to the marketing support group for the south-west operations, and Ted and Frank saw each other frequently. In the process, they evolved the idea of going into business together, 'In good business school fashion', said Frank, 'we established some criteria'; these were as follows:

1. The company couldn't cost anything since they did not have any money.
2. The company had to need what they had to offer — which they thought, at that time, were managerial skills.
3. The industry had to be fragmented and non-oligopolistic. They didn't want to be a small fish in a big pond.
4. They needed to be able to see their way clear to have the company grow at a rate of 20% per year in the first 5-year period.

Ted and Frank looked at a number of businesses over the next year and a half and, in early fall of 1971, located a 'fixed-base operation'* at San Miguel Airport in Texas that was losing money and looking for a buyer. After four months of negotiation , on 29 December 1971, Ted, aged 26, and Frank, aged 28, purchased the stock of the company for $10 000 each, assumed the lease on the building (and all the assets and liabilities) and were in business.

The lease on the facilities had a purchase option at a price considerably less than the market value. By exercising the option and then selling and leasing back the building, Ted and Frank were able to raise the $100 000 for working capital referred to above.

Ted and Frank had discussed the organizational structure at Altex and agreed to decentralize its operations by making each operating activity a profit centre and grouping them by departments. Each departmental manager would be given authority over his operations, including credit granting, purchasing to a pre-determined limit, policy and collection of receivables. He would also be held responsible for its results. Frank was concerned, however:

'I agree with our decision to decentralize this authority, but I am concerned whether now is the time to do it. We will have a tough time when we first walk in the door, and I don't know if the departmental managers can be

---

* Fixed-based operations (FBO) are companies located on an airport that service the non-airline aviation market. They generally sell, fuel and maintain aircraft, as well as provide flight instruction and charter services. These companies can range from small family operations to multiple-location companies with sales exceeding $100 million.

taught some of these management techniques fast enough. After all, some have never finished high school. Maybe we should begin by making all these decisions ourselves for a month or two. I realize that we don't know the aviation business yet, but even though neither of us has been a line manager, maybe we can learn the aviation business faster than some of our managers can learn formal management skills. Either way, we're putting the company on the line and the two-minute warning whistle has already blown.'

During the four months they were negotiating the deal, Frank and Ted spent virtually every weekend together. Of this period, Ted commented:

'We spent something on the order of 10 hours a week, of which maybe 2 or 3 hours would be trying to understand Sarah Arthur's accounting system and accounting statements, and another 2 or 3 hours on discussing pro-forma financial projections and the rest on what we would do when we acquired it. Frank basically did the financial projections and I designed the accounting system. Actually, I dreamt it up one afternoon at McKenzie & Booze. I sat down at their IBM composer and designed the forms, using their artwork. Frank's projections, by profit centre for the next 10 years, showed that things were really tight. Even with the $100 000 from the sale and leaseback of the facilities, Frank projected that we were going to run out of money near the end of the first year. We knew this when we were negotiating for the company, and it made us a bit nervous.

Well, 3 days before the closing, Frank came to me, white as a sheet, and confessed that we had made, not an arithmetic error, but a structural error in the projections. He was computing accounts payable on the wrong basis, and we were going to run out of money in 3 months. We had a little discussion as to whether we should blow the whole deal out of the water right there – knowing that we couldn't survive. He basically turned to me and said, "I will do whatever you want to do". I said, "Let's do it anyway". So we did it, but I have to say we were a bit shaken. We knew it would be an impossible job, no matter how we sliced it, but we were prepared to do it; and I must say we leaned on each other for support a great deal in the first few months.'

Altex Aviation prior to purchase

Altex Aviation was one of 8 fixed-base operations at San Miguel Airport which served Center County, Texas – one of the most rapidly growing communities in the nation. Altex had a loss of $100 000 on sales of $2 000 000 in fiscal year 1971, and this left the company with a negative net worth (see Exhibit 1). The company conducted activities through six informal departments, described below (see Exhibit 2). Altex's location on the airport is shown in Exhibit 3(a).

Fuel (line) activity
This activity employed some 12 unskilled fueling people, with an average tenure with the company of 8 months, and 3 dispatchers

who coordinated their activities via two-way radio. It was managed by Will Leonard, a man in his mid-thirties, who had been the construction foreman for Bill Dickerson when Bill was a real-estate developer. When Dickerson bought Altex in 1964, he brought Will Leonard with him to manage the 'line crew'. Will was enthusiastic about his job, extremely loyal to Dickerson and well liked by his employees. Although lacking in any theory of management (he had a high-school diploma and some junior-college credits), Will was a good first line manager who was instinctively people-conscious while holding them in line. The fuel activity encompassed five operations:

1. *Fueling* – A Phillips Petroleum franchise of underground storage of 60 000 gallons of jet fuel, 20 000 gallons of 'AV-gas', and 5 fuel trucks to serve locally based and transient aircraft.
2. *Wholesale fuelling* – Service of a fuel farm for Tex Air, a regional airline connecting San Miguel with cities in Texas, Louisiana, Arkansas and Oklahoma. Altex charged a gallon-variable fee for this service, and billed Tex Air separately for the fuel, at cost.
3. *Fuel hauling* – An over-the-road fuel truck and a Texas Public Utilities permit to haul fuel on public roads. The truck, in essence, served Phillips, at a price, by delivering its fuel to Altex.
4. *Rental cars* – An agency of a local automobile rental company; basically, this was a service to transient pilots.
5. *Tie-downs* – Storage of transient and San Miguel-based aircraft in 6 hangars and 50 open tie-downs.*

The fuel activity was open 18 hours a day, seven days a week, 365 days a year.

Service and parts
The *service activity* repaired, maintained and overhauled piston-engined aircraft. It employed 6 mechanics and a departmental secretary. The *parts activity*, a separate accounting entity, employed one person and was managed by the head of service, as sales went almost entirely to the service activity.

The manager of these operations was Carl Green, a man in his sixties, who had been chief mechanic for Dove Aircraft at Love Field in Dallas prior to his moving to Altex. Before that, he was the mechanic/co-pilot for a Dallas oil executive. Carl had a high school diploma, aircraft and power plant licences, and multi-engine and commercial pilot certificates. He knew airplanes, engines and aircraft

---

* A tie-down is an area of asphalt or concrete with ropes where an aircraft is parked by tying it down to prevent it from rolling away or from sustaining wind damage; it is the aviation equivalent of a parking lot.

mechanics. He was, in Ted's words, 'not a self-starter, had a bit of retirement mentality, and avoided conflict except when it came to quality: you would never worry about anything he rolled out of his shop'.

Flight training

The flight training activity was managed by Roy Douglas whose pilot's licence was signed by one of the Wright Brothers. Roy had held several world records in aviation's early days and was highly respected by the aviation community. He spent a lot of time 'hangar flying' with old cronies and, while he didn't manage the department in any real day-to-day sense, he hired the 7 instructor pilots and 3 dispatchers, gave check rides[†] to students prior to their Federal Aviation Administration flight examination, and set safety policies. He and his chief dispatcher, who now had been with him for over 10 years, were intensely loyal to both Altex Aviation and the flying community. They had, however, 'seen everything and were surprised by nothing', and they were very resistant to change, be it new aircraft technology, aviation teaching methodology or accounting systems. The flight training activity, which had lost money each year, had two types of operations:

1. *Flight school* – flight training in 18 single-engine light aircraft from eight flight instructors coordinated by 3 dispatchers. Flight ratings were offered from private pilot through air transport ratings.
2. *Pilot shop* – sales of flight supplies, such as logbooks, navigational charts and personal and training flight supplies. Sales were made from 3 display counters by the flight school dispatchers.

Avionics

Avionics was a single-person activity conducted by Leon Praxis. Leon was a college-trained electronics technician whose interests were in repairing radios, and electronic navigational equipment from 8 am until 5 pm every day, however, he left promptly at 5 pm for his non-job-related activities.

Aircraft sales

Altex had been a Piper Aircraft dealer until 2 months before its sale. The owner, Bill Dickerson, was unable to finance the number of air-craft Piper required to be carried in inventory, so he lost the franchise, fired his 2 salespeople and closed down the department.

[†] FAA regulations require a certified instructor to check each student's competence prior to recommendation for the FAA flight examination.

Accounting

The Accounting Department* was central to the company in two ways. First, it was located in a glass-enclosed office in the centre of the building (see Exhibit 3b), where it could be seen by everyone and everyone could be seen from it*. The second part of its centrality was the role that its manager, Sarah Arthur, played in Altex. Sarah had worked for Bill Dickerson for some 20 years. Indeed, in his absence, which was frequent, Sarah managed the company. While her title was accountant, she had no accounting training of any kind and her idea of running the company was to be the central repository of all information. She received and opened all the mail – not just accounting mail – and she would distribute it to the department heads as she saw fit. What she distributed, in Ted's words, 'was typically nothing – bills would come and she would keep them; cheques would appear and she would keep them; and at the end of the day, she would collect cash from all the departments and keep it'. Sarah managed all the receivables and payables.

All accounting information was Sarah's and nothing left her office. The department managers knew nothing about the profitability of their operations. All they knew was that airplanes would fly and that Sarah Arthur would come around at the end of each day and collect their money. Then occasionally she would berate the department managers for their high receivables. Of course, they had no idea how big their receivables were or who they represented; they would just 'be beaten over the head'. Other times, mysteriously, suppliers would put the company COD and somebody would go to Sarah and say, 'I want COD money, I can't get janitorial supplies' or 'I need cash because I can't get aircraft parts', and she would say, 'Okay', and mysteriously, a week later they would go off COD. As Ted described it:

'The management system that was in place when we bought the company was one woman who magically kept everything in her head. There was a limited and almost incomprehensible formal system. There were basic financial statements and a set of reports that were produced for and according to Piper Aircraft's specifications each month but they helped Piper, not the management. We may have negotiated with Bill Dickerson but we were going to take over the management of the company from Sarah Arthur.'

Assuming management responsibilities

The roles of Ted and Frank

Frank and Ted took over the business not only as full and equal

* By contrast, the Aircraft Sales Department was located, according to Ted, 'in an old dark office far away from the action'.

partners, but as best friends who understood each other very well. Frank assumed the chairmanship, and turned his attention to specific and critical projects, the first being the re-establishment of aircraft sales – potentially, a major profit area. Ted took the title of president and chief operating officer and began to manage the rest of the business. As Ted said later:

'I knew Frank wouldn't be at my right side at every decision but I made sure that four times a day I could walk into his office and say, "Frank, I don't really know what I am doing", and he would pat me on the back – symbolically – and put my head in order.'

Frank, in turn, depended on Ted for operational inputs and intellectual support. They both worked 12-hour days, five days a week, with Ted, a bachelor, putting in 10–12 hours each day on weekends, and Frank, a family man, 3 or 4 hours on Saturdays and often on Sundays as well.

Management and control
Beyond the immediate cash crisis, Ted viewed his three most important tasks as:

1. Revamping the management of Altex Aviation.
2. Installing a control system that would:
   (a) support the management, and
   (b) provide information needed in order to make the decisions. (Although the company wasn't large, it was rather complicated in terms of the businesses it was in.)
3. Wresting *de facto* control of the company from Sarah Arthur promptly.

Frank and Ted believed that it was very important to provide an environment where the departmental managers made correct decisions on their own since they had decided they could not make all the decisions themselves – they had neither the time nor the technical knowledge. As Ted put it:

'One of the things I was very concerned about was how to manage by providing an environment that encouraged the managers to make decisions the way I would want them made. That was very, very important to me. I wanted to provide a framework that didn't limit their actions, but certainly provided very fast feedback as to how they were doing and made it personally worthwhile for them to do the right things. I spent a lot of time thinking about how to do that and it occurred to me that there were really two ways to do that. I recognize that there has to be the black hat and the white hat in any of these situations and so I decided to make the control system represent reality and my personal role would then be that of an emotional leader as opposed to a task leaders. I would let the control system be the task leader, and then I could exert more avuncular personal leadership.

I also realized that I didn't have the time to train everyone in the management approach we wanted to use at Altex. Nor did I have the guts to fire everyone and bring in new talent, and that wouldn't have been a good idea anyway. I also realized that unless I changed the basic attitudes in the company, we would never survive. In order to do that, we needed to do a lot of educating, and that would be my personal role. But, if I was going to do that successfully, I couldn't at the same time be berating them about the receivables, so it was necessary to take the nitty-gritty daily tasks of banging people over the head and put them somewhere else. I didn't really feel that Frank should do that and so to provide this environment for decentralized decision making was very, very important.'

Ted began to implement a management control structure incorporating the following policies:

1. Profit centres would be established for each major activity. These profit centres would be combined where appropriate into departments;
2. Revenues and expenses would be identified by profit centre and communicated to the profit-centre manager;
3. Departmental managers would be responsible for their profit centers and receive a bonus of 10% of their profit center profits after administrative allocation;
4. The profit centre managers would have pricing authority for their products or services, both internally and externally; the fuel department manager could, and did, charge the Flight School retail price for the fuel they used whereas he charged the Service Department his cost for its oil;
5. The profit centre managers could buy products externally rather than internally if it was in their best interests to do so. The Flight School manager could, and did, have his aircraft repaired outside Altex's shop when it was unable to fulfill his service needs;
6. The profit centre managers could buy needed capital equipment and operating supplies on their own authority within established purchase order limits.

Ted recalled one of the first times this decentralized authority was tested.

'When we bought the company, it had a mimeograph machine and an old, rotten, obsolete copier. They were under the control of Sarah Arthur and everyone who wanted a copy of anything had to go to Sarah, the Witch of the North, and plead – which was really an awful thing to do. I remember one day, Will Leonard, the manager of the Fuel Department, said, "Can I get a Xerox machine?" I said, "Will, you can do anything you want within limitations of the PO". So he acquired the smallest Xerox machine made, and he let everyone in the company make copies, charging them 10¢ a copy. At the end of the month, he would present bills to every department for the copies they used. He made money on his Xerox machine because everyone else was scared to death to walk into the Accounting Department and face the Witch of the North. Here was a classic entrepreneurial example, and it became almost a *cause celebre*. People were saying, "How did he get a Xerox machine? What right does he have to charge me for the Xerox machine?" I would say, "If you want a Xerox machine, go get one". But with one here at 10¢ a copy, they realized they couldn't really afford one themselves, so they grumbled that Leonard had stolen the march on them.'

7. The profit centre managers had the authority to hire, fire and administer the salary schedule in their departments quite independent of the rest of the company.

Cash management

Cash and accounts payable

When Ted arrived at Altex on the first day of his ownership, he gathered up the cheques Sarah had written and the accounts payable ledger cards, called in his departmental managers one by one and said, 'Who are your most important suppliers?'. Then he looked at the ledger cards to see how old the balances were and called up each of the suppliers saying, 'I'm the new owner of Altex Aviation and I would like to come down and talk to you about our credit arrangement'. Ted stated:

'Over the next six months, I got on good terms with the suppliers. I talked to them, took them out to lunch, and let them take me out to lunch. We paid them a little bit here and a little bit there and we stayed out of serious trouble.'

A direct result of Ted's assumption of the accounts payable decision was that Sarah Arthur began to view her stay at Altex Aviation as being limited to the 4 months agreed upon. As it became clear that Ted was not going to let her make the management decisions anymore, she limited her work for the company strictly to the 4-month transition period agreed upon in the purchase agreement. As Ted put it:

'She effectively said, "I will work from 11.00 a.m. to 2.00 p.m. every day. I will answer your questions and that is all." That was fine with me. I hired a new accounting clerk to be Sarah's assistant. She worked from 8 in the morning until 7 at night. I hired her; she worked for *me*; and when Sarah Arthur quietly packed up and left, after four months, the departure was easy.'

Cash and accounts receivable

With the accounts payable crisis on the road to a solution, Ted turned his attention to cash inflow; in his words:

'My biggest worry was how we were going to control cash, or rather, how I was going to provide a system that would motivate the departments to manage cash. The solution I came up with was to take the receivables and give them back to the departments. That was very controversial: everybody in the whole company fought me on that. Frank didn't like it – I was totally alone. The reason they didn't like it was severalfold. First of all, the managers didn't understand it. They had never seen receivables, they didn't know what they were. They felt as though they were playing with dynamite. "Here they are but what am I to do with them?" Frank, on the other hand, was concerned that things would get totally out of control because our most important asset – our incoming cash flow – had suddenly been handed out to amateurs. Sarah Arthur may not have been perfect but she had a lot of experience.

In the Fuel Department, I handed the receivables to the dispatcher, a 20-year-old surfer who had dropped out of college after two years. In the Flight School, I also gave them to the dispatcher, a 55-year-old, loyal employee. These were the only two departments with significant accounts receivables. In Service and Avionics, I gave them to the managers, but these were not significant.

Literally, one Saturday morning, I went to a stationery store and bought a metal folder and some ledger cards, and I sat down in the Accounting Office while Sarah was not there. I transferred all the balances over to the ledger cards and physically presented them to these two women – the *de facto* departmental heads. Then I sat down and showed them how to use the forms using the current week's transactions. So we started to collect data on the accounts receivable.'

To motivate the department heads to manage their accounts receivables, Ted gave them the credit-granting authority and the responsibility for collections. He also established the following charges against their departmental profits.

Receivables	60 days old or less	1% of the balance
Receivables	60–90 days old	3% of the balance
Receivables	90–120 days old	6% of the balance
Receivables	over 120 days old	Charged the unpaid balance to the profit centre

Cash and the banks

When Frank and Ted acquired Altex, they also acquired short-term bank notes payable of $60 000 from the Center National Bank which had been outstanding for several years. Ted was concerned since if Center National Bank called the notes, it would put the company into bankruptcy. As Ted recalled:

'One of the people I called just before we bought the company was Harold Lattimer, the manager of the branch we did business with. I took him out to dinner, and over dinner and a glass of wine, I told him about myself, what I was doing, my thoughts and I said, "We have this problem of the $60 000 I owe you". He replied, "What do you want to do with it?". I said, "I would love to convert it to a 24-month note to get it out of the short-term category so as to increase our working capital to make us more attractive to our suppliers. That way we can get better terms from them." He looked at me and said, "Fine, I'll do it".

Now, at that point, he had made a gut decision based upon some vibrations. And I was so shocked, since I was prepared to negotiate with him, that I said to myself, "The basis upon which business is done, at least with this man, is total candor and honesty". So I started this programme of giving the bank our internal financial reports every month along with a cover letter summarizing what I was doing. Hal's reaction was superb. He thought it was the greatest thing he'd seen. No customer had ever done that to him before, ever! The result was that whenever I went to him – we paid off the loan ahead of time – and said, "Hal, it looks as if I'm going to need $100 000 for 60 days", he would say, "Yes, I've been following it, I've been watching your receivables growing because of your extra business. I know a growing business needs this money from time to time. It's no problem and I'll put the money in your account this afternoon."'

The accounting system

By the end of the second month, Altex was producing a profit and loss statement on the activities of each department. Each department kept account of its own sales, receivables, inventories, expenses and, through the PO system, expenses initiated by the department.

In order to provide a predictable and simple method of cost allocation which still would be understood and 'managed' by the department heads, Ted established an Administration Profit Centre which paid taxes, borrowed money, paid interest, utilities, bills and other general administrative expenses. The Administrative Department in turn levied a series of monthly charges to each department as follows:

1. Social Security taxes, health, insurance, and other fringe benefits were charged to departments as a pre-determined percentage of wages. Thus, when a manager took on a new employee, he or she knew that it would cost the department, say, 125% of the wage.
2. Accounts receivable – a monthly charge based on the amount and age of the receivables (see above).

3. Operating assets – including the Parts Department inventory and the Service Department's shop equipment – were charged to the departments using them on a pre-determined percentage of the asset's costs.
4. Rent, fire and occupancy insurance, building maintenance and depreciation and other occupancy costs were charged as predetermined rental per square foot of floor or ramp space occupied.
5. A predetermined percentage of sales which represented the cost of Ted's office and the Accounting Department was also charged.

As all the charges were pre-determined, calculated, and announced twice a year, the managers would control their expenses by managing their receivable balances, conserving on equipment purchases, and varying the square footage they occupied. There were never any unanticipated expenses, and the charging rates were set for breakeven. As Ted put it:

'There was an interesting example of the effects of this system. Altex had a total of 5.2 acres of land, of which approx. 3 were tie-downs that accommodated approx. 60 aircraft. The Fuel Department always wanted more space because it meant that they could accommodate more transient aircraft. The Flight School always wanted more space to make it easier to manage their comings and goings. The Shop always wanted more space as a service and convenience to customers leaving or dropping off aircraft to be serviced.

Before the departments were charged for the area they occupied, there was no way to intelligently resolve this conflict. Bill Dickerson, the former owner, or Sarah would have to make what was essentially an arbitrary decision. When we showed up, however, there was a definite price to be paid for demanding more space – and with the manager's bonus system, 10% of that price came right out of the manager's pocket.

The result was that we had very few of these discussions that did not reach a 'natural' compromise. And when, over time, each department truly needed more space and was more and more willing to pay the rent, we raised the rent until demand equaled supply. It was wonderful to see a free market in action!'

The monthly financial statements given the Altex department managers are shown in Exhibits 4–8. These are the same reports Ted gave his banker. Although there is provision for including budget figures, no budgets were projected.

The task guidance system

As an aid towards educating departmental managers in the management of their operations and for keeping them aware of their activities, responsibilities and results, Frank and Ted instituted a Daily

Department Report (DDR) which required the departments to submit internally consistent operating and accounting information. Each department kept the customer ledger cards and central accounting kept only receivables control accounts which would balance to each department's detail. The managers would account for their daily activity in units and in dollars. As an example, the DDR for the Flight School is shown in Exhibit 9 and its projections described as follows.

Flight School's DDR is prepared each morning by 11.00 am and reports the activity of the preceding day. The first set of entries on the report (Exhibit 9) details the sales made by the Flight Department by each type of sales. The total represents all the revenue that should be credited to Sales (1).

The second set of numbers categorizes the flow of funds into the Flight Department by type – cash, credit card slips or reductions in block accounts* or leaseback payments due. The total of these funds (indicated by (2) on the DDR) are the charges (debits), to cash, accounts receivable or the block accounts payable.

The final group of items details the direct costs incurred in the production of revenue; these were:

1. The expenses incurred in utilizing leased training aircraft. These were, by contract, a fixed amount per actual hour of aircraft use.
2. The wages due the flight instructors. These instructors were paid a contractual amount for each hour of instruction given. If the flight student was charged $12.00 per instructional hour by Altex, Altex would then owe the instructor $8.00 for that hour.
3. Cost of supplies – the direct cost of the items sold in the Pilot Shop.

The total (3) represented the direct costs of the Flight Department for that day.

Cash received in the mail and cash collected by the departments were deposited daily. Photocopies of the checks were given to the departments for identification of source and inclusion on their DDRs. Ted commented:

'We would deposit the check and send the photocopies around to the departments. Sometimes a cheque would come into Altex Aviation from someone

---

* A block account represented prepaid flying lessons or aircraft rental. Cash was received in advance and recorded as an accounts payable by Altex. The customer's flying activities were then charged (debited) to this account as they occurred. Altex leased most of its instructional aircraft from private owners. Altex contracted to pay them so much per hour for use of the aircraft. Some leases were 'wet', meaning that the aircraft owner furnished the fuel. Others were 'dry', meaning that Altex paid for the fuel used.

and no-one would know who it was. Sometimes it would take 2 or 3 weeks to find out what it was for. It was passed around the various departments but, in the meantime, we had the money. We couldn't account for it so we put it in a little suspense account. And, interestingly enough, sometimes no one accounted for it and it became administrative profit.

The detail of charge slips, photocopies of cheques and physical currency would be attached to the DDR and by 11.00 am each department would turn them into Accounting – with sales balanced against receipts, inventory against fuel flows, and receivables proven-out. There were still errors but they got corrected at the department level, although at least one department had to hire an additional person to do the DDR.

The system left the Accounting Department with a simple task. They had DDRs from each department but only one sales figure from each. Thus, their postings were trivial. All they had to do was to post the DDRs and then worry about other corporate issues – taxes and that sort of thing. Thus, we only needed one person in Accounting, and the detail was where it should be – in the departments where it could be used.'

Similar systems were put in place for the Flight School, Service Department and Parts Department. For example, in Parts, a physical card was maintained for each inventory item. To purchase, the Parts Department would issue a purchase order. When the parts and invoice arrived, the total inventory balance was increased by the invoice amount, and a copy of the invoice was sent to the Parts Department. They would update their card files with the units and the costs. Similarly, they would decrease the balances for sales made. At the end of each month, Accounting would balance its control account against the sums shown on the parts cards.

Another control was the requirement for each department to submit ageing of their accounts receivables to Accounting. Accounting would compare these amounts against their control totals. Ted commented: 'We balanced the ageing provided by the departments against the books in central accounting down to the penny. That gave us our basic control.'

Aircraft sales
While Ted was implementing the control system, educating the managers, dealing with the creditors, and establishing a better relationship with the bank, Frank was dealing with Aircraft Sales. Frank began by re-establishing Altex's relationship with the Piper Aircraft Corporation. He convinced them that Altex was on its way to financial stability and could not only sell, but be able to inventory the requisite number of aircraft to maintain dealer status. Frank negotiated the terms with Piper, involving Ted only with Piper's reporting requirements.

A few years before, Altex had been the largest Piper dealer in the territory, so Piper was interested in the potential of the new management. Things went well until Piper brought up the subject of their standard accounting reports. Frank and Ted were willing to commit to purchase five aircraft in the first 6 months, but they balked, at the standardized reporting requirements which Ted characterized as 'factory oriented'. He stated:

'I wanted to be basically independent. The reports weren't all that onerous. It might have been childish, but it was partly, "I own this place and no one is going to tell me what to do". It was also partly a feeling that I wanted to establish an equal relationship with Piper. I did not want to come to them as a supplicant. For the past several years, Altex had always been begging Daddy Piper for hand-outs. I wanted to establish a relationship with them that was one of equals. "We have different jobs to do. You help me. I help you." So it was psychological but also I didn't want to waste the time of my people on something that I did not think would be productive. I told them they could have access to any of our reports that they wanted. I said, "Here are our forms. If there is any information that you would like that is not here, we would be happy to supply it, and if you want to transfer this information to a Piper form, go ahead. But we think all the information is here." They didn't like it, but they bought it. I think Frank worked pretty hard on that one.'

After obtaining the Piper franchise, Frank rehired the old salesmen but personally shepherded through the first aircraft sales. The first one was, in Frank's word, 'memorable'. He continued:

'Our first sale was to a local Chevrolet dealer. He wanted to buy the aircraft, but he wouldn't pay for it until it arrived at San Miguel saying, "In my business, you don't pay for a car until you see it". Now we had to pay for it when we picked it up at the factory, so I asked Ted how we stood. He said, "We have enough money although if he doesn't pay for it, we won't make the next payroll, and we will be out $40 000 for however long it takes to get the airplane from Vero Beach to here. But I'm willing to do it. Go do whatever you have to do." So we did. I engaged the son of the aircraft salesman to fly the aeroplane. Unfortunately, there was horrible weather that grounded him in Tuscaloosa, Alabama, for a week – thunderstorms and everything. I nearly lost my mind. I had committed every last cent the company had, and it was sitting in Tuscaloosa. That's how tight things were.'

Profitability of the aircraft sales activity proved to be highly variable between months. For example, while losses were shown in May and August 1972 (see Exhibits 7 and 8), several very high-margin sales, accounting for nearly $100 000 in operating profit, were made in the period June–July 1972.

Exhibit 1

ALTEX Balance Sheets ('000s)

Assets	8/26/71*	1/1/72†	Liabilities and net worth	8/26/71	1/1/72
Cash and Marketable Securities	$ 8	$ 88	Accounts Payable – Trade	$ 62	$ 50
Accounts Receivable	25	49	Accounts Payable – Phillips Oil	112	116
Contracts Receivable – current	51‡	15	Contracts Payable – Current	31	33
Financing Commissions Due	20	20	Customer Deposits	–	2
Receivables from Officers and Employees	68	–	Notes Payable	88	31
Other Receivables	14	–	Accrued Expenses	32	35
Inventory:			Deferred Block Time	5	4
Aircraft	33	103	Other Current Liabilities	2	2
Parts and Flight Supplies	50	45	Total Current Liabilities	332	273
Fuel	13	25	Contract Payable – long-term	41	90
Work-in-Process	7	2	Long-term debt	424	34
Prepaid Expenses	7	30			
Total Current Assets	296	377	Total Liabilities	797	397
Fixed Assets (net)	437	27	Net Worth	(17)	62
Contracts Receivable – long-term	–	26	Total Liabilities and Net Worth	$780	$459
Investments	29	29			
Other	18	–			
Total Assets	$780	$459			

*Fiscal year-end before purchase.
† Just after purchase.
‡ Not split out between current and long-term; no room on Piper aircraft form to do so.

Personnel management

In the second month of Ted and Frank's ownership, Will Leonard, the manager of the Fuel Department resigned. There were two reasons: firstly, a local newspaper had written up Altex Aviation and the new boy wonder owners in a way that seemed to disparage the former owner – a close friend of Will's. The second reason involved Ted and Frank's philosophy of management. As Ted related it:

'One of the fuel drivers came to us about two weeks after we bought the company and said, "The former owner never let us wear mustaches or beards or anything like that. How do you guys feel about mustaches or beards?"

Now there was a lot of feeling about facial hair and long hair during that period and the fuel drivers were in contact with the public. Frank and I wanted to say, "We agree with the former owners". But we were consistent Harvard Business School people and we said, "As long as it does not affect your work performance, you can do anything you want". As a result, beards started cropping up all over the place. The manager of the Fuel Department rightly felt that he had been undercut, and he quit. We really blew that. We were dumb – just from pure inexperience, naivete. He was not that valuable, but that is not the way to get rid of a man – forcing him to quit in a huff.'

Management style

In running the company, Ted took an active role both through long hours of planning and managing and also through learning and doing. He learned to fly and got a multi-engine commercial license, changed the oil in the shop, and worked on the engines. It was as Ted said:

'. . . a part of the process of being an avuncular, emotional leader. In the first couple of years, I deliberately set out to make my role a teacher. The first thing I did in my office was to put up a blackboard and arrange the furniture, so that there was a sofa facing the blackboard and a sidechair canted towards the blackboard. My desk was at right angles to the blackboard – all of us could see it. When departmental managers would come to me with problems, rather than focusing on the problem, we would talk about the process. I would say, "Where is your accounting data? Where are your profit centre reports? What do your profit centre reports tell you about this problem? What thought processes did you go through to extract information from the profit centre reports that would help you solve this problem? What alternatives did you consider?" And I did this in a typical Socratic teaching process. Through Frank's and my personal involvement in the company and through this teaching approach, we could not only obviate Frank's forecast of bankruptcy in 3 months, but we could rely on our managers and build for the future.'

Questions
1. What do you think of the management control philosophy Frank and Ted were trying to implement?
2. Do you think the system they designed will work?
   (a) With four major departments and a sales level of $2 million?
   (b) With growth?
3. Do you share Ted's opinion as to the importance of a control system?
4. What do you think will happen to Altex? To Frank? To Ted?

Exhibit 2
ALTEX AVIATION Pre-Purchase Organizational Chart

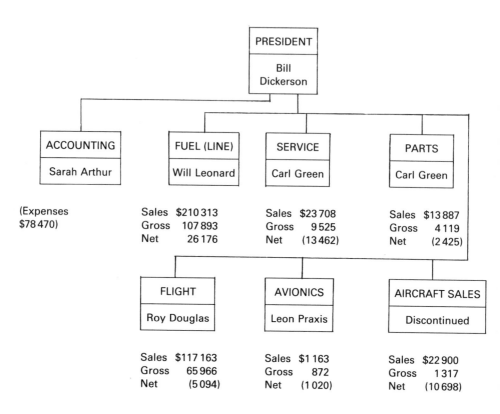

Note:
Sales, Gross Profit Margin and Net Income were for the 4 months preceding purchase:
September–December 1971. Profit was calculated from the extant accounting system
which fully allocated administrative costs. Comparable figures for the 31 August 1970
fiscal year were: Sales $2 073 000, Gross $657 000, Net ($109 000).

Exhibit 3(a)

ALTEX Physical Facilities 29 December 1971

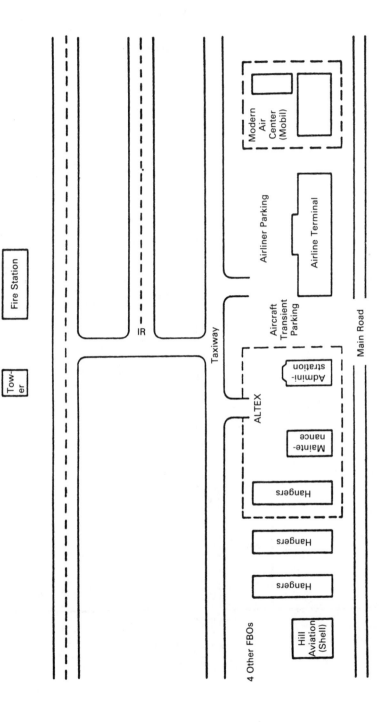

Exhibit 3(b)

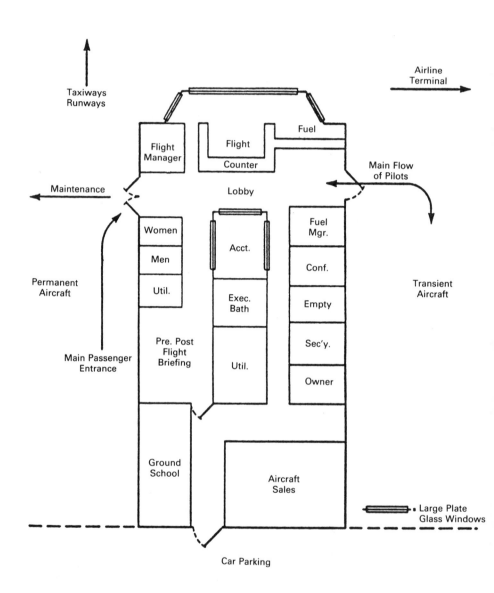

Exhibit 4

ALTEX Summary Balance Sheets (at end of month indicated) ('000s)

Assets	Feb. 1972	May 1972	Aug. 1972
Cash and Marketable Securities	$ 67	$112	$129
Accounts Receivable	52	73	91
Contracts Receivable – current	35	4	4
Finance Accounts Receivable	12	12	12
Inventory:			
Aircraft	103	144	183
Parts	52	52	53
Fuel	20	19	15
Work in process and other	0	2	8
Prepaid Expenses	30	32	39
Total Current Assets	371	450	534
Contracts Receivable – long term	5	4	3
Fixed Assets (net)	28	27	28
Investments and Other	29	32	37
Total Assets	$433	$513	$602

Liabilities and net worth	Feb. 1972	May 1972	Aug. 1972
Accounts Payable – Trade	$ 39	$ 38	$ 47
Accounts Payable – Phillips Oil	103	102	52
Contracts Payable – Current	34	33	46
Customer Deposits	1	4	1
Notes Payable	29	28	27
Accrued Expenses	30	35	14
Deferred Block Time	14	21	20
Total Current Liabilities	250	261	207
Contracts Payable – long-term	85	85	104
Long-term debt	34	104	104
Total Liabilities	369	450	415
Net Worth	64	63	187
Total Liabilities and Net Worth	$433	$513	$602

Exhibit 5

ALTEX Summary Monthly Income and Operating Statements (for period indicated) ('000s)

Corporate summary	Jan.–Feb. 1972	May 1972	August 1972
Sales	$181	$164	$162
Cost of Sales	146	133	113
Gross Margin	35	31	49
Total Expenses	24	28	29
Operating Profit (Loss)	$ 11	$ 3	$ 20
Profit (Loss) by Activity			
Parts	$ (1)	$ (2)	$ 1
Radio*	(2)	–	–
Service	0	(2)	4
Flight School	3	4	3
Flight Supplies	1	(1)	0
Tie-Downs and Hangars	(1)	0	0
Fuel Hauling	(1)	1	2
Retail Avgas	0	(2)	2
Retail Jet Fuel		4	3
Wholesale Fuel	4	7	11
Aircraft Sales	3	(4)	(6)
Car Rentals	(1)	–	–
Charter	–	0	2
Unrecovered Administrative Costs (+ = gain)	6	(2)	(2)
Total Operating Profit	$ 11	$ 3	$ 20
Other Income	0	1	1
Extraordinary Items	(22)	(8)	(2)
TOTAL INCOME	$ (11)	$ (4)	$ 19

*Merged with Service Department in March 1972.

Exhibit 6

ALTEX Summary Income Statements by Activity (January–February 1972) ('000s)

	Parts	Radio	Service	Flight school	Flight supplies	Tie-downs and hangers	Fuel hauling	Retail fuel*	Wholesale fuel	Aircraft sales	Car rentals†
Sales	4.7	0	11.0	23.4	1.7	3.8	2.7	50.0	5.4	87.9	0.7
Cost of Product	3.4	1.4	2.3	10.4	‡	1.2	1.6	37.5		76.4	0.6
Salaries and Commissions	0.5		3.0	5.7	0.3	0.6	0.6	5.8	0.5	0.5	0.3
Payroll-related Expenses	0.1		0.6	1.1		0.3	0.1	0.6			
	4.0	1.4	5.9	17.2	0.3	2.1	2.3	43.9	0.5	76.9	0.9
Gross Margin	0.7	(1.4)	5.1	6.2	1.4	1.7	0.4	6.1	4.9	11.0	(0.2)
Other Expenses	1.6	0.1	5.2	3.7	0.8	2.7	1.6	6.0	0.5	7.9	0.2
Operating Profit	(0.9)	(1.5)	(0.1)	2.5	0.6	(1.0)	(1.2)	0.1	4.4	3.1	(0.4)

* Avgas and jet fuel.
† Discontinued in April.
‡ Could not be captured in January–February because inventory control system not yet in place.

Exhibit 7

ALTEX Summary Income Statements by Activity (May 1972) ('000s)

	Parts	Service	Flight school	Flight supplies	Tie-downs and hangars	Fuel hauling	Retail Avgas	Retail jet fuel	Wholesale fuel	Aircraft sales	Charter*
Sales	4.8	8.2	39.4	2.0	4.4	3.8	26.4	18.9	9.6	45.1	1.6
Cost of Product	3.8	0.1	20.5	1.4	1.3	0.8	18.0	13.2		42.9†	1.4
Direct Payroll	0.7	4.3	8.9	0.4	0.4	0.8	4.8	1.3	1.0		
Commissions							1.0				
Payroll-related Expenses	0.1	0.7	1.1		0.2	0.6	0.8	0.2	0.1		
	4.6	5.1	30.5	1.8	1.9	2.2	24.6	14.7	1.1	42.9	1.4
Gross Margin	0.2	3.1	8.9	0.2	2.5	1.6	1.8	4.2	8.5	2.2	0.2
Other Expenses	1.7	4.8	4.8	0.8	2.7	0.5	4.4	0.6	1.6	6.2	0.1
Operating Profit	(1.5)	(1.7)	4.1	(0.6)	(0.2)	1.1	(2.6)	3.6	6.9	(4.0)	0.1

*Charter activity started in May.
†Costs not broken out after March.

Exhibit 8

ALTEX Summary Income Statements by Activity (August 1972) ('000s)

	Parts	Service	Flight school	Flight supplies	Tie-downs and hangars	Fuel hauling	Retail Avgas	Retail jet fuel	Wholesale fuel	Aircraft sales	Charter
Sales	10.1	16.4	33.4	2.0	4.9	4.3	28.6	13.7	14.0	22.3	12.3
Cost of Product	6.3	3.0	17.4	1.2	1.0	0.8	20.2	11.7		19.9	6.8
Salaries and Commissions	0.6	4.0	7.5	0.3	0.6	0.7	4.6	0.8	1.0		0.6
Payroll-related Expenses	0.1	0.8	0.8	0.1	0.2	0.7	1.8				
	7.0	7.8	25.7	1.6	1.8	2.2	26.6	12.5	1.0	19.9	7.4
Gross Margin	3.1	8.6	7.7	0.4	3.1	2.1	2.0	1.2	13.0	2.4	4.9
Other Expenses	2.0	4.7	5.2	0.8	2.8	0.4	(0.2)*	(1.7)*	1.5	8.6	2.5
Operating Profit	1.1	3.9	2.5	(0.4)	0.3	1.7	2.2	2.9	11.5	(6.2)	2.4

*Includes Inventory Adjustment (end of year).

Exhibit 9
FLIGHT DEPARTMENT DAILY REPORT

DATE: _____

SALES

Primary Ground School . . . .   _____

Flight Instruction (Wait, Ground Training, Pre/Post) . . . .   _____

Leaseback Owner's Rental + Employees Rental . . . . . . (____)   _____
                          + Cost of Sales

Rental (Solo) . . . .   _____

Flight Supplies and Over-counter Sale-Retail Sales . . . .   _____

Sales Tax Collected . . . .   _____

Check Rides . . . .   _____

Waiver . . . .   _____

Mexican Insurance . . . .   _____

Car Wash and Aircraft Wash + Tie-downs . . . .   _____

Student Tuition Refund Fee . . . .   _____

Enrollment Fee + X-C Dues . . . .   _____

Interest Service Charges . . . .   _____

RECEIPTS   TOTAL $_____

Cash or Cheques . . . .   _____

Credit Card Payment . . . . (Phillips_____) . . . . (AX_____) . . . .   _____

Block Accounts and Block Account Supplies . . . .   _____

Altex Charges and Altex Charge Supplies . . . .   _____

Master Charge and Visa . . . .   _____

Leaseback Refunds . . . .   _____

DIRECT COST OF SALES   TOTAL $_____
Leaseback Expenses . . . .   _____
Instructor Wages . . . .
Cost of Supplies Sold Today . . . .   _____

                                           _____

                                  TOTAL $_____

APPENDIX 1   PROFIT CENTRE REPORTS Fuel Department
31 August 1972

RETAIL JET FUEL (August 1972)

	THIS MONTH			2/1/72 TO DATE		
	ACTUAL	BUDGET	VARIANCE	ACTUAL	BUDGET	VARIANCE
SALES	13 686			69 527		
Direct Payroll Commissions Overtime and Vacations	797	n/a		4 502		
Fringe at % Payroll Taxes Cost of Product	12 11 688			160 290 51 659		
GROSS MARGIN	1 189			12 916		
EXPENSES Supervisory Payroll Commissions Fringe at %	341 10			1 796 54		
Payroll Taxes Administrative Use of Assets	547 41			3 339 41		
Advertising Demonstration Flights* Bad Debts						
Telephone, etc. Donations, Dues, etc. Freight, Postage, etc.						
Insurance Inventory Adjustment Maintenance	(3 079)			(5 125)		
Professional Services Rent Supplies	200			800		
Tie-downs† Travel, Entertainment Utilities						
Vehicles Warranty Adjustments	215			860		
Cash O/S Miscellaneous	7			20 7		
TOTAL EXPENSES	(1 718)			1 792		
TOTAL PROFIT (LOSS)	2 907			11 124		
COST OF PRODUCT DETAIL Primary Cost‡ Freight, Delivery§ Taxes¶						
Other Costs ———— ———— ————						
LESS BREAKDOWN‖ ———— ———— ———— ————						

BREAKDOWN OF ADMINISTRATIVE
CHARGES   RETAIL JET FUEL (August 1972)

		RATE		CHARGE
TOTAL DIRECT PAYROLL	$ _____	__ %	=	$ _____
(incl. commissions, overtime, etc.)				
TOTAL SUPERVISORY PAYROLL	$ _____	__ %	=	$ _____
		TOTAL		$ _____

BREAKDOWN OF CHARGES FOR USE OF ASSETS

ITEM	AMOUNT	RATE		CHARGE
Accounts Receivable (less than 60 days)	$ _____	1.0%	=	$ _____
Accounts Receivable (60–90 days)	$ _____	3.0%	=	$ _____
Accounts Receivable (over 90 days)	$ _____	6.0%	=	$ _____
Inventory	$ __2 752__	1.5%	=	$ __41__
Market Value of Physical Assets Used				
_____	$ _____	1.5%	=	$ _____
_____	$ _____	1.5%	=	$ _____
_____	$ _____	1.5%	=	$ _____
_____	$ _____	1.5%	=	$ _____
_____	$ _____	1.5%	=	$ _____
_____	$ _____	1.5%	=	$ _____
TOTAL				$ __41__

*For any use by any department that uses flight school planes for demonstration or promotion purposes. This amount is the same as if a customer rented one of our aircraft and is credited to flight school sales.
†This is a charge for aircraft under your control that used tie-down space and appears as part of the revenue of the tie-down department.
‡Primary cost is:
   Parts: invoice cost of parts sold
   Service: transfer cost of parts used or installed
   Flight: cost of leasebacks
   Fuel: cost of fuel and oil
   Sales: cost of aircraft.
§All freight and delivery charges are added to the inventory cost of products and become an expense when the product is sold. For the fuel department, PUC rates are used.
¶This includes all taxes that we must pay for the products used, primarily excise taxes. These taxes are carried in inventory and are expensed when the product is sold.
‖Each departmental head can specify how he wants his sales broken down. This sub-category should be used for different activities that are not sufficiently separable to warrant becoming a separate profit centre. For example, service might be sub-divided into flat rate sales versus time and material sales. The flight school department might wish to separate instruction from charter.

RETAIL AVGAS (August 1972)

	THIS MONTH			2/1/72 TO DATE		
	ACTUAL	*BUDGET*	*VARIANCE*	*ACTUAL*	*BUDGET*	*VARIANCE*
SALES	28 623	n/a	n/a	105 132		
Direct Payroll	4 605			18 610		
Commissions	910			3 596		
Overtime and Vacations	229			481		
Fringe at %	252			921		
Payroll Taxes	403			1 814		
Cost of Product	20 234			27 142		
GROSS MARGIN	1 990			7 568		
EXPENSES	340			1 813		
Supervisory Payroll						
Commissions	10			55		
Fringe at %						
Payroll Taxes						
Administrative	1 145			4 971		
Use of Assets	376			1 562		
Advertising						
Demonstration Flights*						
Bad Debts						
Telephone, etc.						
Donations, Dues, etc.						
Freight, Postage, etc.				13		
Insurance	200			401		
Inventory Adjustment	(3 935)			(2 042)		
Maintenance	278			1 064		
Professional Services						
Rent	239			596		
Supplies	182			977		
Tie-downs†						
Travel, Entertainment						
Utilities						
Vehicles	865			3 999		
Warranty						
Adjustments						
Cash O/S						
Miscellaneous	68			96		
TOTAL EXPENSES	(232)			13 505		
TOTAL PROFIT (LOSS)	2 222			(5 937)		
COST OF PRODUCT DETAIL						
Primary Cost‡						
Freight, Delivery§						
Taxes¶						
Other Costs						
_____						
_____						
_____						
LESS BREAKDOWN‖						
_____						
_____						
_____						
_____						

BREAKDOWN OF ADMINISTRATIVE CHARGES   *RETAIL AVGAS* (August 1972)

	RATE	CHARGE
TOTAL DIRECT PAYROLL (incl. commissions, overtime, etc.)	$ _____ __ % =	$ _____
TOTAL SUPERVISORY PAYROLL	$ _____ __ % =	$ _____
	TOTAL	$ _____

BREAKDOWN OF CHARGES FOR USE OF ASSETS

ITEM	AMOUNT	RATE		CHARGE
Accounts Receivable (less than 60 days)	$ __6 111__	1.0%	=	$ __61__
Accounts Receivable (60–90 days)	$ __1 903__	3.0%	=	$ __57__
Accounts Receivable (over 90 days)	$ __1 032__	6.0%	=	$ __62__
Inventory	$ __9 187__	1.5%	=	$ __138__
Market Value of Physical Assets Used				
_____	$ __3 902__	1.5%	=	$ __58__
_____	$ _____	1.5%	=	$ _____
_____	$ _____	1.5%	=	$ _____
_____	$ _____	1.5%	=	$ _____
_____	$ _____	1.5%	=	$ _____
_____	$ _____	1.5%	=	$ _____
TOTAL				$ __376__

*For any use by any department that uses flight school planes for demonstration or promotion purposes. This amount is the same as if a customer rented one of our aircraft and is credited to flight school sales.

† This is a charge for aircraft under your control that used tie-down space and appears as part of the revenue of the tie-down department.

‡ Primary cost is:
    Parts: invoice cost of parts sold
    Service: transfer cost of parts used or installed
    Flight: cost of leasebacks
    Fuel: cost of fuel and oil
    Sales: cost of aircraft.

§ All freight and delivery charges are added to the inventory cost of products and become an expense when the product is sold. For the fuel department, PUC rates are used.

¶ This includes all taxes that we must pay for the products used, primarily excise taxes. These taxes are carried in inventory and are expensed when the product is sold.

‖ Each departmental head can specify how he wants his sales broken down. This sub-category should be used for different activities that are not sufficiently separable to warrant becoming a separate profit centre. For example, service might be sub-divided into flat rate sales versus time and material sales. The flight school department might wish to separate instruction from charter.

WHOLESALE JET FUEL (August 1972)

	THIS MONTH			2/1/72 TO DATE		
	ACTUAL	BUDGET	VARIANCE	ACTUAL	BUDGET	VARIANCE
SALES	13 977	8 200	(5 777)	66 746		
Direct Payroll	981			6 716		
Commissions						
Overtime and Vacations						
Fringe at %	39			275		
Payroll Taxes						
Cost of Product				173		
GROSS MARGIN	12 957	6 900	6 507	59 582		
EXPENSES						
Supervisory Payroll	84			882		
Commissions						
Fringe at %	3			28		
Payroll Taxes						
Administrative	559			3 278		
Use of Assets	124			622		
Advertising						
Demonstration Flights*						
Bad Debts						
Telephone, etc.						
Donations, Dues, etc.						
Freight, Postage, etc.						
Insurance						
Inventory Adjustment				(231)		
Maintenance						
Professional Services				1 113		
Rent	159					
Supplies						
Tie-downs†						
Travel, Entertainment						
Utilities						
Vehicles	575			2 875		
Warranty						
Adjustments						
Cash O/S						
Miscellaneous						
TOTAL EXPENSES	1 504	1 500	(4)	(8 567)		
TOTAL PROFIT (LOSS)	11 453	5 400	6 053	51 015		
COST OF PRODUCT DETAIL						
Primary Cost‡						
Freight, Delivery§						
Taxes¶						
Other Costs						
_____						
_____						
_____						
LESS BREAKDOWN‖						
_____						
_____						
_____						
_____						

BREAKDOWN OF ADMINISTRATIVE
CHARGES   RETAIL WHOLESALE (August 1972)

		RATE		CHARGE
TOTAL DIRECT PAYROLL (incl. commissions, overtime, etc.)	$ _____	__ %	=	$ _____
TOTAL SUPERVISORY PAYROLL	$ _____	__ %	=	$ _____
		TOTAL		$ _____

BREAKDOWN OF CHARGES FOR USE OF ASSETS

ITEM	AMOUNT	RATE		CHARGE
Accounts Receivable (less than 60 days)	$ _____	1.0%	=	$ _____
Accounts Receivable (60–90 days)	$ _____	3.0%	=	$ _____
Accounts Receivable (over 90 days)	$ _____	6.0%	=	$ _____
Inventory Market Value of Physical Assets Used	$ 8 257	1.5%	=	$ 124
_____	$ _____	1.5%	=	$ _____
_____	$ _____	1.5%	=	$ _____
_____	$ _____	1.5%	=	$ _____
_____	$ _____	1.5%	=	$ _____
_____	$ _____	1.5%	=	$ _____
_____	$ _____	1.5%	=	$ _____
TOTAL				$ _____

*For any use by any department that uses flight school planes for demonstration or promotion purposes. This amount is the same as if a customer rented one of our aircraft and is credited to flight school sales.
†This is a charge for aircraft under your control that used tie-down space and appears as part of the revenue of the tie-down department.
‡Primary cost is:
   Parts: invoice cost of parts sold
   Service: transfer cost of parts used or installed
   Flight: cost of leasebacks
   Fuel: cost of fuel and oil
   Sales: cost of aircraft.
§All freight and delivery charges are added to the inventory cost of products and become an expense when the product is sold. For the fuel department, PUC rates are used.
¶This includes all taxes that we must pay for the products used, primarily excise taxes. These taxes are carried in inventory and are expensed when the product is sold.
‖Each departmental head can specify how he wants his sales broken down. This sub-category should be used for different activities that are not sufficiently separable to warrant becoming a separate profit centre. For example, service might be sub-divided into flat rate sales versus time and material sales. The flight school department might wish to separate instruction from charter.

FUEL HAULING (August 1972)

	THIS MONTH			2/1/72 TO DATE		
	ACTUAL	BUDGET	VARIANCE	ACTUAL	BUDGET	VARIANCE
SALES	4 335	3 700	635	24 994		
Direct Payroll Commissions Overtime and Vacations	736 568			5 037 2 286		
Fringe at % Payroll Taxes Cost of Product	52 67 775			307 568 6 470		
GROSS MARGIN	2 137	1 600	537	10 326		
EXPENSES Supervisory Payroll Commissions Fringe at %						
Payroll Taxes Administrative Use of Assets	173			-1 197		
Advertising Demonstration Flights* Bad Debts						
Telephone, etc. Donations, Dues, etc. Freight, Postage, etc.				397		
Insurance Inventory Adjustment Maintenance	139			35 1 339		
Professional Services Rent Supplies	80			559 711		
Tie-downs† Travel, Entertainment Utilities						
Vehicles Warranty Adjustments						
Cash O/S Miscellaneous				45		
TOTAL EXPENSES	392	700	308	4 283		
TOTAL PROFIT (LOSS)	1 745	900	845	6 043		
COST OF PRODUCT DETAIL Primary Cost‡ Freight, Delivery§ Taxes¶						
Other Costs ——————— ——————— ———————						
LESS BREAKDOWN‖ ——————— ——————— ——————— ———————						

TIE-DOWNS AND HANGARS (August 1972)

	THIS MONTH			2/1/72 TO DATE		
	ACTUAL	*BUDGET*	*VARIANCE*	*ACTUAL*	*BUDGET*	*VARIANCE*
SALES	4 923	4 800	(123)	31 984		
Direct Payroll	649			3 220		
Commissions						
Overtime and Vacations	134			964		
Fringe at %	31			175		
Payroll Taxes	26			297		
Cost of Product	1 000			8 259		
GROSS MARGIN	3 083	3 000	83	19 069		
EXPENSES						
Supervisory Payroll	85			534		
Commissions						
Fringe at %	3			17		
Payroll Taxes						
Administrative	197			1 587		
Use of Assets						
Advertising						
Demonstration Flights*						
Bad Debts						
Telephone, etc.						
Donations, Dues, etc.						
Freight, Postage, etc.						
Insurance						
Inventory Adjustment						
Maintenance						
Professional Services						
Rent	2 467			17 269		
Supplies						
Tie-downs†						
Travel, Entertainment						
Utilities						
Vehicles						
Warranty						
Adjustments						
Cash O/S						
Miscellaneous						
TOTAL EXPENSES	2 752	2 800	48	19 407		
TOTAL PROFIT (LOSS)	331	200	131	(338)		
COST OF PRODUCT DETAIL						
Primary Cost‡						
Freight, Delivery§						
Taxes¶						
Other Costs						
_____						
_____						
_____						
LESS BREAKDOWN‖						
_____						
_____						
_____						
_____						

HCC INDUSTRIES

Until 1987, HCC Industries, a manufacturer of hermetically sealed electronic connection devices and microelectronic packages, operated with a philosophy of having 'stretch' performance targets for its operating managers. This philosophy was based on the belief that aggressive targets would motivate the managers to perform at their highest possible levels. In planning for the fiscal year 1988, however, this philosophy was changed. Andy Goldfarb, HCC's CEO explained:

[A large consulting firm] designed our old budgeting philosophy and the incentive compensation plan associated with it, but I'm not sure they understand companies smaller than the *Fortune 500*. They gave us 'the great incentive plan of 1982', but it hasn't worked very well.

The problem is that if you're forecasting for stretch targets, you must be thinking optimistically. This concept might work well at some companies of a certain size that understand their markets well enough and are in a position to influence it. But we haven't been in that position. We have just been taking orders, not doing marketing. In the meantime, the corporation has been missing its plans. For 4 years now, we have had some divisions do well and some do poorly, but the corporation never achieved its targets. As a public company, we need that to happen. Also people at corporate haven't earned any bonuses.

Now we've changed our philosophy. We want to judge people first on whether they are hitting a 'minimum performance standard'. Only then can they start earning extra rewards. We've asked our managers to submit budgets with targets that are realistic and achievable, and to make sure the managers have gotten the message about the change, we made it clear to them that missing budget now could cost them their jobs.

Most of our general managers didn't like the change when we announced it. They worried that bonuses aren't automatic and that the amounts they could earn weren't large enough. They might be right, and we may make some changes. And as I look at the actual results for the first quarter of FY 1988, I'm concerned that we haven't yet implemented the new concept quite as we intended. Some of our divisions have missed their minimum performance standards by large margins.

The company

HCC was a small publicly held corporation, headquartered in Encino, California, USA, that designed, manufactured and marketed her-

Research Assistant Lourdes Ferreira and Associate Professor Kenneth A. Merchant prepared this case as the basis for class discussion rather than to illustrate either effective or ineffective handling of an administrative situation.

metically sealed electronic connection devices and microelectronic packages. Revenues totalled $36 million in the fiscal year 1987 (ended 28 March 1987). (A 5-year summary of financial data is presented in Exhibit 1.)

HCC was an industry leader in electronic connectors requiring glass-to-metal and ceramic-to-metal seals, and particularly those requiring unusual or close tolerance machining and the sealing of exotic metals. Many of the companies' products were used for aerospace and military applications requiring high reliability or operation in adverse conditions (such as high temperatures or pressures).

The company was organized into 4 primary operating divisions, each run by a general manager (see Exhibit 2). The general managers were each responsible for all the division's business functions, except that the division controllers reported on a solid line to Chris Bateman, HCC's Chief Financial Officer. Andy Goldfarb explained:

'The division controllers are paid to be controllers. We don't want them to be motivated to 'cook the books'. That is a danger because we base bonuses on division results and because they work at quite a distance from headquarters and naturally develop an emotional attachment to the people with whom they work. The solid-line reporting to corporate helps remind them that their primary job is to protect the corporation's assets.'

Three of the divisions – Hermetic Seal, Glasseal, and Sealtron – produced connectors of various types. Hermetite produced custom-designed, microelectronic packages. Exhibit 3 shows some typical products, and Exhibit 4 provides some summary information about each division.

The three connector divisions were similar, in that they were profitable but growing slowly. Their industry was highly fragmented. The number of potential customers was huge because many products used electrical connectors. Many small competitors served some portions of the market. The connector divisions did not have a solid base of knowledge about their competitors' strengths and weaknesses, their market shares and forthcoming business possibilities because of the dearth of readily available marketing information and limited size of their marketing staffs. Thus, it was difficult for them to make accurate sales forecasts.

The primary difference among the connector divisions was in the degree of standardization of their product lines. Sealtron was at one extreme, as it produced standardized connectors in relatively large volumes. Hermetic Seal, on the other hand, operated primarily as a job shop which designed and produced small batches of custom connectors, predominantly for military customers. Glasseal's operations were between the two extremes.

Hermetite, which produced microelectronic packages, was different from the connector divisions in several important ways. Firstly, its market and competitors were relatively well defined. Customer contacts were typically made at trade shows, and most customers and competitors were well known. There were five main competitors in the industry, and Hermetite's market share was third or fourth in rank. Secondly, Hermetite's potential for growth was great. In contrast with the connector market, which was stable, the packaging market was growing at 20–30% per year. Thirdly, it faced tremendous price competition. A new competitor had entered the market in 1985 and had lowered prices to buy market share. The existing competitors responded by lowering their prices to attempt to fill their production capacity. Fourthly, Hermetite faced significant production technology and control problems. The production processes were complex, and the division had had instability in its engineering and production organizations. This had resulted in half of its $3 million backlog being delinquent, even though on-time delivery was an important competitive factor. Because of the price competition and the production problems, Hermetite had been operating at a loss since before it was acquired in August 1985.

The divisions were all largely self-contained and independent of one another. They served different customers and had different part number systems, product standards and accounting and information systems. Corporate management had never tried to force, or even encourage, synergy between the divisions. As Chris Bateman, HCC's CFO, explained it: 'We want to let the managers be managers. They will do the best for you, that way. Decentralization is a sound business concept.'

Corporate staff had always monitored non-operating decisions closely (e.g., corporate authorization was necessary for any capital acquisition in excess of $500). But they had been providing few direct services to the divisions. This was starting to change. In 1987, a corporate marketing function was created to assist the divisions with market research, advertising and promotions. And a corporate engineering service function was started to develop new product designs that might be used by any or all of the connector divisions. Chris Bateman observed that the division managers were generally not receptive to receiving this support: 'Some of them say that corporate is now dictating when they should brush their teeth.'

Standards for evaluating the divisions' performances

The divisions' performances were evaluated in terms of seven performance areas: (1) profit before tax, (2) bookings, (3) shipments,

(4) returns (as a percentage of total dollars shipped), (5) re-work ageing (number of jobs and percentage less than 30 days), (6) efficiency (net sales/number of employees) and (7) delinquencies (dollar volume and percentage of delinquent orders outstanding). Profit was generally the most important evaluation criterion, but good performance in all of these performance areas was considered necessary for achievement of the profit targets.

Division and corporate management negotiated performance standards in each of these areas during HCC's formal planning process – an annual budgeting cycle. This process began in December (or early January) and concluded in mid-March, just before the start of the new fiscal year.

The process started with the division managers' preparation of sales forecasts. To prepare these numbers, they typically contacted their largest customers directly. Then they worked with their operating managers to prepare budgets for expenses, capital expenditures and cash flow. They summarized the numbers into 13-week quarters that were broken into 'monthly' periods of four, four and five weeks.

In February, corporate officers visited the divisions and conducted thorough reviews of these preliminary targets. They looked at the detailed numbers, such as sales by customer and by product, and challenged the general managers' assumptions and numbers by account. Chris Bateman explained why they conducted such a thorough review:

'There are a couple of reasons. Firstly, most of our managers are not very good at budgeting. They are engineers and generally do not have a lot of business training. Secondly, they tend not to play it straight with us. Some will submit conservative targets. Others will submit numbers they have little chance to make.'

After this review, the revised targets were '95% ready'. Typically, the divisions just needed to work out a few details before their budgets were presented to the board of directors. The board formally approved the budget in March.

After the budget was approved, it became a fixed evaluation standard for purposes of awarding incentive compensation. The division managers were asked to send updated forecasts to corporate monthly, but these forecasts were used for planning purposes only.

HCC managers did some planning for periods greater than one year, but these processes were handled almost exclusively at corporate. Al Berger explained:

'The general managers are not in a position to do what needs to be done 2 years down the road. They compete day-to-day. The corporation needs to do some long-term things, such as improving our marketing and consolidating some of our efforts. We involve the general managers in some of those discussions only occasionally because they are not leading those efforts.'

Monitoring of performance

Corporate managers, particularly Al Berger, who was hired as COO in March 1987, monitored division performances closely. He was in frequent contact with the divisional managers and reviewed performance reports in detail when they were produced. Al was even monitoring quality reports from Hermetite on a daily basis because of the significance of that division's known production problems.

The division managers were acutely aware of the emphasis placed on quarterly results. Each quarter they had to write a commentary explaining their division's results as input to a formal budget review. Considerably less explanation was necessary if they exceeded their performance targets. For example, Mike Pelta, manager of Hermetic Seal noted that:

'If I miss a monthly target, I can always explain that something happened at the last minute, and they accept that explanation. If I miss a quarterly target, that's a big thing.'

And Lou Palamara, manager of Sealtron, explained that: 'If I miss a quarterly budget, Al Berger will visit me immediately asking what I am doing about the problem.'

Performance targets and incentives under the 'stretch' budgeting concept
Until 1987, HCC's philosophy was to have 'stretch' performance targets based on the belief that aggressive targets would push managers to strive to do their best. These targets were 'not unreachable, just tough'. The intended probability of achievement was 75–80%.

The budget targets directly affected bonuses paid to those included in the bonus plan. Each person included in the plan was assigned a bonus potential which, for most division managers, was 30% of base salary. The bonuses paid were based half on profit before taxes (PBT), and half on a subjective rating of performance (which was also influenced by profit performance). The objective portion of the award was paid according to the following schedule:

Actual division PBT (% budget)	Bonus paid (% bonus potential)
<60%	0
60	80
100	100
140	150

The subjective portion of the evaluation was based primarily on top management's judgement of the degree of accomplishment of the targets in all 7 performance areas. For example, if a division manager met the standards for 5 out of the 7 performance criteria, mentioned above, top management would have to judge that importance of the targets that were not met. If the two targets that were not met were judged to be critical, the manager might earn no subjective bonus.

Bonuses were paid based on annual performance, but payments were made quarterly. The interim (quarterly) payments were made only at 80% of the earned rate to protect the company from paying bonuses that might not eventually be earned.

Dissatisfaction with the 'stretch' budgeting concept

Gradually corporate managers became dissatisfied with the stretch budgeting concept. Most important, they felt it was causing the corporation not to achieve its plans. Each year, some divisions achieved their targets and some did not, but the corporation was consistently missing its targets. Chris Bateman explained:

'Since everybody knew that the 'stretch' targets were too optimistic, it became 'OK to miss budget'. For example, from the time when I joined HCC in September 1986 until March 1987 I had to prepare 8 budget reviews because the corporation was not achieving its plans. The problem was that at 60% of budget, the managers were still in bonus territory, so they didn't have to worry much about meeting budget. Their budgets were like a wish. They were too easily blown off.'

There was also dissatisfaction with the bonus plan associated with the stretch budgets. The division managers, in particular, considered it to be too subjective and complex to communicate to their middle managers. Communication of the details of the plan was also hampered at two divisions because the division managers did not want to disclose division-level financial information to their personnel because they feared that the information might be leaked to competitors. As a consequence, most of the division personnel included in the plan never knew their bonus potential, nor the bases on which the bonus awards were made.

Most managers were also dissatisfied with the plan because the awards were typically not made until 3–4 months after the end of the quarter. The delay was caused by the several levels of approvals that were necessary before the payments could be made.

The change to minimum performance standards

In October 1986, Andy Goldfarb met with his divisional managers and corporate staff and announced that from then on the company would operate with a 'minimum performance standard' (MPS) budgeting philosophy. MPS budgets were to be set so that the felt probability of achievement was 100%. In addition, to the MPS, the managers were asked to set 'targets' that reflected a performance level considered to be beyond normal capability. Al Berger explained that these targets might involve a 25–30% increase in something, rather than 5–10%. They represent a level that might be said to have only a 50% probability of achievement.

The change in level of difficulty of standards was coincident with a change in the incentive compensation plan. Under the new plan, a division bonus pool was created based on 20% of the amount by which actual division PBT exceeded the MPS, plus 25% of the amount by which it exceeded the target.

The most important performance measure for bonus purposes was still PBT, but bonuses could be affected by results in the other 6 performance areas. Al Berger explained:

'If they make all their targets, they will be paid the full bonus pool. If they miss only a couple of targets, they may earn 100% or close to 100% of the pool. If they make only half their targets, they may earn only 60% of the pool. I left the details of the plan vague because the importance of particular targets varies over time – for example, this year delinquencies and quality are even more important than profit – and some targets are more important in some divisions, than in others. I did not want to quantify the relationships.'

The division managers were given the discretion to decide (before the year started) which of their subordinates would share in the bonus pool, and how the pool would be allocated among themselves and the others included. Corporate guidelines suggested that they reserve between 30% and 40% of the pool for themselves. At targeted performance levels, the divisional managers were expected to earn bonuses of approx. 20–25% of base salary. Bonuses were still paid quarterly at a level of 90% of that earned. The remaining 10% was accrued to be paid at the end of the year contingent on annual performance.

The 1988 budget negotiation processes and reactions to the change in budgeting philosophy in the four divisions

Hermetic Seal
Mike Pelta, general manager of Hermetic Seal, was a cofounder (with Jack Goldfarb, the current chairman) of HCC. Mike was a major HCC stockholder, owning 15% of the corporation's stock. He had been managing Hermetic Seal since January 1987, after having served a

stint as general manager of Hermetite. Mike was known as an effective, hard-working manager, but one who had a tendency to be autocratic and ineffective at developing his subordinates. This limitation was becoming a more serious problem because Mike was nearing retirement age. Mike's philosophy in setting performance targets was to be conservative:

'Knock on wood, in my 33 years as a manager, I've never missed a budget. I'm not really sandbagging; I'm an upbeat person. When I get a target to meet, I go for it. I do have to be careful with the optimism of my subordinates, however. I often have to lower their estimates when putting together my budgets.'

Mike's reasoning for wanting to achieve budget targets consistently:

'If you keep missing budget, how do you feel? You feel like a failure. If you exceed the budget, you feel proud. You're going to project higher the next year. You can't keep beating down on people. You've got to build them up. Stretch budgets don't make me work harder. They can't make me do something I can't do. If the bookings are not there, the profit targets are impossible.'

Consistent with his philosophy, Mike submitted a conservative budget for fiscal year 1988. Al Berger explained from his point of view:

'Mike was looking for a large bonus. He had good reasons for pessimism, bookings were terrible and the bookings rate had declined in the last 3 months of the year; they were shipping 25% more than they were booking; delinquencies were numerous, as production was inefficient. But he didn't explain his numbers in terms of these problems. He just said he was new in the job and was in the process of rebuilding. I listened to what he had to say and then we went through the customer list a number of times. We finally agreed on sales and bookings numbers, and then quality, delinquencies and profit targets.'

After the revisions were approved, Mike felt between 95% and 98% confident that he would achieve his sales target. And even if he missed the sales target, he expected to meet the profit goal. He explained:

'It would simply be a matter of digging into my backlog and cutting costs here and there. I know this business inside out, so I know what I have to do to make budget. I wouldn't do anything that could hurt the company in the long run, though.'

He noticed the change in budgeting philosophy. He recalled that in the past he used to have only an 85–90% chance of making the 'stretch' profit targets.

Glasseal

Carl Kalish, was the manager of Glasseal. Carl had been vice-president, marketing for Glasseal at the time it was acquired by HCC. He was appointed general manager of Glasseal soon after the acquisition. Carl considered it very important to prepare realistic forecasts:

'It's easy to sit in a staff position and be optimistic, but as a general manager, I have to be right. In the past 4 years I have been tremendously accurate in my market projections. You can't anticipate everything, though. For instance, in the fiscal year 1987 we exceeded our profit budget by 12% primarily because of unusual gains in sales volume. A major competitor was going through some crises, and we were able to pick up part of their share. We exceeded budget during each of the first 3 quarters, but in the last quarter our customers started deferring shipments to use up their inventory, and our sales decreased sharply. We expect our volume to go back to normal in 1988.'

Carl's first budget projected $7.4 million in bookings and $7.2 million in shipments. Corporate managers told him to increase both targets by $200 000, based on their interpretation of market trends. They also increased his PBT target by almost 2%, up to $1.1 million. Carl's reaction to these changes was as follows:

'Personally, I think that my initial forecast was right, but I'm committed to the new budget. It's a number that I'm trying to live with ...

[Under the old system] I used to feel 90% sure that I'd make budget in any given year. Now I'm still only 90% sure, but the difference is that my job depends on it ...

The old plan allowed for bonus payments if you missed budget, so we had something to shoot for, even if we knew we would come out short, and the rewards were also greater than they are now. Furthermore, corporate was not so dictatorial when setting the targets. But I'm trying to stay open-minded and see how it goes. I consider this first year as an experiment.'

Sealtron

Lou Palamara, Sealtron's general manager, was recruited from outside HCC in January 1986. His background was as a ceramic engineer and engineering manager. Lou's initial 1988 budget submission was for sales of $6.4 million and PBT of $900 000. This budget was rejected. Lou explained: 'Andy Goldfarb told me, "Your charter is to make $1 million in PBT next year. Show me a plan to make that much profit".'

Lou then prepared a budget that increased the projected sales and reduced costs of advertising, promotions and other discretionary spending. He discussed this new budget with Chris Bateman (CFO). Neither Lou nor Chris were confident that the $1 million target would be achieved, so Chris agreed to propose the $900 000 PBT target again to Andy. Andy would not budge. He sent Lou a letter stating that: 'Sealtron's target for 1988 must be $1 million'.

Lou felt that while he had perhaps a 95% chance to achieve the $900 000 profit budget, his chance to achieve the $1 million MPS budget was only 60–65%. His PBT target was $1.1 million, a level that he considered impossible to achieve. Lou was somewhat discouraged:

'Mine is a strange plan. If I make budget, which is an 18% increase from our last year actuals, I get no bonus. I really feel that if you put together a plan and don't hide anything and plan capital investments and expenditures for the future, and you feel comfortable with it, then that's the best plan. The plan must be realistic. My plan is a threat. I may even have to lay off some people that we will likely need later. But if I don't do it and I miss my minimum performance standards, I may get fired.'

Lou was concerned because nobody at Sealtron expected a bonus in 1988. Missing budget also prevented salary increases. In the fiscal year 1987, for example, nobody at Sealtron got a salary increase, because the division did not make budget. This situation made him worry about employee retention:

'If this salary freeze persists for 2 more years, I may lose some of my key employees. We missed our profit target last year mainly because I had to hire a new industrial engineer and a production control manager to get our manufacturing operations in shape. Now I know of a local company that wants to hire the industrial engineer, and he is just starting to put our systems in order. I think we should keep people happy if we want them to stay. They should be compensated for their effort.'

Corporate managers' perspectives about the situation at Sealtron were somewhat different. Al Berger thought that the $1 million PBT budget was necessary to change the aspiration levels of Sealtron personnel. He explained that Sealtron's efficiency, measured in terms of sales per employee, was 50% below that of the other connector divisions, even though its production processes were simpler. And Al was particularly annoyed that even though Sealtron had missed its budget by 30% in 1987, the number of employees in the division had actually grown. Al felt that with good management, Sealtron would be certain to achieve its $1 million PBT budget, but this would probably require cutting staff and shipping more product.

Chris Bateman, rated the probability of Sealtron achieving the $1 million target at only 90%:

'Because of the people. The people in that division have historically not been thinking much about costs. Their perspective has always been that they need sales to make money. We're trying to get the message to them that we can't afford any fat in the organization, and I'm not sure how fast they will learn to adjust.'

Lou felt that personnel at Sealtron truly were concerned about costs:

'I recognize that some good comes out of budget pressures. Everybody becomes conscious of overhead costs, and the pressures force expense cuts and productivity improvements faster. But I still feel that hiring the people I did was in the best long-term interest of the company.'

Hermetite

Alan Wong, the general manager at Hermetite, was a MBA/CPA/ lawyer who worked for a major public accounting firm before joining HCC as CFO. He accepted the job as general manager of Hermetite in August 1986, only 4 months before he had to submit his initial budget for 1988.

Alan's first budget showed projections of $13 million in sales, and PBT of $130 000. These figures compared with 1987 actual sales of $7 million and a loss of $2.8 million. Although he knew these were aggressive targets, Alan felt that it was important for him to be optimistic:

'You have to be an optimist in a turnaround situation. If you don't set high standards, you'll never achieve high performance.'

Alan thought that the pressure to make budget every year would encourage him and his personnel to become more efficient:

'We may have to postpone maintenance or purchases of supplies in a tough quarter. If the profit is not there, you shouldn't spend the money. It is my job to provide the profits this quarter. And it is up to corporate to think long term.'

Alan's initial budget submission was also based on a belief that corporate managers would not accept a budget that projected a loss. It had been 2 years since HCC acquired Hermetite and he felt that corporate managers were anxious for it to turn into a profitable operation. This belief was incorrect. Al Berger noted that:

'Alan thought the company wanted profit from him; he thought we would not survive without profit. So he based his budget on what was needed in order to break even or make a small profit. He was naïve. I told him we would not accept a budget from him that showed a profit.'

Al and the other corporate managers considered Alan's first budget 'ludicrous' ('pie in the sky'), and they felt that even his second submission (sales of $11 million) was still too optimistic. During a series of budget reviews, Hermetite's budget was revised sharply downward. The final MPS budget was for sales of $9.2 million and a loss of $400 000. The performance target was set at sales of $10.5 million and PBT of $67 000.

After these reviews, Al was certain that Hermetite had a budget that it would achieve. Alan was not as confident; he felt that he had only a 80% chance of achieving it, and commented:

'This concept of minimum performance standards may be OK for a normal business, but we're not normal. Nobody knows what is the standard for Hermetite. We could make $200 000 in profits or show many times that in losses. Hermetite's track record has been so bad, that we don't know what to expect. Our motivating factor is just to keep our jobs.'

Alan felt he had only a slight (perhaps 5%) chance of achieving his PBT target.

Early experiences with the new system

As described above, the divisional managers were concerned that they were not assured of achieving their MPS budgets. Al Berger was certain that the division budgets were achievable, but as is shown in Exhibit 5, others in the corporation were not so sure.

Events subsequent to the budget approvals caused Al to admit he was wrong in the case of Hermetite, which started the year 1988 very poorly. Only three weeks into the year, Al lowered Hermetite's performance targets (but not MPS) as a gesture of encouragement:

'At the time it was prepared, I was certain that Hermetite's budget would be achieved. But some good things didn't happen. Bookings were so low that we went dry in December and January. This was out of Alan's control. The delinquency problem, created by his predecessor, had caused the reputation of the company to go to pot, and customers weren't placing orders.

I had to admit we were wrong. Although I had intended never to revise the standards, I lowered the performance target to $9 million in sales. The people needed to be reinforced during a difficult time. I wanted to be able to say 'You're doing a good job' through bonuses.'

The first quarter results, which were available in July 1987, caused more concern. As is shown in the summary presented in Exhibit 6, none of the divisions had achieved all of its MPS. These results caused Andy Goldfarb and other corporate managers concern about whether the new budgeting philosophy had been implemented properly.

Exhibit 1
HCC INDUSTRIES Summary Financial Data
(dollar amounts are in thousands, except per share data)

	1987	1986*	1985*	1984*	1983*
Operations					
Net sales from continuing operations	$35 552	$32 554	$25 262	$18 827	$11 177
Earnings (loss) from continuing operations before extraordinary item	(1 028)	793	1 236	735	808
Per Common Share					
Earnings (loss) from continuing operations before extraordinary item	$ (0.58)	$ 0.45	$ 0.68	$ 0.38	$ 0.43
Cash dividends	0.06	0.06	0.06	0.06	0.06
Stockholders' equity	4.98	6.38	6.24	6.05	5.50
Year-end Financial Position					
Current assets	$17 830	$20 993	$20 665	$24 067	$21 629
Working capital	12 145	12 856	14 577	17 166	17 579
Current ratio	3.14:1	2.58:1	3.39:1	3.49:1	5.34:1
Total assets	$32 495	$38 857	$33 039	$36 971	$30 007
Long-term debt	15 998	16 635	13 557	17 334	15 228
Stockholders' equity	8 851	11 332	11 405	11 554	10 512
Return on average stockholders' equity from continuing operations	(10%)	7%	11%	6%	8%
Shares outstanding (in thousands)	1 776	1.776	1.773	1.911	1.910

*Restated for discontinued operations.
*Based on weighted average number of shares outstanding.

Exhibit 2
HCC INDUSTRIES Partial Corporate Organization Chart

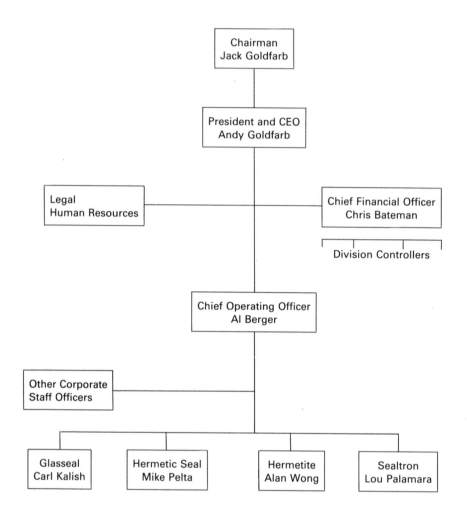

Exhibit 3
HCC INDUSTRIES Typical Products

Hermetically Sealed Connectors

Hermetically sealed
headers and terminals
and ceramic-to-metal
seals used in high
temperature and
pressure requirements
such as jet fuel nozzles

Connector used in
deep-hole oil
exploration

Custom-designed Microelectronic Packages

Kovar fiberoptics
package with
precisely dimensioned
tube designed for
telecommunications

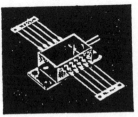

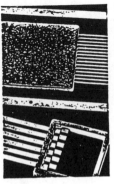

Microelectronic
packages for
hermetically sealed
hybrid integrated
semi-conductor
applications such
as in MX missiles

Exhibit 4

HCC INDUSTRIES Summary Information about Divisions

Division	Products	1987 Revenues ($m)	Location	Other
Hermetic Seal	Connectors	12	Rosemead. California	The original HCC business
Glasseal	Connectors	6	Lakewood. New Jersey	Acquired in June 1983
Sealtron	Connectors	6	Cincinnati. Ohio	Was wholly owned subsidiary of Glasseal when acquired Acquired in August 1985
Hermetite	Microelectronic packages	10	Avon. Massachusetts	

Exhibit 5

HCC INDUSTRIES Felt Probability of Budget Achievement at Time Target Was Set (March 1987)

	Estimate from:		
Division	Al Berger (COO)	Chris Bateman (CFO)	General Manager
Hermetic Seal	100%	100%	95%–98%
Glasseal	100	100	90
Sealtron	100	90	60–65
Hermetite	100	70	80

Exhibit 6
HCC INDUSTRIES First Quarter Results (1988)

Criteria	Hermetic Seal			Glasseal			Sealtron			Hermetite		
	MPS	Target	Actual	MPS	Target	Actual	MPS	Target	Actual	MPS	Target	Actual
Sales												
Bookings	2600	2800	2844	2020	n/a	1645	1500	1600	1513	1811	2000	1234
Shipments	2600	2900	2843	1815	n/a	1742	1400	1450	1442	2351	2200	2323
Quality												
Returns (% of shipment)	10%	7%	14.4%	3%	n/a	3.5%	3%	2%	1.3%	10%	5%	6.3%
Re-work: number of jobs/ percentage less than 30 days	60/ 85	40/ 92	62/ 30	10/ 80	n/a	10/ 80	6/ 70	4/ 75	9/ 67	25/ 50	12/ 80	10/ 82
Productivity												
Profit (before tax)	650	800	843	283	300	192	167	175	195	(410)	(300)	(188)
Efficiency (sales/employee)	60	62	60	57	59	67	38	40	38.7	52	59	53
Delinquency ($, %)	220K, 6%	0	460K, 10.4%	80K	0	48K	70K	0	151K	250K	150K	368K

Key: ◯ Below MPS; ▢ Exceed target.

ES INC.

In 1982, ES Inc. (ESI) was starting a process which could lead to major changes in its planning and measurement systems. Cliff Jamieson, Vice-President, Planning and Services, explained:

The basic thrust of what we are starting to do is very simple, but it has potentially major ramifications. We are changing the basic decision rules by which we evaluate our plans and our accomplishments. We have become convinced, that for ESI, at least, the traditional accounting measures such as net earnings or return on net assets, are neither good criteria on which to base decisions, nor reliable indicators of performance.

The primary objective of our company is to create value for our shareholders. We believe that stock values, like the values of all economic resources, depend on investors' expectations of future cash flows, discounted for time and risk. Consequently, we think that in evaluating possible actions, it is more important to focus on the possible impacts on future cash flows and risk, rather than estimating the impact on the accounting indicators. In addition, we think that it makes sense to judge our performance based on what we accomplish for our shareholders – meaning the amount of value we generate for them.

The company

ESI was a large, diversified corporation with headquarters in New York City. The company's 1981 sales of $2.2 billion ranked it among the largest 300 corporations in the USA. ESI had experienced excellent growth in both revenues and earnings for many years (see Exhibit 1).

ESI was organized into 4 main business groups: Semiconductor, Electrical Products, Industrial Products and Consumer Products (see Exhibit 2). The Semiconductor Group (SG) designed, manufactured and marketed a broad line of semiconductor devices, including electronic sensors (e.g., photodiodes), memory devices, microprocessors and transmission devices (e.g., fiber optics, speech synthesis chips). The Electrical Products Group (EPG) produced such varied products as generators and motors (fractional horsepower only), circuit breakers and electrical connectors. Also included in EPG was the Electrical Supply Division which sold the products of approx. 100 of the leading US electronics and electrical component manufacturers to over 25000 customers worthwhile. The Industrial Products Group (IPG) sold a wide range of products, including

This case was prepared by Associate Professor Kenneth A. Merchant as basis for class discussion rather than to illustrate either effective or ineffective handling of an administrative situation.
© 1982 President and Fellow of Harvard College, Harvard Business School. Case 9-183-061.

custom engineered ball, roller and slider bearings, precision engine parts, mechanical seals, industrial laminates, non-woven materials and some industrial chemicals. The Consumer Products Group (CPG) designed, manufactured and distributed products which used in-house technologies, including electronic watches and calculators, small garden tractors and mowers, luggage, footwear and health and beauty products. A financial comparison of these groups is presented in Exhibit 3.

The groups were divided into a total of 19 divisions which were, in turn, divided into 70 product departments each with profit-centre responsibility.

In 1982, the compensation of a typical manager was expected to be approx. 60% salary and 40% performance incentives. The performance incentives were based 75% on operating income less a capital charge (i.e., residual income), and 25% on the accomplishment of specific MBO (management-by-objectives) targets.

ESI was a growth-oriented company with relatively young management. Most general managers had an engineering education and either technical or marketing experience, or both. The average age of the division managers was approx. 41. Brian Kinney, the Chairman of the Board, was only 51. Top management was interested in maintaining at least moderate levels of overall internal growth and was also interested in acquiring companies with operations that would complement present ESI activities.

Planning processes

Planning at ESI was intended to be a bottom-up process. In March, the strategic planning process was started with headquarters sending general planning guidelines to the business units. These guidelines included an economic forecast and some preliminary estimates of the resources the company would make available to each business unit. The department managers (and lower-level managers, where appropriate) were expected to propose their own goals and strategies. They were asked to prepare 3-year plans with the emphasis on market analysis and identification of strategic alternatives. Quantitative data (including financial) were required in only summary form.

These plans were then reviewed at successively higher organizational levels. The Corporate Management Committee (CMC) reviewed the plans and evaluated the total portfolio of businesses early in September. The CMC rarely made material changes to the strategic plans at this time; changes were usually made only if the resource availability situation changed or if an acquisition or divestment was imminent.

After CMC approval of the strategic plan, the department managers prepared detailed operating plans (budgets) for the next year. The operating plans included targets for sales growth, profit margins and operating earnings and were intended to be consistent with the strategic plans. The operating plans were also reviewed at successively increasing organizational levels, usually with only minor modifications being made.

The shareholder value model

In the late 1970s, corporate staff had begun to use a model called VALUmod as an aid in evaluating strategic plans. VALUmod was developed by Bourne and McIntosh, a Chicago-based management consulting firm, with the help of several leading academics in the fields of finance, accounting and strategic planning. At the heart of VALUmod was a discounted cash flow model which, with the input of estimates of future cash flows and factors for discounting time and risk, could be used to place a value on any business entity at any point in time. For strategic planning purposes, VALUmod could be used to value an entity given the assumptions behind any of a number of different strategic alternatives.

A particular strategy was considered to generate a positive value for shareholders only if it increased the business entity's cash flows in a manner sufficient to more than offset new investments that might be required. Cash flows (and value) might be generated by, for example, increasing the volume of sales, increasing the contribution generated by each incremental sale, or reducing the amount of investment tied up in working capital as compared to the levels in the base period.

In addition to providing the basic value calculations, VALUmod helped in the preparation of the cash flow forecasts themselves by allowing easy manipulation of the parameters affecting future cash flows. This made it easy to ask the 'what-if' questions necessary for performing sensitivity analyses.

In concept, VALUmod was identical to capital investment analysis models based on the net present value method. But with VALUmod, *all* cash outlays required to implement a strategy were considered, not just capital investments which typically comprised only a small fraction of the total.

History of use of the shareholder value model
Diane Avery, Director of Corporate Planning, described how ESI came to use a shareholder value model in strategic planning:

'By all the traditional accounting measures, our performance over the decade of the 1970s was excellent. Take any measure you want – sales growth, earnings growth, return on equity, return on assets and earnings per employee – they all indicate we had done very well. Our shareholders, however, hadn't really derived any benefit from this 'success'. In 1979, our market value was essentially where it was in 1970.* And although we increased our dividends as earnings increased, this never provided shareholders with a return greater than 5%.

In the late 1970s, the merger and acquisition people in our corporate planning department [see organization chart in Exhibit 4] were involved in a lot of value analyses. We were using pretty sophisticated models which helped us analyze the determinants of value – cash-flow potentials and risk – under various business and economic assumptions, so that we could put a value on business segments we were considering buying or selling.

In our planning meetings, my group saw needs for the same types of analyses. One choice our management was often faced with was whether to acquire an existing business or to build one by allocating resources to one of our existing business units. Thus, it was natural that we began to use cash-flow-based value models in our planning analyses.'

ESI first applied the shareholder value models to the plans submitted during the 1980 planning process. The operating managers were not involved in the actual use of the models; corporate staff just took the numbers in the plans and plugged them into the models. The purpose of this exercise was not to use the output in decision making, but just to get some familiarity with the problems that might arise when the models were used to compare internal business units.

In the first year, the corporate planning staff used the model's cash flow-based estimates of changes in 'intrinsic shareholder value' at the corporate level and compared them with the actual ESI market-value changes over the period 1975–79 and the year 1980. The model's estimates were quite accurate. They showed that the net cash returns during the 1975–79 period actually were not sufficient to increase shareholder value, but that the plans for 1980, if they were achieved, should do so. And, indeed, at the end of 1980 when the plans had been achieved, the total ESI market value had risen to over $750 million, up from the $550 million level where it had been for virtually the entire decade of the 1970s.

At this time, top-level ESI managers indicated that they were very comfortable with these findings. Brian Kinney (Chairman) stated that the value concept supported the intuitive feelings that he had.

Later in the year, VALUmod was given a real credibility boost. At

* From 1970 to 1979 the weighted average compound price appreciation of stocks listed on the New York Stock Exchange (NYSE Common Stock Index) was 1.9%.

year-end 1980, ESI stock was selling at about $32 per share; and at mid-year 1981, it was around 40. In June 1981, Dennis Chu, an analyst in the Corporate Planning Department, used VALUmod to analyse ESI's financial performance and concluded that despite continuing improvement in the accounting numbers, company performance did not justify the higher stock price. Dennis estimated that by year-end the stock price would be around $31 per share if the company maintained its current strategy and performance came in as projected. This estimate was shown to the high-level corporate managers, but they did not choose to alter company strategies at that time.

At year-end, with everything going according to plan, ESI stock was selling at $30!† Dennis observed:

'You can't depend on the model showing that kind of accuracy consistently. We have to make a number of assumptions and approximations, nobody really knows how the stock market will respond at any given time, and the market does not have access to the confidential information I used. But the theory behind the model is correct; the intrinsic value of our company should depend on the size, pattern and uncertainty surrounding the cash flows we expect to be able to generate in the future.

The success of this forecast was very important. It gave the model credibility. Everybody is used to thinking in terms of sales and earnings growth, and we have always used those numbers to plan with, even though they are not very good numbers on which to base our decisions or to judge our success.'

VALUmod and strategic planning
Dennis went on to describe how the model could be used to assist ESI's planning efforts:

'Let me show you some examples of why I think we should use VALUmod in our planning processes. Here is an example of a situation where operating managers might be discouraged from investing in, or even proposing, good strategies because of their adverse impact on accounting earnings [Exhibit 5]. Schedule 1 shows pro-forma income statements for a 3-year period in which I've assumed no real growth but 10% inflation. I've called this Strategy 1; it can be considered a 'base case' or a 'maintenance strategy'.

Now, suppose a manager identifies a strategy which requires an investment of $5 million in marketing expenses in each of the next 3 years (1982–84) but which promises 5% real growth in 1983 and 1984. [The projected income statements for this alternative, Strategy 2, are shown in Schedule 2.]

The implication should be clear. With a projected decline in earnings in 1982, this strategy will probably suffer an early death. The division manager

_____

†During the last half of 1981, the NYSE Common Stock Index declined by approximately 6.6%.

will be reluctant to propose it because top management is not likely to look at it enthusiastically, and furthermore if the strategy were implemented, it would adversely affect his bonus.

From the stockholder standpoint, however, this is a good plan. [Cash flow and shareholder value numbers shown in Schedule 3.] As per our standard, conservative procedure, I've assumed the operating cash flows will remain constant at the 1984 level in perpetuity. But even so, the value numbers make it obvious that our shareholders would want us to invest in this plan. An analysis would show that the internal rate of return is over 30%.

The accounting biases can also operate in the opposite direction; that is, a decision that promises excellent profits can be bad for the stockholders. Here is such an example [Exhibit 6].

I've taken the same base case (Schedule 1) and this time assumed that a manager has identified an investment of $25 million in capital equipment and working capital that would increase the operating margin from 20% to 22%. This provides an improved profit picture (Schedule 2), but this is actually a bad investment that yields less than the 18% cost of capital that I've assumed. The net effect is to reduce the value of the earning assets in this business unit by almost $4 million [Schedule 3].

These are very simple examples, of course, but I can assure you that these patterns occur in some of the plans submitted by our operating units. Let me show you one example. During the 1981 planning process, one of our divisions proposed a strategy which showed sharp increases in both sales and earnings [Exhibit 7]. From these numbers, it is easy to conclude that this is a pretty decent plan. In truth, however, it is not.'

'Using VALUmod, I calculated that the pre-strategy value of this division (net of liabilities) is approx. $500 000. But if this strategy is implemented, I figure that the value of this division would actually be a negative $1.2 million [Exhibit 8]. This is true because the strategy requires a considerable up-front investment for items which do not show up in the income statement for some time. I conclude that implementing this strategy would cause a decrease of $1.7 million in the intrinsic value of this division and the value of ESI stock. And if anything, my calculation may be optimistic because for this business segment it would be easy to justify using a risk-adjusted discount rate greater than the 18% that I used in making these calculations. The 18% is the overall corporate weighted-average cost of capital, and this particular business unit is probably one of the riskiest businesses in our portfolio.

I think we should seriously consider selling this business, assuming someone would be willing to pay something close to the $500 000 that it is worth right now. We certainly should not be investing the money proposed in this plan. The increased sales and earnings picture is misleading; this plan will actually be very costly to our shareholders.

Let me make one qualification, however. I am not suggesting that impact on shareholders' value should be the only criterion we should look at when we make our strategic resource allocation decision. What I am suggesting is that impact on shareholder value should be an important financially oriented criterion and that it is far superior to looking at projections expressed in traditional accounting terms.'

Change in statement of objectives

At the end of 1981, the wording of ESI's primary statement of objectives was changed to read as follows: 'The primary objective of ES Inc. is to increase shareholder value. This will be accomplished by focusing on markets where the Company has or can capture a major share, by developing a higher-than-average flow of successful new products, and by continuing to emphasize productivity of Company personnel and assets.'

Formerly, the primary objective had been 'to grow and to improve profitability'. This change in the wording of the statement of company objectives was not brought about by VALUmod directly, but it was motivated by the same logic that the model used.

The future of the shareholder value model

ESI planned to work with and to refine the shareholder value model and eventually to spread its use throughout the organization. Brian Kinney (Chairman) promised to use VALUmod and related models 'more intensively and extensively'.

A number of important issues remained to be solved, however. One issue was the planning horizon. In making the value calculations, all cash flows, no matter how far into the future, had to be considered, but the ESI operating plans only included 3 years of data. To work around this limitation, the planning staff had been making the assumption that the operating cash flows in the last year of the plan would remain constant in perpetuity, in the absence of information to the contrary. While the most immediate cash flows had the largest value impact because of discounting, this assumption was subject to obvious criticisms, particularly for those divisions with products with relatively short product life cycles. Thus, to improve the accuracy of VALUmod's calculations, one possibility that had to be considered was an extension of the planning horizon, from 3 to 5 years, or perhaps even longer.

A second issue was whether the plans should reflect a single point estimate of future results or whether they should reflect a range of possible outcomes and an assessment of the likelihood of each. VALUmod's value calculations were intended to reflect the *expected value* of the future cash flows, and the model could easily accommodate probabilistic cash flow estimates. However, several senior ESI managers thought that single point estimates were necessary for control purposes, so that managers could be held responsible for achieving a specific plan.

Risk presented another problem. ESI's early uses of the model used the same discount factor – the corporate average cost of capital – in all analyses. If ESI had been highly vertically integrated and in a single market, this might have been acceptable, but the Corporate Planning staff felt that the various ESI business units did bear quite different levels of risk. Quantifying the amounts of risk faced in order to reflect them in the discount rates used in the value calculations was not straightforward, however, and more thought would have to be given to this issue before use of the model was made more widespread.

A fourth issue was the speed of implementation, meaning how fast to involve managers at each organization level in the use of the model. Because they were convinced of its worth, top management was inclined to use the 'impact on shareholder value' criterion for evaluating plans immediately. However, this might cause frustration and conflict if the lower-level managers did not understand the bases on which the decisions were being made. All managers were familiar with the net present value concept because they were required to use it in preparing their capital investment proposals, but it was not clear whether they could easily transfer their knowledge of this basic concept to the preparation of whole operating plans.

Finally, if impact on shareholder value became an important criterion in strategic decision making, another issue would arise; that is whether or not to link a value-related performance criterion – impact on shareholder value – to the management reward system. To reinforce the shareholder value concept, some portion of management compensation could be made contingent on value increases – either of the corporation as a whole or of specific business units. The question was: 'should this be done, and if so, how soon?'

Questions:
1. Should ESI use 'impact on shareholder value' as the primary financial criterion on which to evaluate:
   (a) business-unit plans?
   (b) managerial accomplishments?
2. If not, what criterion (or criteria) should be used for each purpose? Should impact on shareholder value be considered at all?
3. If the impact on the shareholder value criterion is used, how should the issues raised in the case be resolved?

Exhibit 1
ES INC. Financial Comparison (1970–81) ($m)

	1981	1980	1979	1978	1977	1976	1975	1974	1973	1972	1971	1970
Net sales	2152	1841	1577	1334	1139	1025	883	762	647	533	458	399
Net earnings	110	96	84	71	61	50	44	38	33	28	23	20
Capital expenditures	98	86	57	59	59	35	40	45	36	19	16	25
Market value (average)	755	769	544	526	551	619	581	563	625	662	574	541
Ratios (%)												
Increase in sales	16.9	16.7	18.2	17.1	11.1	16.1	15.8	17.8	21.3	16.5	14.8	14.3
Increase in net earnings	14.6	14.2	18.3	16.4	21.9	13.6	15.8	15.2	17.8	21.7	15.1	3.6
Net earn as % of sales	5.1	5.2	5.3	5.3	5.3	4.9	5.0	4.9	5.1	5.3	5.1	5.0
Dividends as % of net earnings	29.7	27.4	25.7	26.2	24.1	20.7	19.2	21.8	22.5	24.9	28.3	31.5
Return on average shareholder equity	15%	14.6%	14.6%	13.5%	12.9%	12.0%	12.2%	11.9%	11.6%	11.1%	10.2%	9.4%

Exhibit 2
ES INC. Organization

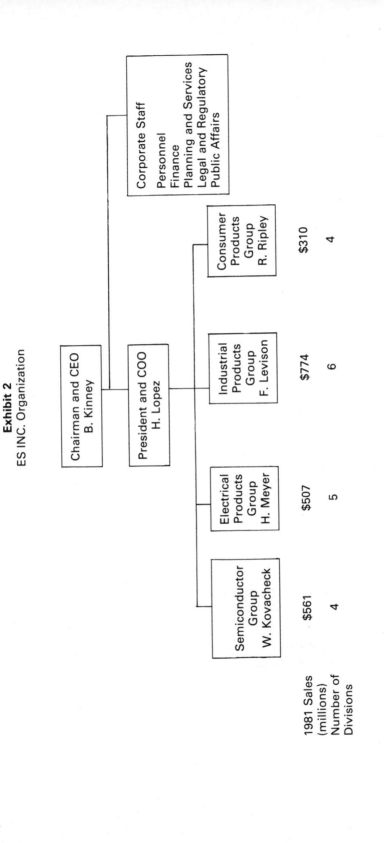

	Semiconductor Group W. Kovacheck	Electrical Products Group H. Meyer	Industrial Products Group F. Levison	Consumer Products Group R. Ripley
Chairman and CEO B. Kinney				
President and COO H. Lopez				
Corporate Staff Personnel Finance Planning and Services Legal and Regulatory Public Affairs				
1981 Sales (millions)	$561	$507	$774	$310
Number of Divisions	4	5	6	4

Exhibit 3
ES INC. Financial Comparison of Major Business Groups ($m)

	1981	*1980*	*% increased*
Semiconductor			
Net Sales	$561	$428	31.1%
Net Earnings	6	5	20.0
Electrical Products			
Net Sales	507	469	8.1
Net Earnings	28	27	3.7
Industrial Products			
Net Sales	774	701	10.4
Net Earnings	63	56	12.5
Consumer Products			
Net Sales	310	243	27.6
Net Earnings	13	8	62.5
ESI Total			
Net Sales	2152	1841	16.9
Net Earnings	110	96	14.6

Exhibit 4
ES INC. Planning Division Organization

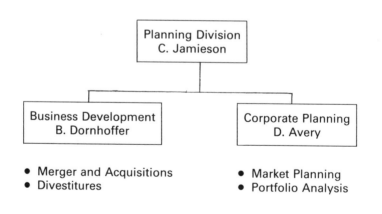

Exhibit 5
ES INC. Example Showing Discouragement of a Good Investment ($m)

SCHEDULE 1: Projected Income Statements, Division A, Strategy 1
('Base case')

| | Actual | | Forecast | |
	1981	1982	1983	1984
Sales	$200	$220	$242	$266
Variable operating expenses	160	176	194	213
Depreciation	10	11	11	12
Discretionary expenses	20	22	24	27
Total expenses	190	209	229	251
Profit before tax	10	12	13	15
Income tax (40%)	4	5	5	6
Profit after tax	$ 6	$ 7	$ 8	$ 9

SCHEDULE 2: Projected Income Statements, Division A, Strategy 2
(Real growth)

| | Actual | | Forecast | |
	1981	1982	1983	1984
Sales	$200	$220	$253	$291
Variable operating expenses	160	176	202	233
Depreciation	10	11	11	12
Discretionary expenses	20	27	29	32
Total expenses	190	214	243	276
Profit before tax	10	7	10	15
Income tax (40%)	4	3	4	6
Profit after tax	$ 6	$ 4	$ 6	$ 9

SCHEDULE 3: Value Calculations

Annual Cash Flows	1982	1983	1984	1985 and beyond
Strategy 1	$ 18	$ 19	$ 21	$ 21
Strategy 2	$ 15	$ 17	$ 21	$ 24

Value of Division A on 31 December 1981 at 18% (ignoring liabilities):
Strategy 1 $112.3 million
Strategy 2 $116.3 million

Exhibit 6

ES INC. Example Showing Encouragement of a Bad Investment ($m)

SCHEDULE 1: Projected Income Statements, Division A, Strategy 1
('Base case')

	Actual		Forecast	
	1981	*1982*	*1983*	*1984*
Sales	$200	$220	$242	$266
Variable operating expenses	160	176	194	213
Depreciation	10	11	11	12
Discretionary expenses	20	22	24	27
Total expenses	190	209	229	251
Profit before tax	10	12	13	15
Income tax (40%)	4	5	5	6
Profit after tax	$ 6	$ 7	$ 8	$ 9

SCHEDULE 2: Projected Income Statements, Division A, Strategy 3
(Improve Operating margins)

	Actual		Forecast	
	1981	*1982*	*1983*	*1984*
Sales	$200	$220	$242	$266
Variable operating expenses	160	172	189	208
Depreciation	10	12	13	14
Discretionary expenses	20	22	24	27
Total expenses	190	205	226	248
Profit before tax	10	15	16	18
Income tax (40%)	4	6	6	7
Profit after tax	$ 6	$ 9	$ 10	$ 11

SCHEDULE 3: Value Calculations

Annual Cash Flows	Investment	1982	1983	1984	1985 and beyond
Strategy 1		$ 18	$ 19	$ 21	$ 21
Strategy 2	$(25)	$ 21	$ 23	$ 25	$ 25

Value of Division A on 31 December 1981 at 18% (ignoring liabilities):
Strategy 1 $112.3 million
Strategy 3 $108.6 million

Exhibit 7
ES INC. Division A, Strategy X
Projected Income Statements ($m)

	1982	1983	1984
Sales	$74	$89	$106
Expenses	70	84	99
Profit before taxes	4	5	7
Income taxes	2	2	3
Profit after taxes	$ 2	$ 3	$ 4

Exhibit 8
ES INC. Division A, Strategy X
Shareholder Value Calculations ($m)

Present value of earning assets at end of implementation of strategy	$ 16.8
Less: Present value of investment required	(7.9)
Less: Market value of debt (net of monetary assets)	(10.1)
Present value of division if strategy is implemented	(1.2)
Less: Pre-strategy value of division	0.5
Shareholder value contribution of strategy	$ (1.7)

References

Accounting Standards Committee (ASC) (1980) *Current Cost Accounting: SSAP 16*. ASC.

Ackerman, R.W. (1970) Influence of integration and diversity on the investment process, *Administrative Science Quarterly*, September, 341–52.

Adelman, M.A. (1961) The Antimerger Act, 1950–60, *American Economic Review*, May, 236–44.

Aharoni, Y. (1966) *The Foreign Investment Decision Process*. Division of Research, Harvard Business School, Boston.

Alchian, A.A. and Allen W.R. (1967) *University Economics*, 2nd Edn. Wadsworth.

Amey, L.R. (1969) Divisional performance measurement and interest on capital, *Journal of Business Finance*, Spring, 2–7.

Amey, L.R. (1969) *The Efficiency of Business Enterprises*. George Allen and Unwin, London.

Amey, L.R. and Egginton, D.A. (1973) *Management Accounting: A Conceptual Approach*. Longman, Harlow, Essex.

Amey, L.R. (1979) *Budget Planning and Control Systems*. Pitman, London.

Amey, L.R. (1980) Interest on equity capital as an ex post cost, *Journal of Business Finance and Accounting*, Autumn, 347–65.

Amigoni, F. (1978) Planning management control systems, *Journal of Business Finance and Accounting*, 5, (3), 279–92.

Ansari, S.L. (1977) An integrated approach to control systems design, *Accounting, Organizations and Society*, 2, 101–12.

Ansari, S.L. (1979) Towards an open systems approach to budgeting, *Accounting, Organizations and Society*, 4, 149–62.

Ansoff, H.I. and Weston, J.F. (1962) Merger objectives and organization structure, *Quarterly Review of Economics and Business*, August, 112–26.

Anthony, R.A. (1988) *The Management Control Function*. Harvard Business School Press, Boston.

Anthony, R.N. (1965) *Planning and Control Systems: A framework for analysis*. Division of Research, Harvard Graduate School of Business, Boston.

Anthony, R.N. and Dearden, J. (1980) *Management Control Systems*, 4th Edn. Irwin.

Argyris, C. (1952) *The Impact of Budgets on People*. The Controllership Foundation, Ithaca, New York.

Argyris, C. (1964) *Integrating the Individual and the Organization*. Wiley, Essex.

Arnold, J. (1973) *Pricing and Output Decisions*. Haymarket, London.

Arnold, J. and Hope, T. (1983) *Accounting for Management Decisions*. Prentice-Hall, Hemel Hampstead, Herts.

Armstrong, M. and Murlis, H. (1988) *Reward Management*, Kogan Page, London.

Arpan, J.S. (1972) International intracorporate pricing: non-American systems and views, *Journal of International Business Studies*, Spring, 56–72.

Arrow, K.J. (1951) *Social Choice and Individual Values*, Yale U.P.

Arrow, K.J. (1964) Control in large organizations, *Management Science*, April, 1–36.

Arvidsson, G. (1973) *Internal Transfer Negotiations – Eight Experiments*. The Economic Research Institute, Stockholm.

Atkin, B. and Skinner, R. (1975) *How British Industry Prices*. Industrial Market Research Ltd.

Bain, J.S. (1956) *Barriers to New Competition*. Harvard U.P., Cambridge, Mass.

Barnard, C. (1938) *The Functions of the Executive*. Harvard U.P., Cambridge, Mass.

Barrett, E.M. and Fraser, III, L.M. (1977) Conflicting roles in budgeting for operations, *Harvard Business Review*, **55**, 137–46.

Barwise, T.P., Marsh, P.R. and Wensley, J.R.C. (1987) Strategic Investment Decisions, *Research in Marketing*, **9**, 1–57.

Batty, J. (1970) *Corporate Planning and Budgetary Control*, Macdonald and Evans, London.

Baumes, C.G. (1963) Allocating corporate expenses, *Business Policy Study No. 108*, The Conference Board.

Baumler, J.V. (1971) Defined criteria of performance in organizational control, *Administrative Science Quarterly*, Sept., 340–9.

Baumol, W.J. and Fabian, T. (1964) Decomposition, pricing for decentralization and external economies, *Management Science*, **2**, 1–32.

Beer, S. (1959) *Cybernetics and Management*, Wiley, Essex.

Beer, S. (1972) *Brain of the Firm*, Allen Lane, Harmondsworth, Middx.

Beer, S. (1975) *Platform for Change*, Wiley, Essex.

Bellah, R.N., Madsen, R., Sullivan, W.M., Swidler, A. and Tipton, S.M. (1985) *Habits of the Heart: Individualism and commitment in American Life*. University of California Press, Berkeley, California.

Benbassat, I. and Dexter, A.S. (1979) Value and events approaches to accounting: an experimental evaluation, *The Accounting Review*, **LIV**, (4), 735–49.

Benke, Jr. R.L. and Edwards, J.D. (1980) *Transfer Pricing: Techniques and Uses*. National Association of Accountants, New York.

Berg, N. (1969) What's different about conglomerate management?, *Harvard Business Review*, November/December, 32–40.

Berg, N.A. (1965) Strategic planning in conglomerate companies, *Harvard Business Review*, May/June, 79–92.

Berry, A.J. and Otley, D.T. (1975) The aggregation of estimates in hierarchical organizations, *Journal of Management Studies*, May, 175–93.

Beynon, M. (1973) *Working for Ford*, Allen Lane, Harmondsworth, Essex.

Bierman, Jr. H. and Dyckman, T.R. (1976) *Managerial Cost Accounting*, 2nd Edn. Macmillan, New York.

Bierman, H. and Schmidt, S.C. (1975) *The Capital Budgeting Decision*, 4th Edn. Macmillan, Basingstoke, Hants.

Birnberg, J.G., Turpolec, L. and Young, S.M. (1983) The organizational context of accounting, *Accounting Organizations and Society*, **8**, 111–30.

Boland, R.J., Jr. (1979) Control, causality and information system requirements, *Accounting, Organizations and Society*, **4**, (4), 259–72.

Boland, R.J. and Pondy, L.R. (1983) Accounting in organizations: a union of natural and rational perspectives, *Accounting Organizations and Society*, **8**, 223–34.

Bonini, C.P., Jaedicke, R.K. and Wagner, H.M. (eds.) (1964) *Management Controls: New directions in basic research*, McGraw-Hill, Maidenhead, Berks.

Boulding, K.E. (1956) General systems theory – the skeleton of science, *Management Science*, **2**, 197–208.

Bower, J.L. (1970) *Managing the Resource Allocation Process*, Division of Research, Harvard Business School, Boston.

Bower, J.L. (1972) *Managing the Resource Allocation Process*. Irwin.

Brealey, R. and Myers, S. (1981) *Principles of Corporate Finance*, McGraw-Hill, Maidenhead, Berks.

British Institute of Management (BIM) (1971) Transfer pricing: A measure of management performance in multi-divisional companies, *Management Survey Report*, No. 8.

British Institute of Management (BIM) (1974) Profit-centre accounting: the absorption of central overhead costs, *Management Survey Report No. 21*.

Brownell, P. (1981) Participation in budgeting, locus of control and organizational effectiveness. *Accounting Review*, **56**, 844–60.

Bruns, W.J. and Waterhouse, J.H. (1975) Budgetary control and organizational structure, *Journal of Accounting Research*, **13**, 177–203.

Burgoyne, J.G. (1975) Stress, motivation and learning, in *Managerial Stress* (eds D. Gowler and K. Legge) Gower, Aldershot, Hants.

Burns, T. and Stalker, G.M. (1961) *The Management of Innovation*, Tavistock Institute, London.

Burrell, G. and Morgan, G. (1979) *Sociological Paradigms and Organizational Analysis*, Heinemann, London.

Burrough, B. (1985) Oil-field investigators say fraud flourishes from wells to offices, *Wall Street Journal*, 15 January, 1–20.

Cable, J.R. (1988) Organizational form and economic performance, *in* Thompson, S. and Wright, M. (Eds.), *Internal Organisation, Efficiency and Profit*, chapter 2. Philip Allan.

Campbell, J.P. *et al.* (1970) *Managerial Behaviour, Performance and Effectiveness*, McGraw-Hill, Maidenhead, Berks.

Caplan, E.H. (1966) Behavioural assumptions of management accounting, *The Accounting Review*, **42**, 496–509.

Caplan, E.H. (1971) *Management Accounting and Behavioural Science*, Addison-Wesley, Wokingham, Berks.

Carroll, S. and Tosi, H. (1973) *Management by Objectives: Applications and Research*, Macmillan, New York.

Carter, E.E. (1971) The behavioural theory of the firm and top level corporate decisions. *Administrative Science Quarterly*, **16**, 413–28.

Caves, R.E. (1980) Industrial organization, corporate strategy and structure. *Journal of Economic Literature*, March, 64–92.

Centre for Business Research (1972) *Transfer Pricing: Management Control Project, No. 3*. Manchester Business School, Manchester.

Chandler, A.D. (1962) *Strategy and Structure*. MIT Press, Mass.

Chandler, A.D. (1977) *The Visible Hand: the Managerial Revolution in American Business*, Belknap, Cambridge, MA.

Chenhall, R.H., Harrison, G.L. and Watson, D.J.H. (1981) *The Organizational Context of Management Accounting*, Pitman, London.

Child, J. (1969) *The Business Enterprise in Modern Industrial Society*, Collier Macmillan, Basingstoke, Hants.

Chua, W.F., Lowe, T. and Puxty, T. (1989) *Critical Perspectives in Management Control*. Macmillan.

Coase, R.H. (1937) The nature of the firm. *Economica*, November, 386–405.

Cohen, M.D., March, J.G. and Olsen, J.P. (1972) A garbage can model of organizational change. *Administrative Science Quarterly*, March, 1–25.

Cook, Jr. P.W. (1955) Decentralization and the transfer price problem. *Journal of Business*, April, 87–94.

Cooper, D. (1981) A Social and organizational view of management accounting, *in* Bromwich M. and Hopwood, A. (Eds), *Essays in British Accounting Research*, 178–205, Pitman, London.

Costello, T.W. and Zalkind, S.S. (1963) *Psychology in Administration*. Prentice-Hall, Hemel Hempstead, Herts.

Cummings, L.L. and Schwab, D.P. (1973) *Performance in Organizations: Determinants and Appraisal*, Scott Foresman, Westminster, Maryland.

Cyert, R.M. and March, J.G. (1963) *A Behavioural Theory of the Firm*, Prentice-Hall, Hemel Hempstead, Herts.

Cyert, R.M., March, J.G. and Starbuck, W.H. (1961) Two experiments on risk and conflict in organizational estimation, *Management Science*, **7**, 254–64.

Cyert, R.M. and March, J.G. (1963) *A Behavioural Theory of the Firm*, Prentice-Hall, Hemel Hempstead, Herts.

Daft, R.L. and Macintosh, N.B. (1978) A new approach to design and the use of management information, *California Management Review*, **2**, 82–92.

Dean, J. (1951) *Capital Budgeting; Top management policy on plant, equipment and product development*. Columbia U.P., Guildford, Surrey.

Dean, J. (1955) Decentralization and intracompany pricing, *Harvard Business Review*, July/August, 65–74.

Dearden, J. (1960) Problem in decentralized profit responsibility, *Harvard Business Review*, May/June, 79–86.

Dearden, J. (1961) Problem in decentralized financial control, *Harvard Business Review*, May/June, 72–80.

Dearden, J. (1962a) Limits on decentralized profit responsibility, *Harvard Business Review*, July/August, 89–90.

Dearden, J. (1962b) Mirage of profit decentralization, *Harvard Business Review*, Nov/Dec, 33–41.

Dearden, J. (1973) *Cost Accounting and Financial Control Systems*. Addison-Wesley, Wokingham, Berks.

Demski, J.L. (1972) Optimal Performance Measurement, *Journal of Accounting Research*, Autumn, 243–58.

Demski, J. (1976) Uncertainty and evaluation based on controllable performance, *Journal of Accounting Research*, Autumn, 230–45.

Demski, J.L. (1980) *Information Analysis*, 2nd Edn. Addison-Wesley, Wokingham, Berks.

Demski, J.L. and G.A. Feltham, G.A. (1978) Economic incentives and budgetary control systems, *The Accounting Review*, April, 336–59.

Dermer, J. (1977) *Management Planning and Control Systems: Advanced topics and cases*. Irwin.

Dew, R.B. and Gee, K.P. (1973) *Management Control and Information*. Macmillan, Basingstoke, Hants.

Doctor, R.H. and Hamilton, W.F. (1973) Cognitive style and the acceptance of management science recommendations, *Management Science*, **19**, (8), 884–94.

Drucker, P. (1961) *The Practice of Management*. Mercury, London.

Drucker, P. (1964a) Control, controls and management, in (Eds. C.P. Bonini, R.K. Jaedieke and H.M. Wagner). *Management Controls: New directions in basic research* McGraw-Hill, Maidenhead, Berks.

Drucker, P. (1964b) *Managing for Results*. Harper and Row, Plymouth, Dever.

Drury, C. (1988) *Management and Cost Accounting*, 2nd Edn. Van Nostrand Reinhold, London.

Dyckman, T.R. (1975) Management accounting: where are we? A critique, *in Management Accounting and Control* (Ed. W.S. Albrecht). Wisconsin.

Earl, M.J. and Hopwood, A.G. (1981) From management information to information management, *in* Lucas, H.C., Jr *et al.* (Eds.), *The Information Systems Environment*, North-Holland.

Eaton, J. and Rosen, H.S. (1983) Agency, delayed compensation, and the structure of executive remuneration, *Journal of Finance*, **XXXVIII**, 1489–505.

Eccles, R.J. (1983) Control with Fairness in Transfer Pricing. *Harvard Business Review*, Nov–Dec, 149–61.

Eccles, R.J. (1985) *The Transfer Pricing Problem*, Lexington, Aldershot, Hants.

Edey, H.C. (1966) *Business Budgets and Accounts*, 3nd Edn. Hutchinson, London.

Edwards, R.C. (1975) The social relations of production in the firm and market structure, *Politics and Society*, **51**, 83–108.

Ehrenberg, R.G. and Milkovich, G.T. (1987) Compensation and firm performance, *in* Kleiner, M. *et al.* (Eds.), *Human Resources and the Performance of the Firm*, pp. 87–122. Industrial Relations Research Association, University of Wisconsin.

Emmanuel, C.R. (1976) *Transfer Pricing in the Corporate Environment*. Unpublished Ph.D. thesis (University of Lancaster).

Emmanuel, C.R. and Gee, K.P. (1982) Transfer Pricing: A fair and neutral procedure, *Accounting and Business Research*, Autumn, 273–8.

Emmanuel, C.R. and Otley, D.T. (1976) The usefulness of residual income, *Journal of Business Finance and Accounting*, Summer, 43–51.

Etzioni, A. (1961) *A Comparative Analysis of Complex Organizations*. Free Press, Basingstoke, Hants.

Ezzamel, M.A. (1979) Divisional cost of capital and the measurement of divisional performance, *Journal of Business Finance and Accounting*, Autumn, 311–29.

Ezzamel, M. and Hilton, K. (1980a) Can divisional discretion be measured?, *Journal of Business Finance and Accounting*, Summer, 311–29.

Ezzamel, M.A. and Hilton, K. (1980b) Divisionalization in British industry: a preliminary study, *Accounting and Business Research*, Spring, 197–214.

Fawthrop, R.A. (1971) Underlying problems in discounted cash flow appraisal, *Accounting and Business Research*, Summer, 187–98.

Fayol, H. (1949) *General and Industrial Management*. Pitman, London.

Ferrara, W.L. (1976) Accounting for performance evaluation and decision making, *Management Accounting (USA)*, December, 13–19.

Ferrara, W.L. (1977) Production costs, *in Handbook of Modern Accounting* (Eds. S. Davidson and R.L. Weil), 2nd Edn. McGraw-Hill, Maidenhead, Berks.

Ferris, K.R. (1977) A test of the expectancy theory of motivation in an accounting environment, *The Accounting Review*, **52**, 605–15.

Financial Accounting Standards Board (FAS) (1979) *Financial Reporting and Changing Prices: SFAS 33*.

Flamholtz, E.G. (1983) Accounting, budgeting and control systems in their organizational context: theoretical and empirical perspectives, *Accounting, Organizations and Society*, **8**, 153–69.

Flower, J.F. (1971) Measurement of divisional performance, *Accounting and Business Research*, **3**, 205–14.

Follett, M.P. (1924) *Creative Experience*. Longman and Green.

Foulkes, F.K. (1985) Why bonus plans are good for business, *Personnel*, **62**, 72–3.

Foucault, M. (1977) *Discipline and Punish*, Allen Lane, Harmondsworth, Middx.

Franko, L.G. (1974) The move toward a multidivisional structure in European organization, *Administrative Science Quarterly*, December, 493–506.

Fremgen, J.M. (1970) Transfer pricing and management goals, *Management Accounting*, December, 25–31.

Galbraith, J.R. (1972) Organization design: an information processing view, *in Organizational Planning: Cases and Concepts* (Eds. J.W. Lorsch and Lawrence, P.R.). Irwin.

Galbraith, J.R. (1977) *Organizational Design*. Addison-Wesley, Wokingham, Berks.

Gee, K.P. (1980) A cash flow measure of divisional performance, *The Accountant's Magazine*, January, 17–20.

Giglioni, G.B. and Bedian, A.G. (1974) A conspectus of management control theory: 1900–1972, *Academy of Management Journal*, No. 17.

Godfrey, J.T. (1971) Short-run planning in a decentralized firm, *The Accounting Review*, **46**, 293–4.

Golembiewski, R.T. (1964) Accountancy as a function of organization theory, *The Accounting Review*, April, 333–41.

Gordon, L.A. and Miller, D. (1976) A contingency framework for the design of accounting information systems, *Accounting, Organizations and Society*, **1**, 59–70.

Gordon, L.A. and Narayanan, V.K. (1984) Management accounting systems, perceived environmental uncertainty and organization structure: an empirical investigation, *Accounting, Organizations and Society*, **9**, 33–47.

Gordon, M.J. (1964) The use of administered price systems to control large organizations, *in Management Controls: New Directions in Basic Research* (C.P. Bonini, R.J. Jaedicke and H.M. Wagner), 1–26. McGraw-Hill.

Gordon, M.J. and Halpern, P.J. (1974) Cost of capital for a division of a firm, *The Journal of Finance*, September, 91–113.

Gordon, M.J. and Shillinglaw, G. (1974) *Accounting: A Management Approach*, 5th Edn. Irwin.

Gort, M. (1959) *Diversification and Integration in American Industry.* Princeton.

Govindarajan, V. (1984) Appropriateness of accounting data in performance evaluation: an empirical examination of environmental uncertainty as an intervening variable, *Accounting, Organisations and Society*, **9**, 125–35.

Govindarajan, V. and Gupta, A.K. (1985) Linking control systems to business unit strategy: impact on performance, *Accounting, Organisations and Society*, **10**, 51–66.

Grabski, S.V. (1985) Transfer pricing in complex organizations: A review and integration of recent empirical and analytical research. *Journal of Accounting Literature*, **4**, 33–75.

Gulick, L.H. (1937) Notes on the theory of organizations, *in* Gulick, L.H. and Urwick, L. (Eds.), *Papers on the Science of Administration*. Institute of Public Administration, Columbia University.

Hall, D.T. and Nougaim, K.E. (1968) An examination of Maslow's new hierarchy in an organizational setting, *Organizational Behaviour and Human Performance*, **3**, 12–35.

Hamner, W.C. (1975) How to ruin motivation with pay, *Compensation Review*, **7**, 17–27.

Handy, C. (1978) *Understanding Organizations*. Penguin.

Harrison, E.F. (1975) *The Managerial Decision-Making Process*. Houghton Mifflin.

Hay Group, Inc. (1987) *Hay Executive Compensation Report*. Hay Group.

Hayes, D. (1977) The contingency theory of management accounting, *The Accounting Review*, **52**, 22–39.

Hedberg, B. and S. Jonsson (1978) Designing semi-confusing information systems for organizations in changing environments, *Accounting, Organisations and Society*, **3**, 47–64.

Heflebower, R.B. (1960) Observations on decentralization in large enterprises, *Journal of Industrial Economics*, November, 114–26.

Henderson, B.D. and Dearden, J. (1966) New sytem for divisional control, *Harvard Business Review*, September/October, 144–60.

Henderson, R.I. (1985) *Compensation Management: Rewarding Performance.* Reston, V.A.

Hertz, D.B. (1964) Risk Analysis in Capital Investment, *Harvard Business Review*, Jan/Feb, 175–86.

Herzberg, F. (1966) *Work and the Nature of Man.* Staples Press.

Herzberg, F., Mausner, B. and Snyderman, B.B. (1959) *The Motivation to Work*. Wiley.

Hill, C.W.L. (1985) Internal organisation and enterprise performance: some UK evidence, *Management and Decisions Economics*, **6**, 210–16.

Hirshleifer, J. (1956) On the economics of transfer pricing, *Journal of Business*, **29**, 172–84.

Hirst, M.K. (1981) Accounting information and the evaluation of subordinate performance, *The Accounting Review*, **56**, 771–84.

Hofstede, G.H. (1968) *The Game of Budget Control*. Tavistock Institute.

Holstrum, B. (1979) Moral hazard and observability, *Bell Journal of Economics*, Spring, 74–91.

Hopper, T.M. (1980) Role conflicts of management accountants and their position within organization structures, *Accounting, Organizations and Society*, **5**, 401–12.

Hopper, T.M. and Berry, A.J. (1983) Organizational design and management control, *in* Lowe, E.A. and Machin, J.L.J. (Eds.), *New Perspectives in Management Control*, Macmillan.

Hopwood, A.G. (1972) An empirical study of the role of accounting data in performance evaluation, *Empirical Research in Accounting, Supplement to Journal of Accounting Research*, **10**, 156–82.

Hopwood, A.G. (1974) *Accounting and Human Behaviour*. Prentice-Hall.

Hopwood, A.G. (1984) Accounting and organizational behaviour, *in* Carsberg, B. and Hope, A. (Eds.), *Current Issues in Accounting*, 2nd Edn., pp. 260–72. Philip Allan.

Horngren, C.T. (1962) *Cost Accounting: A Managerial Emphasis*. Prentice-Hall.

Horngren, C.T. (1981) *Introduction to Management Accounting*, 5th Edn. Prentice-Hall.

Horngren, C.T. (1982) *Cost Accounting: A Managerial Emphasis*, 5th Edn. Prentice-Hall.

Horngren, C.T. and Foster, G. (1987) *Cost Accounting: A Managerial Emphasis*, 6th Edn. Prentice-Hall.

Hoshower, L.B. and Mandel, L.A. (1986) Transfer pricing policies of diversified US multinationals. *International Journal of Accounting*, Autumn, 51–60.

Hunt, P. (1966) The fallacy of the one big brain, *Harvard Business Review*, July/August, 17–25.

Ijiri, Y., Jaedicke, R.K. and Knight, K.E. (1966) The effects of accounting alternatives on management decisions, *in* Jaedicke, R.K. *et al.* (Eds.), *Research in Accounting Measurement*. American Accounting Association.

Istvan, D.F. (1961) *Capital Expenditure Decisions: How They are Made in Large Corporations*. Bureau of Business Research, Indiana University.

Itami, H. (1977) *Adaptive Behaviour: Management Control and Information Analysis*. Studies in Accounting Research No. 15, American Accounting Association.

Ivancevich, J. (1976) Effects of goal-setting on performance and job satisfaction, *Journal of Applied Psychology*, **61**, 605–12.

Jacques, E. (1961) *Equitable Payment*. Heinemann.

Jarrett, J.E. (1978) Estimating the cost of capital for a division of a firm and the allocation problem in accounting, *Journal of Business Finance and Accounting*, **5**, 39–47.

Jensen, M.C. and Meckling W.H. (1976) Theory of the firm: managerial behaviour, agency costs and ownership structure, *Journal of Financial Economics*, **3**, 305–60.

Jensen, M.C. and Murphy, K.J. (1988) *Performance, Pay and Top Management Incentives*. Working paper No. 88-059, Harvard Business School.

Johnson, H.T. (1980) Markets, hierarchies and the history of management accounting. Paper presented in the Third International Congress of Accounting Historians, London Business School, August 16–18.

Jones, C.S. (1985) An empirical study of the role of management accounting systems following takeover or merger, *Accounting, Organizations and Society*, **10**, 303–28.

Kaplan, R.S. (1982) *Advanced Management Accounting*. Prentice-Hall.

Kaplan, R.S. (1984) The evolution of management accounting, *The Accounting Review*, July, 390–418.

Kaplan, R.S. and Atkinson, A.A. (1989) *Advanced Management Accounting*, 2nd Edn. Prentice-Hall.

Kast, F.E. and Rosenzweig, J.E. (1974) *Organization and Management: A Systems Approach*. McGraw-Hill.

Katz, D. and Kahn, R.L. (1966) *The Social Psychology of Organizations*. Wiley.

Keane, S.M. (1983) *Stock Market Efficiency*, Philip Allan.

Kenis, I. (1979) Effects of budgetary goal characteristics on managerial attitudes of performance, *The Accounting Review*, **LIV**, (4), 707–21.

Khandwalla, P.N. (1972) The effects of different types of competition on the use of management control, *Journal of Accounting Research*, **10**, 275–85.

Khandwalla, P.N. (1977) *Design of Organizations*. Harcourt Brace Jovanovich.

King, P. (1975) Is the emphasis of capital budgeting theory misplaced?, *Journal of Business Finance and Accounting*, **2**, 69–82.

Knights, D. and Willmott, H. (1982) The problem of freedom: Fromm's contribution to a critical theory of work organization, *Praxis International*, **2**, 204–25.

Knights, D. and Willmott, H. (Eds) (1986) *Managing the Labour Process*, Gower.

Kohn, A. (1988) Incentives can be bad for business. *Inc.*, January, 93–4.

Kotter, J.P. (1982) *The General Managers*. Free Press.

Lambert, D.R. (1979) Transfer Pricing and Inter-Divisional Conflict. *California Management Review*, Summer, 70–5.

Lawler, E.E. III. (1971) *Pay and Organization Effectiveness*. Addison-Wesley, Reading, MA.

Lawler, E.E. III. (1973) *Motivation in Work Organizations*. Wadsworth.

Lawler, E.E. III. and Suttle, J. Lloyd (1972) A causal correlation test of the need hierarchy concept, *Organization Behaviour and Human Performance*, 7, 265–87.

Lawrence, P.R. and Lorsch, J.W. (1967a) Differentiation and integration in complex organisations, *Administrative Science Quarterly*, June, 1–48.

Lawrence, P.R. and Lorsch, J.W. (1967b) *Organization and Environment: Managing Differentiation and Integration*. Graduate School of Business Administration, Harvard University.

Lawson, G.H. (1978) The rational of cash flow accounting, *in* Van Dan, C.

(Ed.), *Trends in Managerial and Financial Accounting*. Martinus Nijhoff, 85–104.

Lee, T.A. (1972) Cash flow accounting, *Journal of Business Finance*, Summer, 27–36.

Likert, R. (1961) *New Patterns of Management*. McGraw-Hill.

Lindblom, C.E. (1959) The science of 'Muddling Through', *Public Administration Review*, Summer, 79–88.

Livingstone, J.L. (Ed.) (1975) *Management Accounting: The Behavioural Foundations*. Columbus, Ohio.

Locke, E.A. (1968) Towards a theory of risk motivations and incentives, *Organizational Behaviour and Human Performance*, **3**, 157–89.

Lorsch, J.W. and Allen, S.A. (1973) *Managing Diversity and Inter-dependency: An Organizational Study of Multidivisional Firms*. Division of Research Graduate School of Business Administration, Harvard University.

Lowe, E.A. (1970) Budgetary control: an evaluation in a wider managerial perspective, *Accountancy*, Nov, 764–9.

Lowe, E.A. and Chua, W.F. (1983) Organisation Effectiveness and Management Control, in Lowe, E.A. and Machin, J.L.J., *op. cit.*

Lowe, E.A. and Machin, J.L.F. (1983) *New Perspectives in Management Control*. Macmillan.

Lowe, E.A. and Shaw, R.W. (1968) An analysis of managerial biasing: evidence from a company's budgeting process, *Journal of Management Studies*, **5**, 304–15.

Lumby, S. (1984) *Investment Appraisal*, 2nd Edn. Van Nostrand Reinhold (UK).

Lupton, T. (1971) *Mangement and the Social Services*. Hutchinson.

Lupton, T. and Gowler, D. (1969) *Selecting a Wage Payment System*. Kogan Page, London.

Ma, R. (1969) Project appraisal in a divisionalized company, *Abacus*, December, 132–142.

Machin, J.L.J. (1983). Management Control Systems: Whence and Wither, in Lowe, E.A. and Machin, J.L.J., *op. cit.*

Macintosh, N.B. (1985) *The Social Software of Accounting and Information Systems*. Wiley.

Management bonuses: do you need them? (1979) *Chief Executive*, November, 18–21.

Manchester Business School (1972) Transfer Pricing: Management Control Project No. 3.

March, J.G. and Olsen, J.P. (1976) *Ambiguity and Choice in Organizations*. Bergen, Universitetsforlaget.

March, J.G. and Simon, H.A. (1958) *Organizations*, Wiley, London.

Markus, M.L. and Pfeffer, J. (1983) Power and the design and implementation of accounting and control systems, *Accounting, Organisations and Society*, **8**, (2), 205–18.

Marris, R. and Mueller, D.D. (1980) 'The corporation, competition and the invisible hand', *Journal of Economic Literature*, March, pp. 32–63.

Marsh, P. (1976) *Capital Budgeting in Practice: A Summary of Empirical Studies*. LBS working paper (June), 1–28.

Marsh, P.R., Barwise, T.P., Thomas, K. and Wensley, J.R.C. (1988) Managing Strategic Investment Decisions in Large Diversified Companies, in *Competitiveness and the Management Process* (Ed. A.M. Pettigrew), Basil Blackwell, Oxford.

Maslow, A.H. (1954) *Motivation and Personality*. Harper and Row.

Maslow, A. (1965) *Eupsychian Management: A Journal*. Irwin.

Mason, R.O. (1969) A dialectical approach to strategic planning, *Management Science*, **15**, B403–14.

Mauriel, J.J. and Anthony, R.N. (1966) Misevaluation of investment center performance, *Harvard Business Review*, March/April, 98–105.

Mautz, R.K. (1968) *Financial Reporting by Diversified Companies*. Financial Executions Research Foundation.

Mayo, E. (1933) *The Human Problems of an Industrial Civilization*. Macmillan, New York.

McGregor, D. (1960) *The Human Side of Enterprise*. McGraw-Hill.

McNally, G.M. (1980) Responsibility accounting and organizational control: some perspectives and prospects, *Journal of Business Finance and Accounting*, Summer, 165–82.

McRae, T.W. (1971) The behavioural critique of accounting, *Accounting and Business Research*, **1**, 83–92.

Medoff, J.L. and Abraham, K.G. (1980) Experience, performance and earning. *Quart. J. Econ.*, **95**, 703–36.

Mepham, M. (1978) A reinstatement of the accounting role of return, *Accounting and Business Research*, Summer, 178–90.

Mepham, M.J. (1980) *Accounting Models*. Polytech Publishers, Stockport.

Merchant, K.A. (1981) The design of the corporate budgeting system: influences on managerial behaviour and performance, *The Accounting Review*, **LVI**, (4), 813–29.

Merchant, K.A. (1982) The control function of management, *Sloan Management Review*, **23**, 43–55.

Merchant, K.A. (1984) Influences on departmental budgeting: an empirical examination of a contingency model, *Accounting, Organizations and Society*, **9**, (3/4), 291–307.

Merchant, K.A. (1985a) *Control in Business Organizations*, Ballinger.

Merchant, K.A. (1985b) Organizational controls and discretionary program decision-making: a field study, *Accounting, Organizations and Society*, **10** (1), 67–86.

Merchant, K.A. (1985c) Budgeting and the propensity to create budget slack, *Accounting, Organizations and Society*, **10**, (2), 201–10.

Merchant, K.A. (1989) *Rewarding Results: Motivating Profit Center Managers*. Harvard Business School Press.

Merchant, K.A. and Manzoni, J.-F. (1989) The achievability of profit center budget targets: a field study, *The Accounting Review*, **LXIV**, 539–58.

Merrett, A.J. and Sykes, A. (1973) *The Financing and Analysis of Capital Projects*, 2nd Edn. 378–80. Longman.

Meyer, H.H., Kay, E. and J.R.P. French, J.R.P. (1965) Split roles in performance appraisal, *Harvard Business Review*, Jan/Feb, 123–9.

Milani, K. (1975) The relationship of participation in budget-setting to industrial supervisor performance and attitudes: a field study, *The Accounting Review*, **L**, (2), 274–83.

Milburn, J.A. (1976) International transfer transactions: what price?, *CA Magazine*, December, 22–7.

Mintzberg, H. (1973) *The Nature of Managerial Work*. Harper & Row.

Mintzberg, H. (1975) *Impediments to the Use of Management Information*. National Association of Accountants.

Mintzberg, H. (1979) *The Structuring of Organizations*. Prentice-Hall.

Monsen, R.J. and Downs, H. (1965) A theory of large managerial firms, *Journal of Political Economy*, June, 221–36.

Moore, C.L. and Jaedicke, R.K. (1980) *Managerial Accounting*, 5th Edn. South-Western.

Morgan, G. (1979) *Cybernetics and Organization Theory: Epistemology or Technique*. Working Paper, Dept. of Behaviour in Organizations, University of Lancaster.

Morgan, J. and Luck, M. (1973) *Managing Capital Investment*. Mantec.

Murlis, H. (1988) Merit payment systems: the lessons so far, *Manpower Policy and Practice* (UK), Spring, 27–9.

Naert, P.A. (1973) Measuring performance in a decentralized firm with inter-related divisions: profit center versus cost center, *Engineering Economist*, **18**, 96–110.

National Association of Accountants (NAA) (1957) *Costing Joint Products*. Research Report No. 31.

National Industrial Conference Board (NICB) (1961) *Division Financial Executives*. Studies in Business Policy No. 101.

National Industrial Conference Board (NICB) (1967) *Inter-divisional Transfer Prices*. Studies in Business Policy No. 122.

Opsahl, R.L. and Dunnette, M.D. (1979) The role of financial compensation in industrial motivation, *in* Mahoney, T.A. (Ed.), *Compensation and Reward Perspectives*, 79–88. Richard D. Irwin.

Organization for Economic Cooperation and Development (DECD) (1979) *Transfer Pricing and Multinational Enterprises*.

Otley, D.T. (1976) *Budgetary Control and Managerial Performance*. Unpublished Ph.D. thesis, University of Manchester.

Otley, D.T. (1977) *Behavioural Aspects of Budgeting: Accounts Digest No. 49*. ICAEW, London.

Otley, D.T. (1978) Budget use and managerial performance, *Journal of Accounting Research*, **16**, 122–49.

Otley, D.T. (1980) The contingency theory of management accounting: achievement and prognosis, *Accounting Organizations and Society*, 194–208.

Otley, D.T. (1983) 'Concepts of control: the contribution of cybernetics and general systems theory to management control' *in* Lowe, E.A. and Machin, J.H.J. (Eds.), *New Perspectives in Management Control*, Macmillan.

Otley, D.T. (1984) Management accounting and organization theory: a review of their inter-relationship, *in* Scapens, R.W., Otley, D.T. and Lister, R. *Management Accounting, Organizational Theory and Capital Budgeting: Three Surveys*. Macmillan.

Otley, D.T. and Berry, J. (1979) Risk distribution in the budgetary process, *Accounting and Business Research*, **9**, 325–37.

Otley, D.T. and Berry, A.J. (1980) Control, organization and accounting, *Accounting, Organizations and Society*, **5**, 231–46.

Otley, D.T. and Dias, F.B.J. (1982) Accounting aggregation and decision-making performance: an experimental investigation, *Journal of Accounting Research*, 171–88.

Otley, D.T. and Wilkinson, C. (1988) Organizational behavior: strategy, structure, environment and technology, in *Behavioral Accounting Research: A Critical Analysis*, Ferris, K.R. (Ed.), Century VII Publishing Co.

Ouchi, W.G. (1977) The relationship between organizational structure and organizational control, *Administrative Science Quarterly*, March, 95–113.

Ouchi, W.G. (1979) A conceptual framework for the design of organizational control mechanisms, *Management Science*, **25**, 833–48.

Ouchi, W.G. (1981) *Theory Z: How American Business Can Meet the Japanese Challenge*. Addison-Wesley.

Parker, L.D. (1979) Divisional Performance Measurement: Beyond an Exclusive Profit Test. *Accounting and Business Research*, **36**, 309–19.

Pask, G. (1961) *An Approach to Cybernetics*. Hutchinson.

Pendlebury, M.W. (Ed.) (1989) *Management Accounting in the Public Sector*. Heinemann.

Pearce, J.L. (1987) Why merit pay doesn't work: implications from organization theory, *in* Balkin, D.B. and Gomez-Mejia (Eds.), *New Perspectives on Compensation*, 169–178. Prentice-Hall.

Perrow, C. (1970) *Organizational Analysis: A Sociological View*. Tavistock.

Peterson, C. and Miller, A. (1964) Mode, median and mean as optimal strategies, *Journal of Experimental Psychology*, **68**, 363–7.

Perrow, C. (1967) A framework for the comparative analysis of organizations. *Am. Socio. Rev.* **00**, 194–208.

Pettigrew, A.M. (1973) *The Politics of Organizational Decision-Making*. Tavistock.

Pfeffer, J. (1981) *Power in Organizations*. Pitman.

Pfeffer, J. (1982) *Organizations and Organization Theory*. Pitman.

Pfeffer, J. and Salancik, G.R. (1978) *The External Control of Organizations*. Harper and Row.

Pickle, H. and Friedlander, F. (1967) Seven societal criteria of organizational success, *Personnel Psychology*, **20**, 165–78.

Pike, R.H. (1983) The capital budgeting behaviour and corporate characteristics of capital-constrained firms, *Journal of Business Finance and Accounting*, **10**, 663–72.

Pinches, G.E. (1982) Myopia, capital budgeting and decision-making, *Financial Management*, Autumn, 6–19.

Piper, J. (1978) Determinants of financial control systems for multiple retailers – some case study evidence. Unpublished paper, University of Loughborough.

Piper, J.A. (1983) Classifying capital projects for top management, *in Readings in Cost Accounting, Budgeting and Control*, South Western, 189–207.

Plasschaert, S.R.F. (1979) *Transfer Pricing and Multinational Corporations: An overview of concepts, mechanisms and regulations*. Saxon House.

Plasschaert, S.R.F. (1981) The multiple motivations for transfer pricing modulations in multinational enterprises and governmental counter-measures: an attempt at clarification, *Management International Review*, **21**, 49–63.

Preston, A. (1986). Interactions and arrangements in the process of informing, *Accounting, Organizations and Society*, **11**, 521–40.

Price Waterhouse (1984) *Transfer Pricing Practices of American Industry*, P.W., Ohio.

Pugh, D.S. and Hickson, D.J. (1976) *Organisational Structure in its Context: The Astron Programme*. Saxon House.

Puxty, A.G. (1985) The problems of a paradigm: a critique of the prevailing orthodoxy in management control, *in* Chua, W.F., Lowe, E.A. and Puxty A.G. (Eds.), *Critical Perspectives in Management Control*. Macmillan.

Rathe, A.W. (1960) Management controls in business, *in* Malcolm, D.G. and Rowe, A.J. (Eds.), *Management Control Systems*. Wiley.

Read, W.H. (1962) Upward communication in industrial hierarchies, *Human Relations*, **15**, 3–16.

Reece, J.S. and Cool, W.R. (1978) Measuring investment center performance, *Harvard Business Review*, May/June, 28–46 and 174–6.

Rice, A.K. (1958) *The Enterprise and its Environment*. Tavistock Institute.

Ridgway, V.F. (1956) Dysfunctional consequences of performance measure-ments, *Administrative Science Quarterly*, **1**, 240–7.

Robichek, A.A. and Myers, S.C. (1965) *Optimal Financing Decisions*. Prentice-Hall.

Robens, A. (1972) *Ten Year Stint*. Cassell.

Rockley, L.E. (1973) *Investment for Profitability*. Business Books.

Rockness, H.O. (1977) Expectancy theory in a budgetary setting: an exper-imental examination, *The Accounting Review*, **52**, 893–903.

Ronen, J. and Livingstone, J.L. (1975) An expectancy theory approach to the motivational impact of budgets, *The Accounting Review*, **50**, 671–85.

Rumelt, R.P. (1974) *Strategy, Structure and Economic Performance*. Division of Research, Graduate School of Business Administration, Harvard University.

Rutherford, B.A. (1982) The interpretation of cash flow reports and the order allocation problem. *Abacus*, **18**, (1), 40–9.

Ryan, B. and Moloson, J. (1985) *Management Accounting: A contemporary approach*, Pitman, London.

Samuels, J.M. (1970) Divisional performance measures and interest on capital: a contributed note, *Journal of Business Finance*, **1**, 3–4.

Sathe, V. (1978a) Who should control division controllers?, *Harvard Business Review*, Sept/Oct, 99–104.

Sathe, V. (1978b) The relevance of modern organization theory for managerial accounting, *Accounting, Organizations and Society*, August, 89–92.

Sayles, L.R. (1979) *Leadership*. McGraw-Hill.

Scapens, R.W. (1978) A neo-classical measure of profit, *The Accounting Review*, April, 448.

Scapens, R.W. (1980) An overview of current trends and directions for the future, *in* Arnold, J., Carsberg, B. and Scapens, R. (Eds.), *Topics in Management Accounting*, 277–85. Philip Allan.

Scapens, R.W. and Sale, J.T. (1981) Performance Measurement and Formal Capital Expenditure Controls in Divisionalised Companies. *Journal of Business Finance and Accounting*. Autumn, 389–420.

Scapens, R.W. (1984) Management accounting: a survey, *in* Scapens, R.W., Otley, D.T. and Lister, R., *Management Accounting, Organization Theory and Capital Budgeting: Three Surveys*. Macmillan.

Scapens, R.W., Sale, J.T. and Tikkas, P.A. (1982) *Financial Control of Divisional Capital Investment*. ICMA.

Scapens, R.W., Otley, D.T. and Lister, R. (1984) *Management Accounting, Organizational Theory and Capital Budgeting: Three Surveys*, Macmillan.

Schiff, M. and Lewin, A.Y. (1970) The impact of people on budgets, *The Accounting Review*, **45**, 259–68.

Schreyogg, G. (1980) Contingency and choice in organization theory, *Organization Studies*, **1**, 305–26.

Scott, B.R. (1971) *Stages of Corporate Development – Part 1*. Harvard Business School Case Services.

Scott, W.R. (1981) Developments in organization theory, 1960–1980, *American Behavioural Scientist*, **25**, 407–22.

Shavell, S. (1979) Risk sharing and incentives and the principal and agent relationship, *Bell Journal of Economics*, Spring, 55–73.

Sherwood, D. (1983) *Financial Modelling: A Practical Guide*, Gee and Co.

Shillinglaw, G. (1972) *Cost Accounting, Analysis and Control*. Irwin.

Shillinglaw, G. (1977) *Managerial Cost Accounting*, 4th Edn. Irwin.

Shulman, J.S. (1967) When the price is wrong – by design, *Columbia Journal of World Business*, **2**, May/June, 69–76.

Shwayder, K. (1970) A proposal modification to residual income – interest adjusted income, *The Accounting Review*, April, 299–307.

Sihler, W.W. (1964) The capital investment analysis and decision process at the plant level of a large, diversified corporation. Unpublished doctoral dissertation, Harvard Business School.

Silverman, D. (1970) *The Theory of Organizations*. Heinemann.

Simon, H.A. (1957) *Administrative Behaviour*, 2nd Edn. Macmillan.

Simon, H.A. (1966) *The New Science of Management Decision*, Harper and Row.

Simon, H.A. *et al.* (1954) *Centralization versus Decentralizations in the Controller's Department*. Controllship Foundation.

Simons, R. (1989) Strategic orientation and top management attention to control systems. Paper presented at the International Management Control Association, London Graduate Business School, 10–12 July 1989.

Sizer, J. (1978) *How to Develop Hurdle Rates*. Unpublished working paper, University of Loughborough.

Sizer, J. (1979) *An Insight into Management Accounting*, 2nd Edn. Pitman.

Solomons, D. (1965) *Divisional Performance: Measurement and Control*. Irwin.

Solomons, M.B. and Haynes, W.W. (1962) A misplaced emphasis in capital budgeting, *Quarterly Review of Economics and Business*, February, 39–46.

Spicer, B.H. and Van Ballew (1983) Management accounting systems and the economics of internal organization, *Accounting, Organizations and Society*, **8**, 73–96.

Stedry, R.C. (1960) *Budget Control and Cost Behaviour*. Prentice-Hall.

Stedry, A.C. and Kay, E. (1966) The effects of goal difficulty on performance. *Behav. Sci*, **00**, 459–70.

Steers, R.M. (1975) Problems in the measurement of organizational effectiveness, *Administration Science Quarterly*, December, 613–29.

Steers, R.M. (1977) *Organizational Effectiveness: A Behavioural View*. Goodyear.

Stewart, J.C. (1977) Multinational companies and transfer pricing, *Journal of Business Finance and Accounting*, Autumn, 353–71.

Stewart, R. (1970) *The Reality of Organizations*, Macmillan.

Stigler, G.J. and Kindahl, J.K. (1970) *Behaviour of Industrial Prices*. Columbia Press.

Stobaugh, R.B. (1970) The financial strategies of subsidiaries of US controlled multinational enterprises, *Journal of International Business Studies*, Spring, 43–64.

Stone, W.E. (1973) An early English cotton mill cost accounting system: Charlton Mills 1810–1889, *Accounting and Business Research*, Winter, 71–8.

Swieringa, R.J. and Waterhouse, J.H. (1982) Organizational Views of Transfer Pricing. *Accounting, Organizations and Society*, **7**, (2), 149–65.

Tang, R.Y.W. (1979) *Transfer Pricing Practices in the United States and Japan*. Praeger.

Tang, R.Y.W. and Chan, K.H. (1979) Environmental variables of international transfer pricing: a Japan–United States comparison, *Abacus*, June, 3–12.

Taylor, F.W. (1947) *Scientific Management*. Harper and Row.

Thomas, A.L. (1971) Transfer prices of the multinational firm: when will they be arbitrary?, *Abacus*, June, 40–53.

Thomas, A.L. (1974) The allocation problem: Part two, in *Studies in Accounting Research No. 9*. American Accounting Association.

Thomas, A.L. (1978) Arbitrary and incorrigible allocations: a comment, *The Accounting Review*, January, 263–9.

Thomas, A.L. (1980a) *Cash-flow Reporting as Allocation-free Disclosure: A Polemic*. Working Paper No. 136, University of Kansas.

Thomas, A.L. (1980b) *A Behavioural Analysis of Joint-Cost Allocation and Transfer Pricing*, Stipes.

Thomason, G. (1978) *A Textbook of Personnel Management*, 3rd Edn. Institute of Personnel Management.

Thompson, J.D. (1967) *Organizations in Action*. McGraw-Hill.

Tomkins, C. (1973) *Financial Planning in Divisionalized Companies*. Haymarket.

Tomlinson, R.C. (1981) Some dangerous misconceptions concerning operations research and applied systems analysis, *European Journal of Operational Research*, **7**, 203–12.

Tosi, H. (1975) The Human Effects of managerial budgeting systems, *in*

Livingstone, J.H. (Ed.), *Management Accounting: The Behavioural Foundations*. Grid. Columbus, Ohio.

Trist, E.L. and Bamforth, K.W. (1951) Some social and psychological consequences of the longwall method of coal-getting, *Human Relations*, **4**, 3–38.

Turvey, R. (1979). *in* Luck, G.M. *et al.* The management of capital investment, *Journal of the Royal Statistical Society* (Series A, Vol. 134, 485–533. 485–533.

United Nations (1978) Transnational Corporations in World Development: A re-examination, U.N., New York.

Urwick, L.F. (1947) *The Elements of Administration*. Pitman.

Vancil, R.F. (1979) *Decentralization: Ambiguity by Design*. Irwin.

Vatter, W.J. (1959) Does rate of return measure business efficiency, *NAA Bulletin*, January, 33–48.

Verlage, H.C. (1975) *Transfer Prices for Multinational Enterprises*. Rotterdam University Press.

Vickers, G. (1967) *Towards a Sociology of Management*. Chapman and Hall.

Waterhouse, J.H. and Tiessen, P. (1978) A contingency framework for management accounting systems research, *Accounting Organizational and Society*, **3**, 65–76.

Watson, D.J.H. and Baumler, J.V. (1975) Transfer pricing: a behavioural context, *The Accounting Review*, July, 466–74.

Weick, K. (1979) *The Social Psychology of Organizing*. Addison-Wesley, Wokingham, Berks.

Weick, K.R. (1979) *The Social Psychology of Organizing*, 2nd Edn. Addison Wesley, Wokingham, Berks.

Wells, M.C. (1968) Profit centers, transfer prices and mysticism, *Abacus*, December, 174–81.

Wells, M.C. (1978) *Accounting for Common Costs*. Centre for International Education and Research in Accounting, University of Illinois.

Wildavsky, A. (1975) *Budgeting: A Comparative Analysis of the Budgeting Process*. Little Brown.

Wilkinson, E. (1983) *Japan versus Europe: A History of Misunderstanding*. Penguin.

Williamson, O.E. (1964) *The Economics of Discretionary Behaviour*. Prentice-Hall.

Williamson, O.E. (1970) *Corporate Control and Business Behavior*. Prentice-Hall.

Williamson, O.E. (1975) *Markets and Hierarchies: Analysis and Antitrust Implications*. Free Press.

Williamson, O.E. (1985) *The Economic Institutions of Capitalism: Firms, Markets and Relational Contracting*. Free Press.

Williamson, O.E. and Bhargaval, N. (1972) Assessing and classifying the internal structure and control apparatus of the modern corporation, *in* Cowling, K. (Ed.), *Market Structure and Corporate Behavior: Theory and Empirical Analysis of the Firm*, 125–48. Gray-Mills.

Willmott, H.C. (1984) Images and ideals of managerial work: a critical examination of conceptual and empirical accounts, *Journal of Management Studies*, **21**, 349–68.

Willmott, H. (1989) Autocritique II, *in* Chua, W.F., Lowe, T. and Puxty, T. (Eds.), *Critical Perspectives in Management Control*. Macmillan.

Wilson, S.R. (1973) Motivating managers with money, *Business Horizons*, **XVI**, April, 37–43.

Wood, S. (1979) A reappraisal of the contingency approach to organization, *Journal of Management Studies*, **16**, 334–54.

Woodward, J. (1958) *Management and Technology*. HMSO.

Woodward, J. (1965) *Industrial Organization: Theory and Practice*. Oxford U.P.

Woodwards, J. and Rackham, J. (1970) *Industrial Organization: Behaviour and Control*. Oxford U.P.

Wright, P. (1974) Language of British Industry, Macmillan.

Wright, M. and Thompson, S. (1987) Divestment and the control of divisionalized firms. *Accounting and Business Research*, Summer, 259–68.

Wrigley, L. (1970) *Divisional Autonomy and Diversification*. Unpublished DBA dissertation, Harvard Business School.

Wu, F.H. and Sharp, D. (1979) An empirical study of transfer pricing practice, *International Journal of Accounting*, Spring, 71–85.

Yetton, P.W. (1976) The interaction between a standard time incentive payment scheme and a simple accounting information system, *Accounting, Organizations and Society*, **1**, 81–7.

Zannetos, Z.S. (1965) On the theory of divisional structures: some aspects of the centralization and decentralization of control and decision making, *Management Science*, December, 132–50.

Zimmerman, J.L. (1979) The costs and benefits of cost allocations, *The Accounting Review*, July, 504–21.

Author index

Subject index